Global Private Banking and
Wealth Management

For other titles in the Wiley Finance Series
please see www.wiley.com/finance

Global Private Banking and Wealth Management

The New Realities

David Maude

John Wiley & Sons, Ltd

Published 2006 by   John Wiley & Sons Ltd, The Atrium, Southern Gate, Chichester,
West Sussex PO19 8SQ, England

Telephone   (+44) 1243 779777

Email (for orders and customer service enquiries): cs-books@wiley.co.uk
Visit our Home Page on www.wiley.com

Reprinted October 2006, April 2007, September 2007, October 2008

Other Wiley Editorial Offices

John Wiley & Sons Inc., 111 River Street, Hoboken, NJ 07030, USA

Jossey-Bass, 989 Market Street, San Francisco, CA 94103-1741, USA

Wiley-VCH Verlag GmbH, Boschstr. 12, D-69469 Weinheim, Germany

John Wiley & Sons Australia Ltd, 42 McDougall Street, Milton, Queensland 4064, Australia

John Wiley & Sons (Asia) Pte Ltd, 2 Clementi Loop #02-01, Jin Xing Distripark, Singapore 129809

John Wiley & Sons Canada Ltd, 22 Worcester Road, Etobicoke, Ontario, Canada M9W 1L1

Wiley also publishes its books in a variety of electronic formats. Some content that appears
in print may not be available in electronic books.

Library of Congress Cataloging-in-Publication Data
Maude, David.
   Global private banking and wealth management : the new realities / David Maude.
      p.   cm.
   Includes bibliographical references.
   ISBN-13: 978-0-470-85421-1
   ISBN-10: 0-470-85421-9
   1. Private banks. 2. Banks and banking—Customer services. 3. Wealth—Management. I. Title.
HG1978.M38 2006
332.1'23—dc22   2006005378

British Library Cataloguing in Publication Data

A catalogue record for this book is available from the British Library

ISBN 13: 978-0-470-85421-1 (H/B)

Typeset in 10/12pt Times by TechBooks, New Delhi, India.
Printed and bound in Great Britain by CPI Antony Rowe, Chippenham, Wiltshire.

To Francesca and Antonio

Acknowledgements

This book was originally conceived back in 2002, but has taken far longer to bring to fruition than I originally intended. The sheer weight of client work over this period has been the main culprit. I therefore thank Philip Molyneux, Professor of Banking and Finance at the University of Wales, for stepping in to help write several chapters. Anna Omarini, Assistant Professor at Bocconi University, also kindly assisted with one of the chapters.

Several people helped out by reviewing draft chapters, including Helen Avery at *Euromoney*, Marc Kitten at Candesic and Sascha Schmidt at a-connect.

Various executives at the leading players provided insightful discussions and helped refine my thinking. Similarly, many clients, knowingly or unknowingly, have provided input over the years. However, all examples in the text are either drawn from public information or, where based on my professional experience, have been disguised to protect client confidentiality.

Special thanks go to Christian Casal, John Cheetham, Andrew Doman, Hugh Harper, Francesca Rizzi, Purnima Roy, Corrado Ruffini, Frederic Vandenberghe, Martha Whitmore and other former colleagues at McKinsey & Company, who provided extensive comments and source material.

I am also very grateful to a number of other people who generously devoted time and source material, including: Christian de Juniac, Boston Consulting Group; Ian Woodhouse, IBM Business Consulting Services; Bruce Weatherill, PricewaterhouseCoopers; Stephen Jarvis, Alberto Pagliarini and Huw van Steenis, Morgan Stanley; Liz Nesvold and Jennifer Sransky, Berkshire Capital; Gavin Houlgate, KPMG; Alan Gemes, Booz Allen Hamilton; Lauren Taylor, Mercer Oliver Wyman; Dominic Wilson, Goldman Sachs; Marc Rubinstein, Credit Suisse; Javier Lodeiro, Bank Sarasin; Jon Diat, Citigroup; Carolin Deutsch and Dana Grosser, SEI; Anne Bourgeois, Datamonitor; Karen Cohen, Renee Duvall, Petrina Dolby, Ronni Edens and Donie Lohan, Capgemini; Sierk Nawijn, ABN AMRO; Jon Peace, Fox-Pitt, Kelton; Conrad Ford and James Morris, Barclays; Christian Kwek, BNP Paribas; Matt Spick, Deutsche Bank; Daniel Davies, Exane BNP Paribas; Christopher Humphrey, Eden McCallum; Dr Bernhard Koye, Swiss Banking School, University of Zurich; and Richard Drew.

I also thank Sam Hartley, Emily Pears and Viv Wickham at John Wiley & Sons, Ltd, who kept me on the straight and narrow, and ensured that the publication process ran smoothly.

This book could not have been written without the love and support of my family. Extra special thanks go to my wife, Francesca, and to my son, Antonio, who had to put up with his Dad typing away for long hours instead of playing with him.

Needless to say, any errors in the text are mine alone.

DJM

Preface

"Let me tell you about the very rich" (with undisguised envy). *"They're very different from you and me."*

F. Scott Fitzgerald

"Yes" (taking a long pull from a thick Havana and pausing longer for dramatic effect). *"They have more money."*[1]

Ernest Hemingway

It is easy to forget that only a few years ago, wealth management was the darling of the financial services industry. Highly profitable and growing rapidly, everyone wanted a piece of the action. Indeed, come 1999, it was difficult to find a bank of any stripe that was *not* targeting the wealth management business.

Driven by strong global economic growth and buoyant financial markets during the go-go years of the 1980s and 1990s, wealth managers were able to prosper simply by showing up, being there and standing relatively still. There was no great need to have a clear strategy or distinctive client proposition. In many cases, the assets – and profits – just flowed in.

So, what happened? The financial market turmoil of 2000–2002 left many wealth managers – old and new – highly exposed: exposed more than ever to the global equity market; and, in the case of the large number of integrated players, exposed, too, to accusations of inherent conflicts of interest. As Warren Buffet famously said, "It's only when the tide goes out that you learn who's been swimming naked."[2] In short, for many players, at least for a while, wealth management lost its golden lustre.

Today, with the recovery in financial markets, many players are refocusing on wealth management, and growth initiatives are firmly back on management agendas. The industry's profile has never been higher (see Figure 0.1).

Going forward, however, financial markets alone cannot be relied on to grow or even sustain profits. Many wealth managers' strategies are in flux and the pace of change is picking up. New initiatives are appearing by the week.

The main aim of this book is to help wealth management players chart a course through the new, increasingly choppy, waters. I aim to provide a flavour of the key issues at stake,

---

[1] Conversation anecdotally reported to have taken place in a Paris café in the 1920s. In fact, Fitzgerald wrote the first phrases in a 1926 short story, 'The Rich Boy', and Hemingway replied a decade later in an article, 'The Snows of Kilimanjaro', published in *Esquire*. (And Hemingway's glib retort was borrowed from Mary Colum, an Irish literary critic.)

[2] Source: Berkshire Hathaway Inc., Chairman's Letter to Shareholders, 1992.

Number of press articles* including given term
Thousands

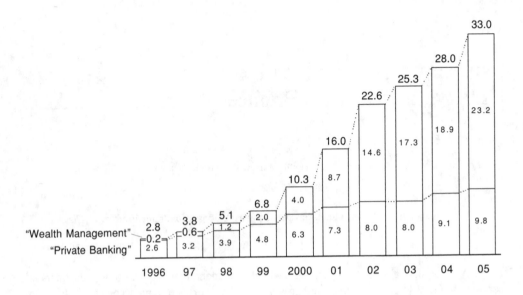

* English language only

Figure 0.1   The rise and rise of wealth management
Source: Factiva; author's analysis.

but the book certainly does not attempt to cover every possible aspect of wealth management. Along route, I hope to blow away some of the myths that have grown up around the industry.

The good news is that, looking ahead, the industry's intrinsic fundamentals are relatively solid. There are still fortunes to be made in wealth management. But one thing is clear: the private banking and wealth management business will not get any easier to manage.

David Maude
Verona, May 2006
david_maude@lycos.co.uk

Contents

1

Global Market Overview

In the late 1990s, wealth management was reported to be the fastest growing sector of the financial services industry. Though the 2000–2002 downturn took its toll on many wealth management providers, looking ahead, the industry remains attractive, with strong fundamentals. Globally, the number of millionaires continues to grow at more than 7% a year – around 6 times the pace of the population as a whole.[1] The industry is certainly up there with investment banking in terms of fun, glamour and glitz. However, to meet the evolving needs of clients, the industry has become increasingly broad and complex.

For decades, the industry was dominated by a select group of sleepy, very traditional players. But during the 1990s, the industry changed almost beyond recognition. There was a huge influx of new players offering a wide range of specialised products and services to a broader, ever more demanding client base.

The aims of this introductory chapter are to:

- Define the wealth management market and provide an idea of its size and recent growth.
- Examine the key drivers of the wealth management industry.
- Outline the economics of the industry.
- Briefly describe the competitive landscape.

Most of the themes introduced here will be explored in more detail in later chapters.

1.1 THE WEALTH MANAGEMENT MARKET

There is no generally accepted standard definition of wealth management – both in terms of the products and services provided and the constitution of the client base served – but a basic definition would be financial services provided to wealthy clients, mainly individuals and their families.

Private banking forms an important, more exclusive, subset of wealth management. At least until recently, it largely consisted of banking services (deposit taking and payments), discretionary asset management, brokerage, limited tax advisory services and some basic concierge-type services, offered by a single designated relationship manager. On the whole, many clients trusted their private banking relationship manager to 'get on with it', and took a largely passive approach to financial decision making.

Private banking has a very long pedigree, stretching back at least as far as the seventeeth century in the case of some British private banks.[2] It is, however, only really over the last 15 years or so that the term 'wealth management' has found its way into common industry parlance. It developed in response to the arrival of mass affluence during the latter part of

---

[1] The compound annual growth rate (CAGR) in the global number of millionaires, 2002–2004, is 7.4% (*source*: Capgemini/Merrill Lynch). The CAGR in the global population, 2000–2005, is 1.2% (*source*: Population Division of the Department of Economic and Social Affairs of the United Nations Secretariat, 2004).

[2] See Maude and Molyneux (1996), Chapter 1, for a discussion of private banking origins and historical evolution.

the twentieth century; more sophisticated client needs throughout the wealth spectrum; a desire among some clients to be more actively involved in the management of their money; a willingness on the part of some types of financial services players, such as retail banks and brokerages, to extend their offerings to meet the new demand; and, more generally, a recognition among providers that, for many clients, conventional mass-market retail financial services are inadequate. Wealth management is therefore a broader area of financial services than private banking in two main ways:

- *Product range.* As in private banking, asset management services are at the heart of the wealth management industry. But wealth management is more than asset management. It focuses on both sides of the client's balance sheet. Wealth management has a greater emphasis on financial advice and is concerned with gathering, maintaining, preserving, enhancing and transferring wealth. It includes the following types of products and services:
  (a) Brokerage.
  (b) Core banking-type products, such as current accounts, time deposits and liquidity management.
  (c) Lending products, such as margin lending, credit cards, mortgages and private jet finance.
  (d) Insurance and protection products, such as property and health insurance, life assurance and pensions.
  (e) Asset management in its broadest sense: discretionary and advisory, financial and non-financial assets (such as real estate, commodities, wine and art), conventional, structured and alternative investments.
  (f) Advice in all shapes and forms: asset allocation, wealth structuring, tax and trusts, various types of planning (financial, inheritance, pensions, philanthropic), family-dispute arbitration – even psychotherapy to children suffering from 'affluenza'.
  (g) A wide range of concierge-type services, including yacht broking, art storage, real estate location, and hotel, restaurant and theatre booking.
  Based on research by BCG, non-cash investments may account for no more than c.36% of the global wealth management revenue pool (see Figure 1.1).

- *Client segments.* Private banking targets only the very wealthiest clients or high net worth individuals (HNWIs): broadly speaking, those with more than around $1 million in investable assets. Wealth management, by contrast, targets clients with assets as low as $100 000, i.e. affluent as well as high net worth (HNW) clients.

Robert J. McCann, President of the Private Client Group at Merrill Lynch, provided a succinct definition of wealth management at a recent industry conference:

[Wealth management] addresses every aspect of a client's financial life in a consultative and a highly individualised way. It uses a complete range of products, services and strategies. A wealth manager has to gather information both financial and personal to create an individualised series of recommendations, and be able to make those recommendations completely tailored to each client. Off the shelf – it won't do. What [wealth management] requires is connecting with clients on a personal level that is way beyond the [retail financial services] industry norm.

When asked to describe the factors that distinguish their services from other types of retail financial institution, wealth managers emphasise the uniqueness of their client relationships – relationships that are *broad*, in that they encompass all areas of a client's financial life, and *deep*

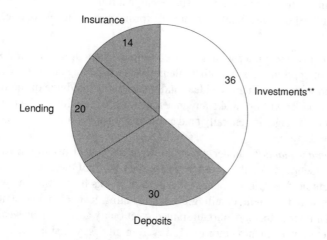

2003
Percent

100% = c.$200 bn–$250 bn

*From households with AuM > $100,000
**Including managed funds and directly held securities

Figure 1.1   Wealth management revenue pool* by product
Source: Boston Consulting Group; author's calculations.

with respect to the advisor's intimate knowledge of a client's values and priorities. In turn, this breadth and depth of relationship enables the wealth manager to develop and implement highly tailored solutions that address all aspects of a client's financial well-being. At a minimum, the following three criteria differentiate a firm as a wealth manager:

- The *relationship* that wealth managers have with their clients, both in terms of breadth (where providers emphasise terms such as 'holistic', 'comprehensive' and 'all-inclusive') and depth ('intimate' and 'individualised').
- The *products and services* provided, with a particular emphasis on estate planning and multi-generational planning services, as well as tax advisory expertise and alternative investments.
- The *specific objectives of wealthy clients*, such as investment performance, wealth preservation or wealth transfer.

1.1.1   Investment mandates

Wealth managers may serve clients under different types of investment mandate. At the most basic level, the wealth manager may act as a pure *custodian* for a client's assets. That involves, essentially, asset safekeeping, income collection, fund disbursement and associated reporting.

Under an *execution-only mandate*, the wealth manager executes, or selects brokers to execute, securities transactions on behalf of the client. The wealth manager does not provide investment advice, so this service is aimed primarily at self-directed clients. The wealth manager is typically required to seek 'best execution' for client transactions, i.e. executing transactions so that the client's total cost, or proceeds, in each transaction is as favourable as possible to the client under the particular circumstances at that time.

The next level of investment mandate is a formal service-level contract, of which there are two types:

- *Advisory mandate*, under which the wealth manager will discuss and advise the client on investment opportunities. The client then makes the buying and selling decisions based on a combination of his or her own ideas and the investment advice of the wealth manager. The wealth manager will not make any investment decision without the client's prior approval. The wealth manager is generally paid a commission based on the volume of executed trades, plus custody fees.
- *Discretionary mandate*, under which the wealth manager usually has sole authority to buy and sell assets and execute transactions for the benefit of the client, in addition to providing investment advice. Discretionary management works by starting off with the construction of a brief with the client, detailing investment aims, level of risk-aversion and other factors that will influence the portfolio. In some discretionary accounts, the wealth manager is given only limited investment authority. However, in all cases, major investment decisions, such as changing the account's investment strategy or asset allocation guidelines, may be subject to the client's approval. The wealth manager is generally paid on the basis of a flat-fee arrangement linked to the value of the assets under management. The gross revenue margin of a discretionary mandate is typically at least double that of an execution-only mandate.

The proportion of clients using advisory mandates is, in general, relatively stable across the various client wealth bands. Execution-only mandates become more prevalent, and discretionary mandates less prevalent, as client wealth rises. That typically reflects a greater degree of financial sophistication among the wealthier clients.

Wealth management can mean different things in different geographic regions. The US and Europe have traditionally stood at two extremes in this regard. In the US, wealth management is more closely allied to transaction-driven brokerage and is typically investment-product driven. In Europe, the term is more synonymous with traditional private banking, with its greater emphasis on advice and exclusivity.

1.1.2   Offshore versus onshore

A fundamental distinction within wealth management is onshore versus offshore. Onshore wealth management is the provision of products and services within the client's main country of residence. Offshore wealth management, by contrast, serves clients wishing to manage their wealth outside their main country of residence for reasons such as: financial confidentiality; legal-system flexibility; tax considerations; the lack of appropriate products and services onshore; a low level of trust in domestic financial markets and governments; and the need for safety and geographical diversification in response to domestic political and macroeconomic risks. Indeed, some clients treat their offshore account(s) primarily as a 'vault'.

Some practitioners go further and refer to four types of wealth management. Take the example of a Swiss wealth manager. It will, of course, have a presence in Switzerland: its domestic business. Its domestic business will typically serve two types of clients. First, there are Swiss clients seeking to keep assets within their own country of residence, which is referred to as the

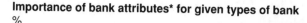

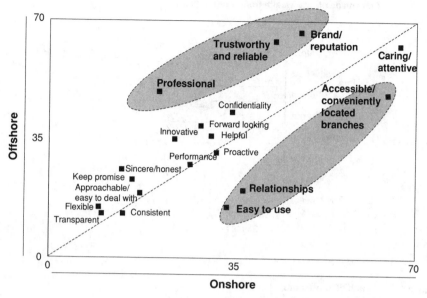

Importance of bank attributes* for given types of bank
%

*Multiple answers possible

Figure 1.2   Wealth manager attributes
Source: McKinsey & Company, 'Annual Investment and Wealth Management CEO Conference, 2005'. Reproduced by permission.

wealth manager's domestic onshore business. Its domestic business may also serve clients from outside Switzerland, which is referred to as the wealth manager's domestic offshore business. The Swiss wealth manager may also have a presence outside Switzerland: its international business. That may include a presence in Italy, serving both Italian clients (i.e. its international onshore business) and non-Italian clients (i.e. its international offshore business).

The onshore/offshore distinction matters because these two types of wealth management have very different client appeal, dynamics, product sets and economics (see below). Figure 1.2 illustrates that offshore private banks need, in particular, strong brands, trustworthiness and a high degree of professionalism. For onshore private banks, there is greater emphasis on local branch presence, strong relationships and 'user friendliness'.

As Figure 1.3 illustrates, the proportion of wealth managed offshore varies significantly across regions. There is a general trend for assets to shift onshore, particularly in Western Europe, which is primarily driven by a series of global tax initiatives (see Chapter 9). But that shift is happening at different speeds, and some regions – including Africa, the Middle East, Latin America and Eastern Europe – continue to have a sizeable offshore wealth component. At the client level, the proportion of wealth held offshore tends to rise in line with the level of wealth. In terms of offshore wealth destinations, the main offshore centres are Switzerland, the United Kingdom (including the UK Channel Islands – Jersey, Guernsey and Isle of Man), Hong Kong, Singapore, Luxembourg, Gibraltar, Monaco, Cayman Islands, the Bahamas, New York

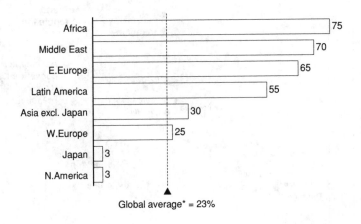

Figure 1.3   Wealth held offshore
Source: Boston Consulting Group; Julius Baer; author's client work.

and Miami. There are different types of offshore centres. Some – such as London, New York and Miami – offer a comprehensive range of private banking services in their own right. Others, such as the Cayman Islands, are principally booking centres, where funds and transactions are registered.

1.1.3   Market size and growth

Primary questions for wealth managers the world over is: who are the wealthy and how much wealth do they have?

Measuring the size of the wealth management market is certainly no easy task. For a start, as noted above, there is no generally accepted market definition. Individual institutions differ widely both in the level of the wealth threshold they use to separate a wealth management 'client' from a mass-market 'customer', and in how they define wealth itself. Frequently used metrics include: annual gross income, liquid financial assets, investable assets, net worth (i.e. assets net of debt) or some combination of these. The thresholds are sometimes defined by the geographic market that the wealth management provider is targeting.

The wealth management market is probably best thought of as a group of distinct submarkets, based on client wealth bands. Again, institutions vary considerably in how they define these wealth bands and in how they label them (see Figure 1.4). Broadly, the market can be divided into two subgroups – affluent and high net worth – with, in turn, further subsegmentation within each.[3]

---

[3] Note that the focus here is on defining the overall market. Chapter 3 provides a more detailed discussion of client segmentation practices at the more granular level.

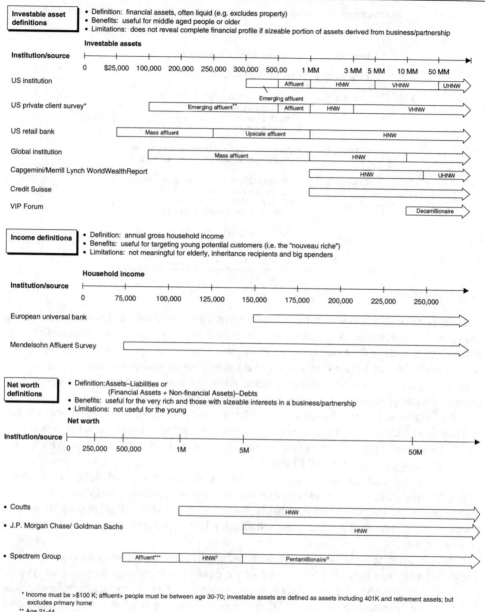

Investable asset definitions
- Definition: financial assets, often liquid (e.g. excludes property)
- Benefits: useful for middle aged people or older
- Limitations: does not reveal complete financial profile if sizeable portion of assets derived from business/partnership

Income definitions
- Definition: annual gross household income
- Benefits: useful for targeting young potential customers (i.e. the "nouveau riche")
- Limitations: not meaningful for elderly, inheritance recipients and big spenders

Net worth definitions
- Definition: Assets–Liabilities or
  (Financial Assets + Non-financial Assets)–Debts
- Benefits: useful for the very rich and those with sizeable interests in a business/partnership
- Limitations: not useful for the young

* Income must be >$100 K; affluent+ people must be between age 30-70; investable assets are defined as assets including 401K and retirement assets; but excludes primary home
** Age 21-44
*** Affluent defined as either >$100K in income or >$500 K in net worth (not including property)
† HNW defined on basis of investable assets, not net worth
†† Not including property
Note: Not drawn to scale

Figure 1.4 What is wealthy? Client indicative wealth threshold definitions
Source: Author's analysis.

EXAMPLES OF DIFFERENT ENTRY CRITERIA APPLIED BY PRIVATE BANKS

Example 1	• Minimum account size USD 1m
Example 2	• USD 5m+of bankable assets
Example 3	• Minimum account size USD 0.5m **or** • Use of derivative products **or** • Use of discretionary mandate **or** • Language requirements
Example 4	• Decision of relationship manager based on assessment of client's financial potential
Example 5	• Minimum USD 0.2m with minimum advisory management services • Minimum USD 0.5m in discretionary management with limits on investment possibilities • Minimum USD 1m in discretionary management without limits

Figure 1.4 (*Continued*)

There is no industry-wide minimum requirement for the bankable assets entry criterion. In any case, the minimum account size often reflects the bank's aspiration rather than reality (even at the most upscale institutions, the average account size is usually below the minimum asset requirement). During the late 1990s, many banks moved down market and accepted clients who did not fulfil their communicated entry criteria. Also, at the industry level, entry thresholds do not tend to change much over time and have not generally kept pace with asset-price inflation: over the long term, real (i.e. inflation-adjusted) entry thresholds for many players have fallen.

There are generally no official government or private statistics on the actual distribution of wealth within individual countries. We are therefore forced to rely on estimates, which come in a variety of shapes and forms (see Box 1.1).

Micro, survey data are often unreliable. Not unnaturally, many individuals deliberately attempt to conceal the exact size of their wealth, and a large proportion of wealth may be held not only in secret accounts and trusts but also in assets that are illiquid and/or not publicly quoted. Furthermore, it is often difficult to draw a distinction between an entrepreneur's corporate and personal wealth.

Hence, in using these data, a 'health warning' applies: clearly, the output, in terms of the wealth estimate, can only ever be as good as the input, in terms of the data and analysis on which the estimate is based; the final estimates will be highly sensitive to the assumptions made; and there can, therefore, be substantial differences in estimates from different organisations. For example, Capgemini/Merrill Lynch estimate that global HNWI wealth as at end-2004 was $30.8 trillion; the corresponding estimate from The Boston Consulting Group was $24.5 trillion; and UBS's published internal estimate[4] was $35.4 trillion. There are also substantial differences within the regional breakdowns and dynamics (see Figure 1.5).

Box 1.1 explores some of the reasons for these differences and examines wealth market-sizing methodologies more generally.

---

[4] *Source*: Presentation by Peter Wuffli, CEO, UBS, at Morgan Stanley European Banks conference, 22 March 2006, page 8. Estimate excludes real estate, private business interests, insurance and other illiquid assets.

Box 1.1   Wealth market measurement methodologies: lies, damn lies and wealth statistics?

Most estimates of the wealth market for a given country (or region) follow a two-step methodology:

- Estimate the stock of total wealth.
- Estimate how that wealth is distributed across the adult population.

To estimate the stock of total wealth, basic source data are typically available from national statistical offices, central banks and investment industry associations. In the absence of wealth-stock data, one approach is to cumulate national accounts-based private savings flow data. Another approach is to rely on the relationship between net private investment assets and nominal gross domestic product (GDP). For both approaches, the financial asset data are captured at book value, so a market-value adjustment is required, based on movements in equity, bond and real estate prices. To the extent that offshore investment flows are not accurately reflected in all national accounts data, a further adjustment will be required.

Total wealth is then distributed within each country using the relevant official statistics for those countries where such data are available. For countries without such data, estimates are made on the basis of the wealth distribution patterns of countries with similar income distributions. Income-distribution data can be summarised by the 'Gini coefficient', which measures the extent to which the distribution of income (or, in some cases, consumption expenditure) among individuals or households within an economy deviates from a perfectly equal distribution. The coefficient falls between zero for perfect equality and one for extreme inequality. Gini coefficients for individual countries vary between close to 0.25 for egalitarian high-income countries such as Japan and Sweden and close to 0.6 for Brazil, which is one of world's most inegalitarian countries. The World Bank (2005) provides estimates of the Gini coefficient for most countries in its *World Development Indicators* publication; its most recent estimates show the US coefficient as 0.41 and the UK coefficient as 0.36. (Calculating the Gini coefficient is based on the Lorenz curve, which plots the cumulative percentages of total income received against the cumulative number of recipients, starting with the poorest individual or household. The coefficient measures the area between the Lorenz curve and a hypothetical line of absolute equality, expressed as a percentage of the maximum area under the line.)

Within this general methodology, approaches vary, particularly with regard to how wealth is defined. For example:

- The Capgemini/Merrill Lynch annual World Wealth Report defines the market in terms of individuals with financial wealth of more than $1 million. Its data include private equity holdings as well as all forms of publicly quoted equities, bonds and funds, and cash deposits. It excludes ownership of collectibles and real estate used for primary residences. Offshore investments are theoretically accounted for but, in practice, only insofar as countries are able to make accurate estimates of relative flows of property and investment in and out of their jurisdictions. It accommodates undeclared savings in its figures. It applies the methodology to 68 countries, which account for 98% of global GDP and 99% of global equity market capitalisation.
- The Boston Consulting Group (BCG), in its most recent annual Global Wealth Report (2005), defines the market in terms of assets under management (AuM). For this it includes listed securities, held either directly or indirectly through managed funds, cash

deposits, and life and pension assets. For larger countries, for 2004 and also for past years, it calculates AuM based on national accounts and other public records. For smaller countries, AuM is calculated as a proportion of nominal GDP, adjusted for country-specific economic factors. It calculates market movements as the weighted-average price changes of the asset classes held by households in each country, factoring in both domestic and overseas equity and bond holdings. To identify asset-holding patterns across different countries and wealth segments, it uses national statistics. When such data are not available, it assumes that countries with similar cultures and regulatory environments have similar asset-holding patterns. BCG defines 'mass affluent investors' as those with $100k–$1 million in AuM, 'emerging wealthy investors' as those with $1 million–$5 million in AuM and 'established wealthy investors' as those with more than $5 million in AuM. It now provides estimates for 62 countries.

- Datamonitor defines wealth by reference to onshore liquid assets only, including cash, equities, bonds and funds. Its typical approach is to use the UK as a base country: the UK is one of the few countries that has relatively robust liquid-asset distribution data (sourced from HM Revenue and Customs). For other countries, it calculates total wealth from public data sources, and then establishes a distribution for that wealth based on a skewed version of the UK's wealth distribution. The degree of skew applied is determined by a series of multipliers, which take into account factors such as population, asset holdings per capita and relative Gini coefficients. Datamonitor defines 'mass affluent' individuals as those with liquid assets of $54k–$360k, HNWIs as those with liquid assets of $360k–$9 million and UHNWIs (ultra-high net worth individuals) as those with liquid assets of more than $9 million.

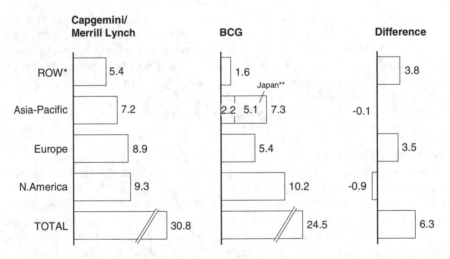

HNW wealth, 2004
$ trillion

*Latin America, Middle East and Africa
**Not disclosed; estimate takes BCG's $4.5 trillion estimate for 2003 (as published in *The Economist*, 10 June 2004), and assumes growth in line with that of non-Japan Asia

Figure 1.5   HNW wealth estimate comparison
Source: Capgemini/Merrill Lynch; Boston Consulting Group; *The Economist*; author's calculations.

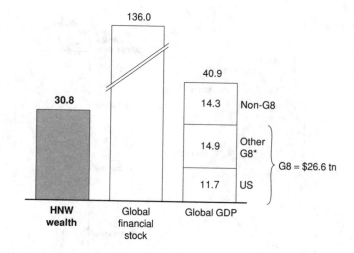

2004, $ trillions

*Japan, Germany, UK, France, Italy, Canada, Russia

Figure 1.6   Global HNW wealth in context
Source: Capgemini/Merrill Lynch; IMF; McKinsey Global Institute.

Regardless of the measurement methodology, the size of the wealth market is large. As Figure 1.6 shows, the stock of global HNW wealth represents around a quarter of the global financial stock (which includes all bank deposits, government and private debt securities, and equities). Also by way of context, HNW wealth is larger than the annual GDP of the G8, and is more than 2.5 times the size of US annual GDP.

Figure 1.7 shows that mass affluent wealth, i.e. the wealth of individuals holding $100k–$1 million of assets, makes up around two-thirds of the global wealth market. Turning to HNW wealth, as one would expect, North America and Europe currently dominate the market, accounting for 59% of the total, representing the wealth of 5.3 million millionaires. The average wealth of the world's 8.3 million millionaires is $3.7 million, but Latin American and African millionaires stand out as having much higher average wealth levels.

How much wealth is booked or managed offshore? That is notoriously difficult to assess with much confidence – and, needless to say, estimates vary substantially. At one extreme, the Tax Justice Network estimated total offshore wealth as at end 2004 of c.$11.5 trillion, or 37% of global HNW wealth, an estimate they consider conservative. Applying the indicative regional onshore-offshore splits given in Figure 1.3 yields an estimated total offshore wealth of c.$7 trillion. The Boston Consulting Group estimate c.$6.4 trillion, or 7.5% of total global wealth, in 2004.

In earlier work, BCG analysed the sources and destinations ('booking centres') of offshore wealth (see Figure 1.8). In terms of sources, they found that Europe accounted for more than half of the total, flowing mainly to Switzerland, Luxembourg and the Channel Islands. Geographic proximity appears to be a key driver in selecting an offshore destination: Latin Americans favour Miami, New York and the Caribbean; Asians favour Singapore and Hong Kong. But

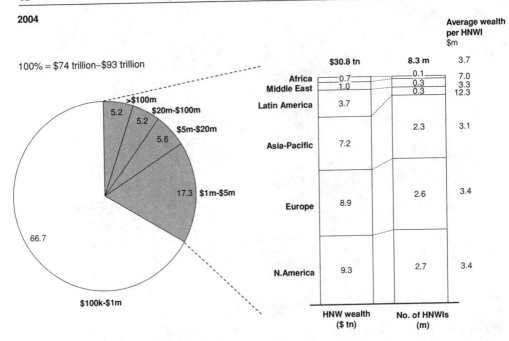

Figure 1.7 Global wealth by region and client wealth band
Source: Boston Consulting Group: Capgemini/Merrill Lynch; author's calculations.

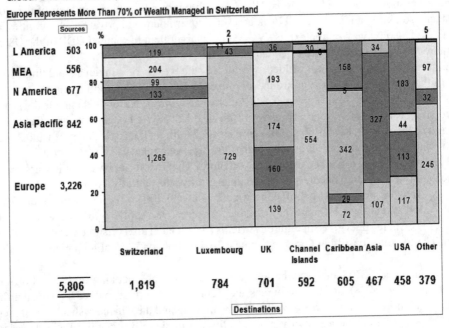

Figure 1.8 Offshore wealth: sources and destinations
Source: Boston Consulting Group; Huw van Steenis, Morgan Stanley. Reproduced by permission.

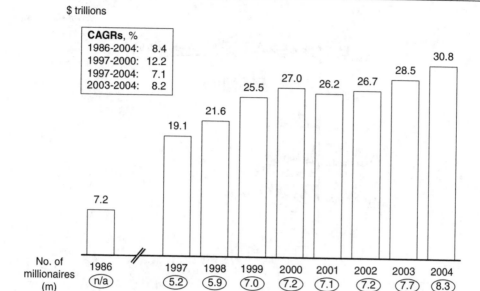

Figure 1.9   Growth in global HNW wealth
Source: Capgemini/Merrill Lynch 'World Wealth Report' (various years); author's calculations.

overall, Switzerland dominates the destinations, managing around one-third of total offshore assets.[5]

Since 1986, global HNW wealth has grown at a compound annual growth rate (CAGR) of 8.4% (see Figure 1.9), substantially higher than the 5.6% CAGR of global nominal GDP. Growth was particularly strong during the late 1990s, linked to strong growth in global equity markets in particular. Market growth faltered during 2000–2002, and there was widespread wealth destruction for the first time in recent history in 2001, driven by asset price falls and the global economic downturn. The market returned to growth in 2003, with further expansion in 2004. But recent growth at 8.2% is well down on that seen in the late 1990s.

Since 1997, the highest growth in wealth has been in Asia, followed by Europe and North America (see Figure 1.10). Recently, however, growth in the Middle East and Africa has picked up very strongly. Globally, the number of millionaires continues to grow at more than 7% a year – around 6 times the pace of the population as a whole.

1.2   KEY WEALTH DRIVERS

What are the key factors driving the growth in the wealth management market? These factors can be divided into a group of drivers that are common to all wealth markets, and those drivers that are region specific. In considering wealth market growth, it is useful to decompose it into appreciation of existing wealth, net new inflows from existing wealth owners and entry of new wealth owners. That, in turn, can have important implications for market accessibility.

There is also a group of less tangible factors at work. Kevin Phillips (2002) in his book, *Wealth and Democracy*, argues that a few common factors appear to support 'wealth waves',

---

[5] Note that this analysis focuses on the *stock* of assets. As discussed in Chapters 9 and 10, the picture with regard to new offshore asset *flows* would look very different.

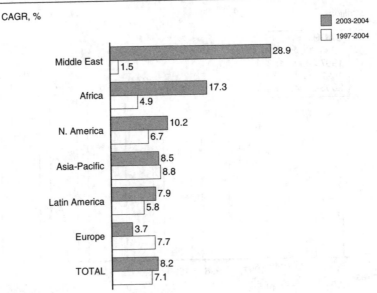

Figure 1.10 Growth in HNW wealth by region
Source: Capgemini/Merrill Lynch 'World Wealth Report' (various years); author's analysis.

including: a fascination with technology, creative finance, supportive government, the rule of law, patented inventions and an international dimension of immigrants and overseas conquests.

1.2.1 Generic drivers

A key driver of the wealth management market is clearly the growth of wealth itself and how it is distributed. In principle, the revenues of most financial services are driven by 'surplus' wealth. As individuals grow wealthier, they make more use of financial services. Wealthy individuals invest and spend more, they seek more protection for their existing wealth and lifestyle, and they feel comfortable borrowing large sums of money. They also seek advice when addressing this collection of financial needs.

Growth in wealth, in turn, is impacted by four main generic drivers: economic growth, asset prices, wealth allocation and demographic factors.

1.2.1.1 Economic growth

From a long-term perspective, the key wealth driver is economic growth (which, in turn, ulti-mately helps drive asset prices). Within aggregate economic growth, its balance/composition, volatility and the pattern of productivity growth also have an impact on wealth creation and allocation.

Figure 1.11 shows that growth in global wealth has exceeded that of global GDP in recent years. Asia Pacific and Latin America stand out as having grown wealth well in excess of their GDP growth rates, while the opposite has been the case in the Middle East. Latin America also accounts for a disproportionately high share of global wealth relative to its share of global GDP; on the other hand, Europe's wealth share is disproportionately low.

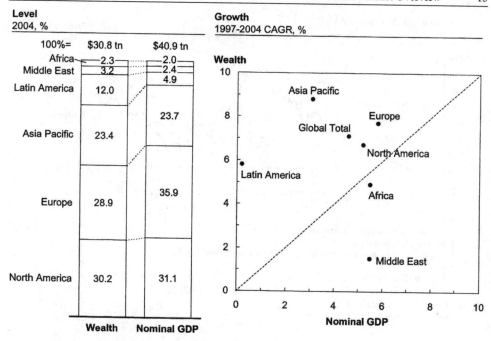

Figure 1.11   Relationship between wealth and nominal GDP
Source: Capgemini/Merrill Lynch; IMF; author's analysis.

1.2.1.2   Asset prices

The 1990s surge in wealth was largely due to the biggest ever bull market in equities, particularly in America. Some of the increase in investable wealth reflects a shift of assets to the market that had previously existed in an illiquid and less measurable form. In recent years, many family-owned companies have been sold, including a growing number through an initial public offering (IPO). To some extent, this merely represents wealth reclassification rather than genuine new wealth creation.

Figure 1.12 illustrates how, despite the equity market downturn from 2000 to 2003, other assets, notably property and commodities, have, to some extent, taken up the slack, and fuelled huge interest in product innovation and asset class diversification.

1.2.1.3   Wealth allocation

Another recent trend has been the increasing income and wealth *concentration* among the more affluent segments of society as a whole. Going forward, BCG expects that the wealth of the world's wealthiest investors (i.e. those with more than $5 million) will grow by 6.6% a year between 2004 and 2009, while that of the least wealthy (i.e. those with less than $100 000) will shrink by 0.3% a year.

Nowhere has this trend been greater than in the US (see Box 1.2). For income, the share going to the top 1% was 15% in 2002 according to a study of tax returns by Thomas Piketty and Emmanuel Saez (2004). That compares to around 13% in the UK and Canada, but compares

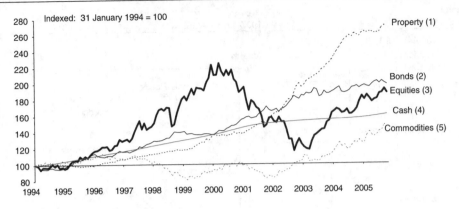

Notes:
1. UK residential property; Halifax house price index
2. Based on US Treasury bonds
3. Based on world equity market index of Morgan Stanley Capital International
4. US Fed funds rate
5. Based on Reuters–CRB index

Figure 1.12   Selected asset prices
Source: Author's analysis.

Box 1.2   US Wealth Dynamics[6]

Recent trends

Every year since 1982, Forbes has published data on what staff of that magazine estimate to be the wealthiest 400 people in the United States. The Forbes wealth data show strong growth *in real terms* across a variety of dimensions from 1989 to 2001. There are, however, some striking differences within the period and across different groups (see Table 1.1).

Table 1.1   The wealthiest 400 people in the US according to Forbes: wealth by rank and average wealth in millions of 2001 dollars

Wealth by Forbes rank	Year							
	1989	1992	1995	1998	1999	2000	2001	2002
1	7 106	7 746	17 002	63 214	89 716	64 318	54 000	42 361
10	3 417	4 303	4 940	11 907	17 943	17 356	17 500	11 723
50	1 736	1 537	2 068	3 139	4 222	4 798	3 900	3 152
100	957	984	1 034	1 840	2 533	2 654	2 000	1 773
200	615	584	689	1 028	1 267	1 531	1 200	1 084
300	478	430	500	731	897	1 000	875	763
400	376	326	391	541	660	740	600	542
Average wealth	921	937	1 025	1 997	2 731	3 057	2 366	2 148
Memo item: Number of billionaires	97	92	107	205	278	301	266	205

Source: Kennickell (2003); US Federal Reserve Survey of Consumer Finances.

---

[6] This box draws heavily on Kennickell (2003).

From 1989 to 1995, overall mean Forbes wealth was relatively stable, as was the level of wealth at most of the ranks of the distribution of this population up to around the top 50. The top 50 showed substantial growth in wealth over this period. From 1995 to 1999, the entire distribution shifted up, particularly at the top. By 1999, the wealth of the wealthiest individual was 5.3 times larger than in 1995, while that of the tenth wealthiest individual was 3.6 times higher. Over the same period, the cut-off point for membership of the Forbes group rose 69%. After 1999, the top end led the way to a general downturn in 2001 that continued into 2002. Nonetheless, even at the end of the period, the entire distribution was significantly above the levels of 1989. The total wealth of the Forbes 400 as a proportion of total individual wealth ranged from 1.5% in 1989 to a high of 2.5% in 1998 to 2.2% in 2001.

The overall growth in the entire distribution of the Forbes wealth masked a considerable amount of composition churning. Of the 400 people in the 2001 list, 230 were not in the 1989 list. Even between 1998 and 2001, nearly a quarter of the people on the list were replaced by others. Although some of the movement is explained by the transfer of wealth through inheritance, the number of such instances appears to be small – only about 20 of the members in the 1989 list did not appear in the 2001 list. Others may have died and fragmented their wealth into pieces smaller than the Forbes cut-off. Persistence of individuals in the list was highest for people who were in the top 100. Of the people in the top 100 in the 2001 list, 45 were included in the same group in 1989 and 23 others were in the lower ranks of the list. Of the bottom 100 in 1989, only 29 remained in the 2001 list.

Historical perspective

Long-term historical wealth data are hard to come by, so most studies have focused on income. What follows focuses on data compiled by Piketty and Saez (2004). Figure 1.13 shows

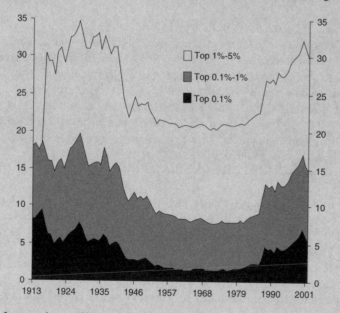

Figure 1.13 Income shares of highest US earners, percent
Source: Picketty and Saez (2004).

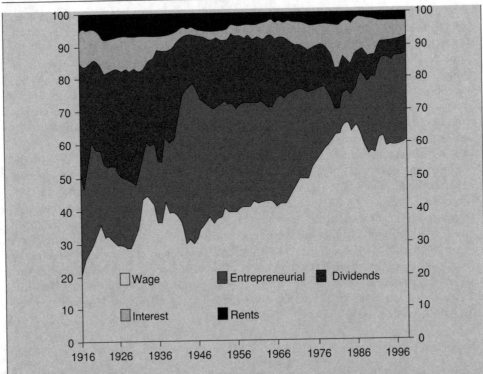

Figure 1.14   Sources of income, top 1% of earners, percent
Source: Citigroup Global Markets (2005), based on Piketty and Saez (2004).

the share of income for the top 0.1%, 1% and 5% since 1913. The fortunes of the top 0.1% (roughly 100 000 households) fluctuate the most, and account for the bulk of the movement of the top 5%. Between World War II and the early 1980s, all of their income shares fell, partly linked to loss of capital income and progressive corporate and estate taxation. But since then, the income shares of these groups have all reverted pretty much to where they were in the roaring 1920s, partly linked again to reductions in taxes. As Figure 1.14 shows, the way in which this income is earned has shifted, because in the earlier period, dividend and rental income were more important than they are now; wages and entrepreneurial receipts now dominate the income of the rich.

with levels of around 8% in Japan, France and Switzerland, for example.[7] Take wealth, rather than income, and America's disparity is even more stark. In 2001, the wealthiest 1% of households controlled 33% of US wealth, while the lowest 50% of households held only 3%, according to the Federal Reserve.

The relative inequality in America reflects the people at the top doing unusually well. The top 10% of Americans are nearly twice as well off as the top 10% of Nordic households. They are also much further away from the US mean. As Robert Frank and Philip Cook (1996) point out in

---

[7] The drivers of these differences are not entirely clear. Tax plays some part, but relative to the US, Canada is a high-tax country and Switzerland a low-tax one. To some extent, the figures may be distorted because they are based on tax returns and in some countries it is easier to park income offshore than it is in others. In addition, people move. There is, for example, a programme in France currently to try to pursuade the rich to move back, as large numbers have apparently decamped to Belgium and the UK.

their book *The Winner-Take-All Society*, new technology, globalisation and market economics have changed the structure of many industries in such a way that their star performers now earn vastly more than the average. That has been most visible in sports (think golf, tennis, soccer, baseball and basketball stars) and the arts (think music, TV and movie icons, supermodels, designers, celebrity chefs, etc.), where the best can become global celebrities and typically earn far more than those who manage and advise them, whereas average performers receive only mediocre pay. Oprah Winfrey, who neatly combines both managing and performing in her company, Harpo Productions, became the world's first self-made billionairess in 2003. But superstar remuneration has also become widespread in less glamorous businesses, including law, investment banking and hedge fund management.[8]

Going forward, government policy, such as the tax policies of the Bush administration, will probably further exacerbate the wide gap between rich and poor. US inheritance tax has been all but scrapped. Marginal rates on top incomes have fallen. Most important may be the 2003 reduction in capital gains and dividends taxes, which will have a disproportionate impact on the top 20% of households.

Continued growth in income inequality is one factor that is expected to support greater future wealth concentration across the globe going forward.

1.2.1.4   Demographic factors

Demographics are also a powerful catalyst to wealth market development. The basic rationale is as follows. The age group that has generally mattered most to the industry from a growth perspective is those aged 45–64. These are the people who are most likely to be accumulating assets for retirement, while at the same time enjoying their peak years of earnings. Because of the baby boom that took place between 1946 and 1965, that age cohort has been growing rapidly from around 1991.

Economic and technological change has also been driving the recent growth in HNWI wealth and has led to a transformation in the profile of the contemporary wealthy individual. Entrepreneurial wealth has become increasingly important, while the significance of inherited wealth has declined somewhat.

Going forward, though, inheritance-related wealth transfers are likely to increase in importance and are expected to peak in 2015. It is important to note that this, of course, is not *new* wealth – merely a redistribution of existing wealth. The baby boomers are poised to benefit from a substantial generational transfer of assets as their parents leave inheritances that could, in the US, easily exceed $41 trillion[9] over their children's lifetime. Boomer parents enjoyed the strongest asset growth rate of any demographic group over the last decade. How these assets will be distributed among the boomer group, and what effect this pending transfer will have on boomer savings patterns and on the industry, both pre- and post-transfer, is not entirely clear. One suggestion is that it will create opportunities in two main ways:

1. 'Money in motion', a chance for wealth managers to grab share ('wealth redistribution') as clients potentially switch providers (one study, Grove and Prince (2003), found that a full 92% of heirs switch wealth managers after receiving their inheritance).
2. Expand the addressable market, because younger clients tend to use wealth managers more than their parents, who often hold securities directly.

---

[8] Dew-Becker and Gordon (2005) show that corporate executives now account for more than half of the incomes of the top 0.1% of the US income distribution. The ratio of the pay of US chief executive officers to average wages rose from 27 in 1973 to 300 in 2000.

[9] This is the lower-bound estimate of Havens and Schervish (1999), confirmed in their 2003 paper.

1.2.2 Regional drivers

Though there are clear differences among the drivers of wealth growth at the individual country level – reflecting, in part, different stages of market evolution and maturity – some regional patterns and stylised facts emerge. Wealthy clients' international lifestyles and business interests mean that a grasp of the regional dimensions is important to serve these clients well. Appendix 1 provides a more detailed country-by-country analysis.

1.2.2.1 North America: Industry shift towards full-service model

In the US and Canada, the key wealth drivers are well known. Chief among them are consistently high economic and productivity growth rates. Wealth has also been driven by strong US financial market returns,[10] particularly equities, in which North American investors hold more than half their assets – far more than the global average. The bulk of the wealth is held onshore, reflecting low domestic tax rates and general economic stability. Though the early phases of economic development were dominated by family businesses, start-up businesses have grown significantly since the 1980s. In the 1990s, there was a further pick-up in the number of entrepreneurs, and the booming IPO market turned many of them into instant millionaires.[11] Most recently, for example, the August 2005 IPO of Google, the Internet search engine company, is reported to have created 5 billionaires and 1 000 millionaires.

The bulk of America's wealthy individuals and families are self-made. During the period from the early 1950s to the mid-1970s, many millionaires were senior corporate executives. However, from the early 1980s the bulk of the newly created wealth has come from entrepreneurs; the market was given a boost during the mid-to-late 1980s as there was a tendency for wealth to be liquidated through leveraged buyouts. The majority of these wealthy individuals are retired business owners, corporate executives or other professionals. A third of respondents to US Trust's June 2002 Survey of Affluent Americans emphasised earnings from corporate employment, private business, professional practice and securities; a quarter emphasised real estate. By far the least important source of wealth was inheritance.

Demographic factors have also played a strong role. There are around 60 million US baby boomers at present, and the cohort is likely to continue growing for the next decade to around 80 million.

US UHNW wealth has recently been growing particularly strongly. Many of the wealthiest families have their own private investment offices, or 'family offices', with a staff of professionals providing a variety of wealth management services.

1.2.2.2 Western Europe: Wealth transfer between generations

Western Europe is one of the most mature wealth management markets. In contrast to the US (see Figure 1.15), it includes a significant proportion of global 'old' wealth – associated with inheritance and more traditional forms of asset growth rather than entrepreneurial wealth creation. A significant proportion of industrial companies remain privately owned, particularly in Germany and Italy. That, together with a tendency for wealth to be tied up in land and property in some countries in particular, has contributed to a degree of wealth illiquidity in

---

[10] Domestic financial market returns are relevant because of investors' well-documented home bias.
[11] During this period, Silicon Valley originated a term to describe the sort of money that frees an individual from ever having to work again: 'fuck-you money'.

Key Differences between North American and European HNWIs

North America   Europe

- Capital market-led, participating in strong equity culture

- Banking-led, protecting capital from war, hyperinflation, and high taxation

- Wealth sources: Highly entrepreneurial, emphasis on technology and finance

- Wealth sources: Inheritance and multiple sectors, including retailing and manufacturing

- Average HNWI age 55–57:
  – Distributed down through younger age bands
  – Increasing female component

- Average HNWI age 59–62:
  – High concentration in upper age bands
  – Fewer females

- Trend towards one principal provider and a more holistic approach

- Use multiple providers and a less integrated approach

- Domestically focused equity culture, mainly in onshore vehicles

- More balanced across asset classes; stronger offshore flavour

Figure 1.15 Key differences between North American and European HNWIs
Source: Capgemini/Merrill Lynch 'World Wealth Report', 2002.

this region. A challenge for private banks with clients in this region is to develop tools for harnessing this wealth.

A significant proportion of European wealth is managed offshore. That reflects relatively high tax rates in most European countries, political instability in some countries and weak domestic investment opportunities.

Until recently, many of the larger individual private banking accounts from this region consisted of fortunes made two or three generations ago with very little new capital being added. It is quite common for individuals who play an active role in the running of their companies to delegate the management of their wealth to private banks or other professionals. In general, private banking clients from this region have tended to be conservative investors.

BCG note that, after several years of decline, exposure to equities throughout Western Europe has stabilised at around 32% of assets, though some countries, such as the UK and Switzerland, have significantly higher shares. A relatively large proportion of Western European wealth is held in property, shipping and privately held businesses. Going forward, intergenerational wealth transfer will be particularly important in this region.

1.2.2.3   Central and Eastern Europe: Strong economic development

There are several key structural drivers of wealth creation in Central and Eastern Europe. Clearly, the stabilising political and economic environment in the post-communist era has been supportive. For some countries in the region, the prospect of European Union (EU) accession, with its associated real economic convergence, has led to high, sustained growth over recent years. That, in turn, has been a result of capital availability (including foreign direct investment, EU structural funds, domestic investment and saving) and gains in capital and labour productivity (linked, in part, to privatisation and restructuring).

Poland, Hungary and the Czech Republic, for example, have recently benefited greatly from an influx of foreign capital as the last hurdles to full membership of the EU were removed. In 2004, GDP growth averaged 4.3% in these countries. Simultaneously, Russia continued the impressive recovery from its late 1990s financial crisis, posting GDP growth of 7.2%; that, combined with the oil price rise, has generated very strong growth in the local equity market.

That the early stages of the transition from communism to market-oriented economies allowed many opportunists to get rich quick is well known. Some did so honestly but, as *The Economist* put it, 'many more cheated, bribed and stole from the state or small investors, using conniving banks as a source of everlasting loans and a place to wash their money'.

In Russia, the wealth market has been supported by a slew of IPOs and by the recent oil price rise, which has helped stabilise the economy, given that it is the second-largest oil exporter in the world. But political instability, and a lack of services aimed at long-term wealth preservation and wealth transfer, have traditionally driven much of the wealth offshore. The Russian Finance Ministry officially projects that capital flight will rise to $10 billion in 2005.

Throughout the region, there is also a legitimate – more onshore-oriented – affluent middle class emerging, supported by market liberalisation, low inflation and interest rates, steadying local currencies, higher risk-adjusted local returns, a growing number of entrepreneurs and small businesses, and broad-based increases in real disposable income. Eastern Europe's newly affluent people are younger, better educated, more familiar with technology and more likely to be entrepreneurs – with an associated greater appetite for credit – than their counterparts in the West.

1.2.2.4 Asia-Pacific: Strong economic development

Strong economic growth and development across Asia has led to considerable wealth accumulation, mainly over the last 25 years. That growth has been supported by high savings rates, young and productive populations, and strong inflows of foreign direct investment.

A key contributory factor has been intense regional entrepreneurial activity, particularly in real estate, banking and trading-related businesses. Throughout the region, some 500 million people are employed in non-agricultural sectors. Of these, around 60% work in small and medium-sized businesses. The entrepreneurs who run these businesses have generally fared well in Asia's rapidly expanding economies.

The ethnic Chinese (diaspora) population stands out as being particularly successful in accumulating wealth. In Asia, there are currently around 2 million Asians of Chinese descent, driven by the large waves of emigration from mainland China during the twentieth century. Initially, they were banned from owning land and often barred from entering local politics, so local commerce and regional trade were their only options. But Chinese communities have consistently managed to turn adversity into prosperity. The cumulative impact of Chinese diaspora accomplishments are dramatic. In Thailand, for example, they comprise 10% of the population, but hold up to 80% of the wealth.

Many individuals throughout the region became wealthy simply by having had family land on the outskirts of Asia's fast-emerging cities. For example, it is not unusual in places like Taiwan or Hong Kong to encounter families whose net worth exceeds US$10 million simply as a result of having owned a plot of land bought before the 1970s, and sold after the mid-1980s. From the mid-1980s, and prior to the 1997–1998 crisis, real estate and financial asset prices rapidly appreciated in the region and capital markets boomed.

The Asian crisis of 1997–1998 had uneven effects within the region. South Korea and Taiwan were particularly affected, but it did not significantly affect Australia or China. For the region as a whole, the number of wealthy clients and their wealth remained remarkably stable over this period. The crisis did have the effect of increasing the investment conservatism of many clients, which enabled them to cope much better with the recent global equity market falls of 2000–2002. Most Asian assets are still held in cash, with equity exposure currently only around 28% of total assets. Most recently, China's huge export industry, along with many successful IPOs of Chinese companies in Hong Kong and New York, have been key wealth drivers.

Indian wealth has been driven mainly by very high economic growth in recent years, which has averaged 6.1% since 1995. India is now a major hub for outsourcing and global manufacturing, linked to its highly skilled workforce. Another driver is India's very high personal savings rate and, more generally, the current and prospective economic deregulation. The 20 million non-resident Indians (NRIs) around the world include around 150 000 dollar millionaires, and represent a particularly attractive segment. NRI remittances and asset repatriation have picked up sharply in recent years as they seek to take advantage of attractive domestic investment opportunities. Other wealth segments include entrepreneurs, corporate executives and professionals.

1.2.2.5 Latin America: Traditional offshore-banking stronghold

Rapid expansion and modernisation of Latin American economies over the last decade has resulted in a substantial increase in personal wealth. Tax systems in the region are, in general, not effectively redistributive so this newly created wealth is very unequally held. World Bank data show that Latin America has the greatest degree of income inequality in the world, with the top 10% of income earners accounting for around 45% of total income (compared to 30% in the US and around 25% in Europe and Asia-Pacific).

Latin American governments have been privatising state assets by selling off state-owned companies. They have also been loosening capital controls, eliminating export taxes, lowering trade barriers and opening up their banking systems to market influences. That, in turn, has encouraged repatriation of capital and boosted foreign direct investment. In Brazil, for instance, investors have recently been allowed to invest more freely abroad. As a result, lower yield and lower risk investments in bank deposits and bonds have been falling from favour.

Investment in local markets has grown, as confidence in some local economies has hardened. Increasingly benign government attitudes towards foreign investors has provided the opportunity for families in the region to increase liquidity by selling family-owned businesses to international investors and multinational companies. For example, in May 2001, Citigroup acquired the first-generation family-owned Grupo Financiero Banamex-Accival, which was Mexico's second-largest bank. During the 1990s, regional capital market development and high equity market valuations encouraged some family-owned firms to seek market listings. Growing numbers of entrepreneurs (e.g. in the offshore trade assembly and services sectors) have also been generating new sources of wealth.

Overall, these drivers mean that Latin America has many substantial wealth management clients. Unlike the rest of the world, Latin America's small pockets of relatively immobile, concentrated wealth have provided an easily identifiable client segment for local and foreign banks to pursue in each country in the region. So far, wealth managers have generally focused on the HNW, rather than the affluent, market, which is not growing as rapidly as in other developing countries.

Though Latin America made substantial progress in handling its macro economy during the 1990s, sustained economic growth and political stability have remained elusive. Mexico, Brazil and, most recently, Argentina have lurched from one financial crisis to another.

Capital preservation has always been the ultimate goal of most Latin American private banking clients. For decades, Latin American HNW investors have been eager to get their money out of their countries and their region. They considered their home and businesses more than ample exposure to their volatile domestic economies and were interested only in the most conservative and discrete US, European and offshore investments. Latin America has very low equity exposure (BCG estimates 14% of total assets in 2004), with the bulk of assets held in fixed income and cash instruments.

Today, however, there appears to be a new willingness among some clients to keep at least part of their money at home. Domestic onshore investment has grown in popularity somewhat as governments try to create a more favourable tax and regulatory environment. Clients have shifted from traditional offshore private banking products to integrated, global solutions that address a complex set of business and personal needs across their entire balance sheet – not just the offshore portion.

There are, however, considerable differences among countries. Real GDP grew by c.4.5% in Mexico and Brazil in 2004, supporting wealth levels in those countries. At the other extreme, Argentina has suffered the greatest value destruction, with a large currency devaluation and a massive default on government and corporate debt in early 2002; its economy shrank at an average rate of 5% a year between 1999 and 2002, though growth has since rebounded strongly. Separately, the oil crisis in Venezuela in 2002–2003 sparked a recession that inhibited wealth generation there, though the economy is now recovering. Onshore providers in these countries have therefore downsized dramatically.

Overall in Latin America, political and economic instability have continued to drive wealth offshore. Latin American clients have generally booked their offshore assets in the United States, the Caribbean or Switzerland. There has been a shift recently towards booking more assets in Switzerland due to the increased transparency requirements under US legislation (e.g. the US Patriot Act – see Chapter 9).

1.2.2.6 Middle East: Oil-driven growth

The wealth of the Gulf region, both public and private, has derived almost entirely from oil and other natural resources such as gas, as well as from property and land. The oil boom reached its peak following the price shocks of the 1970s, creating a vast amount of prosperity. Sustained GDP growth has also supported wealth creation. The region's non-oil exports are small, even though countries such as the United Arab Emirates and Iran have successfully diversified their economies.

Wealth in the Middle East is highly concentrated and predominantly in the hands of relatively few families, who invest mainly in their own businesses. These family businesses act as agents, diversifying into other sectors of the economy and building a chain of dependencies. The majority of these families have inherited their wealth over several generations and continue to control large segments of the domestic economy. Financial institutions managing private wealth have recognised this and have started to meet the needs of these clients by establishing family offices (see Chapter 6). Some of these offices have been known to employ 50 or more people in several locations in the Gulf, Europe and the US.

There are five broad categories of Middle Eastern wealth:

- Classical inherited wealth accumulated over several generations. That is by far the most common form of wealth. This segment mainly consists of long-established wealthy Middle Eastern families who are part of the rulers of the region.
- First-generation oil wealth. These holders of 'old money' tend to be conservative in their choice of overseas investments, with a preference for cash deposits, bonds and real estate.
- Younger generation family businesses. These are usually enthusiastic investors who have been to business school in the US or Europe. Many of them have evolved through the growth of the non-oil sector, including entrepreneurs, traders and holders of important franchises.
- Female inheritors. With the shift of affluence beginning to take place, mainly due to the death of one generation, there are now growing levels of wealth in the hands of women.[12] Views differ as to how much real control and influence these women have over their financial affairs. But there is a growing level of competitive activity in connection with this segment, suggesting that there are enough women who control their own wealth to present a sustained marketing opportunity.[13] An indication of this is the increased presence of female bankers in the region, particularly in the Gulf and Saudi Arabia, where women in business are an innovation.
- Funds held in Islamic institutions. Since its beginnings in the 1980s, the global pool of funds being managed according to Islamic principles[14] now totals around $265 billion. Islamic banking services are in high demand in the Middle East and constitute a rapidly growing segment of the market (see Chapter 4). In Saudi Arabia, for example, Islamic mutual funds have grown at an annual rate of more than 20% over the past few years and now account for some 60% of the total mutual fund market.

Much of the region's wealth has traditionally been held offshore ('petrodollars'). That reflects regional economic and political instability, underdeveloped local financial sectors and, in some cases, the need to support international lifestyles. Most recently, the region is experiencing wealth generation not seen since the 1970s, primarily driven again by the growth in oil revenues.[15] The pick-up in oil revenue initially drives increases in public-sector infrastructure spending and employment which, in turn, feeds through to benefit entrepreneurs, importers and property developers. McKinsey estimates that close to half of new wealth is currently staying onshore, with half of that wealth invested in local equity markets, which have shown staggering gains in recent years.[16] Other recent drivers of wealth market development include greater intra-regional and international economic integration, and the development of domestic financial and other asset markets.

---

[12] In Islamic law, daughters as well as sons inherit, although unequally, on the basis of one part to two parts in the son's favour. Where cross-border wealth is concerned, the beneficial owner dictates how the wealth is distributed, and some international wealth managers detect that a more even-handed approach is now being taken.

[13] In Saudi Arabia, women own 40% of private wealth and account for more than 50% of university graduates – a situation that is unique in the Arab world. Yet they make up only 5% of the country's workforce.

[14] The conviction underpinning Islamic banking is that investments should be put to productive rather than speculative use and that a lender, instead of charging interest, should be compensated with a share of the profits—See Box 4.1 on Islamic Private Banking.

[15] The Middle East accounts for around 65% of global oil exports. In 2005, global oil export revenue more than doubled, and in real terms is now well above its previous 1980 peak. For oil exporters, the current oil shock is in real terms slightly larger than the shocks of the 1970s. See Chapter II of IMF (2006a).

[16] In the two years to September 2005, annual growth in local equity markets averaged 101% in the UAE, 80% in Saudi Arabia, 75% in Quatar and 49% in Kuwait. There have since been partial reversals in most markets – see Box 3 in IMF (2006b).

1.2.2.7   Africa: Commodity-driven growth

Africa has, in recent years, experienced relatively robust growth in wealth volumes and client numbers. That has primarily been driven by oil- and other commodity-related revenues. Other drivers include the pick-up in GDP growth, higher foreign direct investment, the relatively strong performance of local stock markets and local currency appreciation.

The African wealth market is dominated by South Africa, which accounts for around 60% of the region's wealth and has more than 35 000 HNWIs. Other key markets include Nigeria and Egypt. The ruling class, corporate executives, professionals, small and family-run businesses and, in some countries such as South Africa and Botswana, an emerging middle class represent the key target client segments. The bulk of African wealth is held offshore, mainly driven by political and economic instability. The region's wealth is highly concentrated, with levels of inequality very similar to those of Latin America.

1.3   INDUSTRY ECONOMICS

While, again, it is difficult to generalise, this section outlines some stylised facts on wealth management economics. At least on the face of it, the economics of the wealth management industry are extremely attractive, reflecting five key factors:

1. *Large and growing market.* Given the size and growth metrics outlined above it is unsurprising that wealth management is big business. It accounts for a disproportionately large share of the assets under management, revenues and profits of the personal financial services industry – up to 80% of the personal financial services profit pool in Europe, for example (Figure 1.16). Wealth management is also attractive relative to many other areas of financial

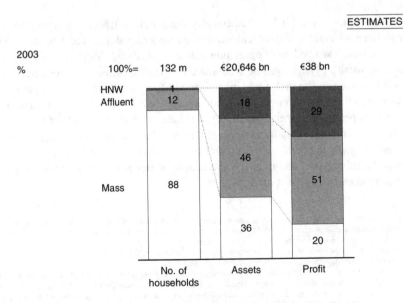

Figure 1.16   Wealth management component of personal financial services Europe
Source: Boston Consulting Group; author's calculations.

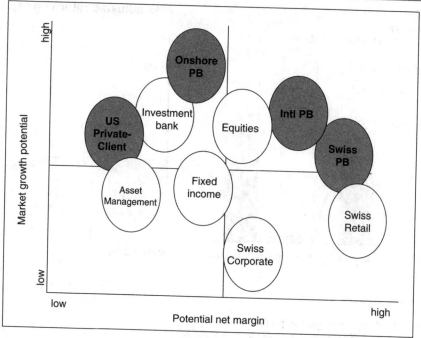

Figure 1.17   Relative attraction of wealth management
Source: UBS investor presentation.

services (Figure 1.17). Citigroup estimates that, globally, wealth management accounts for 20% of the financial services revenue pool, which is higher than investment banking.[17]

2. *High profitability*. This reflects two factors. First, net profit margins are relatively high. Most wealth management players achieve 25 basis points or more, compared to around 5 basis points for instititional asset managment (though institutional earnings are argually even more sticky). Second, regulatory and economic capital requirements are low, linked to very little credit and market risk and a limited need for an extensive branch network. Indeed, on a risk-adjusted basis, wealth management profitability can be spectacularly profitable (see Figures 1.18 and 1.19).

3. *Stable revenue stream*. This reflects a high proportion of fees in the revenue mix, in contrast to more volatile net interest or trading income. When combined with traditionally loyal client relationships, this yields a recurring source of income and cash flow akin to an annuity (Figure 1.20).

4. *A relatively high stock market rating*. The strong economic fundamentals of the industry are reflected in its valuation metrics and implied growth expectations. A premium P/E relative (i.e. the price-earnings ratio of wealth managers relative to that of the market as a whole) of around 1.2 is the norm, compared with a relative of around 0.8 for the financial sector as a whole (Figure 1.21). The best recent example of this is EFG International (see Box 6.1), which was valued at 12% of AuM at the time of its IPO (October 2005).

---

[17] BCG (2005c) estimated the global banking industry revenue pool as $2 057 billion in 2004, split as follows: retail banking 52%, corporate banking 20%, wealth management 12%, investment banking 9%, and asset management 7%.

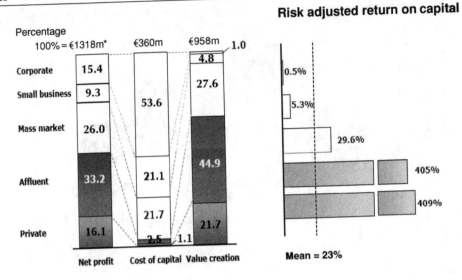

*Excluding other businesses

Figure 1.18 Wealth management profitability
Source: UniCredito Italiano investor presentation, 19 June 2001.

At the time of writing (March 2006), it was trading on c.62 times trailing earnings per share.

5. *Strong intragroup synergies.* Integrated players benefit from their wealth management businesses in two ways. On the revenue side, there are opportunities for wealth management operations to acquire clients from other parts of the group, e.g. the retail and business banking divisions. There are also opportunities for other parts of the group, e.g. investment banking divisions, to leverage the private client base for product sales. On the cost side, there are opportunities to share infrastructure and spread fixed costs, for example (see Chapter 8).

Wealth management economics have four simple components: assets, leverage, fees and costs. From the wealth manager's perspective, an attractive wealth management client has assets that comfortably exceed the stated minimum requirement, that grow steadily with limited volatility and that are invested under a discretionary mandate which produces recurring annual fees. A very attractive client will actively trade a portion of their assets, thus generating additional commission revenue. The truly ideal client will borrow against existing assets to increase the leverage of their investments, with little risk to the bank. If the client is financially sophisticated and understands the products reasonably well, an active portfolio can be effectively managed by a strong relationship manager with reasonably little time devoted to each client. If all goes well, such an account will reward the wealth manager with referrals to other wealthy clients.

Steady assets, consistent revenue streams, a low cost per account and a flow of new business introductions is a strong combination for wealth management economics. These objectives are not incompatible with serving the client's best interests, as long as adequate time is spent up-front to define the client's investment objectives, risk tolerance and service preferences.

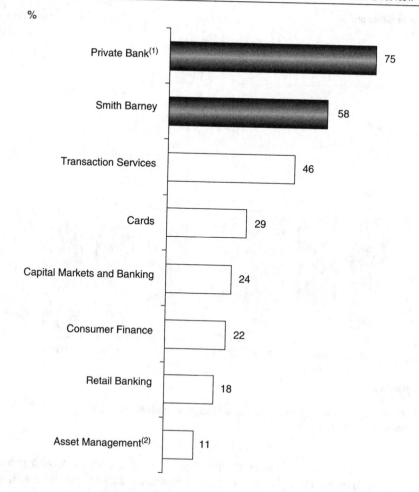

%

Figure 1.19   Post-tax return on invested capital, 2004
Source: Citigroup.

(1) Private Bank ROIC excluding Private Bank Japan Discontinuation Charge of $ 244MM after tax.
(2) Asset Management ROIC excluding Transfer Agent Settlement of $ 151MM after tax.
Note: Does not include Life Insurance & Annuities and Proprietary Investment Activities.

1.3.1   Value drivers and key performance indicators

Wealth management's basic value drivers divide into two: the net profit margin and assets under management (AuM). Figure 1.22 provides a simple value-tree framework. This framework can be applied to decompose current valuation or to identify the drivers of change in valuation over time. On the latter, recent McKinsey European survey evidence shows that, at the aggregate level, revenue generation rather than cost efficiency has been the most critical factor. Within AuM, market performance rather than net new money or a greater share of wallet has been the dominant factor.

Gross revenue margin
Basis points

Type of revenue:

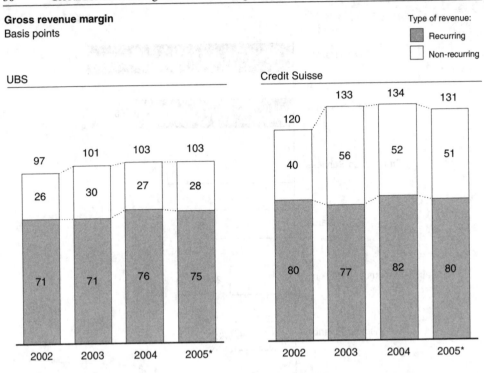

Figure 1.20   High proportion of recurring income: large Swiss bank examples
Source: Company financial reports.

Specific key performance indicators (KPIs) should be tailored to the wealth manager's individual circumstances. They should also be systematically tracked over time and, where possible, benchmarked against competitors.

Surveys have found that healthy profits can be generated across a range of different wealth management business models. The quality of execution is a key differentiator; other factors influencing wealth management economics include:

- *Level and volatility of asset prices.* Indeed, following the post-2000 equity market correction, one UK bank analyst remarked that 'wealth-management economics boil down to a small number times the equity market, less a big number (fixed costs)'. There is more than a grain of truth here as weaker financial markets exposed the fragility of many wealth management models. Merrill Lynch estimated that private banking profits fell by 20% a year on average between 2000 and 2002, driven mainly by falling asset-related revenues and sticky costs. Over that period, private banks' average cost-income ratio surged from 57% to 71%.
- *Scale.* Are there economies of scale in wealth management? As Raoul Weil, head of Wealth Management International, UBS, recently put it, 'Very wealthy clients do not want to entrust their fortune to a bank whose balance sheet is smaller than their own!' (IBM Consulting Services, 2005, p.80). Larger wealth managers certainly weathered the recent downturn better than the smaller firms. To some extent, this reflects their more diversified revenue

Multiples

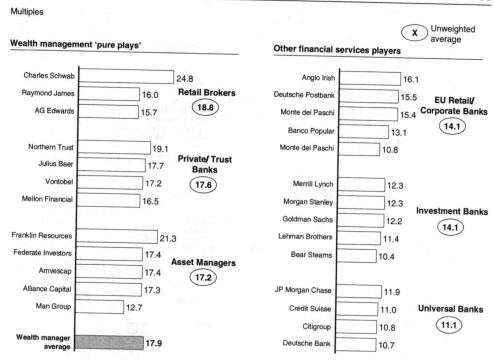

Figure 1.21   Financial services price-earnings ratios, 2005
Source: UBS; IBES; author's analysis.

streams. They also benefited from a 'flight to size', as heightened risk aversion led investors to seek comfort in institutions perceived as being systemically too important to fail. But recent survey evidence shows that smaller players appear to have a *structural* disadvantage with regard to profitability (see Figure 1.23). BCG has said that players with more than $10 billion–$15 billion of AuM are not demonstrably subscale. In IBM's 2005 European Wealth Management and Private Banking Industry Survey, 20% of respondents claim that the minimum threshold is €20 billion, with another 20% of respondents putting it at €50 billion. Larger firms have more bargaining power (and more resources to conduct due diligence) in product sourcing, have greater access to growth markets and, in the case of integrated providers, can lower their client-acquisition costs by using other parts of the group as client-feeder networks. That has contributed to their ability to achieve superior growth in net new money. On the other hand, as an institution grows beyond a critical size, clients can become more wary of potential conflicts of interest; client service quality – which remains the industry's key hallmark – can suffer ('I've become a number', an issue that can apply as much to relationship managers as to clients); greater bureaucracy can increase staff turnover; and the institution can become inherently more difficult to manage. Traditionally, private banking has a reputation for being a non-scalable industry. To the extent that there are economies of scale, most are likely to be found in the back office (see Chapter 7). The Swiss Banking School's International Private Banking Study 2005 (Cocca, 2005) concluded: 'Overall there seems to be some evidence for a moderate level of economies of scale in terms of profitability. However, size [in itself] has no significant influence on efficiency.'

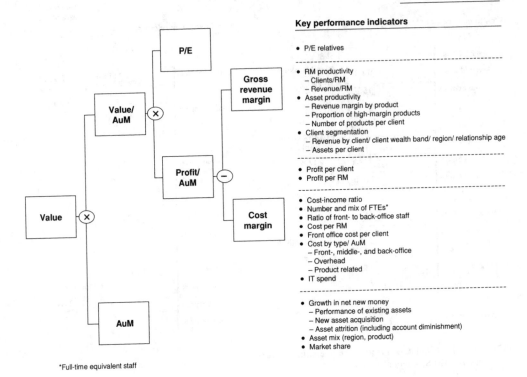

*Full-time equivalent staff

Figure 1.22 Wealth management value drivers
Source: Author's analysis.

- *Business model.*
  (a) *Onshore versus offshore models.* Margins tend to be higher offshore than onshore (see Figure 1.24), reflecting a number of factors. In the offshore business, clients are often less price sensitive and less focused on investment performance; there is a lack of aggressive competition; and client and asset loadings per relationship manager tend to be higher (linked to less frequent client interaction and the prevalence of 'suitcase banking'). In the onshore business, competition is more intense from both incumbents and new entrants; players compete more on price; and costs are higher. Offshore margins are often used to cross-subsidise onshore efforts.
  (b) *Fee- versus commission-based models.* Fee-based models are inherently more stable than commission-based models, which are driven by clients' trading activity. At least in part, that helps to explain why private banks generally have superior economics to those of brokers (see Figure 1.25). Other factors include higher average assets per relationship manager and a lower compensation–revenue ratio. Many US brokers are, in fact, actively focusing on boosting fees, which now account for more than half of total revenue for some players (see Chapter 6).
  (c) *Target client segment and client mix.* Economics vary significantly by client wealth band (see Figure 1.26). Revenue margins tend to be lower for wealthier clients, linked to their greater bargaining power, financial sophistication, more product/deal-driven approach and price sensitivity. Yet for some players, the costs of maintaining a large

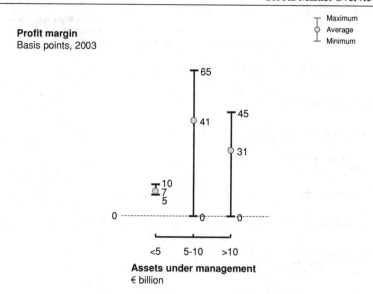

Figure 1.23   Wealth management economies of scale: European survey
Source: McKinsey European Private Banking Economics Survey 2004. Reproduced by permission.

number of low-growth small accounts can offset any revenue advantage, and many of the very wealthiest clients can also be very expensive to serve. Sitting between these extremes, there is a 'sweet spot', which may be client asset levels of around $1 million–$5 million. But it is important to note that *any* client wealth level can, in principle, be profitable. Wealth managers need to pick their target client segments and then tailor their

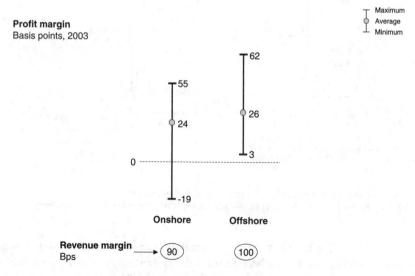

Figure 1.24   Offshore versus onshore economics: European survey
Source: Boston Consulting Group. Reproduced by permission.

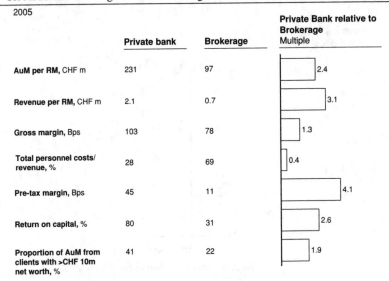

Figure 1.25 Economics of private banking versus brokerage
Source: UBS investor presentation; author's analysis.

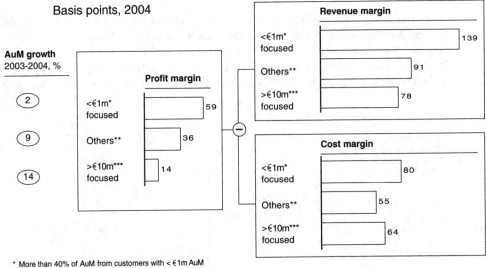

* More than 40% of AuM from customers with < €1m AuM
** Weighted average, excluding <€1m- and >€10m-focused
*** More than 50% of AuM from customers with > €10m AuM

Figure 1.26 Economics of banks focussing on selected client wealth bands
Source: McKinsey European Private Banking Economics Survey 2005. Reproduced by permission.

propositions and operating models appropriately: one-size-fits-all wealth management approaches do not work. A related factor is the proportion of clients with wealth below the bank's stated account minimum, which is around 50% for many players.

• *Other factors*, including asset, product and mandate mix, sales productivity and operational efficiency, each of which is explored elsewhere in this book.

1.4 COMPETITIVE LANDSCAPE

Against this backdrop of historically strong growth and attractive economics, it is no surprise that the number and range of institutions providing wealth management services has been rising dramatically. A decade ago, wealth managers mostly cloaked themselves in secrecy; very few people knew the names of more than a handful of players. Today, the types of players calling themselves wealth managers is truly vast – everyone from one-man-band advisors to companies as large as Citigroup. It is difficult to name a single large bank that is *not* targeting the wealth management market.

Traditionally, the industry was dominated by private banks and stockbrokers. But there were important regional differences in the dominant types of player. To some extent, this reflected differences in the structure and regulation of the financial services industry as a whole. Broadly, there are two main models:

- *North American model*, where the industry is dominated by full-service and discount broker-ages and money managers, whose strengths lie in the investment area, rather than in tradi-tional deposit gathering. As noted above, the traditional emphasis here is on a (transaction-driven) commission-based business model.
- *European model*, where universal and traditional private banks dominate, due to their ability to offer a comprehensive range of wealth management products and services. The emphasis here is on a fee-based business model.

ILLUSTRATIVE

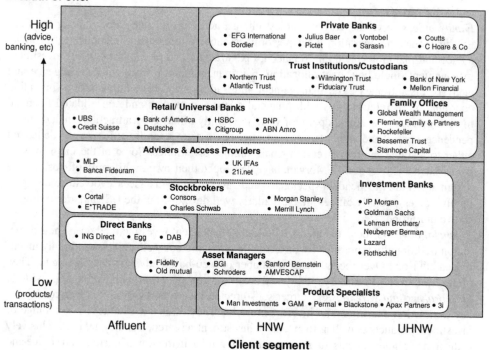

Figure 1.27 Wealth management competitor landscape
Source: Author's analysis.

The following provides a brief overview of the main types of wealth management players. There are huge differences among them in terms of the types of clients served and the types of products and services offered (see Figure 1.27). They also differ in terms of distribution channels, participation within the industry value chain, geographic coverage and scale. It is a complex patchwork. Chapter 6 provides more detail. The main types of player are:

- *Pure private banks* is a broad category of player that includes the classic Swiss private banking partnerships and other independent players. Mainly targeting HNWIs, these institutions offer clients end-to-end capabilities via a relationship with a senior banker (the relationship manager) that is confidential and founded on trust. Typically, the relationship manager is the client's sole contact point and handles all aspects of the relationship. But private banks, though important, are by no means the only player in the wealth management industry. In fact, recent research by Scorpio Partnership shows that private banks manage only around $4.6 trillion, or 16%, of global HNW wealth.

- *Trust banks* are essentially the US equivalent of the traditional European private bank. Most have their roots in providing trust and custody services, but have broadened their product range over the years. They now also provide asset management, insurance and financial, tax and estate planning. Their core target client segment is UHNWIs, but many have also developed tailored propositions for HNWIs.

- *Retail and universal banks* target affluent clients who need comprehensive advice and who value a close banking relationship. Most of them have been shifting their focus up the wealth curve. They offer products across the full client balance sheet, but often struggle to integrate and coordinate them effectively. The emphasis is on 'farming' their existing customer base, including business banking clients. Examples include Citigroup, HSBC, Bank of America and ABN AMRO.

- *Family offices* serve the very wealthiest clients, acting as an integrated hub for the family's financial administration. They perform, essentially, three main functions: (a) specialist advice and planning (including financial, tax, strategic and philanthropic); (b) investment management (including asset allocation, risk management, investment due diligence and analysis, discretionary asset management and trading); and (c) administration (including coordination of relationships with financial services providers and consolidated financial reporting). From the client's point of view, the family office's key attractions include independence, control and highly tailored, specialist expertise. A family office may be dedicated either to a single family or serve a small number of families. Some of the major private banks, such as Pictet and JP Morgan, have developed their own multifamily offices, but the vast majority are independent specialists (and have, in some instances, evolved from single-family offices). Family offices are particularly well developed in the US, and are starting to evolve in Europe.

- *Financial advisors* focus on clients who seek independent investment advice. Their distribution traditionally relies heavily on a mobile sales force of well-trained and highly incentivised advisors. Over recent years, a number of web-based advisors have emerged. They offer above-average advisory quality and act as a gateway to third-party product providers.

- *Stockbrokers and wirehouses*[18] target self-directed investors and traders for their day-to-day transaction execution and investment needs. They offer low-cost access to a range of investment products as well as to extensive investment research. But they are not exclusively dedicated to affluent clients, do not typically offer much in the way of customised advice and

---

[18] US term for the largest brokerage houses.

often lack transaction banking products. It is a diverse group, including firms that have their roots in online broking such as E*TRADE, as well as full-service brokers such as Merrill Lynch.

- *Direct banks* are specialist, low-cost, remote-channel attackers. Although these models are targeted generally at self-directed clients and do not all focus exclusively on affluent clients, some have nevertheless been able to attract and retain significant numbers of mass affluent clients through aggressive pricing and product innovation and simplification. Examples include ING Direct, which now operates in nine countries, and Egg in the UK.
- *Asset managers* include independent money managers and divisions of financial services groups. They serve wealthy clients directly through their own captive sales forces, and act as product providers/packagers to third-party distributors seeking best-of-breed and specialist fund management expertise. Examples include Fidelity, Old Mutual and AMVESCAP.
- *Product specialists* include hedge funds, private equity funds, mutual funds and structured product providers. Lacking their own captive distribution channels, they manufacture products for distribution across a range of HNW channels, including private banks and financial advisors.
- *Investment banks*, such as Goldman Sachs and Lehman Brothers, are stretching their institutional capabilities and targeting it at UHNWIs and, increasingly, the HNW segment. That has been driven, in part, by investment banks' desire to reduce their dependence on volatile trading revenue. To UHNWIs, they offer exclusive access to sophisticated institutional-quality products, including co-investment opportunities. To HNW business owners, for example, they offer sophisticated wealth-diversification products, often as an extension of their corporate finance work. They are also able to leverage their product structuring capabilities (often white-labelling products for private banks) and can connect HNWIs to hedge funds via their prime-brokerage operations.
- There is also a range of *other players*, which include insurance companies, accountancy companies and attorneys. Insurance companies, such as Skandia, primarily target the mass-affluent client segment. In establishing distinct wealth management operations, they have been motivated by the desire to sell additional products to their existing client base, retain maturing life insurance assets and leverage their distribution networks. Accountants, solicitors and other professionals offer financial planning, trusts and fiduciary services, tax advice and specialist services; some also directly manage wealth themselves.

Amid the market turmoil of 2000–2002, private, retail and universal bank incumbents and family offices were arguably the most resilient. Retail and universal banks, in particular, have been able to leverage their large existing customer bases, given that they typically hold up to 90% of the primary bank deposits and up to 80% of the financial assets of all affluent customers.

Financial advisors have made serious inroads, particularly in Europe, but their success has not been consistent across all geographies. In addition, wide differences exist among players following the same broad model. For example, some, such as MLP in Germany, have been able to increase their client base significantly, while others, such as some of the Italian promotori networks, have recently seen a slight fall in client numbers as competition has intensified.

1.4.1 Industry concentration

A consistent feature of the industry's competitive landscape is its high level of fragmentation. Deriving estimates of market share is tricky, driven by issues such as what constitutes wealth management, what types of asset to include (i.e. whether, in addition to AuM, assets under

Global market share of top 10 players, end 2004
Percent

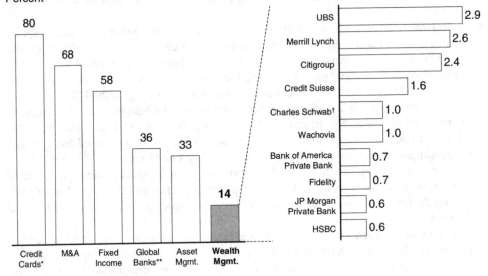

* US market only
** Top 15, based on market capitalisation
† Includes US Trust

Figure 1.28   Wealth management industry fragmentation
Source: Mercer Oliver Wyman; Bloomberg; Global Investor; Deutsche Bank; Datastream; Barron's; Wealth Partnership Review; Datamonitor; Scorpio Partnership; company data; author's analysis.

custody or in transaction accounts should be included), how to strip out non-HNW (and, in some cases, institutional) assets, data availability, etc. In the following, we define market share by AuM, and have used Capgemini/Merrill Lynch data as our estimate of the total market size. We have tried to focus, where possible, only on fee-based assets owned by HNWIs. The analysis should, however, be regarded as indicative of the relative size of key players. Outside the top 20, the degree of accuracy is lower, given the limited disclosure, particularly by some of the privately held players.

In 2004, the market share of the top 10 wealth managers was 14% and that of the top 20 was less than 20%. Wealth management is therefore one of the most fragmented sectors of the financial services industry (see Figure 1.28). With the possible exception of UBS and perhaps Citigroup, HSBC and Merrill Lynch, there are no truly globally dominant players. Seven of the top 10 players are based in the United States. The largest wealth manager in the world, UBS, had wealth management AuM of $878 billion at end 2004, which is equivalent to less than 3% of global HNW wealth. Outside the largest players, there is a huge number of niche players in each regional market.

The fragmented nature of the market is somewhat counterintuitive given the difficulties the industry has faced in recent years, which ought to have led naturally to consolidation. Though there has been recent merger and acquisition activity within the industry, it has largely been limited to players below the top 20 threshold, with similar cultures and/or complementary client bases. As noted in Chapter 9, UBS is one key exception, having made a series of bolt-on acquisitions, i.e. small acquisitions that fit culturally and strategically, without hampering cash generation. Overall, the market share of the top 10 players has remained remarkably stable in recent years.

2

Industry Challenges: New and Old

After years of persistently strong growth, driven in part by booming stock markets, the wealth management industry is emerging from the recent downturn. But it faces a series of huge structural challenges (see Figure 2.1). This chapter introduces these challenges, which form the backbone of the rest of the book.

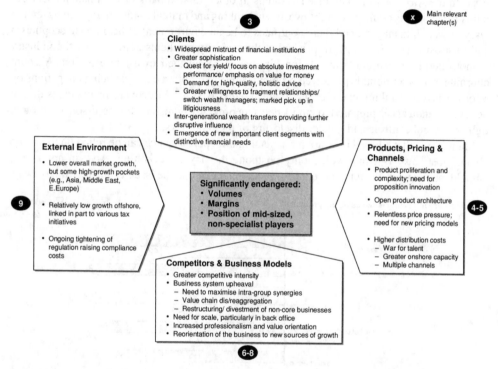

Figure 2.1 Key wealth management industry challenges
Source: Author's analysis.

Of course, not all these challenges are new. Greater client sophistication, for example, has been an industry bugbear for well over a decade. It is the *confluence* of challenges – new and old – and the magnitude and speed of their combined impact that is unprecedented.

In an industry that has been accused of being sleepy, the challenges have been quite a wake-up call. One group of players – the 'early risers' (including the large Swiss banks and some of the brokerage houses) – was quick to spot the need for radical action and is now on the way to tackling the challenges head on. Another group of players (including some of the universal banks), linked to their better positioning or scale, has been content to take a more relaxed approach. But there is a further group of players (including some of the small/mid-sized players) – ironically, the very players that should be best placed to succeed in this business by providing the truly personal service that wealthy clients crave – that has not yet fully come to terms with the new realities.

For all players, life will never be quite the same again. The overall impact is that, despite the recent pick-up in financial markets, high, sustained profit growth is no longer assured for all. Clearly, each of the challenges affects different players in different ways and some players are better positioned to deal with them than others. Mid-sized generalists, in particular, are likely to need to take the most radical action to secure a place in the new world.

2.1 CLIENTS

Arguably, the industry's biggest challenge is the need to restore that most sought-after attribute: trust. In the wake of well-publicised scandals in other, related parts of the financial services industry (including equity research/investment banking and mutual funds), many clients remain wary of wealth managers, and there continues to be an environment of heightened scepticism and mistrust (see Figure 2.2). In particular, the majority of clients believes that the industry is motivated by greed and that relationship managers put their own interests first. Account churning is another notable perceived problem, a recent reported example being allegations by a former private banking client of the Spanish bank, BBVA.[1] Moreover, many clients do not believe the industry is prepared to put its house in order, by punishing transgressors or through tighter internal controls and greater disclosure of fees and risks.

Many argue that a broad pick up in financial market performance can be relied on to restore clients' lost trust. But that would only postpone the day of reckoning. And, in any event, emboldened regulators and a more intrusive media mean that the issue is unlikely to go away.

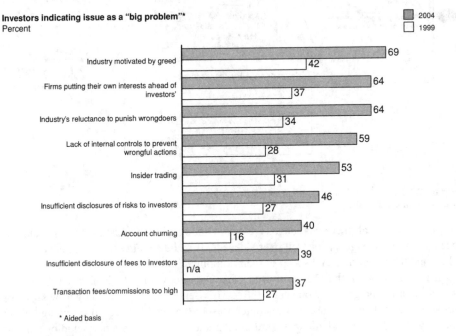

Investors indicating issue as a "big problem"*
Percent

■ 2004
□ 1999

Issue	2004	1999
Industry motivated by greed	69	42
Firms putting their own interests ahead of investors'	64	37
Industry's reluctance to punish wrongdoers	64	34
Lack of internal controls to prevent wrongful actions	59	28
Insider trading	53	31
Insufficient disclosures of risks to investors	46	27
Account churning	40	16
Insufficient disclosure of fees to investors	39	n/a
Transaction fees/commissions too high	37	27

* Aided basis

Figure 2.2   Clients' 'big problems'
Source: US Securities Industry Association annual investor survey, November 2004.

---

[1] BBVA has denied any wrongdoing.

Some firms have been vocal in their efforts to restore trust, a good example being Citigroup's 'Five Point Plan', which involves:

1. Expanded training for employees.
2. Improved internal communications.
3. Enhanced focus on talent and development.
4. Balanced performance appraisals and compensation.
5. Strengthened controls.

In the end, the key test is whether wealth managers can provide clients with high-quality, objective advice.

The composition of the client base is also becoming much more challenging. The well-known shift from old wealth to new wealth continues, and is now relatively evenly balanced in most mature markets. But the changes here go far deeper than that.

The sheer breadth and diversity of the client base is a challenge in itself. It now extends across entrepreneurs of various types, corporate executives, sports and entertainment stars, professionals, inherited wealth, retired people, and a host of niche groups such as lottery winners. Some players have made important strides in adapting their businesses to the needs of specific segments. But there remains a surprisingly large number of players continuing to use essentially a one-size-fits-all approach.

Clients are becoming ever more sophisticated, partly driven by the greater availability of financial news, data and analysis. That is clearly placing very strong product and service demands on wealth managers. The upside of this, however, is that wealth managers can, to some extent, do less in the way of basic 'hand holding' and are able to focus on sales and advice in more complex areas.

Clients are also seeking greater aggregation and control of their wealth. Most clients want to be more actively involved in their wealth management activities and often see their wealth manager as a partner with whom to validate their own investment choices. They are no longer content simply to hand over their wealth and wait for their annual portfolio review ('manage it *with* me, rather than *for* me'). Clients now have far greater demands than five years ago. They are more performance conscious and demand state-of-the-art products and services. At the same time, many clients are increasingly price sensitive and want more value for money.

Turning to investment preferences, the recent stock market downturn left its mark on clients, and many continue to seek guaranteed returns and (full or partial) capital protection. The low-inflation environment has also been influential, with clients increasingly focused on a quest for yield and delivery of absolute (rather than relative) investment performance, at least for a portion of their wealth.

Above all, clients are seeking consistent, high-quality, holistic advice and a means of navigating through the often bewildering array of products (in mutual funds alone, there are more than 54 000 products available globally). Given the greater financial market uncertainty, asset allocation services are in particularly strong demand.

Wealth management clients are complex and typically have international business interests and lifestyles. It is therefore quite typical for clients to have more than one provider, which can also be driven by diversification and secrecy considerations, the need to access specialist expertise and so on. Though some clients have been actively reducing their number of providers in recent years, many have shown an increasing desire to fragment their financial relationships where necessary, across both traditional and non-traditional providers. The IBM European Wealth and Private Banking Industry Survey 2005 found that 40% of clients use more than one provider. That, in turn, offers them a direct way of comparing providers. Indeed, it is increasingly becoming the norm for clients to test out providers by giving them small amounts of wealth to manage. Clients then reward a provider's strong performance by committing more funds.

Clients are also far more prepared to go to law when they feel there has been wrongdoing by their wealth manager. In the United States, for example, the number of investment arbitration cases rose by more than 60% between 2000 and 2003, linked in particular to issues around the omission of facts and investment unsuitability.

IBM found that a client's principal provider typically manages 60%–70% of the client's assets. Client retention for such providers is therefore a key challenge, arguably the single most powerful value driver in wealth management. As a general rule, it costs wealth managers five times as much to add new clients as it does to keep the ones it already has, and every 2% of clients retained is equivalent to cutting costs by 10%. Wealth managers are having to step up their client retention efforts, not least because clients are showing a greater willingness to switch wealth-management providers. In many countries, intergenerational wealth transfer is starting to be a particularly strong disruptive influence in this regard. Wealth managers therefore need to strike early in forging relationships with the younger generation.

New client segments are emerging or are being recognised more explicitly by wealth managers. These include segments such as affluent women, divorcees, young people, sports professionals and various ethnic groups. To capture this new source of growth, the challenges are twofold: first, to acquire these clients, which can require new creative approaches and, second, to tailor existing (or design entirely new) propositions, given that many of these segments have very distinctive needs.

To deepen their overall understanding of client behaviour, satisfaction and the totality of individual situations, wealth managers need to become more systematic in their client learning through regular client surveys or focus groups and by capturing client feedback from relationship managers more comprehensively.

2.2 PRODUCTS, PRICING AND CHANNELS

To meet the needs of clients and strive for competitive differentiation, wealth managers are having to cope with a range of challenges that cut across products, pricing and channels.

2.2.1 Products

As noted above, clients are demanding a broader range of products than ever before. Product requirements span the client's entire balance sheet and beyond, also including non-financial products and services. The willingness of clients to diversify their asset allocation more broadly (across geographies and asset classes) is a further challenge, requiring wealth providers to broaden their product range still further in many instances.

Against this backdrop of product proliferation, it is unsurprising that wealth managers are under pressure to upgrade and renew their product ranges constantly. Thankfully, most private banks have long realised that some services – dog walking, school hunting, jewellery finding – largely destroy value. But the temptation to add products in an undisciplined manner, under the belief that product diversification alone will produce higher margins, is still there in many cases. Unwieldy product ranges increase costs and place a heavy burden on back and middle office infrastructure. Hence, product management discipline is becoming a key challenge.

Driven by commoditisation and shortening product cycles, wealth managers face pressure to develop more innovative propositions as a way of differentiating themselves. To some extent,

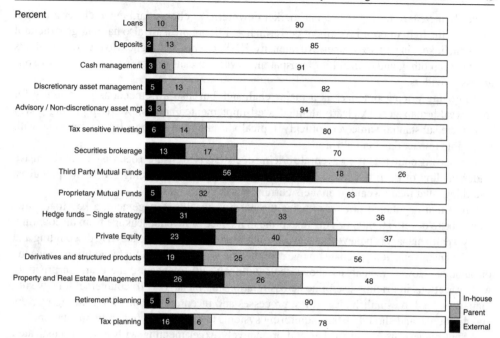

Figure 2.3 Wealth management product sourcing
Source: PricewaterhouseCoopers, Global Private Banking/Wealth Management Survey 2005, p. 10. Reproduced by permision.

this means being able to secure cost-effective, preferential access to the top product providers (see below). It also requires more creative approaches to product structuring and proposition design and packaging.

The necessary modifications in product mix can be challenging to implement, requiring changes in investment policy, revenue-sharing arrangements and nothing short of a major cultural shift in some instances. The changes also require closer, two-way coordination between product development specialists and the front line. The new complex products often take relationship managers out of their comfort zones, and the front line needs specialist training in order to explain and sell these products effectively.

Open architecture is now a reality. Most players do, at least, talk a good game here: 'some of our best clients have none of our products at all'. In practice, however, most wealth managers have not fully embraced the concept, or have done so half-heartedly, preferring to manufacture products either themselves or through their parent organisation (see Figure 2.3). One notable exception is mutual funds, but it is interesting that, in Europe at least, even in alternative investments, the general preference is to source internally where possible. Nevertheless, for those players that have genuinely embraced open architecture, the key challenge is to secure strong relationships and to manage the interface with the very best third-party product providers. That requires substantial resources and skill, and has become a value-added client service in its own right.

2.2.2 Pricing

Wealth managers, in common with players in most areas of financial services, are facing relentless downward pressure on prices across many product and service areas. That pressure naturally increased during the recent market downturn, as clients paid much closer attention to fees in the light of poor investment performance. Pricing pressure also has a large structural element, linked, in part, to competitive intensity, HNW clients' willingness to play off providers against each other, and demand for transparency, which means greater scope for comparisons across providers.

Improving pricing practices is a major challenge but also a tremendous opportunity for most wealth managers. A clearly defined, well-implemented and followed-up pricing policy can create substantial value very quickly, typically to the tune of up to 10% of revenue, with negligible impact on client attrition.

The starting point for taking accurate pricing decisions is to ensure a deep and comprehensive understanding of (a) product and service costs; and (b) current pricing levels and practices, two things that many wealth managers currently lack clear sight of.

Given that negotiated pricing remains the norm in wealth management, a key focus area should be to develop tighter pricing discipline in the face of revenue leakage from discounting. Many wealth managers believe they have established rules to prevent excessive discounting and that, for any given client, a rebate on one revenue line is compensated for by additional revenue on another. However, analysis shows that, within wealth managers, there are surprisingly wide variations in pricing discipline across relationship managers. To counteract this, wealth managers need to establish clear rules, processes and incentive systems for granting waivers and discounts, and should install monitoring systems to ensure effective implementation.

A few players are going further and are actively experimenting with more sophisticated pricing models and a variety of new tactical and strategic approaches. These include value-based pricing and linking pricing to the performance of the client's entire portfolio. Pricing directly for advice has so far met with only limited success, at least outside the very top end of the market (i.e. family offices), with few clients currently willing to pay very much. This suggests that wealth managers seeking to go down that route need to be more forthright in demonstrating the benefits of such an approach to a broader range of client segments.

2.2.3 Channels

Wealth managers face a number of challenges across their distribution networks, which are raising costs.

Given the expansion of the industry, there is strong demand for high-quality relationship managers (RMs) – the so-called 'war for talent'. Nowhere is this battle more fierce than in Asia. To help meet that demand, new institutes are springing up to train private bankers, such as the Wealth Management Institute in Singapore. Players are also having to be more creative in their recruitment approaches, often looking outside financial services altogether, e.g. to other industries, the armed services and the professions. Like their clients, RMs are also more prepared to move firm.

Wealth managers also need to upgrade RM sales productivity using a variety of levers. For example, many players are well advanced in deploying team-based approaches to client coverage, by combining groups of RMs with product and other specialists. As Wells Fargo's Head of Private Client Services put it, 'This isn't about some hero salesperson, but rather the conductor of an orchestra.' Wealth managers are also thinking more carefully about RM roles (such as client 'hunters' versus 'farmers'), optimising client and asset loadings per RM, encouraging best-practice sharing, and providing RMs with dedicated support staff. Yet, despite these and other initiatives, analysis shows that many RMs spend less than half their time in front of clients. It is important, therefore, for wealth managers to tackle the root causes of this problem. Smarter deployment of technology is a key enabler, but is only part of the solution.

Offshore-oriented wealth managers, in particular, face the challenge of securing onshore distribution capacity, through wider feeder networks, linked mainly to changes in the external environment (see below).

Though the RM will remain the dominant channel, wealth managers are also facing the challenge of having to develop and manage multiple channels – something that retail banks have struggled with for some years. This is largely client and technology driven. Online, for example, though very slow to get off the mark, is now a staple channel for some wealth managers, particularly useful for providing interactive consolidated reporting and for payments. But there is more to do here. In particular, mobile devices offer opportunities, and, moreover, there is a pressing need to exploit the full power of broadband technology, with experiments in video-based client consultation delivery now underway.

2.3   COMPETITORS AND BUSINESS MODELS

Competition within the industry is a key challenge, though it is far from new. There was a shake-out of some peripheral players during the downturn but, as the market recovery has gathered pace, competitive intensity has picked up, mainly among incumbents. All players are increasingly focused on growth. There is greater awareness that existing books of business offer a key opportunity at many banks: at least to some extent, much of the banks' 'wealth' will be inherited.

One key overriding theme – unheard of until recently in such a secretive, closeted industry – is collaboration:

- *Within integrated players*, as many large banks are actively seeking ways to maximise intra-group synergies. Key challenges here include breaking down product silos and developing effective interfaces and working arrangements with other parts of the group, whilst overcoming perceived conflicts of interest.
- *Among players*, across an increasing range of areas, driven by factors such as the growing importance of open product architecture, the trend towards operational outsourcing and the need to secure cost-effective onshore distribution.
- *Among clients* themselves, a more recent development that is occurring mainly at the top end of the market with some interesting peer-based models emerging. That is a key challenge for wealth managers because it shifts more of the bargaining power to the client and, particularly when combined with some of the other changes, raises the real threat of disintermediation.

Business system disaggregation is gathering pace, forcing hard choices on competitors as to where and how they should play in the value chain. Not least among them is whether to be a manufacturer, distributor or advisor. This pulling apart of the value chain is creating new roles for specialist players and raising the competitive bar (and IT and other investment requirements) for integrated players. But it also offers significant opportunities for players to reshape themselves in fundamental ways. For example, some players – large and small – have successfully hollowed themselves out through operational outsourcing and offshoring; many others, however, have yet to respond.

Driven, in part, by the downturn and by the need to reduce perceived conflicts of interest, many Swiss players in particular have been restructuring and divesting non-core businesses. The obvious candidates here are institutional brokerage and corporate finance, which are in some cases barely profitable. It is possible that a sustained market recovery will be used to delay the need for radical decisions here. Brokerage houses are also restructuring and, like most other types of player, are converging on the holistic wealth management model. They are shifting away from traditional commission-based securities transactions, driven by slowing organic account growth, limited consolidation opportunities and the relentless decline in trade pricing. Their key challenge is to develop (a) greater advisory capacity and (b) broader product platforms (including asset management, banking and credit), in order to capture a greater share of wallet.

In principle, the high blocks of fixed costs mean that there should be economies of scale in wealth management. There should also be performance-related economies of scale: even without net new money, with the right investment platform, the performance of existing client assets will expand the revenue base and generate higher profits. However, as noted in Chapter 1, the benefits of scale in wealth management can sometimes be overstated. It has yet to be proven that size really does matter in the long term. There is, however, now a growing consensus on the need for scale in the back office, in particular.

Though scale can be achieved organically (albeit relatively slowly), given the industry's fragmentation, many are turning to the inorganic route. Indeed, most players have expressed a desire to make incremental acquisitions and the consolidation process is gaining momentum. One initial challenge here is the scarcity, and hence the high price, of available targets, which makes it difficult for many deals to create genuine value. But the fundamental merger and acquisition (M&A) challenge in wealth management – even more so than elsewhere in financial services – is integration execution: it is not unusual for 10%–15% of client assets (and quality RMs) to walk out of the door as a result of the associated client relationship disruption and cultural clashes. In short, M&A needs to be handled with care, given that client relationships and the personal touch are key in this industry.

As players become larger, small acquisition roll-ups are not enough to 'move the dials'. Meanwhile, revenue synergies can be hard to come by particularly when two large players combine, given the more limited scope for product complementarity. Moreover, it is important to note that consolidation in wealth management will, to some extent, be a by-product of – or, worse still, an afterthought within – the next wave of cross-border universal banking deals. Such deals are motivated by considerations that lie largely outside wealth management (typically by synergies in the broader retail and corporate banking areas). Hence, a key challenge will be for the relevant wealth management unit to fit into, and extract synergies from, the new organisation.

Bluntly, wealth managers need to become more professional in their management of the business. Once the preserve of gifted amateurs and the old-boy network, the quality of the top team has become more critical. Leading retail banking players have actively sought out management talent from other retail industries to enhance their expertise in areas such as pricing, marketing and branding. Similarly, wealth managers need to become less inward looking and more open to attracting talent from outside financial services, including the luxury brands, for example.

Wealth management requires a much more disciplined, value-oriented approach. There has been a shift, by many, away from the furious asset grab and revenue-at-all-costs approach that characterised the late 1990s. Serious long-term players are, at last, focusing firmly on the level and growth of net profit as their primary key performance indicators. The Pricewaterhouse-Coopers Global Private Banking/Wealth Management Survey 2005 found that over the next three years, wealth managers say they plan to focus particular attention on profit per client.

But many face a pressing need to upgrade the quality and sophistication of their management information systems.

Most wealth businesses need to reorientate themselves to capture new sources of growth from, for example, new geographies, client segments and propositions. That, in turn, will require greater flexibility, faster (and smarter) decision making and highly disciplined execution.

So, all in all, the wealth business model is very much in flux. Some have likened the business model challenges to those faced by the investment banks 20 years ago. At that time, investment banks were also struggling with value chain disaggregation, scale, complexity and cross-border expansion issues. Back then it was the US players that seized the initiative, with the emergence of the bulge bracket and an industry shakeout that continues to this day. It is conceivable that the wealth management industry is at a similar inflexion point.

2.4 EXTERNAL ENVIRONMENT

The industry consensus is for wealth market growth of around 6% a year over the next five years, well down on the double-digit levels seen during the late 1990s. In particular, overall net new money growth is low: McKinsey found that it accounted for less than one-fifth of overall AuM growth in 2003 and 2004, with the bulk of the growth being driven by market performance (linked to the stock-market recovery) and share-of-wallet expansion. Looking ahead, as noted above, there is even greater uncertainty than normal as to the direction of financial and other asset prices.

Regionally, there are some projected high-growth pockets (including Asia, the Middle East and Eastern Europe). But many established wealth managers are finding these opportunities difficult and time-consuming to access: they require a greater degree of onshore investment than in the past; cross-border banking is notoriously difficult to execute well; and there are cultural issues to overcome. In Asia, for example, it takes a particularly long time for foreign banks to gain wealthy families' trust – an issue that has been exacerbated recently by Citigroup's fall from grace in Japan. The key challenge is to develop, at speed, a local presence with the necessary critical mass. Collaboration and joint ventures with local players offer a way forward, but require careful handling, as some have already discovered.

Growth in offshore wealth management is expected to remain relatively low, linked in part to global, regional and country-specific tax initiatives. The most important recent one of these is the European Savings Directive, which went live in July 2005. But the imminent death of offshore banking – still projected by many – has been greatly exaggerated: offshore is down, but not out. In any case, there are signs that the 'reinvention' of offshore is underway. Offshore-oriented wealth managers are pursuing a range of strategies designed to defend their existing franchise and deliver growth onshore. And the rapid growth of onshore markets is forcing many players to raise their investments in new resources and distribution capacity and to develop new propositions.

Regulatory resurgence is continuing across a range of areas – from money-laundering to product regulation, and from accounting standards to capital rules. To implement the new regulations, players are having to overhaul their IT systems, adapt their products and, in some cases, rethink their entire strategic direction. Needless to say, this is raising compliance costs, which are up by more than 60% over the last three years. Smaller players are bearing the brunt of the impact, given their more limited resources. But the larger players are also feeling pressure here, given the breadth of their product ranges and greater scope for conflicts of interest.

The New York State Attorney General, Eliot Spitzer, has conducted investigations into investment bank conflicts of interest, illegal trading practices by mutual funds and bid rigging in the insurance industry – and has been a catalyst for industry-wide reforms. As some equity analysts have pointed out, a Spitzer-like investigation into private banking practices cannot be ruled out. For example, just as mutual fund firms have suffered from the fallout over market timing, the private banking industry could face a de-rating if a similar scandal erupted, and client confidence would suffer.

Analysts highlight two areas that could potentially come under scrutiny:

- *Rebates*. This is the industry practice of wealth managers receiving fees from product providers for selling their products. While this is a form of payment for distribution, it clearly creates a potential conflict of interest for wealth managers. Quotes like the following, which appeared in a *Euromoney* article (January 2004) on private banking, do not help the industry: 'You get third-party fund manager A with a good track record, consistent performance, low volatility but that pays [the private client adviser] a rebate of only 20 basis points. Then you get fund manager B in the same strategy and style offering mediocre returns and high volatility but paying a 40 basis points rebate. And guess what? Somehow or other the client ends up with fund manager B.'
- *Fee levels*. Another possible area of concern is the high fees paid on wrap products such as multimanager funds. While the fees on the underlying products themselves are sometimes full, private banks go on to charge a further fee on top. Fees for certain structured products could also come under the microscope. There is nothing illegal here. But private banks' unique pricing structure (where different-sized clients pay different prices for essentially the same service) leaves players open to criticism.

Greater transparency may provide one of the solutions. Initiatives along the lines of the 'Schumer Box', recently introduced (under Parliamentary pressure) in the UK credit card industry, could, at least in principle, be applied in wealth management.

3

Clients

With Anna Omarini

This aims of this chapter are to:

- Understand wealth management clients' key characteristics.
- Discuss the approaches that wealth managers are taking to client segmentation in order to tailor their service levels.
- Outline how client value management can help wealth managers acquire, develop and retain profitable clients.

Wealth management clients are changing and they are growing in number and in complexity. They are more sophisticated, willing to fragment, chop and change their financial relationships and have demanding advice requirements. A host of new niche segments are being targeted – with others waiting in the wings. Needless to say, traditional wealth- and risk-profile-based segmentation approaches are woefully inadequate. The sheer diversity of client segments means that wealth managers are having to become more specialised and to upgrade their relationship management skills.

In the light of these changes, wealth managers are also having to work harder at client value management. Client retention, in particular, could become more of a concern as large-scale generational change gathers momentum in many countries.

3.1 KEY CHARACTERISTICS

This section draws on several recent surveys of wealthy clients and private banks to build a picture of clients' key characteristics. Client needs have changed significantly over the years, as illustrated in Figure 3.1.

3.1.1 Sophistication

Clients are, on the whole, adopting an increasingly sophisticated approach to wealth management. This is being driven, in part, by greater access to financial news, information and analysis, increased familiarity with specialist investments (such as structured products, hedge funds and private equity) and a quest for yield in the current low-inflation environment.

A recent Citigroup/McKinsey survey (2005) showed that even with their superior access to the best advice money can buy, hypersophisticated UHNW clients do sometimes make similar mistakes to those made by the broader population of investors. Examples include chasing performance, excessive risk taking and underdiversified portfolios.

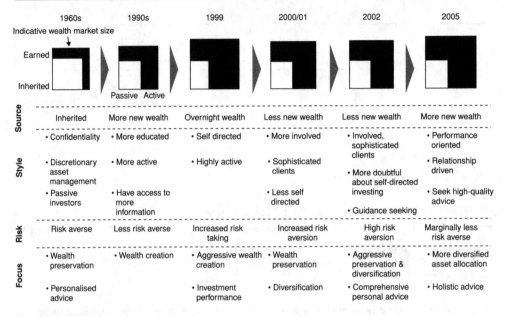

	1960s	1990s	1999	2000/01	2002	2005
Source	Inherited	More new wealth	Overnight wealth	Less new wealth	Less new wealth	More new wealth
Style	• Confidentiality • Discretionary asset management • Passive investors	• More educated • More active • Have access to more information	• Self directed • Highly active	• More involved • Sophisticated clients • Less self directed	• Involved, sophisticated clients • More doubtful about self-directed investing • Guidance seeking	• Performance oriented • Relationship driven • Seek high-quality advice
Risk	Risk averse	Less risk averse	Increased risk taking	Increased risk aversion	High risk aversion	Marginally less risk averse
Focus	• Wealth preservation • Personalised advice	• Wealth creation	• Aggressive wealth creation • Investment performance	• Wealth preservation • Diversification	• Aggressive preservation & diversification • Comprehensive personal advice	• More diversified asset allocation • Holistic advice

Figure 3.1   Client trends: 1960–2005
Source: Capgemini/Merrill Lynch; author's analysis.

3.1.2   Advice

Along with the increased sophistication and complexity of client demands comes 'time poverty' – these days, clients have less time to dedicate to their wealth management needs. But their demands, and the array of products and services on offer, are becoming more varied and complicated.

One area that is of particular interest relates to the observed demand for advisory services. While there is a clear need for private banks to develop such services, particularly in areas relating to intergenerational wealth transfer and alternative investments, it is by no means clear whether clients will be prepared to pay for such services. In fact, the Smith Barney Affluent Investor Survey (2004) suggests that clients will be unwilling to pay for such advice. It goes on to note that a business model based solely on advisory services will not, at least at the moment, be financially sustainable.

We believe this simply reflects the keen interest of clients in obtaining more consistent advice regarding family dynamics and intergenerational wealth transfer planning. These issues, by default, are long-lasting and clients clearly express a need for help with the challenges of raising their children amid affluence and successfully passing their assets on to future generations. Despite this need, however, many individuals seem to express reservations about seeking out advice on family wealth dynamics on their own. Clearly, the intimate nature of these discussions acts as some form of constraint in initiating this type of dialogue with their wealth advisor. One interesting development has been the shift in emphasis in some banks away from providing concierge services towards coaching and educational services that teach potential inheritors (whatever generation) about the responsibilities and how to manage wealth (see Chapter 4).

The advice-seeking pool of wealthy clients is large, but currently underserved. Some clients want advice all the time and all clients want advice some of the time, but many clients are unhappy with the advice they get most of the time. Clients want a different kind of advice from the advice they receive currently – and more of it. That advice is event driven, tiered, and above all, personalised. It includes the human touch/persuasion at the right times. It is also modular, just-in-time and linked to execution, leveraging specialists and other data sources as necessary, with much less hassle for the client.

At the same time, clients are seeking more involvement in their wealth management relationship, more added-value intervention and continuous access to information. Wealth managers have to deal with this greater challenge and consider the various ways to perfect the client experience. They do this typically by offering clients more holistic advice that focuses on a better understanding of the client's personal and business situations while also being more proactive in the relationship.

Wealthy clients continue to seek advice regarding family dynamics and intergenerational wealth transfer planning. The top clients increasingly require advice and services relating particularly to intergenerational wealth transfer planning. That is because these clients are generally elderly, have to consider how to educate their family members as to the responsibilities of wealth, need to plan for retirement and need to find out how to preserve their wealth for future generations.

3.1.3   Buying behaviour

What do clients look for in a wealth manager? In choosing a provider, quality of client service, confidentiality and security are the key characteristics (Figure 3.2).

Clients have increased access to sophisticated financial products through multiple channels and no longer view access to products as a sufficient value proposition from their advisors. That is mainly a result of the larger array of investment services that have been offered to HNW clients via non-traditional providers – especially hedge funds and private equity firms. Services such as strategic asset allocation advice, the coordination of disparate investment offerings and other specialist services such as co-investments are increasingly being offered by non-traditional wealth management firms and often add more value than standard private bank services.

Clients are increasingly interested in hedge funds and other alternative investments, while demanding greater transparency regarding risk and return. Although many private banking clients experienced poor returns during the stock market downturn during 2000–2002, and also in 2004, some types of hedge funds and other alternative investments yielded very strong (double digit) returns over the same periods. That has encouraged HNW clients to focus much more attention on these types of investment opportunities and they have, in turn, required suppliers to provide more advice on the various strategies pursued. There also appears to be a strong demand from HNW clients for greater disclosure from alternative asset managers as to the performance, risks, fees and pricing mechanics of such investments.

UHNW clients have responded to the increased complexity of the investment offering by setting up family offices or have sought out family-office-type services from their private bank or independent advisors. Many of them feel that traditional providers may not offer best-practice solutions or simply cannot meet the demand for new products and services of sufficient quality. That includes such things as strategic asset allocation planning, hedge fund

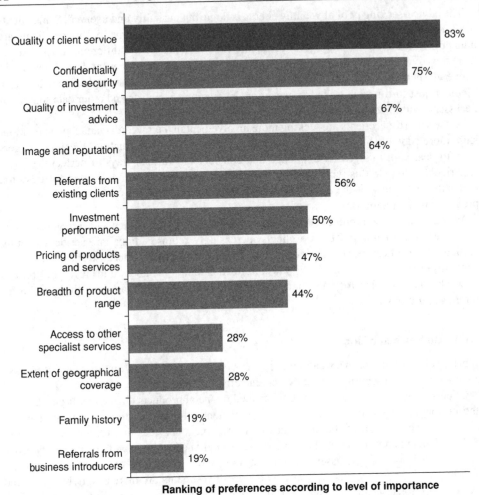

Ranking of preferences according to level of importance

Figure 3.2   Clients' reasons for choosing their wealth manager
Source: IBM Consulting Services, European Wealth and Private Banking Industry Survey 2005. Reproduced by permission.

manager selection, due diligence services and so on. Such services, however, tend to be cost effective only for clients with at least $100 million of investable assets.

3.1.4   Relationship fragmentation

According to the IBM European Wealth and Private Banking Industry Survey 2005, 60% of clients have more than one provider (Figure 3.3), and are therefore increasingly able to compare wealth managers first hand, across a range of dimensions. Clients have also identified a set of unmet needs. They are seeking far greater proactivity and ideas, are less tolerant of providers that do not come up to the mark (whether that be down to poor service, weak investment performance or reporting flaws) and, when necessary, are more willing to switch – and, in the case of perceived wrongdoing, prosecute – providers.

Percentage of client respondents

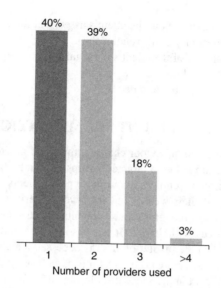

Figure 3.3   Number of wealth managers used by European private clients
Source: IBM Consulting Services, European Wealth and Private Banking Industry Survey 2005.

3.1.5   Regional differences

Despite ongoing globalisation and the fact that they have more international lifestyles than most, the service and products needs of HNW clients vary quite substantially across geographical regions. For example:

- *North American* clients have a strong desire for alternative investments, have multiple wealth manager relationships, are more likely to have family offices and appear less interested in integrating personal and business wealth.
- *European* clients have a stronger focus on tax-efficient investment products, structures and advisory services and are more interested in real assets (real estate, shipping, privately held businesses). They also tend to have fewer wealth management relationships.
- *Latin American* clients emphasise confidentiality and privacy, are more interested in strong offshore banking relationships, hold substantial assets in fixed-income investments and privately held businesses, and also have relatively few wealth manager relationships.
- *Middle Eastern* clients strongly focus on real estate and capital-protected products, and they also manage their assets on a tactical basis, switching regularly between different asset classes. They are less interested in hedge funds and also focus on the strength of offshore banking relationships.
- *Asia-Pacific* clients hold a higher proportion of their wealth in cash, real estate and privately held businesses, and emphasise investment opportunities in their own region (e.g. in China, co-investment deals in fast-growing markets). They tend to require integrated private and

corporate banking services for their closely held business assets and place strong emphasis on confidentiality. Clients tend to make heavy use of multiple banks.

IBM's survey concluded that, looking ahead, clients would like wealth management providers to:

- Propose more holistic advice about the client's assets and liabilities.
- Demonstrate more proactivity in the relationship.
- Deepen their understanding of the client's personal and business situation.
- Propose more innovative solutions.
- Tailor reporting preferences to client needs.

3.2   CLIENT SEGMENTATION

As client's needs, attitude and behaviour changes, there is a greater requirement for banks to focus on delivering relevant value to targeted groups of clients. In this respect, private banks need to make more conscious choices about the type of clients they decide to serve, taking account of the sources of their wealth and the level of service they are expecting. It will be increasingly important to recognise that as clients' needs change, some of the traditional products and profit sources will change. It will also be essential to identify new sources of client value and ensure that the institution has the necessary capability to deliver in full.

As in most other industries, there is no such thing as an 'average' wealth management client. Client segmentation – the art and science of tailoring and delivering products and services to distinct client groups – can therefore be a difficult task. But it is built around a reasonably simple principle: know your client. In the private banking world, this means being familiar with two facets of client needs: the products and services that best meet the client's investment objectives and the style of relationship manager that best suits the client. The trick with client segmentation is grouping clients accurately and easily to differentiate service. If you can easily categorise, anticipate and react to a client's needs by asking him or her a few simple questions, then you have passed the acid test for segmentation.

Few institutions can be positioned to serve all segments equally well. Though some institutions may serve every category, very few individual relationship managers are able to stretch their expertise across such a broad range of client needs. That forces private banks to ask a number of strategic questions. How big is each client segment? How well understood are the needs of each segment? What are the bank's strengths and weaknesses in serving each segment? Which segments are more or less profitable? In which segments is competition more or less developed? Last but not least, which client segments are existing staff best suited to serve?

3.2.1   Traditional high-level segmentation: the wealth pyramid

Given the changing client profile in private banking, the key focus is to understand relationships in order to be able to segment the client base more effectively and to maximise value from every client. Clients will pay more if they feel the products and services on offer are tailored to their specific needs.

While retail banks typically deal with customers with relatively similar needs, private banks have few limitations regarding client's nationality, risk preferences, scope of service, etc. In theory, wealth management clients can be segmented according to a multidimensional range of factors (geography, demographics, wealth, income, asset class holdings and preferences,

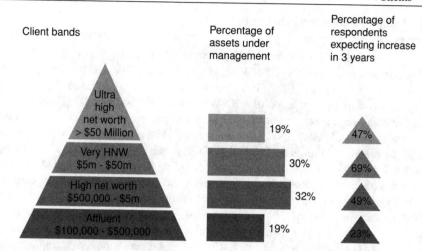

Figure 3.4   The wealth management pyramid
Source: PricewaterhouseCoopers (2005), 'Global Wealth Management Survey'. Reproduced by permission.

domicile and so on); in reality, clients are often lumped together as one client group and do not always receive the tailored services they may have been promised (or think they will receive) at the outset of the relationship. Although they may typically receive more individual attention, their relationship manager has traditionally focused on a relatively large number of clients with very different needs and lifestyles.

Appropriate segmentation is essential if relationship managers are to understand client's requirements fully and will also feed their knowledge base with current and potential future opportunities. In terms of building relationships, effective segmentation strategies should enable teams of relationship managers to build on their expertise and be more proactive in advisory and selling activity from the client base.

The most common basic approach is to segment the client base by wealth – 'the wealth pyramid'. Figure 3.4 illustrates four key segments: 'core affluents', HNWIs, VHNWIs' and UHNWIs (see Box 3.1). Segmentation based on wealth, however, does not adequately address the issue of individual needs, as clients with similar levels of wealth are likely to have substantially different needs. Hence, the level of investable wealth should be used only as an initial indication of the client cut-off 'price' for access to private banking services. In addition to wealth, there is a range of key segmentation criteria that can be used for subsegmentation purposes. Most private banks go further, by identifying similarities between clients, and use them as part of a framework to establish subgroups that can be supported by distinct propositions.

3.2.2   Other segmentation criteria

Some institutions segment clients based on one or more of the following factors: family background, work experience, sex, age, potential profitability of the account and behaviour. Some life insurance companies use what they call life-cycle segmentation, which combines age and behaviour. These companies have determined that the best way to distinguish and predict clients' needs is to assess where they are in their life-cycle: going to university, getting married, having children or retiring. A few simple questions establish a client's life-cycle stage and give a sales agent a reasonable basis for anticipating issues and needs.

Box 3.1   Ultra-high net worth individuals[1]

The expansion of HNWI assets is creating a 'super class' of HNWIs that are known as ultra-high net worth individuals (UHNWIs). Merrill Lynch defines the threshold of wealth required to be considered as UHNWI as $30 million in liquid financial assets. Defined in this way, the worldwide population of UHNWIs stood at 77 500 in 2004 (Figure 3.5) and has risen at an average annual rate of 7% over the last five years. They account for around one-third of the world's total HNW financial wealth. Within the UHNW segment, Forbes estimates there were 691 billionaires globally in 2005. Their combined worth $2.2 trillion, up 16% in 2005. They hail from 47 countries, now including Kazakhstan, Poland and Ukraine.

At this wealth level an identifiable shift in needs and behaviour emerges that calls for a different wealth management approach. Figure 3.6 outlines the key differentiating factors for UHNWI clients as opposed to HNWIs. In particular, most UHNWIs need to be served more as a wealthy *institution*, rather than as an individual. In other words, they need to manage their wealth in a similar way to a business. That has a number of important implications.

First, given the sums of money involved, UHNWIs demand highly structured, personalised products, often linked to their business affairs. A good example is the need to create liquidity from non-liquid wealth. UHNWIs have a clearer vision of short-term developments and are often ready to risk a higher proportion of their wealth in more speculative investments. UHNWIs are, for instance, frequently eager to participate in venture capital and private equity funds. One typical request to a private banker is to 'show me something I couldn't do or structure on my own'.

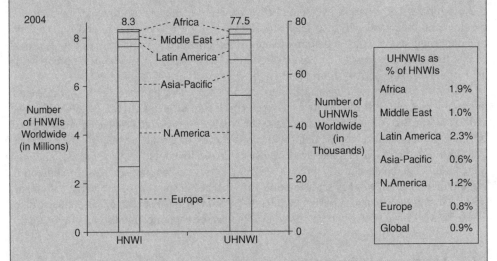

Note: UHNWI is defined as an individual with more than US$30 million in financial assets

Figure 3.5   Geographic distribution of UHNWIs, 2004
Source: Capgemini/Merrill Lynch, 'World Wealth Report' 2005. Reproduced by permission.

---
[1] This box draws heavily from the Capgemini/Merrill Lynch 'World Wealth Report' 2000.

Products	Services
Institutional rather than individual focus	**Consolidation of information**
• Option to invest in products of an institutional nature and calibre: – Bill Gates's wealth of $85bn[a] is equivalent to some smaller banks' total AUM	• Provision of global custodian services • Consolidation of financial performance when portfolios are split or several providers are used
• Increased magnitude of investable assets means institutional spreads are demanded	**Advice on more complex tax and legal matters**
• Ability to leverage business assets and link to personal assets	• Managing tax liabilities across geographies
Greater diversity of product	• Setting up a bespoke legal infrastructure for estate planning (trusts, succession planning, etc.)

• Availability of a wider range of specialist products, e.g.:
  – Access to private equity with high minimum investment thresholds
  – Special allocations at IPOs
  – Option to have custom-made structured products
	• Resolving residency and domicile issues
	
	More personal service

Greater diversification across geographies	• Relationship manager typically becomes a closer, more personal adviser: – With direct access to specialists when requested
• Through offshore asset investment	• More frequent access to, and consultation with, senior management

• Through greater exposure to a wider range of markets:
  – Focus on regional diversification at HNWI level
  – Focus on global diversification at U-HNWI level with greater emerging markets coverage	

Source: Aggregated findings from Relationship Manager interviews.
a. "Sunday Times Rich List 2000", *Sunday Times*, 19 March 2000 (estimate of £53bn taken with an exchange rate of £1:$1.6 used).

Figure 3.6   UHNWIs' key characteristics
Source: Capgemini/Merrill Lynch, 'World Wealth Report' 2000.

Second, UHNWIs usually divide their extensive financial assets across multiple providers, geographies and specialists, and they want consolidated information that conveys a clear picture of overall performance and worth. Tailored statements that can be integrated into the UHNWI's global financial position are essential, along with the ability to handle multicurrency consolidation.

Third, UHNWIs require ready access to specialist advisory services, such as international tax and legal specialists, and a savvy relationship manager who knows what he or she does not know. The relationship manager must have substantial depth and breadth of financial knowledge, as well as the immediate counsel of top-class specialist advisers from a whole range of disciplines, including investment bankers, product specialists and experts in tax, legal, art, estate, trust and property. Many of the new UHNWIs are accustomed to dealing with venture capitalists and investment bankers, and they demand the same type of relationship with their private banker – innovative and fast-paced. Typically, too, the UHNWI expects to deal closely with senior management and receive individual personal service from the highest levels.

Finally, UHNWIs demand quick responses to requests and immediate access to information anytime, anywhere. To serve them effectively, providers need the latest and best technologies available to satisfy these information needs. Account information and performance tracking, leading research, market data, stock recommendations and transactional capability – all delivered 24 hours a day, 7 days a week, 365 days a year online – are an essential entry requirement to serving this market.

What it takes to succeed

Serving UHNWIs is very much a specialist game – and one not for the faint hearted. As already noted, most UHNWIs are exceptionally demanding clients, and negotiate rigorously over fees. Success in serving new UHNWIs will belong to those players who offer unparalleled service in terms of product, advice and technology, and can link these areas of expertise to both personal and corporate wealth.

To succeed in offering the best institutional-quality products (covering all asset types, geographies and risk preferences), providers will first need to determine how to source each product. An in-house approach involves the difficult challenge of integrating and cooperating across the provider's diverse business areas, ranging from asset management to corporate finance. Sourcing from third parties brings challenges of its own – managing the relationship with outside providers and ensuring seamless delivery to clients are necessary, but not trivial, requirements.

Similarly, providing the range of expert advice UHNWIs routinely need will not be easy. Successful players will have to provide up-to-date expertise not only in investments, tax and legal, real estate, inheritance planning and insurance but also potentially in personal offerings such as education, healthcare and general 'concierge services'. This advice will also need to be delivered quickly, clearly and at the client's convenience.

From a technology perspective, the best providers will differentiate themselves by offering the most up-to-date methods to track, monitor, analyse and display individualised financial performance data by asset type. Sophisticated UHNWIs also want detailed attribution statements that specify not just whether investment managers have reached their performance targets but how. Have they, for instance, strayed from an agreed risk profile to achieve the returns?

Finally, successful players will leverage their UHNWI clients' business assets to maximise personal wealth. First, they will exploit IPO/private equity deals to provide interesting products in which new UHNWIs can invest. Second, by linking corporate finance activity to private banking, they will identify potential UHNWIs early, and be in the best position to retain them as clients when they enter the superwealthy league.

Overall, the winners here will be those players who offer the most highly developed, customised, high-tech services that precisely meet these sophisticated UHNWIs' needs, while delivering expertise, convenience and – most of all – top performance. In *Euromoney*'s Private Banking Survey 2006, the top 10 global private banks for UHNWIs were: JP Morgan, Goldman Sachs, UBS, Citigroup, Credit Suisse, HSBC, Pictet, Merrill Lynch, Rothschild, and ABN Amro.

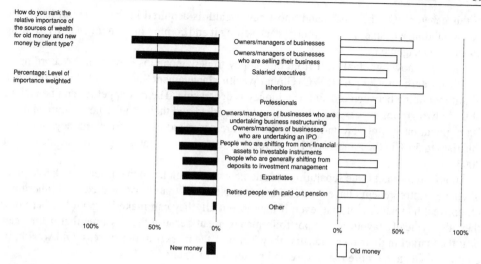

How do you rank the relative importance of the sources of wealth for old money and new money by client type?

Percentage: Level of importance weighted

Owners/managers of businesses
Owners/managers of businesses who are selling their business
Salaried executives
Inheritors
Professionals
Owners/managers of businesses who are undertaking business restructuring
Owners/managers of businesses who are undertaking an IPO
People who are shifting from non-financial assets to investable instruments
People who are generally shifting from deposits to investment management
Expatriates
Retired people with paid-out pension
Other

100%   50%   0%   0%   50%   100%

New money   Old money

Figure 3.7   Sources of wealth: new money versus old money
Source: IBM Consulting Services, European Wealth and Private Banking Industry Survey 2003. Reproduced by permission.

3.2.2.1   Source of wealth

The source of an HNW individual's wealth is an extremely important additional factor in determining investment profile, product and service demands. There are many ways to classify clients in terms of their source of wealth. The classic approach here is to distinguish between 'old money' and 'new money'. As shown in Figure 3.7, the former largely relates to inherited wealth whereas the latter focuses on recent wealth creation via entrepreneurial activity and through various types of highly paid employment (such as senior executives).

Furthermore, a distinction is often made between first-generation and second-generation wealth. In general, first-generation HNWIs are the wealth creators, whereas second-generation HNWIs are the inheritors of this wealth. But this analogy may be too simplistic. Some commentators argue that the focus of second-generation wealth inheritors may be similar to the first generation as they have experienced the hard work associated with the creator generation. As such, it is only in the third generation that the cause-and-effect relationship between work and money really disappears. Since wealth creators were traditionally relatively disinterested in wealth management per se, second-generation clients have no one to teach them about managing money. They generally learn on their own and provide the third and fourth generations with a model to follow.

Old money can be further broken down into two different types: active and passive. The active category refers to inheritors leading a productive and purposeful existence. Though not necessarily wealth producers, they are high achievers. Some of these clients are entrepreneurs, while others can be philanthropists. The class of clients grouped into passive old wealth may be identified (perhaps unfairly) as the idle rich who never quite manage to answer the question, 'What do I do when I wake up today?'

New wealth can also be further divided into 'sudden' and 'slower' new wealth. Sudden new wealth involves any instant acquisition, whether by lottery winning, court settlement or unexpected inheritance. Wealth created during the dot-com IPO bubble can also be included in this category. On the other hand, most new wealth is acquired in the slow, old-fashioned way – building a business over twenty years, selling it and coming into liquid wealth requiring financial management.

The well-known gradual shift from old money to new money is continuing. According to the PricewaterhouseCoopers (PWC) Global Wealth Management Survey 2005, the importance of differentiating between old and new money is decreasing. The risk appetites and behaviour of these two groups appear to have become less marked and their requirements more similar. On a global basis, only around 40% of clients are described as being new money, although this rises to 50% in the Americas. That is roughly the same percentage split as was the case in 2003.

Another important issue separating old and new wealth relates to the different risk tolerance of clients. Entrepreneurs have much higher risk tolerances than those of trust fund inheritors. Often wealth creators feel that, even if they lose it all, they can make it again. Furthermore, they also typically favour active portfolio management because they assume that if they can beat the market in their own industry, they can beat the market in other areas. Old wealth, in contrast, tends to be more risk averse and protection orientated.

The source of wealth also can have a significant impact on clients' current needs. For example, an individual that is affluent and a business owner will often find it difficult to separate their personal from business needs. That is evident in the common organisational alignment of business banking and private banking units within many large retail banks (see Chapter 8).

Another advantage of segmenting the market by the source of wealth is that there can be specific product needs that can be met if one focuses on this feature of client characteristics. For example, land and property owners may well have issues with liquidity, while lottery winners will initially need taxation advice and basic financial planning services.

3.2.2.2   Other criteria

Booz Allen Hamilton (2003) identify four distinct segments of private clients: the delegators, the selectors, the participators and UHNWIs:

- *Delegators* seek out low involvement solutions for their wealth management and they also hope to outsource all the activity to a private bank. The parameters of service excellence for them are: a reliable and empathetic professional adviser, effortless fulfilment of requests, simple effective reassurance, and disciplined financial and investment management.
- *Participators* view investing as their hobby, and enjoy working with their banker to manage their portfolio. They expect service excellence to entail: fun value, enablement of performance through a stream of relevant investment ideas, time and attention, and financial expertise.
- *Selectors* are financially sophisticated investors, who pick and choose the products and services they want. Their expectations for service excellence are: product and investment innovation appropriate to them, highest standards of service delivery, long-term investment in the relationship and excellent performance.
- Finally, the *UHNW clients* (which Booz Allen defines as having more than €50 million in investable assets) have rapidly changing expectations, purchase services in an almost

institutional manner and have very demanding standards. Their expectation on service excellence is: superb professionalism, management of complexity, networking and getting the simple things right.

3.2.3   Multiple segmentation criteria

More advanced players are using multiple segmentation criteria, such as those shown in Figure 3.8. A particularly good example is Coutts (see Box 3.2).

There is no right method of segmenting the private banking market. But at a number of wealth managers around the world, a model that combines personal background, age and behaviour has proved to be a very effective means of understanding and penetrating clients. One possible model segments HNW clients into six categories globally within a given region/country: active retired business owners, passive heirs, entrepreneurs, professionals and UHNWI. The logic behind these groupings is that HNW clients choose their investments and display different levels of financial sophistication based on age and source of wealth.

- *Retired business owner.* The business owner is likely to be in his or her sixties or seventies, and no longer involved in day-to-day business. The primary investment objective is capital preservation and smooth distribution of wealth to heirs. The business owner is interested in working with a mature relationship manager who can sensitively handle the delicate details of family finance, trusts and wills over the long term.
- *Passive heir.* The passive heir is typically middle aged and has inherited money within the past decade. He or she seeks investments that provide steady returns and ensure a certain lifestyle for the heir and his or her family. Most clients in this category look for a European or US private bank which is perceived as very secure. The ideal relationship manager has

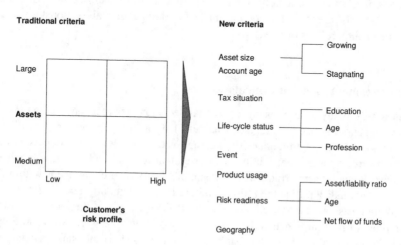

Figure 3.8   New segmentation approaches
Source: Author's analysis.

a strong grasp of the overall portfolio and can provide guidance on key decisions, such as financing a home and optimising tax status.

- *Entrepreneur.* A self-made individual, the entrepreneur is looking for instruments to both protect and grow capital. He or she is looking for a private bank that can provide performance and flexibility. For performance, he or she wants a constant flow of interesting investment ideas and tends to test the skills of private bankers before giving them extensive business, monitoring investment advice for some time before acting. But once a decision has been made, the private banker is expected to be available and responsive. Access to the trading desk, for example, is important to this client, as he or she takes a hands-on approach to investments. The link between personal and business wealth is thin and credit will be required in order to leverage investments and to finance the business. A relationship managers' knowledge, rather than reputation, is key.

- *Professional.* The professional is typically a young to middle-aged executive in a local conglomerate or large multinational corporation. He or she is MBA educated and financially astute, but has little time to handle personal investments, preferring a private bank that can provide a systematic approach to financial planning. The professional needs an investment strategy with the right mix of capital preservation and growth. He or she is likely to be interested in packaged products that have a clear performance record and transparent pricing, and require little or no input. Relationship managers will need to understand their products and clients, but need not be as well versed on individual markets and securities as those serving the entrepreneurs.

- *UHNWI.* Client needs in the UHNW segment are not necessarily driven by age or background. Typically possessing more than $50 million, this client functions more like a financial institution than an individual. The scale of wealth enables this person to employ in-house financial experts to determine investment needs, set portfolio allocations and even execute transactions directly on exchanges. As such, private banks are intermediaries used only when they can provide access to specific investment expertise or possibly loans for leveraged investing. In these instances, private banks function as contact points to refer specialists or execute transactions. Unlike the other client segments, relationship managers serving UHNWIs rarely have the opportunity of building personal relationships or advising across the client's full set of needs.

3.2.4 New segments and subsegments

In the late 1990s, many wealth managers emphasised strategies focusing on the mass affluent segment with generally poor results (see Chapter 6). Typically, the costs of providing limited private banking services were underestimated and value-adding target products and services were difficult to promote – especially as the segment already had access to such services through other financial firm arrangements. Also, the diversity of client needs within the mass affluent segment made it difficult to promote tailored private banking services at the traditional retail banking costs expected by clients. The strategic emphasis of the industry nowadays is to let the retail arm of large banks deal with the mass affluent segment with more upmarket services being provided via the private bank. The main focus of private banks is to target clients with $1 million–$10 million of investable assets as these are perceived as the segment that will provide the greatest profit opportunities.

Box 3.2   Client segmentation at Coutts[2]

Coutts, a private banking subsidiary of Royal Bank of Scotland, pioneered a new client segmentation approach in 2001. As Figure 3.9 shows, this segmentation takes into consideration the lifestyle of an individual ('situational need') and the way in which the individual has become wealthy ('source of wealth').

Coutts describes the various segments as follows:

- *Executives.* 'Demands on your time are increasing and corporate life probably allows you scant time for your own financial affairs. We understand this and offer an efficient and informed service that fits in with your schedule.'
- *Professionals.* 'Whether you are a lawyer, accountant, consultant or medical professional, our team is dedicated to looking after the financial affairs of professionals. We understand the likely career path within your profession and the implications this could have for your personal financial needs. Our goal is to help to protect and grow your wealth, allowing you to concentrate on your career.'
- *Entrepreneurs.* 'We understand that owning your own business presents a unique set of personal financial challenges. Maybe you're in the early stages of building your business, considering selling, or perhaps you're planning to pass it on to your children.'
- *Acquired wealth.* 'If you have received an inheritance, acquired assets as a result of a divorce settlement or won the lottery, you will understand that such an event can present you with countless financial questions, options and decisions. Wealth can, of course,

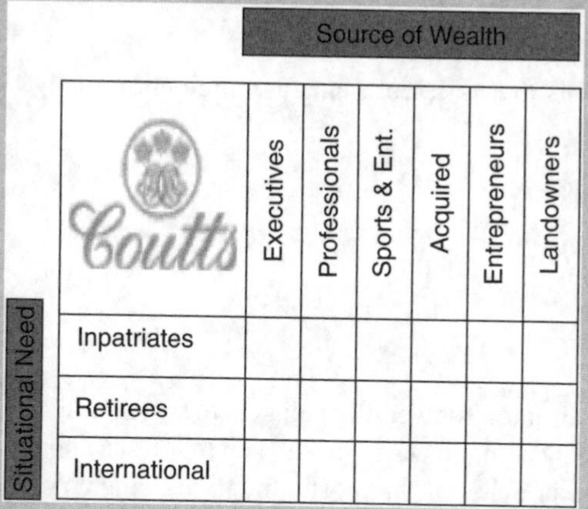

Figure 3.9   Client segmentation at Coutts
Source: Datamonitor (2005), 'Best Practice in Wealth Management – Asia-Pacific', May. Reproduced by permission.

[2]This draws heavily from Datamonitor (2005), 'Best Practice in Wealth Management – Asia-Pacific', May 2005.

come from numerous sources and at any stage of life. But if it comes as a large sum it can be particularly daunting, and having someone to trust, and who has an independent view, is essential.'

- *Sports and entertainment*. 'Your career means you are often in the limelight and that you may have little time to consider managing your wealth for even the immediate future, let alone the longer term. Having a financial adviser who truly understands your world and the demands it makes on you can therefore be invaluable, whether you are an entertainer, an artist or a professional sports person.'

- *Landowners*. 'As an owner of land or property, you may be interested in exploring ways of diversifying your business in order to maintain your lifestyle now, but still be able to pass on your family's assets to future generations. At Coutts, we want to ensure that we can provide the best solutions for you."

- *Inpatriates*. 'If you are resident but are not domiciled in the UK, you can face a bewildering array of financial options and decisions. Our team of private bankers is dedicated to, and experienced in, looking after international clients living and working in the UK. Whether you're a business owner, a professional working for a major international organization, a sports person or an entertainer, and have UK resident status, we understand the unique financial implications for you and your family.'

- *Retired*. 'More than anyone, you know that early planning for retirement pays dividends. But you also know that it does not stop there. Whether you are just getting close to retirement or already enjoying more time at leisure, you'll want to ensure that your financial plans are robust and that they can be flexible during your retirement. We are ideally placed to help you control your financial future whilst maintaining a high quality of life for you and your family.'

- *International*. 'As well as being the UK's leading private bank, throughout our history we have looked after clients who are either non-resident or non-domiciled in the UK, or who are UK citizens living and working abroad.'

Datamonitor suggests that this represents a combination of five separate segmentation criteria:

- Source of wealth.
- Sophistication.
- Geographic situation.
- Lifestage.
- Customer value.

While it is relatively common for wealth managers to target similar client niches, most tend to do so in a much less systematic way. The key benefit of this approach is that it has enabled the bank to gain share in many of the most attractive segments of the UK private banking market. It has done so by organising its relationship managers around these various client groups, which has given team members a very deep understanding of their clients' needs.

Box 3.3 discusses one relatively new important segment: professional sports players. Merrill Lynch is reported to be targeting the UK gay community; it has also had much success with a team covering North African expatriates in France. Chapter 10 discusses two other emerging segments: wealthy women and US ethnic groups.

Box 3.3   Professional sports players

An example of a segment targeted by a growing number of wealth managers is professional sports players. Scorpio Partnership estimate that there are more than 8 500 European sports players each with wealth in excess of $1 million.

Sports professionals have the potential to earn substantial amounts of money in a very short period, and require customised financial services. There is also the opportunity for sports people to leverage collateral such as media and other promotional rights as a source of wealth. Furthermore, a large number of professional sports players become wealthy when they are young and typically have limited financial knowledge. This increases the potential for a single financial institution to become the primary provider to this client, and also enables these institutions to capitalise on annual management fees charged over a long-term period because of the short career span that requires various financial planning services to generate a certain level of income in retirement.

A sports professional is also likely to require a sophisticated level of cash management services because of their large cash earnings. Advanced insurance products are a another key part of the offering, since injuries almost always have an impact on a sports professional's income. Linked to their general lack of financial sophistication, sports professionals like to invest in areas that are relatively simple to understand and are tangible, such as residential property.

In *Euromoney*'s Private Banking Survey 2006, the top providers of services to sports players included: UBS, Coutts, Citigroup, HSBC, Credit Suisse, ABN Amro, Merrill Lynch, Deutsche Bank, ING and JP Morgan. Examples of approaches include:

- *UBS,* which launched its sports and entertainment group in 2000, offers a special offshore fund targeted at European and American sports professionals, run by its former GAM subsidiary.
- *Coutts* provides services geared towards UK sports professionals from football, golf, motor racing and tennis. This segments accounts for around 8% of its AuM. The bank states that professional footballers and agents often refer team-mates to the bank, something that it encourages through dinners and other events. Coutts follows a strategy of providing a structured financial plan to the sports client, based on a career span involving early retirement and the potential for early injury.
- *Credit Suisse Private Banking* offers sports professionals a package titled 'Dream Team'. The package is tailored to each sports person and takes into account insurance cover, current contracts with clubs, sponsors and managers and any special risks associated with the particular sport. Credit Suisse has an alliance with a specialist sports insurance provider which creates tailored policies for each sports professional.

One key client acquisition route is to form alliances with sports agents. Another acquisition route is to use (current and former) sports professionals as business introducers, typically by hiring former sports stars. Merrill Lynch, for example, has a joint venture (JV) with IMG (a world-leading sports management and marketing firm), and recently made a further push into the tennis subsegment by hiring two former professionals.

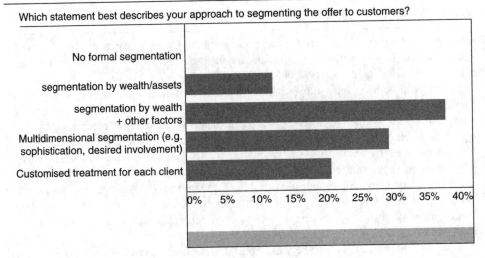

Figure 3.10   Client segmentation approaches used by wealth managers
Source: Mercer Oliver Wyman (2005), p. 16. Reproduced by permission.

Implicitly, client segmentation forces prioritisation. An institution is compelled to evaluate where it can add the most value and then identify the clients who will appreciate what it has to offer. In a competitive and growing market, effective client segmentation enables a bank to know who it is going after and to demonstrate quickly to the selected clients that it is in a strong position to meet their specific needs. Efforts to build tailored products and services that clients need most, and to educate clients, will result in increasing client awareness of a given bank's strengths. It is this client awareness that provides banks with recognition and distinctiveness, and it is this distinctiveness that gives aspirants the opportunity to stand out from the competition and penetrate the HNW market or capture a deeper share of the existing private banking market. Done well, client segmentation is a key to growth.

The Mercer Oliver Wyman European Wealth Management Survey 2004 provides an indication of segmentation approaches used in the industry (Figure 3.10). Though all respondents segment their client base to some extent, less than one-third use multidimensional segmentation. Overall, the results suggest that the industry has more to do in this area, particularly when compared with segmentation approaches used in other sectors of financial services (such as corporate banking and consumer finance) and other consumer-facing industries.

It is worth noting that not all relationship managers are in favour of segmentation, particularly when it is centrally imposed. EFG International, for example, is very strongly opposed to client segmentation, not least because under its unique franchise-like business model, its relationship managers are very firmly in the driving seat (see Box 6.1 in Chapter 6). Indeed, its Chairman has reportedly gone as far as to say[3] 'on our premises, there is no more a distinction between onshore and offshore, or between affluent customers, rich customers or the ultra rich. All that is rubbish'.

---

[3] Speech at the British–Swiss Chamber of Commerce, Geneva, 24 November 2005.

3.3   CLIENT VALUE MANAGEMENT

Having segmented the client base and adapted the service model accordingly, the next step is to consider how to create value by managing clients effectively. This involves using client insights (from the targeted application of databases, simple statistics and in-house business knowledge) to boost profits by:

- *Acquiring new profitable clients*, via initiatives to generate and convert high-quality leads and reduce acquisition costs.
- *Developing existing clients*, via initiatives to increase cross-selling and share of wallet.
- *Retaining profitable clients*, via initiatives to manage client and asset attrition.

This is known as client value management (CVM), or customer relationship management (CRM).

By identifying how value is distributed across the client base, wealth managers can pinpoint the most attractive segments in targeting prospective clients and help to plan an approach to existing accounts by highlighting the priority areas/means by which it can extract additional value from its current clients. Figure 3.11 illustrates a typical distribution of private banking clients' profitability. It shows that there is a small proportion of clients that generate the bulk of the total profit and that almost one-third of clients are currently unprofitable.

Simply ranking clients by profitability is not sufficient, however. Rather, segmentation needs to lead to an understanding of the fundamental drivers of profitability. For example, for a given

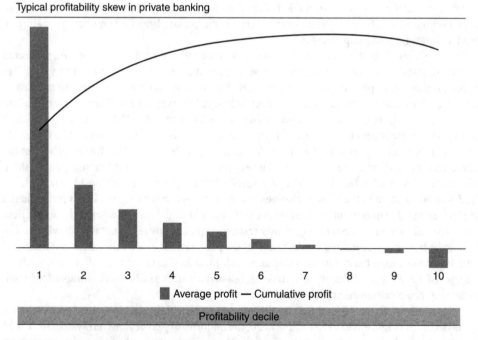

Figure 3.11   Typical client value skew in private banking
Source: Mercer Oliver Wyman client example (2005). Reproduced by permission.

CUSTOMER PRODUCT USAGE ALONG LIFE CYCLE (DOMESTIC CUSTOMERS)

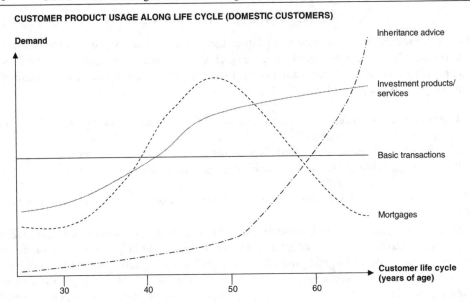

Figure 3.12   Client life cycle (illustrative)
Source: Author's analysis.

client or segment, are they unprofitable because of low revenue or high cost to serve? One bank uses a segmentation based on relationship size (footings) and breadth (number and nature of product holdings) to group clients.

One problem with this approach is that it is static: it makes no allowance for expected future profitability. Clients with limited assets today may represent little current value. But clearly, if they are expected to accumulate assets rapidly, they are more valuable to the wealth manager. Conversely, a client whose product holdings fall over time will tend to become less valuable. The concept of client lifetime value, or net present value (NPV), is key because it allows wealth managers to view their client base strategically. There are several key tangible and intangible factors that will give an initial indication of the client value for the private bank. These factors include: current revenues, current footings, duration of relationship, age, share of wallet, number of referrals, meeting requirements and potential relationship size. Figure 3.12 is an illustration of the kind of changes in product usage that happen over a typical client's life-cycle. It is also important to take into account two additional factors when estimating client value: (a) links among accounts, e.g. family relationships and business contacts (in which case, it could be best to group them together), and (b) the potential for client referrals as an additional source of value. One bank that uses this approach produced data showing that clients within the ages of 19–25 were currently loss-making, but had a positive NPV. This prompted the bank to develop products aimed at increasing loyalty.

Mercer Oliver Wyman found that wealth managers essentially fall into two camps when it comes to CVM (Figure 3.13). On the one hand, the majority of players have no systematic CVM approach beyond a simple client-contact history. The majority of wealth managers seem to make no regular or systematic attempt to measure the effectiveness of marketing campaigns; very few

CVM
Which statement best describes how you use CVM to manage contact with customers?

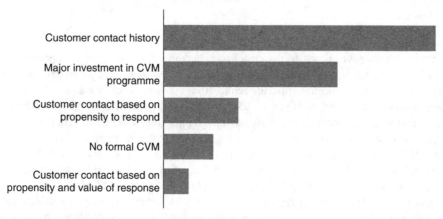

Figure 3.13   Wealth managers' approach to CVM
Source: Mercer Oliver Wyman (2005). Reproduced by permission.

rigorously evaluate their financial effects.[4] This links in with their relatively underdeveloped client segmentation approaches. On the other hand, around 30% of wealth managers, typically the larger ones, have made major investments in CVM programmes.

While many retail banks have recognized the power of CVM and invested heavily in this area, wealth managers have typically been put off by the perception that CVM is expensive and unnecessary. But experience shows that a *tactical* CVM programme can produce significant and immediate results with limited up-front investments and no risk for the organisation. This approach identifies business areas in which CVM knowledge can translate into quick-to-market performance improvements. It can achieve returns within compressed timeframes because it uses existing information and processes, rather than inventing new ones. The approach moves the organisation forward via a series of incremental steps, each of which rings the cash register, builds capabilities and creates profits that can fund succeeding steps.

This tactical CVM approach uses the following rigorous three-step process to profitably cultivate these types of opportunities:

1. The first step is to identify and prioritise the key area(s) of focus – client acquisition, development or retention – leveraging industry knowledge and senior management intuition, as well as strategy. Many players choose to focus on client retention initially as this can give the greatest 'bang for buck'. Once the opportunity set is identified, prioritising the action steps is next. Criteria for prioritisation include economic upside, ease of implementation, expected time to realise impact and frequency with which decisions need to be made.
2. Assess existing information and processes to determine which specific opportunities within the area(s) of focus can be addressed in the shortest time-frame and with the greatest impact.
3. Develop and implement 'quick-win' actions to impact near-term earnings, without building extensive new technology. A disciplined and thoughtful approach can actually

---

[4] For more details see Mercier Oliver Wyman (2005), page 37.

institutionalise key processes and capabilities while yielding short-term benefits, bypassing efforts that do not yield results.

3.3.1 Client acquisition

Acquiring profitable new clients from scratch can be time consuming and, depending on the acquisition channel, relatively expensive. BCG data show that, taking into account lead generation, referral fee and meeting time, the acquisition cost of a referral (via an existing client, elsewhere in the group, or a referral agent) is 65% of the cost of a non-referral. Universal banks, with their retail feeder networks, are clearly advantaged here (see Chapter 8). There is a wide variety of sources of prospective clients – both internal and external (Figure 3.14).

One novel form of 'worksite-type' marketing is MLP (a German financial adviser offering its own and third-party products), which builds its pipeline of high-value clients by establishing relationships at universities. It thereby attracts clients at the point in their life-cycle when the demand for advice is particularly high. MLP advisers gather information on final-year students and invite them to career-specific financial seminars where the different options that best address their particular needs are explained. The seminars are often combined with training on how to apply for a job and other relevant skills. After the seminar, the students are invited to individual consulting sessions where concrete product offers are made. MLP has an 80% closure rate after these sessions, partly due to the strong fit between students and their adviser, who usually studied the same subject. More than 60% of the contacted graduating medical students became MLP clients and the rate is approximately 38% for other core target groups such as engineering, law and business studies.

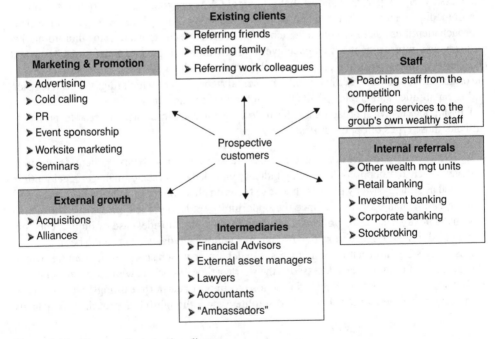

Figure 3.14   Sources of prospective clients
Source: Datamonitor (2002), 'Client Acquisition in Wealth Management Survey', September 2002. Reproduced by permission.

3.3.2 Client development

It is apparent from surveys and other evidence that many private clients find that their expectations are not met: they are dissatisfied with their private banking relationship – the loyalty and inertia that has kept clients with a bank is breaking down. As loyalty is becoming weak among private clients, many private bankers and wealth managers are looking for ways to increase loyalty, such as through the development of life-style services, differentiating their offerings and so on.

Traditionally private bank marketing has been relatively unrefined but this is changing. The marketing emphasis will need to take on board relationship managers' views as to the appropriate value propositions on offer and emphasis will need to be placed much more on targeted client segments as well as complementary brand image approaches.

There is also the opportunity to develop approaches based on client's price sensitivity because private bank pricing is based on a combination of pricing strategies. For this reason, if we lower prices/fees on particular services or other gift-related rewards we can also grant some cross-selling. From an operational perspective, this means that it is important to support advisors with pricing tools, not least because it affords them a better understanding of the choices they make. These tools should also help private banks to optimise the product mix. Advisors or relationship managers can start by attempting to shift clients to products with higher margins. This will help them address some of the pricing inefficiency in their portfolios. Mercer Oliver Wyman suggest that wealth managers often underprice smaller clients, making the bottom 20%–30% of clients unprofitable on a fully costed basis. Addressing this issue through re-pricing can create a 15%–20% improvement in overall profit.

Management should review and adjust the balance of client contact to ensure that the service requirements of the most valuable clients are suitably met and that accounts with potential growth and sales opportunities are targeted by relationship managers (see Chapter 5).

Cross-selling opportunities need to be emphasised. Sales of existing products represent marginal revenues with limited additional costs and are therefore a key way of improving profit margins. Wealth managers should therefore identify these opportunities and develop a process for ensuring these are flagged up to relationship managers in their meetings with clients. The cross-selling initiatives should also be coupled with incentives to encourage multiple product holdings in terms of lower prices/fees on particular services or other gift-related rewards. These should be conditional upon having a number/combination of products with the wealth manager and should be designed to increase client value through a greater number of product holdings. Product bundling and 'staircases' of offers for clients of different wealth bands has proved very effective, at e.g. Merrill Lynch. Relationship manager training and incentivisation will also have a role to play here (see Chapter 5).

Value-destroying clients, such as small clients, need to be either sensitively 'managed out' by increasing minimum investment thresholds or alternatively charged prices that generate value to the bank. Care is needed here to avoid any potential reputational damage.

In order to be successful, private banks should use a range of metrics in order to improve value creation per client while aligning resources to meet various client demands. Examples include: number of client contacts, number of sales conversions, products per client, client profitability and client satisfaction. On the latter metric, very few private banks currently engage in regular structured client research assessments designed to enhance client propositions or marketing techniques. To the extent that they currently measure client satisfaction at all, banks currently typically rely on crude, ad hoc measures such as complaint monitoring, relationship length and staff perceptions. Banks should make the effort to track client satisfaction comprehensively and systematically.

3.3.3   Client retention

The IBM 2005 survey found that clients' top three reasons for leaving their wealth manager were: dissatisfaction with service, poor investment advice and poor investment performance (Figure 3.15). Departure of their relationship manager was a surprisingly long way down the list, at number 10, indicating that some clients may now perceive themselves to be clients more of the bank than the relationship manager.

Experience shows that client and asset attrition is becoming a real problem for many wealth managers, linked to client behaviour and the start of the large-scale intergenerational 'changing of the guard'. Yet the PricewaterhouseCoopers Global Wealth Management Survey 2005 found that nearly 46% of respondents had no client retention process whatsoever.

3.3.3.1   The basic toolkit

Many wealth management institutions should implement the systematic registration and analysis of complaints, although this step is often taken too late to retain dissatisfied clients. If implemented well, client win-back programs can be extremely effective, but they come at a price. The trick here is to take a proactive approach to uncover the root causes of attrition at an early stage.

The starting point should be to track asset attrition systematically. That will make it easier to at least size the problem, identify trends and any key affected segments, and to start to prioritise the retention effort and implement some quick wins. The report should be formally reviewed by senior management and exit interviews introduced. Ideally, an early-warning system should

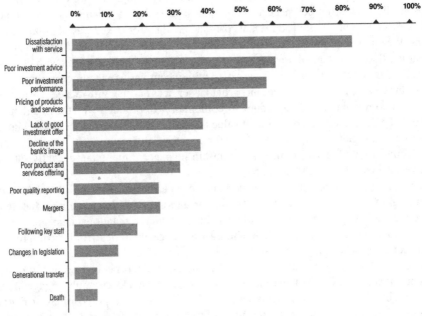

*Sum of percentage of respondents with 'strongly agree' and 'agree' responses.

Figure 3.15   Clients' reasons for leaving their wealth manager*
Source: IBM Consulting Services, European Wealth and Private Banking Industry Survey 2005. Reproduced by permission.

be implemented, incorporating data on, for example, unusually low transaction volumes and increasing asset outflows. There may also be a role for new product packages, designed to increase relationship stickiness.

As discussed in Chapter 5, team-based relationship management approaches can be effective in helping wealth managers with their own succession-planning issues: overall, relationship manager churn continues to be a key driver of asset attrition.

Banks may need to consider spending more time with certain high-risk clients. Implemented well, a retention scheme will strengthen ties and can support cross-selling possibilities. The need to ensure that client requests are carried out more reliably, efficiently and effectively – without unnecessary hand-offs and delay – may sound an obvious point. But it is surprising how, in the process of trying to add value in more elaborate ways, wealth managers can often lose sight of the need to get the basics right.

3.3.3.2   Intergenerational transfers

One client segment for which private banks have noticeably developed their retention focus relates to retired HNWIs. A recent survey by Northern Trust found that 51% of US HNW clients are already retired.

Recall that in the list of clients' reasons for leaving a wealth manager, generational transfer and death came, well, last. Going forward, it is conceivable that they could move up the list, not least because of the sheer scale of the generational change, which still has a long way to go (Figure 3.16). That represents an unprecedented amount of wealth that private banks have the opportunity to grab (or, on the other hand, lose).

Robert Elliott, senior managing director at Bessemer Trust, recently said that 'We sometimes joke that death is the ultimate competitor, because kids are then free to pick their own adviser. If we do our job well, they will already have done so – and it will still be us.' He is not alone.

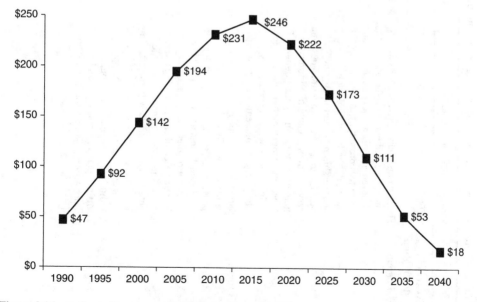

Figure 3.16   Estimated bequests to US baby boomers ($ billion)
Source: AMVESCAP.

Table 3.1 An overview of 'new generation' client retention strategies

	Sporting and social events	Education activities	Involvement activities
Events description	Different events	Conferences, seminars and workshops	Real-time mentoring of wealthy children, both from parents and the private bank
Main goals	These events enable private banks to encourage and entertain the passion that children of their wealthy clients pursue. Despite representing an absolute cost to the bank, the benefits of such sponsorship represent intangible benefits in the medium term. These may serve as an invaluable opportunity to gain popularity among the younger of these offspring, which in turn may lead to invitations at family occasions, ultimately strengthening relationships.	These events intend to educate the client's family on the complex world of wealth management and wider issues such as family governance and succession planning. They also permit private banks to host internships for the offspring of their wealthy clientele to provide an insight into their world. Some of these events put more emphasis on promoting product knowledge to increase revenue.	These events intend to generate both immediate revenue for the bank but also provide precious opportunities to reinforce relationships as a trusted advisor. This has been achieved by training these young adults in the management of wealth and the development of a macroeconomic view of how things work in finance.
Examples	Atlantic Trust Company in the USA entertains wealthy families and prospects at sporting events such as the US Open Tennis and Golf, the Master's Golf Tournament and various major league baseball and football games. Gerrard's investment managers in the UK entertain and mingle with the offspring of wealthy clients at a range of events such as horse races, polo, opera, art exhibitions and even rock concerts. Banif in Spain organises golf and horse-riding tournaments for wealthy families.	Banif in Spain runs seminars on family governance and succession planning and offers the opportunity for children of wealthy families to visit and get an insight into how a private bank functions. Citigroup Private Bank conducts conferences to encourage debate and thought on the issue of protection of wealth to engage with the children of wealthy families. Deutsche Private Wealth Management in the USA hosts an annual, three week Summer Seminar, which offers the young adult offspring of their clients the opportunity to learn about finance, business philanthropy and financial responsibility from industry experts.	Banif in Spain encourages clients to appoint their grown children (early twenties onwards) as board directors of their SICAV companies. Kleinwort Benson Private Bank in the UK encourages its clients to set up trusts with 'shelter amounts', which allow their offspring aged 18 years and above to 'cut their teeth' with making investment decisions. Coutts Private Bank in the UK has had a branch at the prestigious Eton College since 1961, where it offers basic banking services (current accounts, cheque books, etc.) to all students.

Kleinwort Benson Private Bank organizes events such as Harry Potter and James Bond themed evenings. A cinema is hired and staff are dressed up as characters in the movie to engage with the children prior to and after the movie. The bank also organises visits to places of interest such as the London Eye for its international clientele visiting the UK.

Gerrard (UK) regularly organises seminars for its wealthy families, educating them on issues of relevance to the offspring.

JP Morgan Private Bank (twice a year) globally hosts a Next Generation program dealing with a range of wealth management issues.

Rothschild Private Bank (UK) brings in children (late teens–early twenties) of wealthy clients for up to a fortnight, giving them an insight on how a private bank and the 'investment management' business works.

Source: Personal elaboration from Datamonitor (2004), 'Client Retention Strategies for the Next Wealth Generation. A Global Perspective on Practices', August 2004. Reproduced by permission.

Indeed, many are already going out of their way to target the children of existing clients, so as to be the bank of choice for managing the wealth transfer and beyond (see Chapter 4).

Wealth managers are engaging with the next generation in a variety of ways, with the aim of deepening relationships with inheritors. Typically, 'next generation' client retention approaches fall into three broad categories:

1. Education events.
2. 'Involvement' activities, e.g. mentoring.
3. Sporting and social events.

Table 3.1 provides more detail. Education events, in particular, represent an invaluable opportunity to explain the complicated world of finance and to promote the private bank.

4
New Products and Pricing

With Philip Molyneux

There has been an explosion in wealth management products and services in recent years, much of which has focused on asset protection using derivatives and other investment vehicles. Most noticeable is the growth in the use of structured products and alternative investments (such as hedge funds, funds of hedge funds, private equity and real estate investments) together with the development of a range of advisory services. The aim has been to offer a more diverse array of products and services to meet the life-cycle wealth management demands of an increasingly sophisticated and price conscious clientele. This chapter details these developments and identifies issues associated with the product sourcing. As the product offer becomes more complex and clients more demanding, this raises pricing issues – especially performance-related and other relationship-based fee structures.

The private banking product offering has altered substantially in recent years in response to changing demands of clients, greater volatility in capital markets and growing economic uncertainty. Given the downturn in capital markets in 2000–2002, many private clients witnessed a decline in their wealth, which increased demand for capital-preservation products and higher value-added services. These include alternative investments, and credit services, which enable clients to leverage both liquid and illiquid asset holdings.

Morgan Stanley have argued that, within the asset management industry as a whole, there is a growing 'polarisation' between alpha and beta investment products (see Figure 4.1):[1]

- *A core of largely passively managed or low tracking-error 'beta' instruments* (e.g. index, enhanced index, exchange traded funds, or ETFs, etc.), shown as group A in Figure 4.1. These products are typically manufactured by the large quantitative specialist asset managers such as BGI, State Street, Northern Trust, Vanguard and Pimco.
- *Higher risk/return, 'alpha' strategies to achieve yield pick-up and greater diversification,* which is the 'satellite' around this passive, low-tracking error core. As a result, we see strong growth in innovative, alternative and structured investment products and portable alpha structures (group C in Figure 4.1).

As a result of this polarisation, traditional core investment strategies (such as low-tracking-error mandates run actively, e.g. benchmark +1%), shown as group B in Figure 4.1, have recently been in relative decline, as clients demand absolute returns and non-correlated investment strategies, at least for a portion of their assets.

Recent surveys suggest that this overarching dynamic is also being played out in the wealth-management component of the asset management industry (see Figure 4.2). Top-performing European private banks now have on average around 15% of their AuM in structured products

---

[1] See, for example, 'European Asset Management Industry Update', Spring 2005, and other research by Huw van Steenis of Morgan Stanley, from which this section draws.

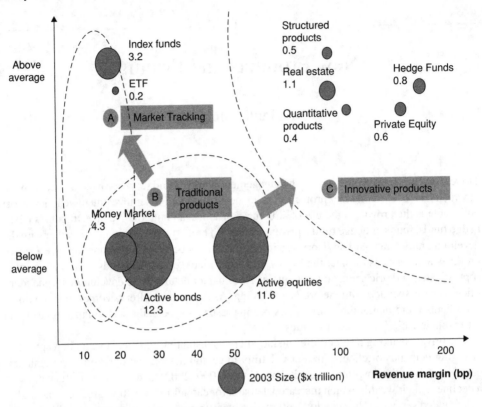

Projected Market Growth: 2004–2006e

Figure 4.1 Polarisation of the asset management industry
Source: National statistics; BCG analysis; Reproduced by permission of Huw van Steenis, Morgan Stanley.

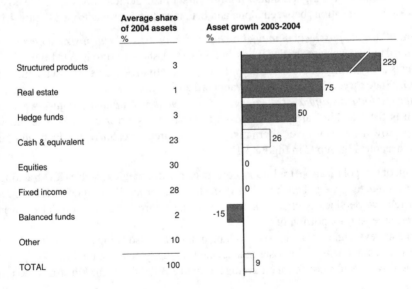

Figure 4.2 Polarisation dynamic also applies to wealth management
Source: McKinsey 'European Private Banking Economics Survey' 2005. Reproduced by permission.

and alternative assets. At end-2004, UBS had 12% of its AuM in 'other' assets, up from 3% in 2000, which has contributed to a widening in its profit margin.

Within wealth management, there has also been an increased emphasis on providing insurance and pension solutions to HNWIs, which is another reflection of the growing focus on protection-related services. As clients have become more sophisticated, they also increasingly seek value-added services that are presented as part of a broad investment philosophy that matches their overall wealth management aspirations. This means that the wealth management industry in general has had to emphasise 'holistic' investment advisory services, making use of a wider range of 'best-practice' in-house and third-party products and services to meet these growing complex service demands.

The need to provide an extensive array of products and services has encouraged the private banking industry to embrace (to varying degrees) the so-called 'open architecture' approach where best-practice products are sourced both in-house from various parts of the bank and also from third-party providers. As clients clearly understand that no wealth management firm can offer 'best practice' solutions entirely in-house, the move towards an open architecture structure is simply a reflection of the increased complexity and sophistication of client demands.

Successful wealth management players have an increasingly modular investment platform that can manage different client wealth levels, use segregated accounts to offer scale with a personal touch and includes a greater proportion of third-party products. Figure 4.3 illustrates how UBS segments its offering despite having a common investment platform.

Another observable trend has been the growing emphasis on managing family wealth. The family office concept/philosophy has been a major feature of UHNWI wealth management in the US for some time but has been traditionally less developed elsewhere. This is changing,

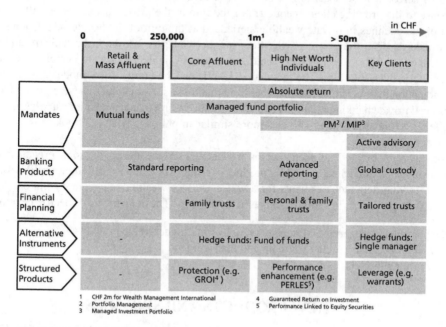

Figure 4.3   Modular investment platform
Source: UBS.

and various large banks such as Deutsche Bank and UBS have developed special arms to deal specifically with this client segment (see Chapter 6). While the cost of establishing stand-alone family offices may be prohibitive for many firms, the main point to emphasise is that the wealth management industry in general is having to embrace the style of services and products as well as investment philosophy that traditionally was mainly the preserve of the family office. The aim is to offer (though not necessarily manufacture in-house) the full range of solutions that are unambiguously in the best interests of clients and their families. This means focusing on individual client, family, client–business relationships, identifying clients' investment and other needs and meeting them with value-added solutions. Such services can range from basic bank transaction services to alternative investments, estate planning, financial education of family members, philanthropic opportunities, etc.

The range of products and services on offer obviously will vary according to the wealth of clients served. Though some wealth managers have created explicit product and service tiers for clients in different wealth bands, in practice it is surpising how little difference there now is among the various tiers. To some extent, the demarcation lines between the services on offer to the various client wealth segments of the private banking client base are breaking down – a phenomenon described by marketing types as 'democratisation'. As has been the case at the top end of the retail banking market, where mass affluent and other limited private banking style services are now on offer, this type of 'product and service spiral' is now a feature of the wealth management industry. Hedge funds, for example, were once only available to UHNWIs, but are now available almost across the board, helped by the development of hedge funds-of-funds.

Private banking firms also now promote all-embracing 'family office style' wealth management services to a broader range of clients, emphasising value-added 'holistic' investment services across a wide spectrum of areas. To a certain extent this broad development is a response to the growing client scepticism of the role of the private banker, especially in the light of the declines in private wealth experienced at the turn of the last decade. Clients often wondered what they were paying their private banks for and both the industry and the clients themselves looked to other wealth management models that were perceived to offer better alternatives/solutions. The fact that UHNWIs use the family office model was an obvious indication that wealthiest families believed that these sorts of solutions were preferable to traditional private banking relationships. As such, the wealth management industry has moved to offer investment and other services more similar in philosophy and outlook to the family office approach.

Another notable trend has been towards product and service 'tiering' by some private banks. This involves private banks designing product packages for clients at different wealth levels.

The growing demands of clients for a wider array of wealth management solutions have forced New approaches to various changes in the industry. The main focus has been to develop:

- New products and services, focusing on delivering higher-value products.
- New approaches to product sourcing and management.
- New pricing models.

4.1   NEW PRODUCTS AND SERVICES

The development of new products and services has been driven not only by changing client demand but also by an industry emphasis on building brand image and differentiating service

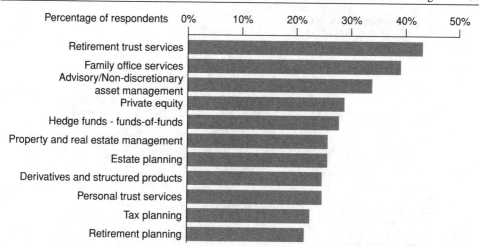

Figure 4.4   Private banking product differentiators. What products will enhance differentiation over the next three years?
Source: PricewaterhouseCoopers (2004b). Reproduced by permission.

offerings. Given the growing number of firms in the wealth management business, and particularly the increased competition between the private banking arms of large groups and specialist operators, all have sought to both expand and differentiate their product and service capabilities. Figure 4.4, taken from a recent survey of global wealth managers, illustrates the sorts of areas that are believed to enhance differentiation, and includes both the offer of relatively new products or services, as well as more traditional services.

4.1.1   The advisory process

Advice remains at the heart of the wealth management industry. But particularly for the larger firms, which operate in multiple geographies, advice has often been ad hoc and of variable quality. For clients with similar profiles and needs, there can be a surprising degree of divergence among the portfolios and advice dished out both within individual players by different relationship managers and across different players. That, in turn, puts individual client relationships in jeopardy and risks damaging the reputation of private banks. Many wealth managers have therefore been focusing on achieving improvments in the quality and consistency of their advice delivery. In particular, the aim has been to put in place a systematic advisory approach that is more structured, capable of being tailored to clients' needs and preferences, and that is supported by a range of related analytical and research tools. There is also a greater overall emphasis on advising across the entire balance sheet, i.e. liabilities as well as assets.

The basic approach is illustrated in Figure 4.5, which is split into four steps:

1. *Client profiling.* The advisor gathers information to build up a comprehensive picture of the client's existing wealth, including all financial and non-financial investments, liabilities (visible and hidden), income, tax profile and expected wealth transfers. The client's assets can then be split into those that are dedicated to covering specific liabilities, which need to

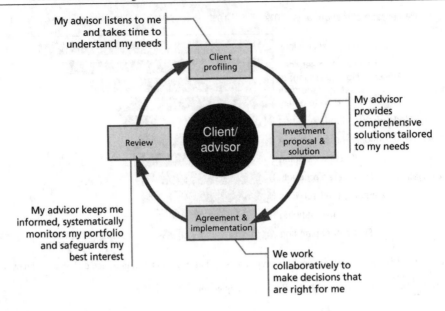

Figure 4.5   Systematic advisory process
Source: UBS.

be invested according to a low-risk profile, and those assets that can be invested according to the client's risk profile and preferences. The advisor then assesses the client's risk tolerance, typically based on a questionnaire that asks the client to respond to a series of risk-related statements. The output determines a set of wealth management preferences relating to type of investment mandate, types of investment to include or exclude, frequency and mode of contact, and client expectations.

2. *Investment proposal and solution.* On the basis of the client's service preference and risk profile, the advisor devises an asset allocation strategy, using an asset allocation model (proprietary or non-proprietary). Advisors often involve specialists to help develop the more technical aspects of the client's strategy. The output is a comprehensive proposal summarising the asset allocation information and all of the financial solutions recommended to fulfil the client's needs. That may include scenario and risk analysis.

3. *Agreement and implementation.* The advisor consults the clients and seeks input and agreement to the solutions presented. The next step is to construct the portfolio, execute the relevant transactions and ensure proactive maintenance. Portfolio tracking software can be used to alert the advisor when the portfolio deviates from the prescribed asset allocation.

4. *Review.* The advisor reviews the client's risk and service profile continuously, and conducts a regular formal review with the client covering the client's complete balance sheet, progress towards longer-term goals and necessary portfolio adjustments.

Relationship managers typically have a range of analytical tools, but these are not all primarily sales focused. For example, Merrill Lynch uses two proprietary programmes: (a) 'Assessing Your Goals' for client profiling and (b) 'Client Review Centre' for periodic performance reviews. These programmes are designed to give relationship managers the tools required to be more thoughtful and comprehensive in their approach.

4.1.1.1   Asset allocation of HNWIs

Given the wide array of investment opportunities available to private banking clients, the wealth management industry needs to face substantial challenges in the asset allocation process. In particular, asset allocation is becoming more granular, and is moving away from broad-brush equities versus fixed-income versus cash treatments. Within each asset class, including alternatives (private equity is not the same as hedge funds – and within hedge funds there is a huge number of different styles), it is necessary to split assets into different catagories based on characteristics such as risk, return and geography.

The way in which HNWIs allocate their investments can change rapidly over time, client type and region. Figure 4.6 illustrates Cap Gemini and Merrill Lynch's assessment of HNWI asset allocation over the last few years, highlighting the reinvigorated interest in equities and the recent preference for alternative investments.

There are, however, substantial regional differences in HNW asset allocation:[2]

- In North America, equities are the asset class of preference among HNWIs, accounting for 41% of their investments. In fact, North American portfolios remain the least balanced

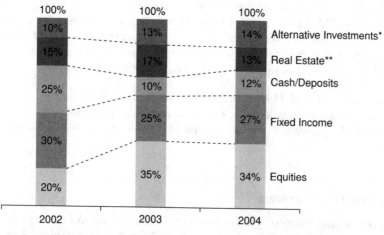

*Includes structured products, hedge funds, managed funds, foreign currency, commodities (including precious metals), private equity and investments of passion (fine art and collactables).

**Includes direct real estate investments and REITs, which are not common instruments outside the United States.

Figure 4.6   Asset allocation of HNWIs
Source: Capgemini/Merrill Lynch, 'Relationship Manager Surveys', March 2003, April 2004, April 2005; 'World Wealth Report' 2005. Reproduced by permission.

---

[2] *Source*: Capgemini/Merrill Lynch (2005), 'World Wealth Report'.

among asset classes, with HNWIs here showing substantially less interest/allocation in alternative investments than their counterparts in Europe, Asia-Pacific and the Middle East. Canadian hedge funds performed well in 2004 and as such they form a greater share of HNWIs' financial assets (7.5%) than in either the United States or in Europe. Hedge funds and private equity were among the fastest growing assets held by Canadian HNWIs in 2004. There has also been an increase in the holding of offshore assets (mainly due to investment opportunities in emerging markets) to 30% of overall asset allocation. Another trend has been the move by US HNWIs away from domestic tax-efficient holding vehicles towards the increased use of offshore centres.

- Asia-Pacific HNWIs held the most equally distributed asset classes of wealthy individuals in any region. Real estate allocations were relatively high in this region, accounting for 19% of HNWIs' portfolios. Around 28% of HNWI assets from the Asia-Pacific region are held offshore.
- European HNWIs have diversified well, with 25% in equities and 24% in fixed income assets. They have the highest proportion of assets allocated to the property sector – around 21% – of which the bulk is in direct real estate investment (e.g. not funds). European investors are also showing a greater interest in managed futures for diversification purposes, but relatively high fees are deterring growth in this segment. European HNWIs have increased their use of offshore centres for tax minimisation purposes, especially Bermuda, the Cayman Islands and the British Virgin Islands. Other centres, such as Panama, Liechtenstein, Hong Kong and the Isle of Man, are attracting more HNWI business for tax protection associated with specialist financing and various asset classes.
- Latin American HNWIs are limiting their exposure to equity (only 18% asset allocation) and focusing on various revenue-generating, risk-balancing products such as hedge funds and managed futures. Private equity accounts for around 25% of their assets with around a third in traditional bond investments, mainly held offshore in the US.

Other major features of HNWI asset allocation relate to a decline in exposure to US markets and growing interest in using foreign exchange transactions as an asset class. The latter has been the preserve of various institutional investors but is of growing interest to HNWIs.

4.1.2 Tracker-related products

Index trackers, as their name suggests, are designed to track the performance (both the upside and downside) of certain markets or indices. The index being tracked may be passive, such as tracking the FTSE 100, or (less common) could be actively rebalanced by the investment manager subject to such changes being stated up-front.

Tracker products are usually long-dated (or may even have indefinite time-spans) and are referred to as tracker, benchmark or (in the case of a tracker looking to benefit from upside risk) bull certificates.

There are a wide range of tracker-related instruments available on offer via many banks and other financial service firms. They include:[3]

---

[3] See the London Stock Exchange website http://www.londonstockexchange.com/ for an excellent description of the main types of tracker products available.

- *Accelerated trackers*, which typically offer a greater share on upside gains compared to the downside. For instance, Société Générale offers a Nikkei 225 accelerated tracker, which offers 200% participation in any rise in the Nikkei 225 index, with just a one–one downside.
- *Reverse trackers* provide returns to the investor based on falls in the underlying index being tracked. They are similar to standard trackers but have an inverse relationship with the underlying asset: should the price of the underlying asset fall, the price of the reverse tracker will rise. They are otherwise known as bear certificates.
- *Bonus trackers* replicate the performance of the underlying index with bonus payment on expiry if the underlying index remains within a particular range.
- *Discount trackers* replicate the performance of an underlying index, but this exposure is given at a discount and gains are capped.

4.1.3   Structured products

One of the most clearly identifiable recent features of the wealth management product offer relates to the development of structured products. Structured products are nowadays widely offered by the private banking industry and are generally used for reducing risk or enhancing returns on conventional (equity, bond) investments. Standard applications include providing full or partial capital (principal) protection to underlying investments while offering the opportunities to make returns on market movements. They can be used to protect investment positions, create liquidity for concentrated equity positions and also provide various tax-efficient solutions.

Demand for structured products varies substantially by region. Though North America is the largest wealth market, it is not a market that has historically been keen on structured products – indeed issuance fell below €10 billion in 2004 (Figure 4.7). Europe, on the other hand, has a persistently strong propensity to use structured products in both the retail and the HNWI areas. 2004 was a strong year, with growth in structured product issuance of 15%. The biggest potential comes from Asia, which saw 58% growth in structured product issuance in 2004, particularly in Hong Kong, Taiwan and Korea.

While there is no consensus as to the classification of such products one can categorise them into two main groups:

- Principal protected products.
- Single-stock hedges.

4.1.3.1   Principal protected products

Capital protected products are instruments that offer the safety features of bond investments but offer the opportunity for investors to make gains based on market movements. They protect an investor's principal at maturity and returns are linked to the performance of such market variables as equity indices, baskets of stocks, commodities and even property prices. While the structures vary the main principle is that investors subscribe to effectively what is a zero coupon bond (thus purchased by the bank at a discount to face value), and the discount element is invested in a call option (if the expectation is based on rising market prices) based on some index. The investor receives the principal on maturity (so capital is protected) and returns are related to the performance of the call option. If the market increases and the call option is

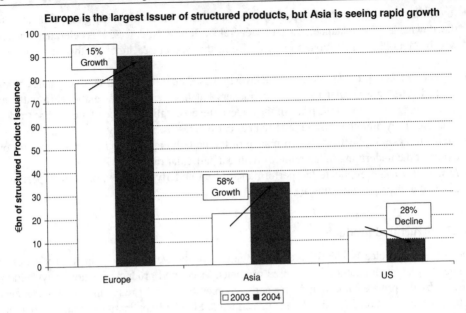

Figure 4.7   Structured product issuance by region
Source: BNP Paribas (2004); Morgan Stanley. Reproduced by permission.

in-the-money at the expiration date, then the investor obtains capital protection and a positive return linked to the performance of the index. Note that capital protection does not necessarily mean 100% protection – in reality capital protection can be higher or lower – although the range 80%–110% is common for most structured products.

While capital has been preserved, the potential risks associated with this type of product relates to the opportunity cost associated with income foregone compared with a standard bond investment (e.g. there is no annual or semi-annual coupon). Inflation will also erode the value of the principal amount collected at maturity.

The various structures and names of such capital protection products vary enormously, which can lead to confusion for clients. Structures vary according to:

- *Time horizons.* They typically vary from one year to seven or eight years but can have any time horizon depending on investor appetite.
- *Product vehicle.* Products can be structured as deposits, notes, certificates, funds, bonds and have names such as: principal protected notes, guaranteed equity bonds, etc.
- *Structuring techniques.* There are an extensive array of derivatives, asset allocation and leveraging techniques that are used to create the desired return structure that meets client requirements. Products are structured to appeal to investors who have a view to future market movements. The structures can include a wide range of underlying indices (equities, commodities, property, precious metals, etc.), those based on market rises or falls (in the case of expectations of falling markets the discount is used to purchase a put option to generate returns), protection involving caps (limit to returns based on positive market movements), collars (limits on downward movements), structures for individual client portfolios, etc.

Participants in the wealth management industry are increasingly looking to new structures to promote their product offerings. Such developments include:

- *Foreign exchange linked notes.* This type of instrument pays a return linked to a global foreign exchange (FX) market. It is usually a short-term note that pays out a fixed minimum rate of interest determined by the movement in foreign exchange rates over the life of the note. On the maturity date, the note pays the initial principal amount plus a return.
- *Hedge fund linked notes.* Investors are paid a return linked to the performance of a portfolio of hedge funds. On the maturity date, the note pays the initial principal amount plus a return, if any, based on the percentage change in the underlying hedge fund.
- *Sharia linked notes.* These pay a return linked to the performance of Islamic law compliant investments. Such a product is available in the US via a basket of equities drawn from the Dow Jones Islamic Market Index (DJIMI). On the maturity date, the note pays the initial principal amount plus return, if any, based on the percentage change in the DJIMI. (Box 4.1 provides more details on Islamic private banking.)
- *Commodity linked notes.* These pay a return linked to the performance of a commodity or basket of commodities over a defined period. On the maturity date, the note pays the initial principal amount plus return, if any, based on the percentage change in the underlying commodity (or basket). Commodities include: WTI crude oil, heating oil, gasoline, NYMEX natural gas, lead, copper, nickel and aluminium.
- *Precious metal linked notes.* Investors receive a return linked to the performance of a precious metal (e.g. the price of gold or silver) over a defined period. On the maturity date, the note pays the initial principal amount plus a return, if any, based on the percentage change in the price (for example) in the underlying precious metal at maturity or an average over time. Goldman Sachs, for example, has launched a variety of call-and-put warrants linked to gold and oil prices, and various Swiss banks and the Dutch ABN AMRO have launched gold-linked guaranteed funds. The latter, known as the ABN AMRO Gold 110% Guaranteed Fund, launched in Hong Kong, offers full capital protection plus a guaranteed return of at least 10%.
- *Structured deposit accounts.* These are similar to standard bank deposit accounts but provide depositors/investors with the opportunity to earn a higher return as compared to conventional fixed deposits. Structured deposits pay a return linked to the performance of an underlying benchmark such as interest rates, equity markets or foreign exchange markets. Typically these deposits are relatively short term (under a year) but can be longer, require the deposit to be held for the full term and have different participation rates depending on what proportion of the (usually) upside risk is to be taken. Rothschild, for instance, offered a structured deposit account linked to the FTSE 100 with only an eighth month term up to April 2003.
- *Property linked products.* These products have essentially the same sort of structures as other capital guaranteed products but use a property or house price index on which to generate potential returns for investors.
- *Actively managed structured products.* One noticeable development in the structured product arena has been the increasing use of linking returns to the performance of actively managed funds. Products are typically linked to high-performing funds and offer the usual capital guarantee with different participation rates. All the main banks involved in wealth management products are currently in the process of offering such services. Some commentators believe that this market will constitute the bulk of structured products over the coming years, given the plethora of actively managed funds on which to base structured product performance.

One can see that there is an extensive array of capital protected products available and the market is changing rapidly. While some commentators view the mass affluent market as the main target segment for these products, there seems to be a consensus that structured products now form an integral element in wealth management provision, across a wide spectrum of clients. However, it should be stressed that there are various limitations associated with the attractiveness of structured products. Fees are typically high; private banks pick up margins of about 1.5% and for independent advisers these can be higher. In addition, many pay no dividends and do not protect investors against inflation. Various commentators have noted their reservations about selling such products. For example, Helen Avery notes (*Euromoney*, January 2005, page 123):

> Private bankers don't seem particularly happy with the new found interest in structured products. Although high net worth individuals seem to be convinced that they should be investing in them, most private bankers and advisers claim to be of the opinion that structured products are of no great value, and should be avoided if possible.

The market for structured products is large and growing rapidly (estimates from Morgan Stanley and Boston Consulting Group as to the size of just the retail European market stood at around $400 billion in 2002, with a forecast annual growth of 8%) and private banks are offering an increasing array of structured instruments to meet buoyant client demand. However, the reservation about offering such products relates to private bankers' perceptions that these products probably do not always best match the risk-return needs of HNW clients. The fact that HNWIs are demanding such services also reflects a general lack of client confidence in a private bank's ability to generate decent investment returns. While some argue that structured products may be a useful tool for tactical asset allocation for new clients (e.g. those that have sold companies and are taking a first major investment step into equities, etc.) or as part of a diversified investment portfolio, there remain concerns that the focus on such products may not be good for the industry in the longer term.

4.1.3.2   Single-stock hedges

Many clients, particularly those that own businesses, have wealth that is insufficiently diversified. There are entrepreneurs who were worth $500 million at the height of the dot-com bubble, but were bankrupt a year later because they did not diversify.

Clients may receive large blocks of stock as part of their compensation or in payment for businesses they may have sold, and they may have restrictions on what they can sell after an IPO. Various structures, using a combination of derivatives and leverage, can help insulate clients from the risks associated with holding large amounts of a single stock.

In the case of single-stock hedges, banks typically recommend a zero-premium collar, which secures protection against adverse price moves while enabling the client to hold on to their stock. In this case, the hedge involves the purchase of a put option (ensuring a price floor for the stock), which is financed by selling a call option (price cap) on the same stock. The client locks-in a range of stock prices based on the floor and cap price levels, which reduces downside risk but limits upside gains (those that would have been received if the stock price exceeded the cap).

Once the range of the stock price is locked-in the concentrated stock position becomes more attractive as collateral on which credit can be extended. The aforementioned structure therefore converts the relatively illiquid concentrated stock position into a more liquid asset. Cash can be extracted and reinvested elsewhere, voting rights are preserved and the client can also gain a degree of tax protection.

Single-stock hedges, as in the case of similar hedges for individual client portfolios, are really only available (and commercially worth pursuing) for relatively large transactions.

4.1.3.3 Recent and expected trends

Between 2001 and 2004, innovation in the payout structures were key, as clients sought both capital guarantees and upside participation. BNP Paribas, for example, has over 46 different capital protected products, including the Cliquet Call, Napoleon and Twister, most of which can be used with a large array of underlying assets and funds.[4] This level and frequency of innovation has helped prevent downward margin pressure.

However, current trends suggest that many clients are seeking simpler structures, with the 'exotic' feature coming from the underlying asset. Many clients are also willing to take more risk of capital loss. Examples of non-capital protected structured products include Airbag, Athena and Kilimanjaro. In these structures, the client participates in the upside, but is at risk if a certain number of assets in the basket fall below a given reference value. In some countries, such as the UK and Germany, clients have also been demanding greater transparency in payoffs and more control over their investments (e.g. secondary liquidity, structures wrapped in certificates, active management, etc.). Many distributors are now sourcing structured products on a global basis, and then adapting them to meet local client needs.

Looking ahead, BNP Paribas anticipates four key developments, driven from both the demand and supply sides:

1. *Increased product segmentation.* For example, simple products with full principal protection, minimum guaranteed returns and longer maturities for less experienced clients; more flexible products, with partial principal protection (typically 70%–90%), a higher risk/return profile often with shorter maturities, for more experienced clients.
2. *Dynamic product management.* Offering clients more possibilities for product repurchase and early exit. If well executed, this can increase client satisfaction by providing comfort that the product exit was well timed given prevailing market trends. It is therefore an opportunity for the wealth manager both to demonstrate proactivity and to increase revenue.
3. *Increasing popularity of mutual funds as underlyings.* Mutual funds offer clients and product providers a number of advantages, including (a) diversification and the ability to access a much broader range of underlying assets, especially those of emerging markets; (b) greater flexibility and the capacity to manufacture in greater size than conventional equity structures; and (c) opportunities for distributors to generate profits by retroceding additional management fees.
4. *Further product extension to new asset classes.* Fluctuating equity market volatility and greater correlation between different equity markets is prompting product providers to use other asset classes such as alternative investments, real estate and inflation as underlyings for their structures. There will also be an increase in the use of combinations ('hybrids')

---

[4] See BNP Paribas (2004) for more details on these and other fantastically named products and associated innovation across the key markets.

of different asset classes as underlyings. That will enable clients to benefit from the return on the best-performing asset class from a basket of, for example, equities, interest rates, exchange rates, commodities and inflation.

Box 4.1   Islamic private banking[5]

The accumulation of wealth by Muslims around the world, and the trend for Muslims to shift assets away from the United States, is driving increased demand for Islamic private banking. Globally, there are now some 270 Islamic banks (including pure-play Islamic banks and the Islamic subsidiaries of – and the Islamic windows within – conventional banks). Together, they hold assets estimated at more than $265 billion. The International Islamic Finance Forum estimates that Islamic banking assets are growing on average by 15% a year, driven primarily by oil wealth. In the UAE, McKinsey estimates that Islamic banking assets grew by 29% a year between 2000 and 2003, around 4.5 times faster than the country's total banking market. Within 8–10 years, as much as half the savings of the world's 1.3 billion Muslims could be held in Islamic banks.

Islamic banking differs from conventional banking in three main ways (see Figure 4.8). The key relevant Sharia (Islamic law) principles include the shunning of interest, or 'riba', and the equitable distribution of income and wealth.

Islamic private banks have created a range of products to meet surging client demand. Islamic investment products span relatively low-risk, low-return murabaha and sukuks to higher risk/return, but less liquid, real estate and private equity. Innovative new product structures include RaMIs (range murabaha investments), a short-term product, with returns linked to gold and a selection of currencies, and offering 100% capital appreciation. Several Islamic hedge funds and funds-of-funds have recently been launched, with more in the pipeline. Other products include actively managed Islamic portfolios, Ijarah investment structures, Sharia trust services and optimised equity-index trackers. To help serve this market, Dow Jones is expanding the number of its Islamic indices around the world from the current 44. Indeed, tracking Shariah-compliant investments is interesting not only for Islamic investors, since many of these investments have outperformed in recent years.

One issue is that the different Sharia schools of thought make it hard to develop a single product type that can be rolled out globally. Malaysia, for instance, which is a thriving market for Islamic finance, is generally thought to adopt a more lenient interpretation of Sharia law. The use of derivatives in Islamic transactions and products is therefore more acceptable, and more common, in Malaysia than in the Middle East. Key product-related challenges included product standardisation, streamlining the product development process and reducing time-to-market.

Islamic banking clearly plays into the hands of local players, such as the Dubai Islamic Bank. The challenge there is for such institutions to increase their skills and product ranges to meet the needs of HNWIs. Foreign banks are also entering the market. Some have done so by joining forces with local players; Pictet, for example, entered an Islamic private banking JV with a Kuwait-based finance house, The International Investor. Other banks

---

[5] See Sawyer (2005) for a more detailed overview of most of the products mentioned here.

Islamic Shariah principles prohibit...	... and allow/encourage	Implication
• **Riba**: An increase; any return of money on money	• Risk-sharing/ co-investments	• Interest is not allowed
• **Gharar**: Uncertainty; any speculative investments	• Profit margin on transactions	• There must be an underlying transaction and exchange of commodity
• **Maysir**: Gambling, investment in forbidden areas (e.g., alcohol, weapons, pork, etc.)	• Transparent transactions	• Many derivatives and speculative instruments can not be used

Other relevant terms

- *Sukuk* – Participation securities; Islamic banking alternative to conventional syndicated finance.
- *Murabaha* – Mark-up financing, similar in structure to a conventional repo. Contract of sale in which payment is made at some point after the delivery of goods transacted; amount charged for deferred payment is in excess of current market price (usually by amount approximately equal to prevailing rate of interest).
- *Tawarruq* – Literally, 'monetisation'. The most popular Islamic alternative to the cash loan. A bank sells its customer a commodity at a marked-up price to be paid over a predetermined time period. The customer then resells it for cash at the market's current spot price.
- *Salam* – A contract for deferred delivery; enables, for example, an Islamic hedge fund to short a stock.
- *Takaful* – Meaning 'mutual support', a product (similar to life insurance) that works on a strict shared-risk system across policyholders.
- *Ijara* – Islamic lease agreement. Allows the bank to earn profits by charging rentals on the leased asset.

Figure 4.8 Islamic Sharia principles
Source: McKinsey & Company (2005); author's analysis. Reproduced by permission.

have developed their own Islamic banking windows and some have developed their own separately branded subsidiaries, which operate on a global scale. Examples include:

- UBS, with its Noriba (literally, 'no-interest bank') global Islamic banking platform, established in Bahrain in 2002. UBS plans to integrate Noriba with the rest of the group by the end of 2006. The aim is to provide Noriba clients with more effective access to the full range of UBS products. The group's investment bank will take over responsibility for Sharia-compliant investment products.
- HSBC, with its Amanah subsidiary, established in 1998, operates private client services in many countries, including Saudi Arabia, Singapore, Malaysia, Indonesia, the United Kingdom and the United States.
- Citigroup, whose Islamic private banking origins go back to the 1980s.
- Deutsche Bank, which has an Islamic banking window.

Though Islamic orientation is an important requirement for some HNWIs, it is, however, important to bear in mind that the primary requirement for most clients continues to be superior service and product performance. After all, Muslim investors, have long used conventional banks. McKinsey research shows that many of the wealthiest clients are, in fact, not willing to compromise returns (Figure 4.9). This, plus rising competition, suggests that Islamic banks should focus on boosting service quality and product innovation to capture a greater share of the private banking market.

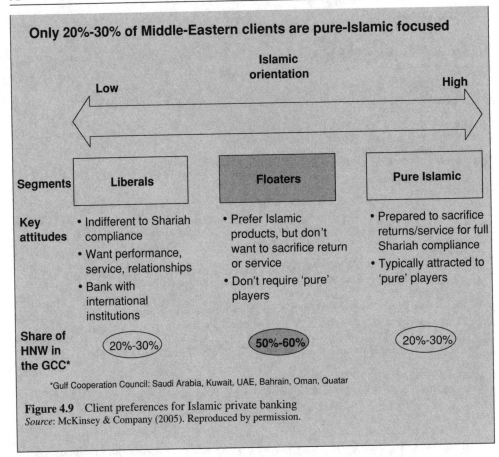

Figure 4.9   Client preferences for Islamic private banking
Source: McKinsey & Company (2005). Reproduced by permission.

4.1.4 Alternative Investments

Alternative investments are typically less individually tailored than structured products and comprise a broad range of investment opportunities in non-traditional areas. The main products that tend to be discussed when talking about alternative investments include hedge funds, private equity and managed futures funds, although the spectrum of such products can also be broadened to include various credit structures (investing in high yield debt or investment grade arbitrage vehicles) and other specialist investments, as shown in Figure 4.10.

4.1.4.1   Hedge funds

Hedge funds have been one of the 'boom' investment products in recent years and all banks are seeking to develop such services to offer to private clients. HNWIs are also increasingly demanding such products, especially given that many clients had their fingers burned on equities between 2000 and 2002 while returns on hedge funds surged. Nowadays, hedge funds are viewed as virtually a standard private client offering along with the more usual equities, bond and fund products.

Credit Structures	Hedge Funds	Real Estate	Private Equity/ Exchange Funds	Managed Futures	Special Investments
Investment Grade Debt	Single-Manager	Fund Offerings	Single-Manager Funds	Multi-Advisor	Municipal Arbitage Funds
Investment Grade Arbitrage Vehicles	Multi-Manager	Direct Equity	Concentrated and Fully Diversified Funds	Single-Advisor	Credit Enhancement Products/
Market Value Leveraged Loan Fund	Multi-Strategy	Co-Investment Opportunities with	of Funds	Separately Managed Accounts	Repackaging Vehicle
High Yield Debt	Style-Specific	Citigroup	Principal Protected Investments		Synthetic CDOs
High Yield and Emerging Market Cash Flow	Sectar-Specific		Direct Co-Investment Opportunities with Citigroup		
	Strategic Investment Portfolios				
Hybrid Products	Principal Protected Notes		Exchange Funds		

Figure 4.10   Alternative investments
Source: Citigroup Alternative Investments (2003), Reproduced by permission.

HNWIs were the first and the traditional investors in hedge funds. It is only over the last three years that institutional investors have really started allocating to the asset class. (Institutional investors held around one-quarter of assets invested in hedge funds in 2005.) This has raised concerns for HNWIs as many hedge funds consider institutional money to be 'stickier' and have lowered their capacity to HNWIs and upped it to institutions. With capacity constraints and only a few consistently superb hedge fund managers, the competition that HNWIs face in getting into these funds has steepened. This has played into the hands of private banks, which pool their clients' money and invest in funds acting like institutional investors and enabling HNWIs access to quality hedge fund managers.

Hedge funds have various features that distinguish them from other investment products such as mutual funds. They are generally unregulated investment vehicles that allow the managers of such funds significantly more freedom than regulated alternatives. This is because hedge funds are typically structured as partnerships for wealthy investors, the view being that sophisticated investors do not need the same level of regulatory protection as firms that detail with mass-market retail investments. (Note that new Securities and Exchange Commission, SEC, rules that come into force in February 2006 require managers of both onshore and offshore hedge funds who have more than 14 US investors, over $30 million in assets and lock-ups of less than two years to register with the SEC. By mid-2005 it was believed that around 50% of US hedge funds had registered. The new registration process will provide greater regulatory oversight to the industry but is not expected to constrain the current activities of the industry.)

While the new SEC rules present an increase in regulatory oversight to the US hedge fund industry the business is still viewed as effectively unregulated compared with other investment firms. This means that hedge funds are less restricted in their use of leverage and derivatives and may hold less liquid assets than would be the case if subject to more formal regulation. In the US, hedge funds are not subject to traditional investment regulation if the number of investors does not exceed 100 and typically the minimum entry level investor is at least $1 million.[6]

The hedge fund industry has grown dramatically in recent years and by the start of 2005 the industry had attracted around $970 billion of assets. The major market is the US onshore business, accounting for around 50% of the total, with 20% accounted for by offshore funds focusing on US clients. The bulk of the remainder is made up of mainly European funds (the

---

[6] The first hedge fund was established in New York in 1949.

Table 4.1 Largest global hedge funds

Rank firm/fund name	Firm/fund capital end-2004 ($ million)
1 Farallon Capital Management	12 500
2 Bridgewater Associates	11 500
3 Goldman Sachs Asset Management	11 242
4 GLG Partners	11 200
5 Man Investments	11 081
6 Citadel Investment Group	11 000
7 Caxton Associates	10 800
7 D.E. Shaw Group	10 800
9 Och-Ziff Capital Management Group	10 700
19 Vega Asset Management	10 700
11 Tudor Investment Corp.	10 400
12 Perry Capital	10 217
13 Moore Capital Management	9 635
14 Maverick Capital	9 600
15 Barclays Global Investors	9 545
16 Cerberus Capital Management	9 500
16 ESL Investments	9 500
18 Wellington Management Company	9 000
19 Campbell & Company	8 764
20 Angelo Gordon & Company	8 500
21 Soros Fund Management	8 300
22 Highbridge Capital Management	8 000
23 Brevan Howard Asset Management	7 700
24 UBS	7 432
25 BlueCrest Capital Management	7 207

Source: Institutional Investor (2005a). Reproduced by permission.

UK-based Man Group being the largest operator in Europe with total AuM of c.$48 billion[7]).
The largest 100 hedge funds account for 58% ($568 billion) of the total estimated hedge fund
AuM (Table 4.1 lists the top 25).

The growing interest in the hedge fund industry by both institutional and retail clients has
resulted mainly from their strong absolute and relative performance compared with traditional
markets in recent years. For example, in the market downturn in the US between April 2000 and
September 2002, hedge funds generated positive returns of around 2.1% while the S&P 500 lost
43.8%.[8] This emphasised the potential capital-protection features of hedge fund investments
and although in certain years, 1998 and 2004, hedge funds performed less well than various
market indices, over time there is evidence that such investment vehicles tend to outperform the
market and (depending on the strategy of the type of hedge fund in question) can have returns
with low correlation to overall market movements, thus providing potential diversification
benefits. An indication of the returns generated by hedge funds compared with other market
indices is shown in Figure 4.11.

Hedge funds use many different investment styles to (typically) generate absolute returns
for investors. Figure 4.12 summarises the main features of the different types of hedge fund

---

[7] As at 31 March 2006; this includes single-hedge-fund and multi-manager assets (multi-manager fund structures are covered later
in the chapter – see Box 4.5).
[8] See George P. Van (2005).

Return, %

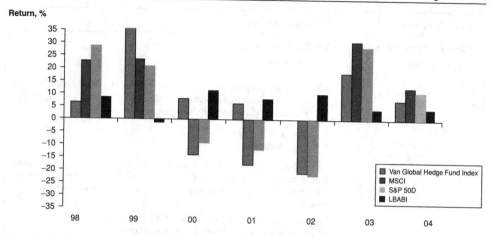

Figure 4.11   Performance of hedge funds and market indices, 1998–2004
Source: George P. Van (2005), see www.vanhedge.com. Reproduced by permission.

investment approaches. It can be seen that they are extremely wide and varied. Market Neutral Arbitrage and Value Funds are the largest segment of the market and in 2004 the best performing types of fund were those focusing on distressed securities (Figure 4.13).

Another product closely related to hedge funds are known as managed futures funds, which invest in a broad range of global markets but solely through futures, options and currencies. They invest in a wide range of derivative products that cover both financial futures (fixed income, equity, foreign exchange, etc.) as well as a growing number of commodity-related instruments (oil, gold, silver and other commodities). The number and variety of markets traded in managed futures investments may add substantial diversification to an investment portfolio and can enhance risk-adjusted rates of return. Historically, managed futures returns have been non-correlated to those achieved by stock and bond investments. Typically, managed futures investments are speculative and involve a high degree of risk and can have substantial charges. These funds are tailored to both retail investors (known as private offerings) with relatively low entry levels (minimum investments around $5 000) and those tailored to private clients (entry levels of $250 000 are not uncommon).

The universe of hedge funds provides substantial investment opportunities for private clients and the relatively recent development of funds-of-hedge funds also allows for investors to benefit from diversification as well as the lower costs associated with entry into this segment. The fund-of-hedge fund product is viewed as the best entry point for private clients wishing to access this market. Recent developments in the hedge fund industry have seen managers focusing on 'new' investment segments including: energy, real estate, private equity, corporate lending to mid-market firms (under $500 million in assets), exchange traded funds and other areas. As the range of fund strategies continues to grow, and performance and protection attributes look attractive, it is likely that private clients will increasingly use types of hedge fund investments as parts of their overall portfolios.

Over the last few years the increased focus of private clients (and institutional investors) means that demand continues to outstrip supply for high-quality hedge fund products, and this is putting an upward pressure on charges: 'We're seeing a tendency towards increasing costs and regard it as a sign of danger,' says Markus Gonseth, Julius Baer's head of investment

Hedge Fund Type	Investment Approach
Market Neutral Group **1. Event-Driven** • Distressed Securities • Special Situations	**Market Neutral Group** **1. Event-Driven** Managers seek to profit from 'extraordinary' events in a firm's life (such as takeovers, mergers, liquidations). Managers focus on profiting from the event itself while normally hedging out market risk. • Distressed Securities • Special Situations Funds that focus on *distressed securities* invest long or short in the debt and/or equity of companies likely to declare bankruptcy in the near future, currently in the bankruptcy reorganization process or emerging from bankruptcy. *Special situations* managers invest in the following areas, among others: a broad range of merger arbitrage transactions (as described elsewhere); convertible debt; company spin-offs; distressed securities (debt); company liquidations; capital structure arbitrage; companies in restructurings; companies with out-of-favour equities.
2. Market Neutral Arbitrage • Convertible Arbitrage • Fixed Income Arbitrage • Merger/Risk Arbitrage • Statistical Arbitrage	**2. Market Neutral Arbitrage** The manager seeks to exploit specific inefficiencies in the market by trading a carefully hedged portfolio of offsetting long and short positions. By pairing long positions with related short positions, market risk is greatly reduced, resulting in a portfolio that bears a low correlation and beta to the market. The four main types of strategy include: • Convertible Arbitrage • Fixed Income Arbitrage • Merger/Risk Arbitrage • Statistical Arbitrage *Convertible Arbitrage* is when the manager buys a convertible security and shorts the common stock of the company in similar proportion and attempts to profit from a perceived mis-pricing of the conversion option in the convertible security. *Fixed Income Arbitrage* is when the manager takes offsetting positions in fixed income securities and their derivatives in order to exploit mis-pricings between interest rate securities; these include, for example, interest rate swaps, government and corporate debt, mortgage-backed and asset-backed securities, etc. *Merger/Risk Arbitrage* is when the manager takes positions in companies expected to be involved in a merger or acquisition. A frequent trade is 'long the acquiree, short the acquirer'. *Statistical Arbitrage* is when managers use mathematical methods to examine the current value of a security relative to its historical mean. If the difference is determined to be statistically significant (generally measured by the number of standard deviations from the mean) an 'arbitrage' opportunity exists.

Figure 4.12 Types of hedge fund
Source: Adapted from George P. Van (2005). Reproduced by permission.

Long/Short Equity

- Aggressive Growth
- Market Neutral Securities Hedging
- Opportunistic Value

Long/Short Equity Group

Long/short equity managers buy stocks they expect to outperform the market and go short on stocks they expect to underperform in the same portfolio. The aim is to decrease market sensitivity (Beta) by being less than 100% exposed to the market and generating returns from out-performance in both directions.

- Aggressive Growth
- Market Neutral Securities Hedging
- Opportunistic
- Value

Aggressive Growth strategies involve investing in companies experiencing or expected to experience strong growth in earnings per share. The manager may consider a company's business fundamentals when investing and/or may invest in stocks on the basis of technical factors, such as stock price momentum.

Market Neutral Securities Hedging is when managers invest similar amounts of capital in securities both long and short, maintaining a portfolio with low net market exposure (+20%). Long positions are taken in securities expected to rise in value while short positions are taken in securities expected to fall in value. Often, quantitative multifactor models are used to identify investment opportunities based on factors such as the underlying company's fundamental value, its projected rate of growth, or the security's pattern of price movement (e.g. momentum). Due to the portfolio's low net market exposure, performance is generally insulated from equity market volatility.

Opportunistic strategies refer to when a manager's investment approach changes over time to take better advantage of current market conditions and investment opportunities, rather than consistently selecting securities according to one strategy's guidelines. Characteristics of the portfolio, such as asset classes, market capitalization, etc., are likely to vary significantly from time to time. The manager may also employ a combination of different approaches at a given time.

Value strategies refer to when managers focus on the price of a security relative to the intrinsic worth of the underlying business. Managers takes long positions in stocks that they believe are undervalued and short positions in stocks believed to be overvalued. Possible reasons that a stock may sell at a perceived discount could be that the company is out of favour with investors or that its future prospects are not correctly judged by Wall Street analysts. If the manager is correct and the market comes to understand the true value of these companies better, it is expectsed that the prices of undervalued stocks in the portfolio will rise while the prices of overvalued stocks will fall. The manager often selects stocks for which a potential upcoming event can be identified that will result in the stock price changing to reflect more accurately the company's intrinsic worth.

Figure 4.12   (*Continued*)

Directional Trading Group

- Macro/Futures
- Market Timing

Directional Trading Group

- Macro/Futures
- Market Timing

Macro funds relate to when managers construct portfolios based on a top-down view of global economic trends, considering factors such as interest rates, economic policies, inflation, etc. Rather than considering how individual corporate securities may fare, the manager seeks to profit from changes in the value of entire investment sectors. For example, the manager may hold long positions in the US dollar and Japanese equity indices while shorting the euro and US treasury bills. Views are generally implemented using derivatives in equity, interest rate, currency and commodity markets.

Futures strategies involve managers utilising futures contracts to implement directional positions in global equity, interest rate, currency and commodity markets. Managers use either systematic models or their own discretion to identify investment opportunities in various markets. Discretionary strategies utilise futures contracts to implement trades based on the manager's judgement on the direction of futures prices. Systematic strategies employ quantitative models to identify investment opportunities using historical prices of and relationships between futures contracts.

Market timing relates to when managers attempt to predict the short-term movements of various markets (or market segments) and, based on those predictions, move capital from one asset class to another in order to capture market gains and avoid market losses. A more recent definition refers to a manager's trend to follow mutual funds that have a favourable price momentum.

Specialty Strategies Group

- Emerging Markets
- Income
- Multistrategy
- Short Selling

Specialty Strategies Group

- *Emerging Markets.* Managers invest in companies and government instruments based in emerging and less-developed countries.
- *Income.* Investment in yield-producing securities (mainly bonds).
- *Multistrategy.* The manager typically utilises two or more specific, predetermined investment strategies, e.g. Value, Aggressive Growth and Special Situations.
- *Short Selling.* The manager maintains a consistent net short exposure in the portfolio, meaning that significantly more capital supports short positions than is invested in long positions (if any is invested in long positions at all). Unlike investing in long positions, which are expected to increase in value, short positions are taken in securities the manager anticipates will decrease in value.
  In order to short sell, the manager borrows securities from a prime broker and immediately sells them on the market. The manager later repurchases these securities and returns them to the broker. If the stock price falls, the manager profits by keeping the difference between the price at which the stock was sold and the price at which it was repurchased. In this way, the manager is able to profit from a fall in a security's value. Conversely, if the stock price rises, the manager is forced to make up the difference between the price at which the stock was sold and the price at which it was repurchased. Short selling managers typically target overvalued stocks; these are characterised by prices the manager believes to be too high, given the fundamentals of the underlying companies.

Figure 4.12   (*Continued*)

	2004		2000-2004			1988-2004		
	Assets (USD) in Strategy	Strategy as % of HF Universe	Return	CARS	Sharpe Ratio	CAR	Sharpe Ratio	Correlation with S&P
Market Neutral Group								
Event Driven								
–Distressed Securities	69 b	7.3%	18.4%	12.7%	1.6	18.8%	1.4	0.3
– Special Situations	90 b	9.5%	10.4%	8.5%	0.9	17.5%	1.7	0.7
Market Neutral Arbitrage	188 b	19.8%	3.6%	8.2%	2	13.0%	2	0.4
Long/Short Equity Group								
Aggressive Growth	49 b	5.2%	6.0%	1.4%	0	17.5%	0.9	0.8
Market Neutral Securities Hedging	18 b	1.8%	6.0%	9.7%	1.7	15.3%	2.5	0.4
Opportunistic	39 b	4.1%	7.7%	9.3%	0.7	19.7%	1.5	0.7
Value	141 b	14.8%	11.5%	10.2%	0.7	16.9%	1.2	0.8
Directional Trading Group								
Macro	99 b	10.4%	2.1%	5.8%	0.5	16.4%	1.2	0.4
Futures	81 b	8.5%	6.9%	11.7%	0.8	17.9%	0.9	-0.2
Market Timing	1 b	0.1%	3.1%	4.8%	0.3	16.2%	1.4	0.7
Specialty Strategies Group								
Emerging Markets	67 b	7.1%	13.6%	10.5%	0.6	16.8%	0.7	0.5
Income	14 b	1.5%	8.8%	9.4%	2.2	10.1%	1.7	0.3
Multi-Strategy	91 b	9.6%	5.9%	5.7%	0.4	14.9%	1.3	0.7
Short Selling	3 b	0.3%	-9.7%	3.2%	0.2	1.3%	0.1	-0.8
Van Global Hedge Fund Index			7.7%	8.0%	0.8	16.0%	1.5	0.7
Comparative Benchmarks								
S&P 500			10.9%	-2.3%	-0.2	12.4%	0.7	1
MSCI			12.8%	-3.8%	-0.2	6.4%	0.3	0.9
LBABI			4.3%	7.7%	1.3	8.1%	1.3	0

Figure 4.13 Hedge funds – assets under management and performance
Source: Adapted from George P. Van (2005). Reproduced by permission

services. 'Whereas you once saw a 1% management fee, and a 10% performance fee, you can now see anything up to 3% and 50%. We're recommending to our clients to keep an eye out' (*Euromoney*, July 2004[9]).

However, there is some recent evidence that the attractiveness of hedge funds to private clients has waned. Morgan Stanley[10] reports that at Man Group, one of the major structurers and distributors of hedge funds, net private client inflows have halved from 35% annualised growth in the six months to March 2004 to around 15% in the same period in 2005, although positive inflows are expected at the industry level at a more 'measured' pace. The main reason for this fall is put down to the general decline in returns – 'aggregate hedge fund' returns have been falling from around +14% in 1995–97 to around 4%–6% over the last couple of years, as shown in Figure 4.14. There is also evidence that HNWIs are moving away from funds-of-hedge funds as they have had enough of the double fee structure and want to go back to investing directly. Swiss HNWIs, for instance, have recently been reported to be redeeming funds-of-hedge funds. To some extent private banks can mimic funds-of-hedge funds as they spread the allocation of money across several managers, but without the double fees in most cases – a big plus for them.

---

[9] Helen Avery (2004), 'Is There Room at the Hedge Fund Table?', *Euromoney*, 1 July 2004.
[10] Morgan Stanley (2005c), Morgan Stanley European Investment Research.

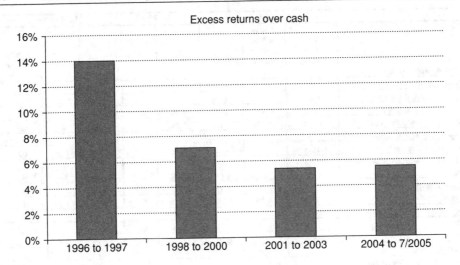

Figure 4.14   Decline in hedge fund performance
Source: Huw van Steenis, Morgan Stanley (2005e), Reproduced by permission.

The key for clients is to use a private bank with very deep relationships with quality hedge fund managers. Just how niche these private banks are in selecting best-practice hedge fund services is also worth considering. Every large private bank has access to the Citadels of this world, but have they got their finger on the pulse of new upcoming hedge funds managers? Are they seeding them? Are they looking out for new hedge fund strategies as traditional ones (such as convertible arbitrage) come off the boil.

Going forward, Morgan Stanley suggests that, in their quest for higher returns, many hedge funds will adopt new strategies. These include (a) *moving down the liquidity spectrum*, by investing in, for example, distressed securities, unrated bank loans, structured credit, small-/mid-cap equities and emerging markets, where the potential for finding mis-priced securities is higher; and/or (b) what it calls '*going freestyle*' with a bias towards long positions, by investing in, for example long-only positions, specific industry sectors, and 'best ideas'.

4.1.4.2   Private equity

Along with hedge funds, private equity investments have become increasingly popular with private clients. Private equity products simply comprise investments in private companies. Investments can be made at any stage of a company's life but are usually divided into two types: venture capital and buy-outs. The venture capital stage covers the early life of a company, from the initial start-up capital to the pre-IPO stage. In general, around 50% of all companies are sold through IPOs while the other half are acquired by established businesses ('trade buyers'). The buy-out stage covers the many types of later-stage financing in a firm's life, such as leveraged buy-outs, management buy-outs, recapitalisations, mezzanine finance (investments through debt instruments including some equity participation) and various forms of growth financing. In short, private equity firms acquire, own and exit private companies. Their basic business model is summarised in Figure 4.15.

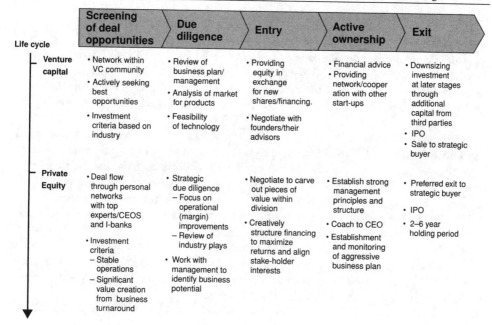

Figure 4.15   Private equity firm business model
Source: McKinsey & Company. Reproduced by permission.

In general, private equity investments are usually made through four main types of investment vehicle:

- *Limited partnerships*, where investors become limited partners in a limited partnership. Capital contributions are invested by an investment manager in a portfolio of private companies in line with agreed investment objectives. The ability of limited partners to transfer their investments in the partnership is limited and subject to the approval of the investment manager (known as the general partner).
- *Funds-of-funds.* These are structured as limited partnerships and the general partner invests capital in one or more other limited partnerships and other poled investment vehicles. The aim is to obtain diversification across a wider range of companies and investment styles. (These private equity funds-of-funds have clear similarity to hedge fund-of-funds products.) For private clients wishing to enter the private equity arena funds-of-funds are generally recommended as a good place to start.
- *Closed-end companies.* These are investment vehicles formed as closed-end limited liability companies. The firm's assets are invested directly in a portfolio of private companies and in limited partnerships. Closed-end companies may be listed or unlisted.
- *Direct investment.* As the name suggests this involves investing directly into a company (not indirectly through limited partnerships or via closed-end companies). In general, direct investment has traditionally been the preserve of institutional investors or private clients who are in some way connected through the firms concerned (e.g. relationships with managers or other shareholders, etc.).

Box 4.2   Co-investment

We noted above the broadening of access to alternative investments and other products to a wider range of client wealth bands. One area that largely remains exclusive to the very wealthiest clients only is co-investment. This is where the private bank (or its parent) invests its own capital alongside that of one or more if its clients. Indeed, co-investment, either with the wealth manager itself or with other HNWIs, has become a growing trend within the industry.

Citigroup is said to be particularly active in the co-investment area. The former chief executive officer (CEO) of Citigroup's private bank used to call this 'investing alongside Sandy [Weill, chairman emeritus of Citigroup] and Bob [Robert Rubin, the chairman of its executive committee]'. Clients with $100 million or more get access to Citigroup Private Capital Partners, which provides an exclusive range of investment opportunities. Examples of the types of co-investment opportunities include private equity deals, hedge funds, corporate investments and single real estate transactions.

Co-investment is particularly relevant in the current mistrustful environment. Clients want to know that those advising them to invest in certain areas are themselves invested in them. The private bank's own financial commitment aligns incentives, gives the clients added comfort and ensures a closer working relationship.

The private equity industry has grown substantially since the late 1990s. The US venture capital market at the start of 2004 constituted over 1 000 firms and nearly 2 000 funds managing somewhere in the region of $260 billion in assets. Buy-out firms and funds were smaller in number (around 560 and 1 000 respectively) but they managed a larger amount of assets (just under $450 billion). Recent evidence suggests that since the peak of the high-tech boom in 2001 both venture capital and buy-out funds (on average) have yielded negative returns, although there is evidence that buy-out funds focusing on small- to medium-sized companies have produced strong returns over the last couple of years.[11] For example, the US Private Equity index outperformed other broad market indexes in 2004, as shown in Figure 4.16.

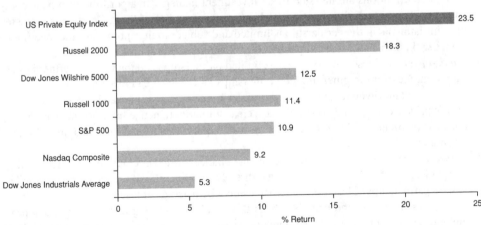

Figure 4.16   US private equity outperformed other market indices in 2004
Source: Capgemini/Merrill Lynch, World Wealth Report 2005. Reproduced by permission.

---

[11] See Thomson Venture Economics (2004).

Box 4.3 Structured products and alternative investments – success in advice-led selling

So far we have discussed the main features of structured and alternative investment products. A key feature of many alternative investment vehicles is that their evolution is typically characterised by starting as being relatively illiquid vehicles and then, as the respective market expands, various derivations of the original concepts emerge to provide greater liquidity and investor access over time. This is highlighted by the growing appearance of fund-of-fund and publicly traded vehicles, which at one time were anathema to these industries. Again we witness the 'product spiral', whereby products that were originally developed to meet the investment needs of institutional and UHNWIs are gradually being developed to access a wider client base. Given this general trend, it is inevitable that a wider range of alternative investments will become a more important element in the private client product offerings in the future.

Both structured and alternative investments enable clients to access specialist products that can have strong diversification and returns potential. The major challenge to the industry relates primarily to educating clients about the benefits of such products and overcoming the perception that they are too risky. Recent high-profile crises and failures of firms engaged substantially in derivatives (e.g. Refco) or hedge funds (Long-Term Capital Management) do little to assuage investors' concerns.

For success in delivering structured products private banks need to:

• Ensure good communication between client relationship managers and the investment bank (or alternative investment provider) so as to make sure that clients needs are met and that they are fully informed on all the terms and conditions (illiquidity, early redemption penalties, etc.) of their investments. Such a process requires flexible and responsive credit policies (e.g. meeting margin calls) and policies to evaluate illiquid position and collateral.
• Have state-of-the-art management information systems to be able to present real-time information to clients so as to calculate security values, positions, collateral and credit limits to manage risk.
• Develop appropriate incentive structures for both the investment banker and client relationship manager so as to encourage a flow of structured product business. In addition, clients interested in these sorts of products will expect expert advice from experienced private bankers.

For success in delivering alternative investment products private banks need to:

• Educate clients as to the features of such investments, explaining clearly the benefits and costs of such investments.
• Offer 'best-practice' solutions combining both in-house and third-party products and services.
• Develop improved ways to prepare information on alternative investments and communicate these to clients more effectively. Consolidated reporting features on such instruments will need to be incorporated into standard reporting lines.

For both types of products, the main challenge to the private bank is to educate their clients and to respond, communicate and coordinate their selling/distribution activities with top-rate support systems. Anecdotal evidence suggests that many relationship managers cannot explain clearly structured products or hedge funds and some banks are trying desperately to educate their client-facing staff. This is a difficult task given that the individuals who typically design these products are maths geniuses but do not have the skills to explain the underlying investments to the relationship managers. SG Private Bank, for instance, runs an education programme for its relationship managers. Most wealth managers should. An expert client relationship manager who understands these types of products and can communicate their features to potentially interested clients is a key success ingredient.

As with hedge funds, returns generated by different companies, funds and partnerships can vary dramatically. While clients may be familiar with the broad investment strategies of various companies, it is difficult to find out the precise details of their activity and this lack of transparency (particularly for unquoted fund providers) increases the risk for investors.

For wealth managers, there are a number of ways of participating in private equity. Each role has different economics, with the highest rewards by far going to direct fund managers (Figure 4.17).

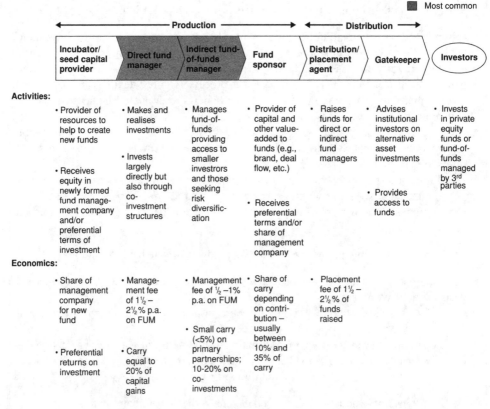

Figure 4.17   Participation options in private equity
Source: McKinsey & Company.

4.1.5   Property and real estate

As we have seem, there is growing interest among clients in real estate investments, which is becoming a very broad area. The following focuses on two areas: real estate advisory services, and real estate investment trusts.

4.1.5.1   Real estate advisory

Property management advisory services is an area that is rapidly developing. Many private banks now provide real estate advisory services that offer their clients the range of services needed to acquire and sell property (both residential and commercial), ranging from management, renovation, valuation, surveys and facility management to financing (through up-market mortgage services) and real estate investment opportunities.

4.1.5.2   REITs and real estate investment

In addition to these advisory services real estate is widely being touted as an important investment class given surging property prices in recent years and the rapid growth of property-related investment vehicles, particularly in the US. One major success story has been the development of the real estate investment trusts (REITs) business, which now amounts to an industry managing around $550 billion in assets. This market is underdeveloped in Europe although the UK authorities are currently (September 2005) considering proposals for the introduction of REIT products and various commentators believe it will be a trend emulated elsewhere.

According to the US National Association of Real Estate Investment Trusts:

> A REIT is a company that owns, and in most cases, operates income-producing real estate such as apartments, shopping centers, offices, hotels and warehouses. Some REITs also engage in financing real estate. The shares of many REITs are freely traded, usually on a major stock exchange. To qualify as a REIT, a company must distribute at least 90 percent of its taxable income to its shareholders annually. A company that qualifies as a REIT is permitted to deduct dividends paid to its shareholders from its corporate taxable income. As a result, most REITs remit at least 100 percent of their taxable income to their shareholders and therefore owe no corporate tax. Taxes are paid by shareholders on the dividends received and any capital gains. Most states honor this federal treatment and also do not require REITs to pay state income tax. Like other businesses, but unlike partnerships, a REIT cannot pass any tax losses through to its investors.

The industry has a diverse profile, which offers various alternative investment opportunities to investors. REITs are often grouped into one of three categories, equity, mortgage or hybrid:

- Equity REITs own and operate income-producing real estate. Equity REITs increasingly have become primarily real estate operating companies that engage in a wide range of real estate activities, including leasing, development of real property and tenant services. One major distinction between REITs and other real estate companies is that a REIT must acquire and develop its properties primarily to operate them as part of its own portfolio rather than to resell them once they are developed.

	PUBLICLY TRADED REITs	NON-EXCHANGE TRADED REITs	PRIVATE REITs
Overview	REITs that file with the SEC and whose shares trade on national stock exchanges.	REITs that file with the SEC but whose shares do not trade on national stock exchanges.	REITs that are not registered with the SEC and whose shares do not trade on national stock exchanges.
Liquidity	Shares are listed and traded daily on stock exchanges with minimum liquidity standards.	Shares are not traded on public stock exchanges. Redemption programs for shares vary by company and are limited. Generally a minimum holding period for investment exists. Investor exit strategy generally linked to a required liquidation after some period of time (often 10 years) or, instead, the listing of the stock on a national stock exchange at such time.	Shares are not traded on public stock exchanges. Existence of, and terms of, any redemption programs varies by company and are generally limited in nature.
Transaction Costs	Broker commissions typically range between $20 and $150 per trade, depending on brokerage service. Investment banks receive a 2–7 percent fee to underwrite initial or follow-on offerings. Offering expenses vary based on deal size.	For each share purchased from the REIT, 10-15 percent of gross offering proceeds typically go to pay broker-dealer commissons, offering expenses and up-front acquisition or advisory fees (fees typically split between a related intermediary and third-party broker-dealer)	Varies by company.
Management	Typically self advised and self managed.	Typically externally advised and manged.	Typically externally advised and managed.
Minimum Investment Amount	One share.	Typically $1,000-$2,500.	Typically $1,000-$25,000 private REITs that are designed for institutional investors requires a much higher minimum.
Independent Directors	New stock exchange rules require a majority of directors to be independent of management. New NYSE and NASDAQ rules call for fully independent audit, nominating and compensation committees.	Subject to North American Securities Administrators Association (NASAA) regulations. NASAA rules require that boards consist of a majority of independent directors. NASAA rules also require that a majority of each board committee consist of independent directors.	Not required.
Investor Control	Investors re-elect direrctors.	Investors re-elect directors.	Investors re-elect directors.
Corporate Govenance	Specific stock exchange rules on corporate governance.	Subject to state and NASAA regulations.	Not required.
Disclosure obligation	Required to make regular financial disclosures to the investment community, including quarterly and yearly audited financial results with accompaying filings to the SEC.	Required to make regular SEC disclosures, including quarterly and yearly financial reports.	Not required.
Perforamance Measurement	Numerous independent performance benchmarks available for tracking public REIT industry. Wide range of analyst reports available to the public.	No independenty source of performance data available.	No public or independent source of performance data available.

Figure 4.18   Features of REITs
Source: National Association of Real Estate Investment Trusts. Reproduced by permission.

- Mortgage REITs lend money directly to real estate owners and operators or extend credit indirectly through the acquisition of loans or mortgage-backed securities. Today's mortgage REITs generally extend mortgage credit only on existing properties. Many modern mortgage REITs also manage their interest rate risk using securitised mortgage investments and dynamic hedging techniques.
- Hybrid REITs both own properties and make loans to real estate owners and operators.

These investment vehicles can be either publicly traded, non-exchange traded or private (see Figure 4.18).

The main attraction of REITs is their focus on yield generation as they must distribute at least 90% of their taxable income to shareholders annually. They are therefore perceived as attractive investments for clients who require relatively stable income as well as exposure to various aspects of the property market. The risk-adjusted returns are also comparable to other broader-based non-property indices (and a number of REITs are actually included in the S&P 500) (see Figure 4.19).

The growing interest in real estate investment vehicles is also highlighted by the creation of a new (February 2005) property index – the FTSE EPRA/NAREIT Global Real Estate Index – which is designed to track the performance of listed real estate companies and REITs worldwide. It is hoped that the creation of this index, which covers 274 stocks across 28

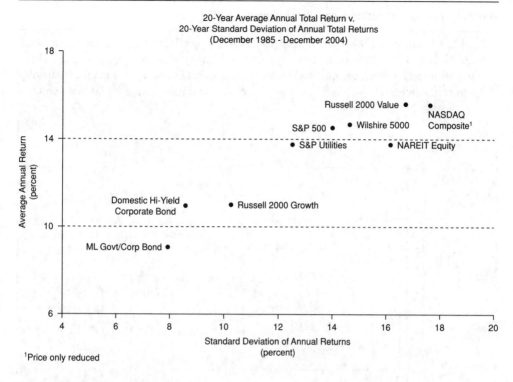

Figure 4.19   REITs risk-adjusted returns versus other industry benchmarks
Source: National Association of Real Estate Investment Trusts®; Ibbotson Associates. Reproduced by permission.

countries, will facilitate trade in structured and other products for clients interested in exposure to global property price movements. The attractions of such an index are illustrated in Figure 4.20, which indicates significant growth since 2003.

PERFORMANCE

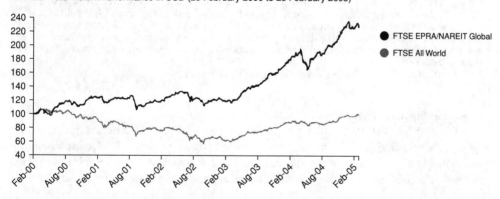

Figure 4.20   Returns on the FTSE EPRA/NAREIT Global Real Estate Index. Reproduced by permission.

Box 4.4   Investment performance measurement

What has my private bank's investment performance been like? Would I have done better going elsewhere? Performance transparency is a major issue for wealth management clients. But this has been complicated by an absence of established performance measures due to confidentiality constraints and the inherent difficulties of using traditional market-capitalisation-based techniques.

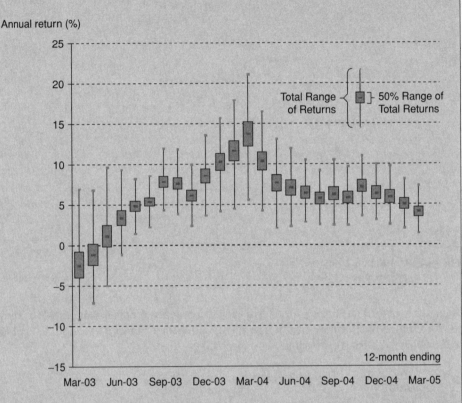

Figure 4.21   ABN AMRO's Private Banking Index – low-risk European private client euro portfolio. The chart shows the distribution of 12-month returns for the low-risk European portfolio held in Euros. The range of returns for each month is determined by the spectrum of possible asset combinations permitted within that portfolio. The flanks represent the highest and lowest achievable return over the period and the box significantly from month to month acccording to performance of asset class over the past 12-month period.
Source: ABN AMRO Private Banking Index. Reproduced by permission.

Various firms are attempting to meet this need. A recent example is the ABN AMRO Private Banking Index (PBI),[12] which provides private bank clients with a transparent multiasset class benchmarking tool to measure the absolute and the relative performance of their investments and, hence, the wealth manager itself. Published monthly and viewable online, the ABN AMRO PBI uses Monte Carlo simulations to provide objective returns measurement

---

[12]See www.wholesale.abnamro.com/abnamropbi.

for typical cross-asset class allocations used by private client investment managers. These are determined semi-annually from a survey of international private banks. The index provides a range of performance levels that reflect both prevailing market conditions across a range of different asset classes and the breadth of investment mandates used in private banking.

The index can be used as a tool to assist with a client's initial profiling and asset allocation. It can also be used as a unique measurement system to compare relative performance across geographies. The total index is broken down into 27 different subindices, based on three base currencies (US dollar, euro and Swiss franc), three risk profiles (high, medium and low) and three regional investment styles (Asia, Europe and the Americas). An example of the ABN AMRO PBI for a low-risk European client euro portfolio is illustrated in Figure 4.21. Figure 4.22 shows an example index for a high-risk Americas client US dollar portfolio.

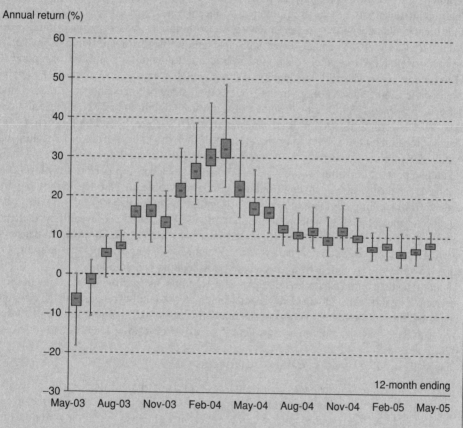

Figure 4.22   ABN AMRO's Private Banking Index – high-risk Americas private client US$ portfolio. The ABN AMRO PBI for 31 May 2005 for an Americas investor holding a high-risk portfolio denominated in USD shows 50% of expected returns over the prior 12 months of between 7.3% and 8.6%. The returns assume that asset allocation parameters remained constant for this period based on current asset allocations received from selected private banks. The range of high-risk portfolio returns for the period was higher due to a significant allocation to more volatile assets such as equities that performed very well over this period. Returns for the period, though benefiting slightly from limited euro currency exposure, were offset by allocation to lower performing US sovereign bonds.
Source: ABN AMRO Private Banking Index. Repreduced by permission.

Separately, a new FTSE Private Banking Index is expected to be launched in 2006 – a combined effort by FTSE Group and Private Banking Index Limited. In addition to performance benchmarking, the index will create opportunities for the development of innovative investment products, such as index-linked funds, ETFs and derivatives. Its constituents and asset allocation will be determined by a dedicated group of private bank index members and will be calculated in a range of currencies to meet investor demand.

Going forward, these two private banking indices are likely to be integrated.

4.1.6 Lending services

Lending services are surprisingly common in the product offering of many private banks. Their significance has grown in importance in recent years, given low interest rates, more sophisticated clients and the greater emphasis on exploiting cross-selling opportunities from within large integrated financial services groups. Credit Suisse Private Banking was among the first private banks to widely push this facility, and it now has a loan book of around $35 billion according to Merrill Lynch equity analysts, which is around 20% of the risk-weighted assets of the Credit Suisse Group. In the US, HNWIs' share of total debt has remained stable at around 5% since 1989. But in absolute terms, it was $346 billion in 2001, up by $50 billion since 1998 according to Federal Reserve estimates. HNWIs are, by definition, rich, but that does not mean they are always very liquid. One of the best-known examples is Elton John, who in 1999 reportedly borrowed $25 million from HSBC Private Bank.

Lending penetration differs significantly among private banks. Top-performing players have managed to make it a significant contributor to profitability, obtaining around 15% of their total revenue from lending, compared to only 3% at bottom-quartile players. This is a direct consequence of much higher product penetration (particularly among lower wealth-band clients). Lending represents a significant growth opportunity particularly for non-universal banks (see Figure 4.23). Julius Baer, under its new management, is a recent example of a non-universal bank that aims to leverage its balance sheet to boost lending penetration.

Lending can also contribute less directly – for example, by improving client retention. As Citigroup's wealth management CEO recently remarked, 'A lending relationship allows you to understand the picture better. It changes the relationship; you become much more of a trusted advisor to the client. We find on average that if we give $1 worth of loan, we get [over time] $4 back in assets.'

Typically, lending services cover two main areas:

1. *Lending to finance lifestyle purchases*, such as second or third vacation homes, private jets, racehorses, art and yachts (see below). Borrowing to buy big-ticket items can free up cash-flow, which can then be used to fund higher-return investments. The lending product offerings are largely conventional, though tweaked to give them an HNW feel. Some clients also demand greater flexibility in repayment terms. A typical product is the 'jumbo' mortgage.
2. In addition, private banks offer *strategic debt*, a range of collateralised loans (to leverage investment and other positions) and other private financing solutions. The most common and widely known collateralised lending facility is the so-called Swiss Lombard or margin loan.[13] This can be used to bridge clients' short-term liquidity requirements and also for

---

[13] In the US, standardised lending against eligible securities is known as Reg-T lending.

Decomposition of revenue margin by business model

Basis points, 2004

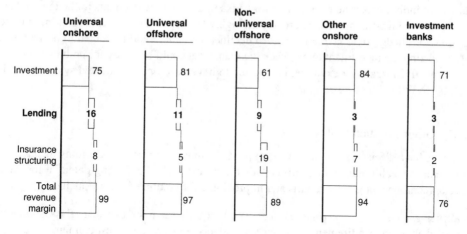

Figure 4.23   Private banks' lending penetration by business model
Source: McKinsey European Private Banking Economics Survey 2005. Reproduced by permission.

leveraging various asset positions. These loans can be backed by pledging securities, bank deposits or other realizable assets. Income and any voting rights from the pledged assets are retained by the pledgor. Pledged assets can be switched at any time subject to the lending limit. The loan can be used as an overdraft facility or in the form of a fixed advance in Swiss francs or in a commonly used foreign currency. In addition, such lending can be used to diversify single-stock exposures.

Other types of lending include loans for lawyers and other partners in professional firms to fund capital contributions. Another popular lending product is the humble credit card. While most people these days qualify for gold and platinum cards, private banks have developed distinctive cards targeted at genuine HNWIs, often on an invitation-only basis. Typical benefits include concierge services, exclusive events and comprehensive travel benefits. These cards include the American Express Centurion card, the Stratus card (which offers clients the opportunity to earn free private jet flights) and Coutts' World Signia card. One of the most exclusive is the Citigroup Chairman's card. Offered by personal invitation only, it offers access to any airport lounge and a free companion ticket for any airline ticket purchase. It was described by its wealth management CEO as 'by far the coolest, sexiest card out there today. You want one.'

A key feature of developments in the provision of lending products is the wider array of collateral that can be used to back such loans. Coutts (a private banking arm of the Royal Bank of Scotland), for example, has introduced a service for landowners that enable them to pledge a portion of land as collateral and draw down credit lines. As we noted earlier in this chapter, single-stock hedges can be created to improve illiquid stock positions for collateral purposes, and various banks will offer a host of lending services based on the valuation of illiquid assets, including art, livestock, property, family business wealth, etc.

There should, in principle, be almost no limit to the type of assets that can be pledged as security for such lending. The trick for wealth managers is to ensure that they have the expertise in valuing the (mainly) illiquid assets in question, and in assessing their own and clients' risk tolerance to such business. As noted in Box 9.1 on Basle II in Chapter 9, a key issue for private banks here is concentration risk, linked to large exposures to a relatively small number of individuals. The recent trend for banks to lend money to clients for hedge fund and private equity investments (which are, recall, highly leveraged themselves) represents another key risk. If a hedge fund goes into a steep decline, the bank could be forced to protect itself by liquidating the investment to pay back the loan. That could be costly for both the bank and the client. JP Morgan, for example, is reported to have developed a patented system to assist it in its HNW lending decision making.

4.1.7   Other products and services

So far we have discussed the main types of products that are viewed as becoming increasingly important to wealth management firms. Other areas often cited as having potential for future development, boosting bank returns and improving a differentiated service include:

- *Retirement planning and trust services.* While it may seem strange that HNWIs are concerned about their retirement plans survey evidence appears to suggest that family business and entrepreneurial clients (as well as top-level executives) seem to be very concerned about this element of wealth management/lifestyle planning. One area that is gaining attention (especially by US clients) relates to the establishment of retirement trust accounts. A retirement trust account is established for the benefit of a corporation's employees. The corporation acts as trustee and manages the record-keeping of the corporate retirement plan. Retirement trusts have a number of advantages, including: flexibility, as retirement trusts may be structured as money-purchase, profit-sharing, pension, defined-benefit or defined-contribution plans; simplicity, as all tax reporting is the responsibility of the trustees; and covered call writing (provided all trustees sign an option agreement). Such services are clearly of interest to business HNWIs whose families may be employed in the same firm. Other pension planning routes and various structures are available to protect the pension wealth of executives and other HNWI clients.
- *Life-cycle tax planning services.* Another area, viewed by many as key, but not particularly profitable, relates to the development of life-cycle tax planning services. The focus on life-cycle tax planning goes hand-in-hand with a strategic emphasis on life-cycle product planning for clients. Given that tax is a major consideration for many HNWIs , the growing array of investment vehicles and structures available is reflected in increased complexity associated with managing the tax situation of clients. Such services are generally outsourced to tax specialists. Figure 4.24 outlines the main issues associated with the provision of such services to HNWIs.
- *Insurance services.* As with most individuals, private clients have the usual range of insurance demands ranging from life cover to property and casualty insurance. However, the demands of HNWIs are likely to be more complex as they typically have multiple residences (therefore multiple property insurance), various types of property (land, estates, ski lodges, etc.) in different jurisdictions and other items to insure. Some may be faced with the risk of kidnap and other less common risks that can be insured against. Identifying the wide range of risks that clients face is likely to result in a multitude of insurance services that private banks can offer. In addition to these types of services, there has recently been a strong growth in so-called 'insurance wrapper' products. Here clients pay premiums on variable

Tax expertise is now as crucial as investment expertise for credible wealth mangement solutions.

A major ingredient for success in providing service to private client and the rise in life-cycle products is a comprehensive understanding of rapidly-changing taxation, including cross-jurisdictional tax, and the ability to harness tax-efficiency in client solutions through appropriate tax wrappers. What matters to clients is after-tax return, and a good investment return can be eradicated by inappropriate tax structuring.

Our survey indicates that wealth managers find tax planning an area of low profitability, it is provided as a client courtesy, although some wealth managers do build tax consequences into products, Leaving clients to work out the consequences of having invested in a complex product is not 'good' service from a wealth manager. With regulatory changes and more sophisticated clients, wealth managers must be proactive in providing up-to-date and often complex) tax structuring solutions, particularly for high-net-worth clients who might previously have held assets in low tax jurisdictions.

Tax expertise,whether in-house or accessed externally, is now as crucial as investment expertise for credible wealth

management solutions. Products are no longer best sourced from the home jurisdiction but need to be accessed internationally. Therefore knowledge of the effects of tax and regulatory regimes across the world is required both now and in the future. UCITs III and the European Savings Directive, for instance, will have a huge impact on European product delivery.

As Asia is a highly fragmented region, having different tax regulations across different countries, tax planning has become integral to the wealth management solution offering. The importance of tax planning is recognised with 45% of wealth managers expecting to offer this service in three years' time, up from 39% currently.

Experience we have had with clients shows that tax implications are not well understood and this could disadvantage private clients and call into question the expertise of wealth managers. Failure of product design to take account of AML, KYC requirements and consideration on product location will be critical in determining whether product provision should be onshore or offshore or even provided at all.

Figure 4.24   Issues relating to life-cycle tax planning
Source: PricewaterhouseCoopers (2004b).

life insurance and these payments are invested in investment reserves segregated from the insurance company's general investment portfolio. Policyholders are not taxed on the growth of the cash values held within their policies and the beneficiaries receive tax-free death benefits. In addition, policyholders may access funds within these policies through loans and withdrawals, usually without immediate tax consequences. Private placement variable life policies, also known as private insurance wrappers, offer various options. The more advanced options allow the policyholder to designate a personal asset manager. In essence, this means that clients can freely determine the strategy with which they would like their investments managed. Traditionally, the minimum premiums have been substantial, usually in the range of $5 million–$10 million. This has restricted the market's exposure to all but the very wealthy. However, these minimums have fallen substantially, as more and more firms discover these products' potential. Hedge fund managers, for example, have recently linked up with life insurance companies to wrap hedge funds in the private placement variable life insurance structure in order to minimize tax generated by high portfolio turnover.

- *Family office (or quasi family office style) services.* The concept of the family office, where UHNWIs set up their own offices to manage their financial affairs, has been a key feature of wealth management to the super-rich in the US and is rapidly developing in Europe (see Chapter 6 for more detail). Various banks such as ING, Deutsche Bank, UBS and various others have established family office divisions to deal with the ultra-rich (typically clients with investable assets greater than $30 million). The aim is to focus on offering family wealth management services with an aggressive focus on best-practice advice-led service. Other wealth management firms are delivering more tailored services which have a flavour of the family office but are directed to less wealthy clients.

- *Non-financial asset acquisition, finance and management.* Various private banks offer specialist services that deal with a variety of non-traditional investments (including art, wine and other collectables such as rare coins, stamps, etc.). Banks such as Citigroup Private Bank and UBS have provided such services, which include advisory, collection management and art banking/finance. However, ABN AMRO's recent decision to close its one-year-old art advisory investment service underscores how tricky it can be for some players to make the economics of this type of service work.

  Another specialist area being developed by various banks relates to the financing of private jets – a job perk that many top executives regret losing when they retire. Bank of America (BofA), for example, has combined its aircraft finance operation with the aircraft leasing unit of its global corporate and investment bank. This allows BofA's private banking clients to secure the use of a private jet through various leasing facilities. Fractional private jet ownership schemes are also becoming increasingly popular (particularly in the US). Firms such as Calibre, part of the wealth management arm of Wachovia Corporation, provide specialist advice on private jet finance and wine investment. Fortis Private Banking (within its MeesPierson Intertrust unit) has a dedicated yacht and aircraft group, which offers tax-efficient ownership planning, financing, registration, insurance, crew provision and management services. Another interesting trend has been the growing co-branding relationships being formed by wealth management firms and luxury goods providers. UBS Warburg, for instance, have arranged co-branded events with Sunseeker (maker of luxury yachts) to promote financing options and to develop client networking.

- *Socially responsible investing.*[14] The growing awareness of ethical and socially responsible issues associated with the operations of firms has encouraged the development of a range of ethical investment funds and various indexes that track socially responsible companies. For example, Dow Jones offers a range of sustainability indexes that track the financial performance of the leading sustainability-driven companies worldwide. By mid-2005, 56 Dow Jones sustainability indexes (DJSI) licences were held by asset managers in 14 countries to manage a variety of financial products including active and passive funds, certificates and segregated accounts. In total, firms holding these licenses manage over $3.3 billion. There is a growing number of ethical investment opportunities available to private clients – in Europe, the UK has by far the largest number of such listed funds – and many commentators believe that this market segment has strong future potential.

- *Philanthropic planning.* Philanthropic advisory services have long been a key element in the product offer to the UHNW segment, but it has not traditionally been the focus of lower-end HNW clients. This is changing, as many private banks seek to be able to offer a wider range of advisory services that differentiate their offering.[15] Many wealth management firms are developing such services, and employing dedicated staff with expertise in strategic planned

---

[14] See Datamonitor (2004), 'Socially Responsible Investing for European Private Clients: Implications for Wealth Managers', June 2004.

[15] See, for example, Bishop (2006)

giving, and in establishing, structuring and managing private foundations and charitable trusts, for example.

- *Education programmes for clients and their families.* As the product and service offer of the wealth management industry becomes increasingly varied and complex, there is a growing realisation that clients need to be made aware of new investment opportunities, wealth management solutions and other services that are available. Also, given the fact that the industry attracts most new businesses via referrals of existing clients, it is important that they are aware of current and future opportunities for both their own purposes and also able to convey these developments to potential new clients. Wealthy individuals also need to be able to convey information to their children about the responsibilities of wealth and issues relating to family business wealth management. A growing trend is for banks to offer such educational services. Coutts, for example, offers an education programme for family businesses. Typically, the nature of these education programmes is wide and varied but the main focus is educate current and potential clients, provide networking opportunities and emphasise the role of intergenerational wealth planning. Banks also run specialist programmes for clients that focus on specialist areas such as art investment, philanthropy and new products.

Another trend is for banks to offer financial training courses (or financial 'boot camps') for the children of wealthy clients. The aim is to teach children about everything from stocks and funds to business start-ups and philanthropy. For the firms, it is a chance both to cultivate the next generation and to solidify their client relationships with wealthy families. As Alvavo Martinez-Fonts, head of the Latin American Practice at JP Morgan Private Bank, recently noted, 'you do something for [a client's] kids and they remember it for ever'. The courses range from half-day retreats and crash courses to ongoing workshops that can last several years. Most of the programmes are geared to young people in their teens, although some go as young as seven. Credit Suisse runs a one-week course in Zurich. JP Morgan has, for more than a decade, run a two-week programme called 'NextGen' in locations such as Miami, Tokyo, Los Angeles and Paris. It focuses on investments and leadership in family-owned businesses. (Another one-week programme called 'investment principles' teaches clients' children about financial basics.) Citigroup Private Bank hosts around 50 of its clients' children each year as part of its 'Children of Wealth' programme. This includes a foreign exchange trading simulation game, classes such as 'Capital Market Economics' and 'Fundamentals of International Estate Planning', as well as sessions covering softer issues such as confidence building, communications and etiquette. It also includes a visit to an art gallery to learn about collecting. Other firms run more individualised tutorials. The courses are extremely popular. Some banks are currently setting up satellite programmes focused on Asia; others are rolling their courses out globally.

4.2 PRODUCT SOURCING AND MANAGEMENT

As the range of expertise needed to produce and distribute an extensive product and service offering increases this has encouraged the wealth management industry to source such services from outside. This is referred to as the development of an 'open architecture' structure where private banks claim to offer best-practice value-added services from different divisions within their own organisation (if part of large groups) or from third-party providers.

Given that the product and service requirements (and expectations) of clients continues to grow rapidly it is becoming very difficult for many firms to provide value-added solutions from their own proprietary offerings. In addition, HNWIs recognize that no individual provider can provide 'best-in-class' solutions for every product and service. This has resulted in the increased use of 'in-sourcing' products and services that typically are not produced by the firm in question. While the desire of firms in the industry is obviously to sell as much proprietary solutions as possible, the reality remains that as product sets and solutions expand, and clients become more demanding, it is almost impossible for any provider to offer all solutions in-house.

These trends tend to favour the largest financial institutions that have an established product innovation capability and typically those having links to investment banks.

> This allows them to leverage the skills of managing multiple product lifecycles and the ability to manufacture products which can benefit from the highs and lows of the capital markets. It also allows them to manage a short time to market capability, and as a result helps them achieve first mover margin and growth advantages. Those players who do not have the capability to manufacture such products are able to insource them from external product providers. The rapid development of a large number of product specialists now enables all private banks (but particularly the small- and medium-size ones) to fill these gaps by outsourcing the manufacturing of a selected number of products and services (IBM Consulting Services, 2005).

An open product architecture is the 'name of the game' in the wealth management industry and even the largest players recognise its importance in having a major structural impact on the industry.

As clients (especially high-end ones) recognize that no single provider can offer best solutions across all areas they have a clear preference for those providers that provide access to products and services from the largest number of sources. Even major players such as Citigroup Private Bank, JP Morgan Private Bank and HSBC Private Bank, which have substantial expertise in fund management, for instance, offer third-party fund products that add value to clients. This may be because these funds are of a certain investment style or generate performance better than those provided in-house. The argument goes that it is best that wealth management firms offer value-added services that they can demonstrate are best practice in the market and rely on third-party providers to deliver other solutions that they cannot match from proprietary products.

Smaller operators, who typically cannot rely as much on proprietary offerings, increasingly have to outsource their wealth management solutions. Firms such as Schwab International and Fidelity in the US, for example, provide a plethora of fund and other services to financial advisors, enabling them to offer a wide range of wealth management services to HNWI clients. In Europe the discount brokerage arm of Direkt Anlage Bank (DAB) is also gradually developing its mutual fund business in order to offer financial advisers the same sort of third-party offering as that of Charles Schwab in the US.

This provides only a handful of examples of how the distribution of wealth management products and services is changing. The focus is now on advice-led sales where 'product' can be manufactured in-house or obtained from third-party providers. The main value driver, therefore, is gradually moving away from production to distribution of wealth management services. Few private banks now really solely on 'in-house' production and distribution of services, as shown in Figure 4.25. However, it should be emphasised that the survey evidence reported in the diagram indicates that outsourcing is mainly focused on 'speciality products' (typically funds, structured products and other alternative investments), suggesting that the bulk of services on offer are proprietary in nature.

Value chain focus

Which statement best describes your approach to participation in the value chain?

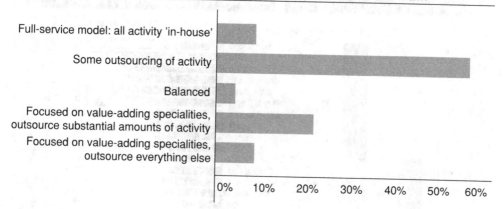

Figure 4.25   Open architecture driving third-party solutions
Source: Mercer Oliver Wyman (2005). Reproduced with permission.

Box 4.5   Multi-manager fund structures

The extensive array of investment fund products on offer has led to the development of multimanager services, which enable wealth management firms to offer a bundle of products to clients sourced from both within and outside the bank. This reflects the clients' desire to be offered a broader array of products. The terminology used to explain this phenomenon is a little confusing as terms such as 'multimanagers', 'manager-of-managers' and 'fund-of-funds' are often used interchangeably.

From the client's perspective, the main benefits include:

• Greater access, particularly to closed funds.
• Enhanced liquidity.
• Diversification.
• Lower minimum investments (typically as low as $50 000).
• Due diligence performed by in-house or external specialist teams (for example, it is not unusual these days even for mid-sized private banks to have as many as a dozen people finding, managing, actively controlling and divesting from third-party investment managers).

Essentially, finding quality managers at the right time is the name of the game. But as David Solo, Head of Asset Management at Julius Baer, recently remarked, 'Selecting the best managers is much more complicated than having three client advisors who aren't good with clients subscribe to the Lipper database, look to see who is in the upper quartile and is still willing to take money and, by the way, pay the high retrocession.'

In general, there are two main types of multimanager products: fund-of-funds and manager-of-managers. Fund-of-funds invest in a range of other funds. The provider monitors the performance of the portfolio of funds, changing them when necessary. It charges for the fund selection, adding perhaps 75 basis points or more to the annual charges clients would pay for the underlying funds. Many wealth management firms use fund-of-fund structures, including: Credit Suisse, UBS and HSBC.

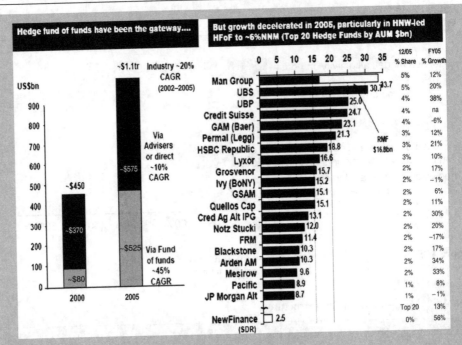

Figure 4.26   Hedge fund-of-funds landscape
Source: Huw van Steenis, Morgan Stanley. Reproduced by permission.

With a manager-of-managers fund, the private bank appoints investment managers (often on an asset class or geographic basis) to invest in the underlying securities. The private bank retains full control over the asset allocation, the choice of managers and the investment style, and is responsible for monitoring the overall portfolios on both the individual stock and investment manager levels. In many cases, the private bank outsources the selection of investment managers to a specialist such as Frank Russell, Northern Trust and SEI. Another key role of the specialist is to aggregate demand and hence achieve buying economies across private banks. Those offering manager-of-managers include Coutts (in-house), C Hoare & Company, EFG International and Pictet (using selection specialists). A study by Cerulli Associates in 2004 suggested that there were 512 global operators in the multimanager arena, which they predicted will grow to around 700 managing some $800 billion by end-2006.

Hedge fund-of-funds are a key gateway to the hedge funds for first-time investors, and now account for around half of hedge fund industry assets (see Figure 4.26). However, research by Morgan Stanley suggests that UHNWIs are showing greater confidence in going directly to the large multistrategy hedge funds, which are increasingly seeking to disintermediate funds-of-funds. (This underscores why multistrategy hedge funds such as Highbridge and Bluecrest are a key focus for industry M&A.)

A major criticism of multimanager fund products is that they double charge: the use of an umbrella structure with a main fund and a group of subfunds adds an extra layer of costs. Typically, the charges of fund-of-funds can be around 1% higher than that of alternative actively managed funds. A lower cost option is the so-called balanced managed funds, referred to as asset allocation funds in the US. These have no charges for the subfunds but they tend to be more expensive than standard index trackers and performance is obviously influenced by the mix of assets involved and expertise of managers.

In general, the offer of such services enables private banks the ability to class themselves as using open architecture to offer a wider range of fund products to their clients and to increase diversification. However, given the high costs associated with such structures, there is little compelling evidence of consistent outperformance relative to direct investments.

The main point to make is that while all market participants in the wealth management industry recognise the attractions of open architecture structures, this is mainly used for specialist services and does not constitute the bulk of private banks' business. Figure 4.27 illustrates the open architecture trend in various areas by showing that a substantial proportion of European wealth management firms source some of the value-added services, in particular, from outside. Figure 4.28 shows a breakdown of various alternative and real estate investments, also illustrating that hedge fund and private equity products are often sourced from third parties whereas derivatives and real estate products are often provided by other parts of the bank.

Suppliers of wealth management services have to recognise the opportunities and threats of the open architecture structure:

- Main threat. This reduces the margins for the supplier and may highlight a lack of 'best practice' in proprietary service provision, resulting in negative client perceptions.
- Main opportunity. This allows suppliers to offer a wider spectrum of best-practice solutions, strengthening client relationships and promoting advice-led sales.

While these threats and opportunities are common to all wealth management firms the fact that the largest operators (and particularly those with substantial investment banking expertise)

Basic banking products and services		Private banking products and services		Wealth management products and services	
Custody services	11	Insurance products	33	Hedge funds	33
Money market	7	Third party mutual funds	27	Private equity	33
Term deposits	3	Real estate investments	22	Structured products	19
Portfolio valuation reporting	3	Investment research	19	Trust and foundation	19
Lending products	2	Brokerage services	12	Derivatives	14
Foreign exchange	2	Securities lending	3	Tax and estate planning	14

Figure 4.27   Products and services offered through third parties
Source: IBM Consulting Services, European Wealth and Private Banking Industry Survey 2005. Reproduced by permission.

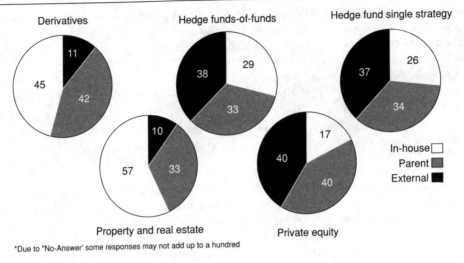

Figure 4.28   Sources of alternative and real estate investments
Source: PricewaterhouseCoopers (2004b). Reproduced by permission.

can produce a larger 'best-practice' product set in-house provides them with an obvious advantage.

All operators are aware of the possible adverse impact that open architecture is having on revenue generating potential and this is forcing them to:

- Develop new product manufacturing arrangements that ensure the continued presence of their products within proprietary channels.
- Focus more on improving sales performance (as noted earlier) by deploying and managing client-facing sales staff with a greater emphasis on value-added solutions.
- Identifying profit opportunities from new manufacturing approaches.
- Extending distribution channels including in-house and third-party client-referral programmes.

A major challenge to private banking firms is to manage the interface between the third-party product provider, choosing the appropriate set of products and distributing these as effectively of possible. In general it seems apparent that private banks have to develop the open architecture approach if they are to be effective in offering a full range of value-adding products and services that meet the increasingly complex product life-cycle demands of HNWIs.

Having said all this, however, various industry commentators have suggested that wealth managers are very much 'all talk and no action' when it comes to open architecture. No matter what they say, banks would always rather offer in-house products and pressure will be on relationship managers (even from just the point of view of a more pleasant working environment with colleagues) to offer home-grown products. In fact, anecdotal evidence suggests that between 70% and 80% of products sold are in-house products. For indexed products this seems reasonable, but for actively managed products and alternative investments we believe the figure is far too high. There is also a huge conflict of interest in promoting third-party products, and the limited embrace of best-practice open architecture products and services may be irritating clients. (Some have argued that HNWIs feel as if they are being treated as fools.) In the words of one family office, 'you are better off putting your money with Goldman

Sachs and knowing that they manage your money in-house, than giving it to a major competitor who champions open architecture and have no idea who the manager is, or even whether they are selecting the best products from third parties!'

Box 4.6   Product management discipline

Many wealth managers are realising that there is a large opportunity both to cut costs and raise revenues through more effective product management. This box focuses on two specific areas: product range rationalisation and the product development process.

Product range rationalisation

As we have seen, there has been a vast cumulative expansion in product and service ranges in recent years. Many wealth managers pursued an undisciplined 'product rush' in the belief that product diversification and customisation would drive volume and margin expansion and be a key competitive differentiator. Overall, however, the impact has too often been (a) disappointing incremental revenue realisation, linked to weak client targeting (e.g. across-the-board product entitlement with little differentiation in pricing) and poor sales effectiveness; and (b) higher costs, linked to misaligned resources, excessive product customisation and the need for multiple product platforms and complex support infrastructure. Handling the fallout from this product rush is therefore a key opportunity area.

The first step is to agree on the relevant product set, which, perhaps surprisingly, is not always as straightforward as it sounds. It is best to think in terms of product hierarchies or trees, starting with high-level product groupings (deposits, lending, investments, etc.) at the top, with subsequent levels capturing greater detail.

The next step is to segment the individual products, based on revenue and popularity (i.e. the number of clients who have bought the product) (see Figure 4.29, sourced from the Boston Consulting Group). It is typical to find that a large number of products collectively account for only a small proportion of total revenue.

This product segmentation informs the final step, which is to devise the rationalisation action plan. For non-core products, options suggested by BCG include discontinuing, raising the rate of cross-selling, repricing and alternative sourcing. Other options include managing client access to these products more effectively, product standardisation and aligning resources more closely to the relevant product economics. The latter strategy should be based on a rigorous analysis of staff (and cost) deployment by product and along the value chain.

Product development

A disciplined, well-executed product development process is the key to a successful product launch. Yet many wealth managers plough ahead with new product development based on the needs of only a very small number of clients and, in some instances, even without a supporting business case. Process governance can also be slack, with no clear ownership or end-to-end accountability. Other typical weaknesses include:

- Product specialists developing ideas with only limited input from the clients, the front line, marketing and elsewhere
- Insufficient focus on commercial aspects – with risk, infrastructure and legal issues often dominating the go/no-go decision
- Slow decision making and extended time to market
- Limited performance tracking, post product launch

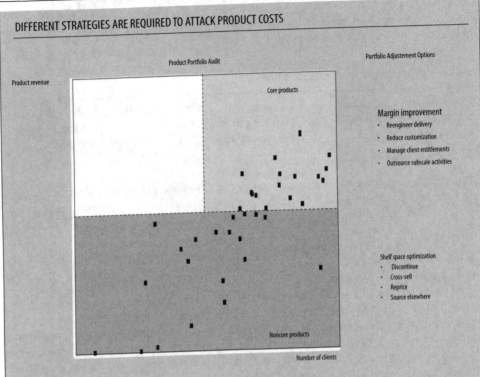

Figure 4.29 Product segmentation
Source: Boston Consulting Group (2003b), p.19. Reproduced by permission.

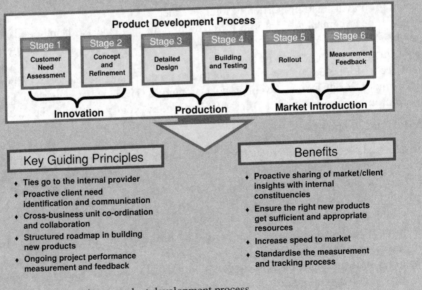

Figure 4.30 Implementing a product development process
Source: UBS.

Figure 4.30 illustrates some of the key elements of a disciplined product development process. One essential enabler is an enhanced, two-way, ongoing dialogue between the product specialists and the front line. This should ensure that (a) the front line is aware and knowledgeable of the new product pipeline and can integrate product management into the account-planning process and (b) the product specialists receive timely, 'on-the-ground' feedback about clients' product needs and demands, and on the latest product moves by competitors.

4.3 PRICING

The pricing of private banking products and services has long been shrouded in mystery mainly because many prices were negotiated and these varied according to the range of products on offer and the type of client being serviced. As shown in Figure 4.31, negotiated pricing forms the basis of wealth managers' pricing strategies, with fixed prices only constituting a small part of overall pricing structures. Although many individual products may have fixed prices (such as a set management fee on fund products), these are ultimately negotiable as part of the package on services offered to the client.

While there is much talk about value-based pricing, in reality the value element typically focuses much more on enhancing the value of client relationships rather than on risk-adjusted pricing aimed at maximising returns to the wealth management firm. The reason why private banks are constrained from pursing aggressive pricing strategies is that HNWIs usually have multiple relationships through which they can compare pricing and use alternative offers to negotiate down fees and other charges. Unlike in retail banking where there is substantial inertia in the customer base (facilitating aggressive pricing in certain segments like credit cards), this is not the case for HNWIs. They are mobile, the transaction costs of moving wealth management provider are low, many are financially sophisticated and understand the costs incurred by undertaking certain transactions, and they all know they have a strong negotiating

Pricing
Which statement best describes how you set prices for custormers?

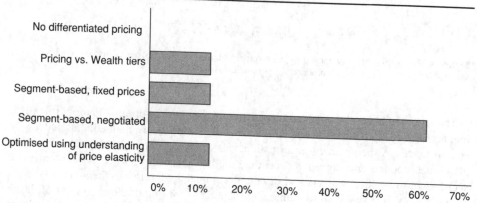

Figure 4.31 Pricing of wealth management services
Source: Mercer Oliver Wyman (2005). Reproduced by permission.

position. Having said this, however, some providers are at least considering more sophisticated pricing models, e.g. examining the elasticity of price demand for their products and services, so as to see the responsiveness of price changes on client demand.

Box 4.7 Pricing discipline

Given that negotiated pricing remains the norm in wealth management, a key focus area should be to develop tighter pricing discipline in the face of revenue leakage from discounting. Many wealth managers believe that they have established rules to prevent excessive discounting, that all relationship managers give comparable rebates and that, for any given client, a rebate on one revenue line is compensated for by additional revenue on another. But analysis shows that, within wealth managers, there are surprisingly wide variations in pricing discipline across relationship managers – by up to a factor of four in some cases (see Figure 4.32). In many cases, it turns out that 'one-off' discounts have become systematic and unrelated to client profitability. To counteract this, wealth managers need to establish clear rules, processes and incentive systems for granting fee waivers and discounts, as well as installing monitoring systems to ensure their implementation.

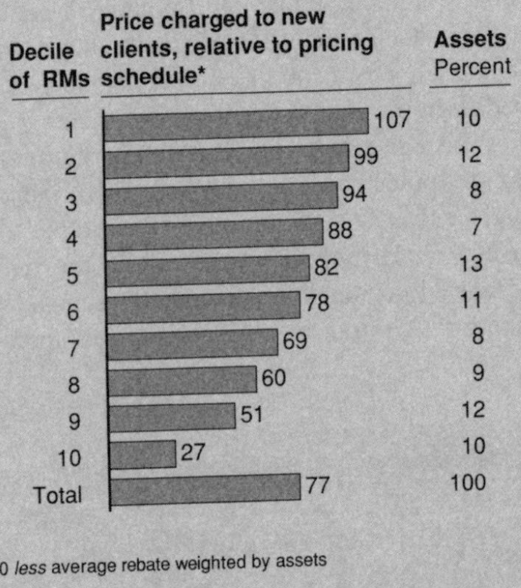

Decile of RMs	Price charged to new clients, relative to pricing schedule*	Assets Percent
1	107	10
2	99	12
3	94	8
4	88	7
5	82	13
6	78	11
7	69	8
8	60	9
9	51	12
10	27	10
Total	77	100

* Indexed to 100 *less* average rebate weighted by assets

Figure 4.32 Actual prices charged by relationship managers: illustrative example
Source: McKinsey & Company. Reproduced by permission.

The first step is for the wealth manager to understand the current situation, investigating, account by account, what sort of discounts and waivers are granted, and under what circumstances. Armed with this information, wealth managers can develop sets of rules for individual products and segments depending on their price elasticity. If a wealth manager decides not to prohibit waivers and discounts completely, but to use them actively in the pricing policy, it is essential to define a clear process for granting discounts at all levels of the organisation – from the frontline relationship managers, with limited authority to reduce prices, to senior management, who must approve any deep discounts. The incentive systems must be aligned accordingly, ideally discouraging discounting behaviour no matter how small the discount might seem. Suggested approaches include: transparency on historical and new discounts per team and per relationship manager, and holding teams accountable for the bottom-line impact of their pricing decisions.

In the implementation phase, training the frontline is vitally important in order to dispel the belief that discounts are the most important means of capturing new business and retaining existing clients. This can be done by demonstrating unequivocally that clients are willing to purchase products without these crutches (internal benchmarking, in particular, has proved to be extremely powerful here), as well as providing support tools to help frontline staff make the best discount decisions. Lastly, tools to track and monitor discounts need to be developed with sales force incentives tied to their use. This type of strategy can have a significant impact on revenues relatively quickly, and without appreciably increasing client attrition. Client experience suggests a revenue uplift of five basis points should be achievable within one year.

The industry focuses very much on a relationship pricing framework although the extent to which individual fees for specific products are bundled together and the total fee discounted to benefit the client are unclear. However, it is not within the scope of this chapter to focus on the pricing of all the individual products described earlier. Table 4.2 illustrates a range of prices for various product classes obtained from a survey of European wealth managers.

Table 4.2 illustrates the fact that fees charged to retail banking clients tend to be higher than those charged to private clients. More interesting is the fact that fees on traditional areas of investment business tend to be relatively low compared with the much higher fees for alternative (including structured) products. Of course, this is not really too surprising given that a lot of banks source alternative investments from third parties as well as the fact that they are most costly to set up. The growing emphasis on advisory services also typically requires substantial outside input suggesting a relatively high fee structure – fees on tax, legal and other advice can be levied on an hourly, relationship or product purchase basis.

One factor that has had an impact on the pricing strategy of many private banks resulted from the losses that many clients experienced in the downturn in the markets at the turn of the decade. Typically, clients were unhappy that they were still subject to substantial fees despite the poor performance of wealth managers. This has resulted in the growing use of various pricing structures including:

Table 4.2 Asset class fees (basis points)

	Retail	Private banking
Alternatives	278	253
Real estate	85	84
Active equity	61	46
Active fixed income	38	26
Money market	28	19
Passive	11	8
Overall	49	38

Source: Mercer Oliver Wyman (2005). Reproduced by permission.

- *Performance related fees.* Such fee structures are relatively common for various fund products where a set annual fee is levied and an additional fee is charged subject to the fund exceeding a benchmark level of performance. Performance structures vary; some funds offer rebates if they fail to hit a stipulated benchmark level of returns. Such pricing strategies tend to be rather uncommon in the case of covering all the asset activity of a client, although there are some specialist firms that do charge a set management fee plus a performance fee on returns generated by the whole HNWI portfolio.
- *Wrap account pricing.* Wrap accounts charge the overall account an annual fee irrespective of how often the stocks or other investments within the account are bought or sold. Wrap accounts were developed as a way to avoid brokers churning a client's investment to generate higher fees. Generally wrap account fee structures can vary depending on the amount of funds under management and the type of assets being managed. Traditionally pricing benchmarks are in line with mutual fund fees – although the development of such services in the private banking industry (are far as we are aware) are rare.
- *Active advisory fees.* These are fees that link advisory services to transactions activity. For example, clients will be informed that if they pay for the advice then any fees or transactions on services purchased thereafter based on this advice will be discounted. Various banks, such as BNP Paribas, have pioneered this type of service.

The above approaches provide an indication of the sort of new pricing approaches and directions that wealth management firms can consider in developing their service proposition. Another challenge relates to the identification of product and service specific costs associated with pricing. Private banking firms have traditionally been poor in implementing systems aimed at identifying costs across product and service lines. This makes it difficult for them to consider various pricing models, such as cost-plus pricing, average-cost pricing, marginal-cost pricing and relationship-based pricing, across the whole wealth management spectrum. The greater emphasis on creating value-added propositions means that much greater attention needs to be paid to this dimension if more effective and profitable pricing models are to evolve.

5

Distribution Channels

With Philip Molyneux

The attraction and retention of clients are key elements in the growth strategy of any wealth management business. We have also seen that the product and service demands of clients are becoming increasingly diverse and complex. That poses substantial challenges to the private banking industry in the context of how firms should deliver such products and services. Traditionally, the main distribution channel has been through face-to-face meetings via bespoke physical offices or branches of the firms in question. However, with the Internet and telecommunications revolution, a broader array of complementary distribution channels now exists.

Value creation within the industry is currently largely driven by product distribution, rather than by manufacturing. Figure 5.1 shows that, in Europe as a whole, distribution captures a full 62% of gross revenues (and this is slightly lower than a few years ago). That reflects the dominance of distributors in wealth management, linked to control of the client relationship, the ability to influence clients' product choice, and the growing demand for advice.

This chapter outlines recent developments and best practices across the key distribution channels, covering:

- Relationship managers:
  - (a) Roles.
  - (b) Organisation and structure.
  - (c) Sales effectiveness.
  - (d) 'War for talent'.
- Other traditional channels:
  - (a) Referral agents.
  - (b) Branches.
  - (c) Client reporting.
- New and emerging channels:
  - (a) Online.
  - (b) Broadband and beyond.
- Multichannel management.

5.1 RELATIONSHIP MANAGERS

As the main interface between the client and the supplier of wealth management services, the relationship manager performs an essential function in attracting new clients, servicing existing clients and generating value from such relationships. That, of course, is easier said than done. Wealth managers not only have to define their target markets and related product offerings but

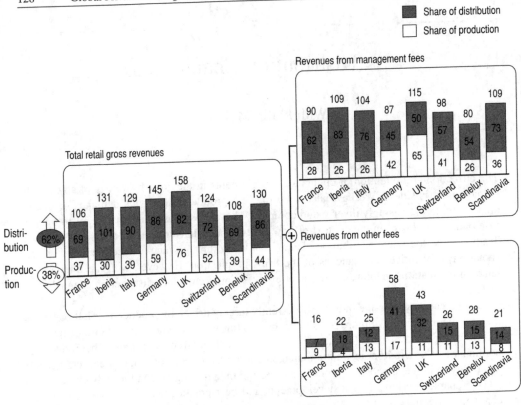

Figure 5.1 Value decomposition: distribution versus manufacturing
Source: McKinsey European Asset Management Survey 2005. Reproduced by permission.

also have to be extremely diligent in attracting top-calibre relationship managers who have to perform a multitude of demanding tasks. Figure 5.2 illustrates this point, emphasising the fact that HNWIs increasingly view wealth managers as 'chief financial officers' dealing with a broad spectrum of banking, investment, advisory, financial reporting and other services. It is through the relationship manager that information and advice on products and services are provided – reactively and proactively.

The new model means that relationship managers need to have deeper knowledge, collaborate more effectively with other relationship managers and specialists, and be more results oriented.

5.1.1 Roles

The relationship manager has the difficult task of (a) acquiring new clients ('hunting') and (b) serving and retaining existing clients ('farming'). Clients that work well with their relationship manager are more likely to make referrals to the same firm. By understanding client needs and aspirations, relationship managers are best placed to learn about potential new clients and their wealth management requirements. Relationship managers are therefore encouraged to prospect for new leads, learn about clients' experiences with other firms (as most HNWI clients have multiple banking relationships) and identify potential new products and services that may help to attract new clients.

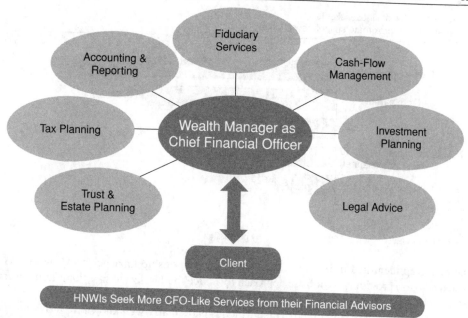

Figure 5.2   Wealth manager as chief financial officer
Source: Capgemini/Merrill Lynch World Wealth Report 2004.

As noted in Chapter 3, new clients can be acquired through various channels, including:

- Referrals from the wealth manager's existing clients and staff.
- For universal banks, internal referrals, i.e. from clients and staff in, for example, the retail, business and investment banking subsidiaries.
- External referrals from third parties (referral agents), such as financial advisors, attorneys, asset managers and accountants.
- Acquisitions or alliances with other banks and financial firms.
- Marketing and promotional events, e.g. sponsorship of up-market sporting, entertainment and cultural events, seminars for HNWIs, cold calling, etc.

For most wealth managers, referrals from existing clients, typically generated by their relationship managers, is the main acquisition channel. That is backed up by industry surveys, including that of Mercer Oliver Wyman (Figure 5.3), and by firm-level data (Figure 5.4). Referrals from existing clients are less costly than external or internal referrals as there is no need for referral fees.

Excellent client relationships are the key value driver in private banking. Various studies[1] have sought to identify the main features of these relationships, highlighting key areas and levels of service delivery. One example, by Booz Allen, is shown in Figure 5.5. This illustrates that, at a minimum, private banks must be able to execute transactions, comply with regulations (including 'know your customer", KYC, rules) and provide accurate reporting services. These, of course, are the basic entry requirements. In reality, the client relationship is enhanced as the relationship moves from being mainly reactive to proactive, including active management of clients with 'high personal engagement' and 'personalised attention to investment performance'.

---

[1] See, for example, Mercer Oliver Wyman (2005) and PricewaterhouseCoopers (2005).

Source of new business: clients
What is the approximate split of new clients?

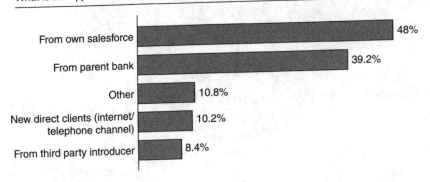

Figure 5.3   Sources of new clients
Source: Mercer Oliver Wyman (2005). Reproduced by permission.

The final step identified in Figure 5.5 relates to the relationship manager being viewed as a trusted advisor, providing a 'holistic approach to advice' and reflected in a 'long-term investment in clients . . . that bring no [immediate] gain to the bank/relationship manager'.

A good example here is Northern Trust, which is particularly well known for providing exceptional, high-touch client service. It emphasises its close proximity to clients by encouraging its relationship managers to reside in their clients' communities.

Many wealth managers find that relationship managers typically neglect referrals as a major source of new business. In practice, a proactive approach of asking clients for referrals can be surprisingly effective. The key here is to make the request in a sensitive way. Sample scripts include:

- For clients with children: 'Does your family bank with us?', 'What account arrangements have you made for your children?'
- For executive clients: 'How would your colleagues feel about this product/service?'

One recent trend is for the relationship manager's role to become more specialised. Some banks, for example, are removing most investment management responsibilities from relationship managers (see Chapter 8). Also, a number of banks are moving to split some or all of

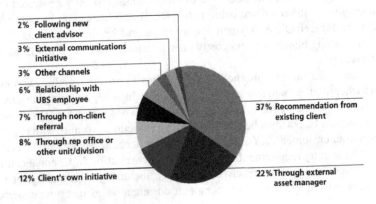

Figure 5.4   Client acquisition at UBS
Source: UBS.

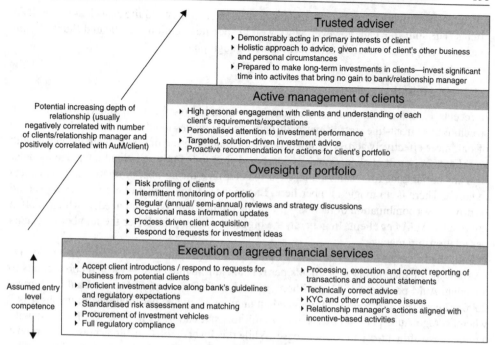

Figure 5.5   Steps to excellence in client relationship management
Source: Booz Allen Hamilton and Reuters (2003). Reproduced by permission.

their relationship managers into dedicated 'hunters' (sometimes called business development specialists) and 'farmers'. The McKinsey European Private Banking Economics Surveys find that this practice is less prevalent at top-performing (high margin and/or high growth) banks (Figure 5.6). The breadth of client needs makes it difficult for a split hunter-farmer model to succeed. That is because of the discontinuity in relationship just after the critical initial client profiling ahead of the first investment proposal. In general, relationship managers who need to cover large retail or business banking networks can build more effective trust-based

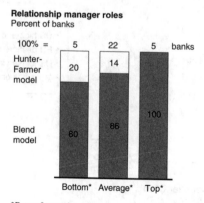

*By profit margin

Figure 5.6   Relationship management specialisation
Source: McKinsey European Private Banking Economics Survey 2004. Reproduced by permission.

relationships with branch managers and business bankers if they acquire as well as serve HNW clients. The split role can, however, work well in specific situations. Dedicated 'hunter' units can, for example, be effective for attacking new geographies.

5.1.2 Organisation and structure

In recent years, there has been substantial innovation in how wealth managers organise and structure their front-line staff. Key trends here include moves to allocate the number and type of staff more effectively across the client base (e.g. matching senior relationship managers with key clients or potential clients) and a widespread shift to team-based client coverage models.

A key initial issue for wealth managers is to determine the number of relationship managers required. There is no magic number here. Experience suggests that client resourcing should be driven by a combination of factors – including client value, type and needs – which is often proxied by AuM per client. In general, the bigger the client, the lower the number of clients per relationship manager.

Published data here are hard to come by, but Figure 5.7 provides some indicative benchmarks. Overall, the median number of clients per relationship manager is 84 (which corresponds to a median AuM per client of $1.8 million), according to *Euromoney*'s Private Banking Survey 2006. The survey also found that the median number of clients per relationship manager is 5 when average AuM per client exceeds $30 million, but can be as high as 325 for those with a more mass-affluent-oriented client base. While this inverse relationship is reasonably robust on average, there is, however, substantial variation across wealth managers serving similar client wealth bands. Part of this variation is linked to the business model. For example, more relationship managers will typically be required for onshore clients than for offshore clients of a given size, given the differencies in the frequency and intensity of interaction.

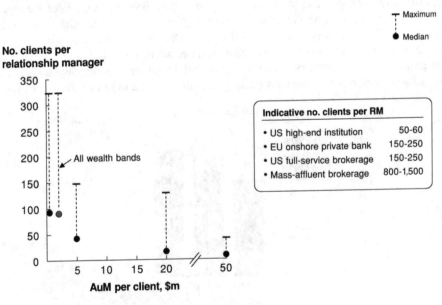

Figure 5.7 Indicative relationship manager client loadings
Source: Euromoney; Boston Consulting Group; author's client work.

Team Based Client Service Model

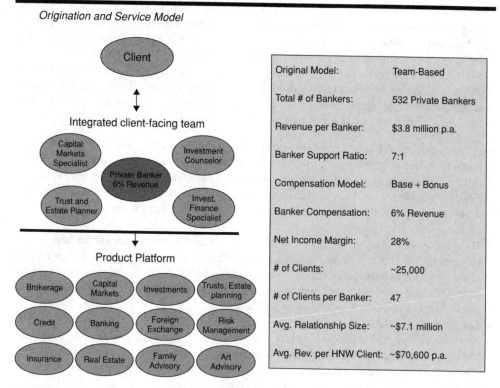

Origination and Service Model

Original Model:	Team-Based
Total # of Bankers:	532 Private Bankers
Revenue per Banker:	$3.8 million p.a.
Banker Support Ratio:	7:1
Compensation Model:	Base + Bonus
Banker Compensation:	6% Revenue
Net Income Margin:	28%
# of Clients:	~25,000
# of Clients per Banker:	47
Avg. Relationship Size:	~$7.1 million
Avg. Rev. per HNW Client:	~$70,600 p.a.

Figure 5.8   Citigroup Private Bank service model and key metrics
Source: Citigroup (2004).

That is supported by data published by Citigroup Private Bank in 2004 (see Figure 5.8). At 47, its average number of clients per relationship manager is relatively low, which reflects its high average client relationship size of $7.1 million. Note also that its relationship managers are each supported by an average of 7 support staff. Experience elsewhere suggests that these support staff are likely to be split roughly equally between specialists and administration staff.

In the past, relationship managers were perceived as self-driven professionals who could be left to function essentially independently. But as Figure 5.8 also illustrates, there is a growing trend among private banks to develop team-based approaches to serving clients. In part, this reflects the growing complexity of the role of the relationship manager and the view that relationship managers should dedicate themselves solely to client-facing activity – marshalling, as necessary, appropriate expertise and resources from around the firm. In other words, the relationship manager should be part of a group of experts, including product and other specialists. In some respects, this is a reflection of private bankers aiming to emulate the family office concept, whereby UHNWIs have their own dedicated teams of advisors providing wealth management solutions. For large, integrated wealth management firms, establishing team-based client coverage models can be a way of leveraging resources from other parts of their parent organisation more effectively. The team-based approach also helps to 'institutionalise' the client relationship, reducing the bank's dependence on individual relationship managers.

In terms of team size, again approaches vary within and across firms. McKinsey research shows that the majority of successful wealth managers use relatively large teams of relationship managers (i.e. more than five relationship managers per team). That not only fosters an effective coaching environment but also broadens the skill base of the whole team by encouraging individual relationship managers to develop specific areas of expertise ('cell splitting').

Merrill Lynch is a good example of a firm that has developed various team-based approaches to the provision of wealth management services. Its Global Private Client Group recognises that there should be no single approach to team-based development, and focuses on developing successful teams of various shapes and sizes. The team structures it employs include:[2]

- *Law practice model.* In this model teams are organised like a law firm, with one or more partners at the top of the practice supported by a range of associates who often specialise in different areas of expertise. The latter are typically paid using a salary and bonus structure. For the associates, it can be a good training ground to establish their own practice eventually, or there is the possibility of progressing to partnership status. For the team, that can provide a natural succession plan.
- *Hub-and-spoke model.* At the centre of the team is one or more relationship managers who focus on the areas in which they personally have the strongest skills. Around them is a circle of specialists who are organised and brought in on an ad hoc basis to complement the team's core skills and address specific wealth management requirements. That provides an added level of expertise and differential value for the team.
- *The corporate model.* These teams are organised like companies, with a CEO, a chief operating officer and a structure below performing very specific, well-defined functions. Merrill Lynch notes that some of their most successful teams serving corporate executive clients have organised themselves in this way. It provides a service structure that corporate executives are often familiar and comfortable with.
- *The family office group.* This group is organised to serve the specialist requirements of a small number of UHNWIs and families, whether it be in estate planning, trust management, alternative investments, etc.

In order to develop the effectiveness of these teams, Merrill Lynch has a Practice Management Group. That is what it describes as a 'SWAT team', which specialises in advising relationship managers. Part of the role of this group is to analyse the role and effectiveness of client-facing teams, and they have identified a number of factors that appear to impact on team performance/productivity. These success factors include:

- *Professional alliances.* Successful teams have good formal or informal relationships with other professionals, such as accountants, lawyers and high-end financial planners, which act as a source of two-way referrals (see below).
- *Niche marketing.* Teams can increase their effectiveness by focusing on particular niche client segments including: professionals, medical practices and corporate executives, as well as needs-based clients such as those seeking retirement planning, or specific ethnic or affinity groups.
- *Situational teaming.* This relates to reaching out on an ad hoc basis, as needed, to deliver specific expertise to a client. The focus here is to 'deliver the firm', i.e. to bring all the

---

[2] See remarks by Robert J. McCann, (Merrill Lynch, 2005), Vice Chairman and President, Global Private Client Group, Merrill Lynch & Co., Inc., on 'Creating Differential Value in a Commoditized World: The Evolving Role of the Wealth Manager', presented at the Investment Management Consultants Association, 2005 Spring Conference, Palm Springs, California, 10 April 2005.

resources and expertise of the organisation to bear, so as to deliver appropriate wealth management services in a focused and organised manner.

- *Open communication within the team.* Good communication between team members is essential for effective team-based delivery and best-practice sharing. That often does not come naturally to wealth management personnel, given the industry's traditional emphasis on discretion. Productive teams realise that it benefits all if there is open, meaningful, two-way ongoing dialogue between team members – 'not a meeting for the sake of a meeting mentality, but constant, effective communication on what they're doing and how they're doing it with our clients'.

It is important to keep team structures as flat as possible, without introducing unnecessary management layers. Among other things, that helps to ensure that leadership teams do not become distant from the client. Many successful private banking heads continue to maintain a limited number of ongoing client relationships themselves, rather than only having client contact only during the acquisition stage or when things go wrong. Other pitfalls include employing team leaders mainly on the back of their sales skills, rather than for their management or coaching prowess and with insufficient coordination with product and other specialists, e.g. in client account planning.

5.1.3   Sales effectiveness

Given the renewed emphasis on growth by most players in the industry, many players are turning their attention to sales effectiveness. There are large differences in the sales productivity of individual relationship managers, which can create opportunities. BCG found that relationship managers in the top quintile generate 10 times more revenue than those in the lowest quintile. A key starting point, then, is to understand the drivers of those differences by decomposing the revenue of each relationship manager (or team) into:

- Number of clients per relationship manager.
- AuM per client.
- Gross margin.

While it is important not to try to do everything at once, a complementary approach to improving the sales effectiveness of relationship managers is to focus on the time that relationship managers spend with clients, using the following three-step plan:

1. Increasing the overall amount of time spent with clients ('sales capacity').
2. Allocating that time more effectively across the client base.
3. Maximising the effectiveness of time spent with a given client.

For the first step, an example of the typical time allocation of relationship managers is presented in Figure 5.9, from the IBM Consulting Services Survey (2005).

Though there is some variation among firms and across countries, this survey (and first-hand experience) finds that relationship managers devote only around 50%–60% of their time on average to client-facing activity. The remainder of their time is split between internal administration and other non-client-related activities. In some instances, there may be valid reasons for this. For example, relationship managers who serve offshore clients may dedicate more of their time to non-facing client business because the associated compliance and regulatory issues are more complex. This poses a problem for the industry because, unsurprisingly, there

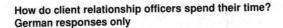

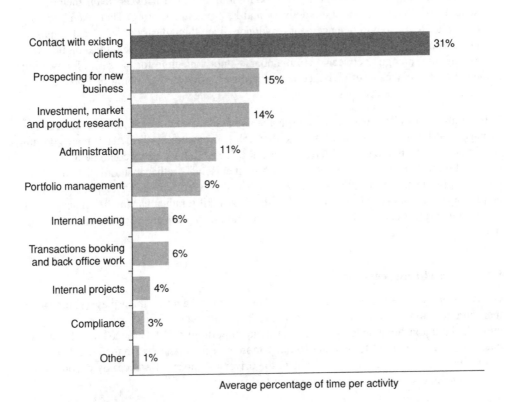

Figure 5.9 Client relationship managers – time allocation analysis
Source: IBM Consulting Services, European Wealth and Private Banking Industry Survey 2005. Reproduced by permission.

is a reasonably strong positive relationship between the time spent with clients and growth in AuM, as shown in Figure 5.10.

Building a trust-based relationship with clients is time consuming, but is ultimately the key to success in wealth management. Therefore, it is important for wealth managers to increase the amount of time spent with clients and ensure that relationship managers become more proactive and disciplined in their approach. Box 5.1 provides some suggestions as to how this issue can be tackled.

Having increased the amount of time relationship managers are able to spend with clients, the next step is to ensure that the time is allocated effectively across the client base. McKinsey research shows that undifferentiated service often ties up a significant share of resources (Figure 5.11). At many firms, it is the clients at the extremes of the value spectrum that receive disproportionate amounts of the relationship manager's time: too much time for the lowest-value clients; too little time for the highest-value clients.

Wealth managers therefore need to align relationship managers' time to clients' needs, attractiveness and potential, as illustrated in Figure 5.12. One way of helping achieve this is

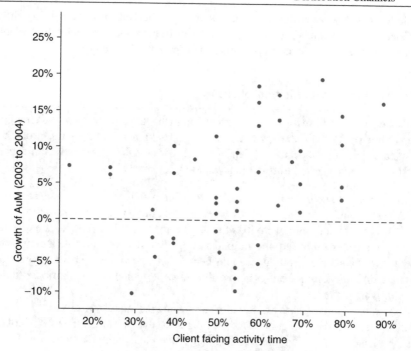

Figure 5.10   Client-facing time versus AuM growth
Source: IBM Consulting Services, European Wealth and Private Banking Industry Survey 2005. Reproduced by permission.

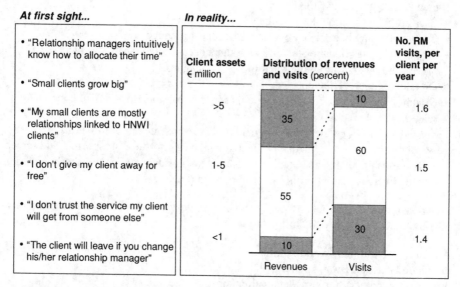

Figure 5.11   Distribution of relationship managers' time across clients: illustrative example
Source: McKinsey & Company. Reproduced by permission.

to introduce a tiered service offering, which is the approach taken by Merrill Lynch, among others. Client segmentation is best performed at the institutional level as individual relationship managers are not well positioned to prioritise and segment effectively.

Box 5.1   Increasing the time in front of clients

There is a wide range of reasons why relationship managers are not spending enough time in front of clients. The key starting point in devising a strategy to tackle this problem is to understand its specific root causes. Eden McCallum, a consulting company of independent professionals, has suggested four initial areas to investigate:

1. *Organisational structure and activity.* Relationship managers may be unclear as to their specific role within the team. They may be spending time on compliance, administration and other non-client-facing activities that could, for example, be reallocated, standardised, automated, centralised or eliminated altogether. It is conceivable that approaches to risk management and compliance may be too 'belt and braces'. There may also not be a standardised division of duties across the network, which could contribute to a large variability in performance.
2. *Compensation and incentives.* Relationship managers may not do what is required of them because there is poor alignment between the overall business objectives, on the one hand, and individuals' targets, objectives and compensation, on the other. In addition, a value-oriented culture may not be driven throughout the organisation and poor relationship manager performance may not have traditionally been penalised.
3. *Training and development.* Relationship managers may not believe that they can have much influence on client income streams. In particuar, they may avoid spending sufficient time with clients because they:
   - Lack sufficient product knowledge (as noted in Chapter 4).
   - Cannot adequately explain poor investment performance.
   - Do not delegate client-related tasks to others because they want to protect their client base or they worry about the reliability of colleagues.
   - Do not feel equipped/supported.
   - Do not know what is expected of them (due, for example, to a lack of concrete client relationship standards).
4. *Tools and technology.* Client development processes may be unclear in terms of: existing versus new clients and segments, product and service priorities, prospecting and screening. Relationship managers' existing tools may not be adequate, or are simply not being used effectively for client profiling, prompting and review.

On relationship manager tools, Booz Allen have suggested that, ideally, relationship managers should have access to the following:

- Administration of their working time:
  (a) Shared calendarising, planning and management
  (b) Search capability through data – client profiles and notes
  (c) Client profiling
  (d) Client notes – creation, storage, search and sharing
  (e) Intelligent form pre-filling

- Information processing and filtering
  - (a) Pricing and movements of financial products relevant to the client's portfolio
  - (b) New and current reviews focused around the client's interests and portfolio
  - (c) Fundamental financial data and performance
  - (d) Fund holdings ownership
  - (e) Research
- Analytical tools to view, analyse and click through portfolios
  - (a) Review true asset allocation (see through funds and other products) by type of asset, geography, industry or currency
  - (b) Top news and movements relevant to the client and their portfolio
  - (c) Financial calculations on risk, asset allocation, etc
- Alerts that prompt the relationship manager to proactively contact their clients
  - (a) New investment ideas relevant to client's risk profile and life cycle
  - (b) Market movements (stop-losses) having a major impact on client's portfolio
  - (c) Calendarised reminders (e.g., major life events)

Overall, to help solve this problem, a combination of focus groups, activity value analysis, and internal and external benchmarking has proved very effective. In doing so, it is, of course, essential to secure buy-in from the relationship managers themselves (some can be highly resistant to change). Only once the root causes of the problem have been identified will it be possible to identify 'quick wins' and devise a coordinated plan of longer-term action. It is, however, well worth the effort. The value-creation impact can be dramatic.

Within each targeted segment, time and resources should be allocated according to client attractiveness

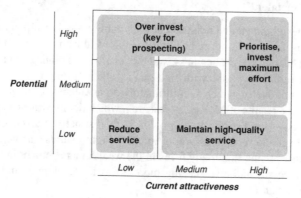

Figure 5.12   Relationship management resource allocation framework
Source: McKinsey & Company. Reproduced by permission.

The final step is to enhance the sales effectiveness of the time spent with clients. That involves relationship managers developing a deeper understanding of clients' goals and aspirations. Relationship managers, in turn, need to help clients gain a clearer perspective of their own financial needs, and suggest appropriate solutions. Account action planning, prioritisation and monitoring should be developed, with earlier and more extensive involvement from product specialists. Ahead of client meetings, relationship managers should devote time for preparation and pre-scripting. In addition, sales coaching and skills transfer within and across teams should be encouraged. One relevant success story from a relationship manager is as follows:

> I conducted pre-contact preparation for a meeting with a client prospect. In half an hour, we learned his family story, and the fact that he sold a company recently. We learned that he has the majority of his business with Bank A, with whom he is no longer satisfied, and is in the process of moving to Bank B. We were able to take his business [AuM] away from Bank B, which for the client we estimate at $25 million, plus up to $90 million from additional business with his family.

More generally, sales effectiveness needs to be reinforced and monitored using appropriate targets, incentives and performance evaluation/review. While client relationship managers are faced with the tasks of building long-term relationships and attracting new business, their performance is increasingly being appraised by various metrics. A survey by IBM Consulting Services in 2005 reveals that, 'to measure the performance of their relationship managers (in the European wealth and private banking industry)...the prevailing factor is now net new asset growth, highlighting again the industry's preoccupation with achieving growth. It is followed by revenue targets, number of new clients and profitability targets'. The survey also comments that it is surprising that few relationship managers are assessed on client satisfaction criteria, though unsatisfied clients would be expected to be associated with client, asset and revenue attrition.

The more advanced players are focusing increasingly on profit (in addition to revenue) per client as a key performance indicator. Given that the bulk of a client's cost is accounted for by the relationship manager's time, it is critical for relationship managers to keep an accurate record of the time spent with each client. That should include all meetings, phone calls and client-dedicated tasks. Other useful key performance indicators here include: number of client contacts (reactive versus proactive), sales closure rate, cross-selling rate and volume per sale.

5.1.4 The 'war for talent'

The recruitment, development and retention of high-calibre relationship managers are viewed by many as among the most important issues in the wealth management industry. Wealth management is, at heart, a people business, and the relationship managers are perceived as essential brand differentiators. A bank with high-quality client-facing staff will generate superior client experience and loyalty, which will ultimately drive enhanced growth and profitability. Figure 5.13 shows the results of McKinsey research, which demonstrates a clear link between good talent management and strong asset growth. Truly distinctive players excel at all aspects of talent management and receive disproportionately high rewards. In such an environment, therefore, it is not surprising that many firms in the wealth management industry are upgrading their hiring processes and also placing more effort in developing and training existing relationship managers and teams.

5.1.4.1 Recruitment

Finding suitably qualified personnel with the appropriate commercial banking, investment and other advisory expertise is a major industry bottleneck. Increasingly, wealth managers are requiring individuals with product skills more often found in investment banking than traditional commercial banking. Yet remuneration structures remain, in many cases, closer to those in commercial banking. Client-facing employees also require competence in many of the 'softer' areas of client management, which are difficult to find in any part of the financial

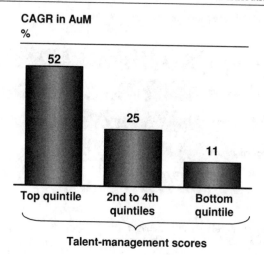

Figure 5.13   Strong talent management works
Source: McKinsey Global Asset Management Talent Survey, 2000–2001. Reproduced by permission.

services industry. That creates major challenges for the private banking industry as most firms are looking for the same kinds of high-calibre staff.

Given the clamour to recruit suitably qualified staff, considerable managerial effort is devoted to sourcing high-calibre relationship managers through various routes. The survey of European wealth managers by Mercer Oliver Wyman (2005) and other evidence suggests the following main sources:

- Competitors – individual relationship managers or team 'lift-outs'.
- Graduate schemes, i.e. the 'grow-your-own' approach (e.g. Citigroup's wealth management business actively competes against its investment bank for new MBA graduates).
- Other parts of the parent bank, such as retail, business and investment banking (combined with in-house training/re-orientation programmes).
- Financial services recruitment agencies and headhunters.
- Other sources, including the professions, other industries, diplomats and the armed forces.

The relative importance of these sources of relationship managers are illustrated in Figure 5.14.

An interesting finding of the aforementioned survey is that European wealth managers obtain around 80% of their relationship managers via hiring from outside the bank. The survey notes that (Mercer Oliver Wyman, 2005, page 27):

> . . . only 17% are trained for the job in-house. Nearly a third come from competitors – a trend that will drive up advisors' compensation as growth-fuelled industry competition mounts. Forward-thinking participants are already ramping up their in-house training capabilities to avoid the hiring crunch that will result.

Increasingly, private banks are resorting to specialist global headhunters to seek out the best talent; examples include Private Banking Search and Selection International and Sulger Buel. There is a real lack of talent in the market, and private banks are looking to fund management houses and further afield to recruit. Sadly, relationship managers are seen by many as glorified

Where do you get Relationship Managers from (approximate %)?

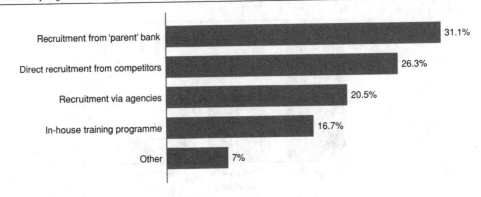

Figure 5.14   Recruiting client relationship managers
Source: Mercer Oliver Wyman (2005). Reproduced by permission.

sales people and it has not traditionally been an area that attracts the best talent. In the high-growth Asian markets there are particular difficulties in finding talent. Many of the business schools now run wealth management classes. Singapore, for instance, which is desperate to become the big wealth management centre of Asia, launched the Wealth Management Institute in 2003. Sponsored by the government and run in conjunction with the Zurich-based Swiss Banking School (which runs its own wealth managemement MBA programme), its main aim is to develop the local wealth management talent pool. In the United States, a number of universities are also adding courses in wealth management, including the Wharton School and New York University.

Another relevant issue touched on earlier relates to remuneration packages for relationship managers. As the demands of these key staff are becoming increasingly complex, the issue of appropriate remuneration packages becomes increasingly important. For example, the skill set required to sell a range of complex structured products and other alternative investment products is somewhat different to those needed to sell more traditional private banking services. Given the increasing requirement for client managers to act in a proactive and holistic investment advisory environment, a more complex skill set is required and base remuneration needs to reflect these increasing demands.

To a certain extent, base-level remuneration of client managers in recent years has increased to reflect these changes and there is a growing emphasis on fixed salary and bonus structures, which are being used to entice and incentivise a broader range of staff (relationship managers, specialists and support). Figure 5.15 illustrates the types of remuneration structures that are present in wealth management firms. For most wealth managers, remuneration schemes also take into account factors such as the degree of sales support and account type. With the aim of aligning incentives more fully, some wealth managers also explicitly take into account client retention and a range of other factors (appropriately weighted), through balanced-scorecard-type approaches.

Figure 5.15 shows that the bonuses for relationship managers are usually tied to a mix of sales and assets under management, although it should be emphasised that the weightings associated with this mix can vary among firms. It is also surprising that there appears to be little evidence of bonuses relating to value created for the bank, which perhaps would be more appropriate

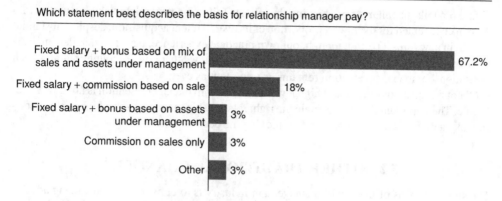

Which statement best describes the basis for relationship manager pay?

Figure 5.15   Remuneration of client relationship managers
Source: Mercer Oliver Wyman (2005). Reproduced by permission.

given the overriding strategic focus on shareholder value creation in banking. There is also little evidence that bonuses are related to measures of client satisfaction – although again, sales and increases in assets under management are probably good proxies for client satisfaction.

5.1.4.2   Development

Evidence suggests that relationship managers recruited via agencies or competitors are often slower to enhance value than those obtained via in-house recruitment, providing a strong incentive for wealth management firms to develop training and other internal recruitment mechanisms. With regard to training, one key issue is the need for a more integrated curriculum. Another issue is that there is generally little regulation overseeing wealth management professional qualifications. In the United States, for example, there are some 90 different acronyms that convey some wealth management know-how, though the best-known ones are the ChFC (chartered financial consultant), the CFP (certified financial planner) and the CFA (chartered financial analyst). Clients are confused, and there is a pressing industry need for greater standardisation here.

Some have moved to improve in-house courses. Credit Suisse, for example, has invested heavily in employee training; it has its own business school, with offices in Switzerland and Singapore. Citigroup's in-house courses cover a variety of product areas (inluding derivatives, asset allocation, alternative investments, trust and estate planning, and credit and other banking products). All private bankers are required to take at least the first level, which is repeated several times a year.

5.1.4.3   Retention

Conventional wisdom holds that clients tend to be loyal to their relationship manager, and hence that relationship manager retention and continuity is important for client and asset retention. But recent survey evidence demonstates that this link may be less clear-cut. For example, the IBM wealth management survey of 2005 noted that relationship manager departure ranked among the lowest reasons why clients changed wealth manager. Its 2003 survey found that two-thirds of banks lose less than 10% of the relevant client assets when a relationship manager leaves.

Figure 5.4 tells a similar story, showing that clients following new relationship managers into the bank accounted for the lowest proportion of its overall client acquisition, despite substantial growth in new hires. Overall, though, our own practical experience, based on detailed analysis of micro-level data at a number of wealth managers, shows that a well thought out approach to relationship manager retention remains as important as ever.

Of course, an across-the-board high level of relationship manager retention is not always desirable. The important thing is to retain the right relationship managers – the high performers – and take a more proactive approach to removing the dead wood.

5.2 OTHER TRADITIONAL CHANNELS

The strategic focus of the wealth management industry is to deliver value-enhancing advice-led sales and service via an array of different distribution channels. The other main channels include:

- Referral agents.
- Branches.
- Client reporting.

5.2.1 Referral agents

In addition to using proprietary distribution channels, most market participants develop networks of external partners to generate client referrals. There is a wide range of professional advisers that are linked in some way to HNWIs, and these can provide access to new business. These include:

- Professional firms, such as accountants, lawyers, surveyors and architects, and their associations.
- Business-oriented professionals, such as entrepreneurs, venture capitalists and investment banks.
- Product specialists, such as hedge fund advisers and insurance firms.
- Real estate companies and advisers.
- Other specialist advisers, such as art experts, equine advisers, career and business coaches, and physicians.

Traditionally, lawyers and accountants have been the main source of referral business for private banks, although in recent years there have been growing links with real estate advisers, given the higher use of property as an investment class in many clients' portfolios. Private banks that offer up-market mortgage and insurance services often have greater opportunities to develop referral programmes through a wider range of third-party advisers. Members of the third-party firms themselves also sometimes become clients. Practices differ somewhat by region. In the US, many of the largest wealth managers have well-developed arrangements with top attorneys, while in Germany, links between tax advisors and small banks are particularly well developed.

The key benefits for the wealth manager are that it can be a very cost-effective acquisition channel. The relationships with some types of third parties also provide opportunities to outsource various services, such as trust construction and tax optimisation.

In most cases, referral programmes have been developed on an ad hoc basis, given the relationship-based, specialist nature of the referrals. However, these links are becoming more formalised, with introducer agreements increasingly being used. Other key issues here include the need to ensure that the referral agent is reputable, with formal vetting procedures used by many players. Another issue is how to structure the associated incentivisation structure. Many players have begun to simplify referral-fee arrangements in order to reduce the associated administration burden; one-off up-front fees are increasingly common.

To make the most of this channel and ensure effective cooperation, wealth managers should be guided by a range of key success factors, including the need for:

- Distinctive and well-communicated value proposition.
- Strong reputation for high-quality relationship managers and products, to provide confidence that referred clients will receive a high-quality service.
- Reciprocal business referral flow.

Private banking firms are increasingly developing these links as a source of new business. They do this by promoting their brand and service offering via the usual advertising and public relations routes, sponsoring high profile up-market sporting and cultural events, professional conferences and so on. Wealth managers will continue to develop such relationships to complement proprietary channels, particularly in the light of increased competition for clients.

5.2.2 Branches

Driven by the relatively rapid growth in onshore wealth management, many players are developing branch infrastructure. Universal banks have not traditionally made the most of their branch networks to acquire and serve wealth management clients. For example, in the past, issues associated with transfer pricing and other organisational obstacles have hindered intra-group referral programmes. But, as discussed in Chapter 8, the retail client base is increasingly viewed as a strong potential source of new wealth management business. Another approach is for wealth managers to share retail branch space, in some cases using dedicated counters for affluent clients, which offer priority service. In Japan, for example, Tokyo-Mitsubishi recently opened its first members-only private banking office, designed by a prominent architect, within one of its retail branches in Tokyo.

In addition to using the branches of other parts of their parent groups to acquire and service clients, some wealth managers with enough critical mass are developing their own dedicated branch structures, often using innovative formats. Some of these branches are up-scale, high-tech-looking advice centres, with real-time market information offering investment-focused advice and a limited range of banking services. In many cases, the advisers are based not in the investment centre itself but in a separate cheaper location (e.g. on an office building floor rather than at street level).

One of the best examples is E*TRADE's flagship financial services superstore, the E*TRADE Center. Launched in New York in 2001, it is designed to offer clients financial services and educational content in a 'high-tech, high-touch experience'. Over 30 000 square feet, it provides visitors with the ability to execute financial transactions, participate in educational seminars, interact with advisors, browse through financial books, purchase items at the E*TRADE gift store and dine in the Mangia Café. The Center also contains a full-service media production studio, from which it broadcasts daily live financial news on plasma screens throughout the store. It also includes a professional trading services area with over 200 state-of-the-art PCs, a forum for affluent clients to conduct transactions and meet with advisors, and a wireless demonstration area. Going forward, E*TRADE plans to have 36 (smaller but similar) branches in the major US cities by the end of 2006. Charles Schwab has also been busy with its build out programme, and now has around 290 branches across the United States.

Following the trend of the 1990s in the US, this concept has recently been deployed by a few European players. For example, Unicredit's Xelion in Italy offers a small network of 'financial studios' in the major cities; HSBC Premier, ING and parts of Deutsche Bank also offer dedicated branches. McKinsey has suggested that, given the narrowness of the target market and the centres' relatively high costs, high-profile branches may serve more as flagships to convey an image of financial sophistication to the client base, rather than as profitable sales-growth vehicles in their own right.

While private banks (whether part of large groups or independent) typically do not have extensive branch networks, there has been a general move to reorganise branch architecture to reflect client demand and to enhance the wealth management advisory function. HSBC Private Bank is building-out its branch presence globally, with recent openings in some of the major cities in the UK and France. Coutts has also opened a number of new branches over the years, most recently in northern England; 16 of its 24 branches are now outside London. Some recent examples of other branch reorganisations are shown in Figure 5.16.

At the very top end of the market, the development of exclusive branch facilities offering a wide range of advisory services (along family office lines) is a key trend. Dealing with top-end clients requires a different branch structure than for other segments. Goldman Sachs, for example, offers a small number of elite offices in select locations such as New York, Miami, Los Angeles, San Francisco, Singapore, Zurich, Geneva and London. Northern Trust has 84 offices in 18 US States, and is in the process of refurbishing and remodelling its facilities. It claims to have offices within a 45-minute drive of approximately half of all US millionaire households.

5.2.3 Client reporting

Many wealth managers are focusing on improving the quality of their client reporting, tailoring it to clients' more compex needs across the various segments. The key trends here have been along the following lines:

- *Content.* Banks are, where necessary, providing more detailed information, including a greater emphasis on client needs, investment performance and benchmarking, portfolio analysis (such as the impact of specific investment decisions), risk assessment (including scenario analyses, simulations and value-at-risk), market developments and explanatory comment. Some players are also using statements to help boost cross-selling by, for example, raising the client's awareness of relevant products or specific offers. Some are also using the statement as a formal means of soliciting client feedback and for measuring satisfaction.
- *Personalisation.* Clients typically now have choices such as whether to receive full or summarised statements, reporting frequency (anything from transaction-by-transaction to annual), base currency and language. Higher-value clients also typically have direct access to the portfolio manager.

Bank	Branch Reorganisation
HSBC Premier	HSBC has established a number of dedicated branch services for customers belonging to its HSBC Premier mass affluent service. This serves clients with incomes greater than £70 000 (approximately € 100 000). The branches are mainly located in major cities, offer cashier services in addition to ATM and Internet channel access, meeting areas, interview rooms and a 'business focus area'.
Deutsche Bank	In 2002, Deutsche Bank reorganised its retail and private banking branch network, combining retail branches with private banking branches to create investment and finance centres. Deutsche closed 470 business and private banking branches in Germany (approximately one-third of the total 1240), replacing the remainder with a combination of self-service centres, mobile consulting units and a new genre of 'investment and finance centres'. All investment and finance centres will have retail banking facilities, while 170 will offer private banking services (and 150 business banking). Deutsche plans to roll the new centres out across Europe, creating 1300 investment and finance centres across the Continent.
JP Morgan Chase	In 2003, JP Morgan Chase opened a prototype branch to attract HNW and mass affluent clients with US$250 000 to US$10 million in assets. The up-market branch, located in Manhattan, offers amenities such as plasma TV screens, artwork, private meeting rooms, a coffee bar and a concierge service. Depending on the success of this facility J.P. Morgan is contemplating other branches in New York, New Jersey, Connecticut and Texas.
Morgan Stanley	Morgan Stanley's Private Wealth Group, which serves clients with more than US$10 million in assets, has eight dedicated offices housing a total of 150 advisors in the United States. Clients are usually referred from Morgan Stanley's affluent brokerage network, which counts over 10 000 brokers across the country.
Mellon Financial	Mellon Financial sold its network of over 300 retail branches to Citizens Financial as part of a new strategic focus on HNW customers with more than US$1 million in assets. While Mellon has been able to successfully serve HNW clients remotely without a branch network, it is now replacing the 300 retail branches with 25 private wealth centres. The main aim of the new centres is to develop client acquisition.
Merrill Lynch	Merrill Lynch employs a hybrid structure to serve UHNW clients within its Private Banking and Investment Group, which serves those with more than US$10 million in assets. Four specialist private banking offices are located in major cities, while teams located in other regions share offices with advisors that serve mass affluent and emerging affluent customers. The specialist offices have onsite experts in banking, trust and estates, restricted stocks and family office services.
Smith Barney (Citigroup)	Smith Barney Private Wealth Management (PWM), which serves clients with more than US$25 million in assets, uses retail branches to advise HNWIs. While most PWM clients are served by nominated advisors with advanced credentials, these highly qualified advisers also serve a small number of lower-value clients. In addition, their presence in the same office as advisors serving lower-value clients allows them to transfer their knowledge.

Figure 5.16 Private bank branch reorganisation
Source: Adapted from www.thevipforum.com.

- *Delivery.* The emphasis here is on more frequent and faster delivery, through a wider range of formats, particularly online but also through greater face-to-face interaction. Frequency is often varied for some types of reporting; market analysis, for example, is often despatched more frequently during times of particular stress. Transaction-level reporting is typically provided monthly, with analysis typically performed on a quarterly basis, ahead of a face-to-face meeting with the relationship manager. Statements are also becoming simpler and easier to understand, with improved layout and greater use of graphics and colour for harder-hitting communication.
- *Pricing.* Some banks have introduced fees, particularly for ad hoc and more frequent reporting. Fees for regular reports are typically included within the general account charge.

One example of the new style of client reporting is Citigroup Private Bank's Relationship Report.[3] That provides clients with online information on transaction history, asset allocation and investment performance, with various customisable reporting formats and links to Reuters news, internal and external investment research, and other information.

For UHNW clients and family offices, reporting requirements become more complex. That is because a typical UHNWI's assets tend to be in many different entities, financial institutions and geographies, and their needs are more akin to those of an institution. Above all, these clients need (a) simplified reporting of complex investment structures and (b) consolidated reporting of global wealth holdings. Various systems have been developed to assist clients in tracking and controlling their wealth. One impact of such systems is to make it easier for clients to separate their financial advice from the products they buy.

Such systems enable clients to track their entire holdings, including business and personal financial assets, real estate, art and collectables. The systems also allow clients to impose 'permission' levels. For example, heirs to a family fortune might be able to see their own accounts, but not those of their siblings; staff who manage the family's property, private jet or yacht will have access to data relevant to their specific responsibility; trustees and accountants may have access to only certain data; while the patriarch or matriarch could see every cheque above $5 000 written out of any account. The computer programs are also set up to cross-check holdings, such as whether multiple-asset managers own the same stock, bond or other investment. Examples of such systems include Northern Trust's customised Private Passport system, which provides online access to banking, trust, investment management, mutual funds and brokerage information, and enables the client to monitor compliance with her on her instructions;[4] RockIT, developed by the Rockefellar & Company family office; and the new system from Fidelity's Family Office Service Group, which is currently being piloted for launch later in 2006.

Overall, many wealth managers are therefore having to invest in improving report production processes and supporting infrastructure. Many of the issues are covered in Chapter 7.

5.3 NEW AND EMERGING CHANNELS

A range of new and emerging channels offer opportunities for wealth managers to provide clients with greater convenience and choice. Call centres, for example, are now being used to handle (largely reactive) communication with clients, particularly among the affluent client

---

[3] http://www.citibank.com/privatebank/client/index.htm.
[4] Northern Trust has also used this system as a tool to attract custody assets, many of which it has subsequently converted into AuM through targeted product offerings.

segment. In some countries, such as the UK, a significant proportion of wealth managers are using call centres as a communication channel for wealthier clients. Here we discuss two other channels: conventional online services and broadband's potential to transform advice delivery.

5.3.1   Online

As in other parts of the financial sector, the private banking industry has embraced the technological revolution. That has had two main impacts on the business. First, it has contributed to a reduction in the costs associated with the management of information (collection, storage, processing and transmission) by replacing paper-based and labour-intensive methods with automated processes. Second, it has created new delivery channels, with further opportunities to network with third parties. It has also accelerated competition and raised transparency, making it easier for clients to compare products and services within and across providers.

In theory, the embrace of new customer-facing technologies should enable private banks to develop multichannel delivery systems, where wealth management services can be offered more effectively via the branch, telephone, mail, Internet and through third-party providers (such as lawyers, accountants, independent financial advisors and so on). That has led some commentators to talk about the possibility of the development of the 'network bank', whereby multichannel delivery systems are integrated with back-office and middle-office systems, with the ultimate objective of providing lower-cost and higher-quality client service.

But relative to their retail banking counterparts, private banks have been relatively slow to develop online services. Much of this reflects clients' preference for face-to-face contact to discuss the bulk of their wealth management business and also the fear of private banks that any attempt to commoditise their services will lead to a decline in brand image. Also, whereas basic transactions (such as payments) can be conducted online, services that are relatively complex and require a substantial advisory input are simply not particularly suited to the conventional Internet.

Most private banks have websites that provide information relating to their products and services. But very few include information on pricing and past investment performance (at least to prospective clients). Although private banks offer various online transaction services, these are more likely to be offered by other arms of the parent bank than by the private bank itself. Hence, overall, private banks still primarily use the Internet as a device to raise awareness of their services and to inform prospective clients.

While the bulk of clients do not wish to conduct *all* their wealth management business online, most will be familiar with the Internet, value the convenience and will expect the private bank to provide information and other basic services online. That is particularly true of the many HNW clients who have fast-paced, mobile lifestyles. More generally, private clients are quite likely to be familiar with conventional online retail financial services, including payments, transfers between accounts, purchase of insurance, mortgages and basic savings products.

Various private banks offer services beyond 'informational' websites, but the extent to which transactions can be conducted online is still relatively limited. Such services include:

- Information on financial markets, news, analyst reports and data feeds, although these types of services are not always restricted to private banking clients.

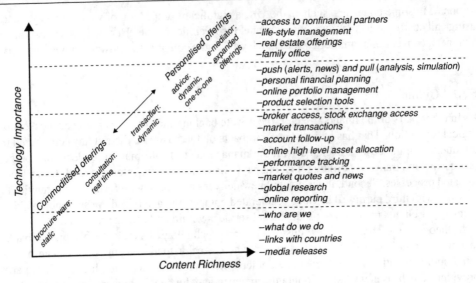

-access to nonfinancial partners
-life-style management
-real estate offerings
-family office

-push (alerts, news) and pull (analysis, simulation)
-personal financial planning
-online portfolio management
-product selection tools

-broker access, stock exchange access
-market transactions
-account follow-up
-online high level asset allocation
-performance tracking

-market quotes and news
-global research
-online reporting

-who are we
-what do we do
-links with countries
-media releases

Content Richness

Figure 5.17   e-Private banking website maturity
Source: Magrini and Thomas (2001). Reproduced by permission of PricewaterhouseCoopers.

- Online account statements and online reporting for clients' investment portfolios (discussed above).
- Online product/service application forms and detailed product information.
- Online broking and securities transactions.
- Fund supermarket/fund comparison services and associated analytics.

While banks such as UBS, Citigroup Private Bank and HSBC probably have the most developed online private banking services, no bank, as far as we are aware, currently offers a broad wealth management service using the online channel alone. Chapter 6 discusses the failure of several online wealth management ventures. Clients currently prefer face-to-face (or telephone) contact with a dedicated relationship manager for most transactions.

Figure 5.17 provides an illustration of the expected life-cycle of a private bank's website. The industry still appears to be providing 'commoditised offerings' and has not really evolved to the 'personalised offerings' stage.

Traditionally, private banking emphasises a deep personal relationship with the client by making available the full range of financial products through the relationship manager alone. This approach aims to highlight the importance of service and advice, brand quality and, above all, trust. Advice is growing in importance, driven, in part, by the sheer breadth of financial products available. Provision of advice traditionally requires face-to-face contact, however, and is therefore not suited to delivery via conventional narrowband Internet alone.

5.3.2   Broadband and beyond

Advances in broadband technology, including greater and more stable bandwidth availability, could make online advice delivery much more appealing. Remote advice has the potential to address two fundamental problems in selling advice-based financial products. For the wealth manager, the opportunity is to strip out some of the high costs of client prospecting and to improve radically the effectiveness of advice delivery. For clients, many of whom mistrust heavy-handed advisors and have turned to the Internet for self-help, remote advice is a welcome balance of personal but lower-pressure relationships. Meetings that used to take place in person could move online, supported by sophisticated advice algorithms and instant access to specialists. In effect, broadband could allow personal financial services currently available only at the top end of the market to be offered more cost effectively to the affluent as well.

Remote advice scenarios vary. Imagine clients watching a financial programme on interactive television. One could use the remote control to get information on the products mentioned or to ask to discuss them with an on-screen advisor. Another might schedule a regular remote meeting with an on-screen advisor, via a PC video link, to review the progress of a personal financial plan. A third might download a video brochure of the latest stock market outlook and then check the conclusions with an on-screen industry expert. Broadband networks can deliver advice in this way because of their capacity and their rapid, secure data transfer, enabling them to offer video on demand, high-speed Internet access and videoconferencing on a PC or mobile device.

The success of these models rests heavily on whether clients feel comfortable receiving advice in this way. Some consumers will be attracted by the convenience and tailoring of remote advice. However, unsurprisingly, few will feel they could establish a relationship with a provider through remote channels alone.

By exploiting broadband, wealth managers could benefit in two ways:

1. *Deliver better-quality advice.* Gathering advisors in one place makes it easier to ensure that advice delivery is consistent and conforms to standards. Broadband will make it feasible to deploy standard algorithms and decision trees to support clients' financial decisions and to give them online access to appropriate experts.
2. *Win productivity gains.* The time an advisor spends interacting with clients could increase dramatically. Travel costs will decline and meetings could become shorter, because clients will have already provided much of the information they currently pass on in face-to-face meetings. In addition, tools for working out a client's options, such as portfolio calculators and scenario software, will be available for the advisor and client to use together. Factor in savings in overhead expenses such as recruitment, training and supervision, and the direct variable costs of delivering advice could fall by as much as 60%–90%. There will be additional fixed costs, most notably in brand building, content provision and technology infrastructure. But even if adoption levels are no more than modest, the economics of client interaction could be transformed.

By changing the industry cost curve for distribution, broadband will accelerate the recent trend towards unbundling advice from transactions and thereby change the competitive landscape. The stuff of James Bond? A broadband reality in wealth management is probably closer than you think. Experimentation by some private banking players is already under way.

5.4   MULTICHANNEL MANAGEMENT

Serving clients through multiple channels is a reality. Going forward, wealth managers will need to offer whatever access channel is demanded by their clients, be that face-to-face or remote. Clients will also expect a consistent experience. McKinsey research shows that 57% of European mass affluent clients are already using three or more channels. Wealth managers, particularly those targeting mass affluent clients, must therefore start to master multichannel management to improve their economic position and generate significant value.

That means cutting costs in channels where possible and exploiting income generation opportunities. Intelligent multichannel management builds on monitoring and steering client behaviour, makes the best use of channels and provides the right incentives for the frontline to work towards a common goal. Although the hype of online channels has subsided, more and more clients will be using these and other direct channels – at least in a supporting role.

A multichannel strategy requires, on the one hand, a thorough understanding of current and future client behaviour in each of the bank's segments and, on the other, comprehensive knowledge of the economics and levers of multichannel management. As a starting point, banks must clarify the role that each channel will play and hence the level of integration required. The new multichannel strategy will require banks to redefine their management concept, which is likely to entail organisational changes and often a redesign of their major sales and service processes. IT architecture also needs to be designed to provide clients with a transparent, consistent interface that contains the same information at any one time.

6

Players

If you see a Swiss banker jump out of a window, jump after him. There's bound to be money in it.
Voltaire (1694–1778)

Chapter 1 provided a brief overview of the wealth management competitor landscape. It explained that there is a broad range of players and that the industry is extremely fragmented.

The objective of this chapter is to add more colour and discuss some of the recent key trends. In particular, the aim is to:

- Provide more detail on the main types of players currently operating in the industry and some of their more interesting recent strategic initiatives.
- Examine recent business system upheaval within the industry in three main areas:
  (a) Business system disaggregation – unbundling and rebundling by players across the value chain.
  (b) Business model convergence.
  (c) Divestment of non-core businesses.
- Describe the what, why and how of ongoing consolidation within the industry.

6.1 TYPES OF PLAYERS

By way of introduction, Table 6.1 provides a snapshot of the latest performance metrics across a range of private banks. (The Addendum to this chapter contains 5-year runs of cost-income ratios, revenue margins and net new money, as well as current valuation data.) Key points to note include:

- The largest Swiss players have performed strongly, as has EFG International, a small Swiss-based private banking specialist (see Box 6.1 below).
- The other large universal banks tend to have relatively high cost–income ratios, but that is offset to some extent by higher AuM growth or higher revenue margins.
- Julius Baer has continued to struggle across the board.

6.1.1 Private banks

As noted in Chapter 1, private banks come in a variety of shapes and sizes. They include: mid-sized listed groups such as Julius Baer and Sarasin; hundreds of privately owned companies such as Union Bancaire Privée; family-owned banks such as Sal. Oppenheim, Les Fils Dreyfus, B. Metzler and B. Carl Spängler; and independent private banking subsidiaries of universal banks such as Coutts (owned by Royal Bank of Scotland). They also include the Swiss private bankers, which industry purists, such as the Swiss Private Bankers Association, argue are the only true private banks. These it defines as:

> Banks whose legal status is one of sole ownership, registered partnership, limited partnership or limited partnership with shares. The specific status of private banker is justified by the presence within the bank of at least one partner with unlimited liability for the bank's commitments.

Table 6.1 Private banks: comparison of operating metrics (1H 2005) (local currency in millions, unless otherwise stated)

	HSBC	Citigroup	UBS	CSPB	Deutsche Bank	Société Générale	ABN AMRO	Julius Baer	Vontobel	EFG Intl.
AuM (local currency in billions)	183	98	890	602	118	55	125	60	20	23
AuM (SFr in billions)	235	126	890	602	183	85	194	60	20	23
Asset growth 1H 2005	3%	−3%	14%	12%	11%	14%	9%	−2%	9%	15%
o/w net new money	5%	na	4%	4%	4%	7%	na	−10%	0%	6%
Revenue (local currency in millions)	1,163	957	4,236	3,722	na	256	581	290	100	141
Revenue (SFr m)	1,401	1,152	4,236	3,772	na	396	898	290	100	141
As % group revenues	4%	2%	17%	12%	na	3%	5%	47%	35%	100%
Gross margin (%)	1.29%	1.92%	1.02%	1.30%	na	0.99%	0.97%	0.96%	1.03%	1.29%
Cost-income ratio (%)	62.3%	70.3%	55.5%	57.6%	na	68.8%	70.6%	73.3%	62.8%	57.2%
Number of CROs	na	477	3,992	2,600	na	na	na	na	na	180
Total employees	na	na	10,901	12,722	3,000	na	4,003	824	358	636
Number of clients	na	26,000	688,000	600,000	70,000	na	na	na	na	16,000
AuM per CRO (SFr m)	na	263	223	232	na	na	na	na	na	130
Annualised revenue per CRO (SFr m)	na	4.8	2.2	2.9	na	na	na	na	na	1.7
AuM per client (SFr m)	na	4.8	1.3	1.0	na	na	na	na	na	1.5
Clients per CRO	na	55	172	231	na	na	na	na	na	89
Non-CRO employees per CRO	na	na	1.7	3.9	na	na	na	na	na	2.5

Notes: EFG International excludes impact of four acquisitions announced but not yet completed as at 30 June 2005 (SFr 10.7bn of AuM). EFG International AuM excludes loans; UBS client data is CSFB estimate; CSPB CRO data is as at end 2004; Deutsche Bank AuM data excludes PCS, but employee and client data includes PCS; Citigroup AuM data relates to client business volumes, excluding custody and investment finance; Citigroup client data relates to number of families; Julius Baer and Vontobel total employees include employees allocated from corporate centre.

Source: Company data; CSFB research. Reproduced by permission.

There are now 17 Swiss Private Bankers firms, down from 67 at the end of World War II, driven by mergers among them and by conversions to joint stock companies. Most can look back on around 200 years' worth of history.

Among the most successful is Pictet, which is run by the direct descendents of the founding family. Its partnership status limits the rate at which it can grow, but in terms of AuM and AuC, it ranks just outside the global top 10 wealth managers – and is four times bigger than it was 20 years ago. It is currently consolidating and developing its onshore private banking presence, particularly in Eastern Europe, the Middle East and Asia. In addition to private banking, it has, over the years, extended its footprint into three related business lines: institutional asset management, global custody and family office.

At the smaller end of the Swiss Private Bankers spectrum, successful players tend to focus on specific product or client-segment niches. For example, Wegelin & Company, founded in 1741 (Switzerland's oldest surviving bank), has carved out a successful niche in structured products.

Sticking with partnerships, another example of a private banking dynasty is the UK's C. Hoare & Co. Founded in 1672, and continuously owned and run by the Hoare family for 11 generations, it is one of the UK's oldest private banks.[1] Prestige is not the word. Would-be clients need recommendations from at least two existing ones before the bank will consider taking them on; this explains why the bank was recently described as 'the bank that likes to say maybe'.[2] Its core business is traditional banking, discretionary asset management, tax planning, trusts and, since 2003, multimanager investments (leveraging relationships with Northern Trust, Russell and SEI). The bank prides itself on meticulous service: it even keeps a guest room on the top floor of its Fleet Street office, which clients are welcome to make use of. Clients are mainly drawn from the aristocracy, landed gentry, expatriates and the legal profession. The bank is rumoured to be doubling in size every five years, constrained mainly by the size of its capital base.

One of the more innovative business models among the private banks is that of EFG International, which has recently come to prominence on the back of its recent IPO and its stellar financial performance (see Box 6.1). Another example is New York Private Bank & Trust, which is being built from scratch. The owner is the real estate baron Howard P. Milstein, and the basic idea is that no one knows millionaires better than a fellow millionaire: 'we understand the needs of wealthy families because we are one'. The bank will focus on New York City area clients with more than $50 million in investible assets.

6.1.2   Universal banks

The universal banks represent another broad group of wealth management players. Table 6.1 above included data on the contribution of wealth management to group revenue. Figure 6.2 shows the contributions to group pre-tax profits, which are generally larger. Credit Suisse and UBS stand out as deriving the highest shares (around one-third) of their group profits from wealth management. For many players, the shares languish at 3%–5%, which can mean that the wealth business does not always get the senior management attention (and hence the resource quantity and quality) it deserves.

---

[1] The oldest surviving private bank is Child & Co., which has goldsmith origins that can be traced back to 1584. It was acquired in 1924 by Glyn Mills, which was in turn acquired by Royal Bank of Scotland in 1939.
[2] *The Times*, 22 October 2005.

Box 6.1   EFG International

EFG International (EFG) is a global 'pure-play' private bank, with an innovative, franchise-like business model. Founded in Zurich in 1995, EFG is unique in the industry in that its relationship managers (which it calls 'customer relationship officers', CROs) – not the client, not the brand, not the product and not the location of the booking centre – are at the very heart of the organisation and its business strategy.

Decentralised CRO model

The basic idea is that, in private banking, the best way to look after the client is to look after the CRO. Some have gone as far as to say that CROs are, in a sense, effectively the real client base of EFG. In mid-2005, it had 226 CROs,[3] with an average experience of 20 years in private banking. Indeed, an offer to work at EFG is typically regarded as the pinnacle of a CRO's career.

The CROs are not subject to client account size or any form of segmentation, and are given flexibility to tailor offerings, pricing (subject to bank-determined caps) and conditions to their clients. Each CRO runs his or her own profit centre: EFG effectively comprises around 150 'micro companies', each with up to four people (CROs and support staff). CROs have a global mandate and can book assets in any of EFG's 12 booking centres, so the conventional onshore/offshore divide is irrelevant for EFG. Hierarchy is kept to a minimum, and management and CROs own 25% of the bank's equity. EFG's lack of bureaucracy means that CROs are able to spend a high proportion of their time with clients.

The CRO is not product driven. EFG offers genuine open product architecture,[4] with only 7% of clients' assets invested in its own funds, compared with 19% at UBS, for example. In addition, only around 5% of AuM are under a discretionary mandate. EFG does not encourage discretionary mandates because of the associated risks to the client relationship when markets fall.

The success of the bank is linked to its ability to ramp up the number of CROs, since they are the key drivers of asset growth (and margins tend to be quite stable). EFG's approach to CRO recruitment is that all new hires must be known to management or to existing CROs. Recruitment specialists are rarely, if ever, used. CROs join individually or in teams. They come from all the major names in the industry, including: Coutts, Citigroup, HSBC, Deutsche Bank, Credit Suisse and UBS. Some are recruited into existing EFG offices; others are recruited to expand the network into new geographies. It plans to grow to around 500 CROs in the medium term.

The goal for each CRO is to bring/win/grow assets (including lending) by CHF 30 million per year, with a target gross margin of 110 bps. By focusing on overall AuM production, looking after the performance of existing clients' assets is as important as winning net new money. CROs are paid a fixed salary plus a fixed 15%–20% of his or her net profit – not revenue – contribution.[5] That is defined as revenue less salary less directly attributable variable costs (e.g. travel, entertainment, office space, assistants, etc.) less client transaction costs (CHF 100 per transaction, which is high but helps charge out some

---

[3] Including 46 newcomers from announced acquisitions during 2005.
[4] Some have argued that EFG's February 2006 acquisition of Capital Management Advisors, a fund-of-hedge-fund manager, may compromise its independence here.
[5] Clariden (owned by Credit Suisse) is, we believe, the only other private bank that uses a similar renumeration scheme.

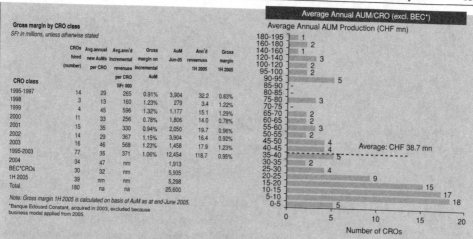

Gross margin by CRO class

SFr in millions, unless otherwise stated

CRO class	CROs hired (number)	Avg.annual new AuMs per CRO	Avg.ann'd incremental revenues per CRO (SFr 000)	Gross margin on incremental AuM	AuM Jun-05	Ann'd revenues 1H 2005	Gross margin 1H 2005
1995-1997	14	29	265	0.91%	3,904	32.2	0.83%
1998	3	13	160	1.23%	279	3.4	1.22%
1999	4	45	596	1.32%	1,177	15.1	1.29%
2000	11	33	256	0.78%	1,806	14.0	0.78%
2001	15	35	330	0.94%	2,050	19.7	0.96%
2002	14	29	367	1.15%	3,904	16.4	0.92%
2003	16	46	568	1.23%	1,458	17.9	1.23%
1995-2003	77	35	371	1.06%	12,454	118.7	0.95%
2004	34	47	nm		1,913		
BEC*CROs	30	32	nm		5,935		
1H 2005	39	nm	nm		5,298		
Total	180	na	na		25,600		

Note: Gross margin 1H 2005 is calculated on basis of AuM as at end-June 2005.
*Banque Edouard Constant, acquired in 2003, excluded because business model applied from 2005.

Figure 6.1 CRO asset production
Source: EFG; CSFB (2005); Fox-Pitt, Kelton (2005). Reproduced by permission.

of the overhead). It is this profit-sharing system that aligns the interests of shareholders, the CROs and the clients.

As Figure 6.1 shows, with the exception of the class of 1998, all CRO classes have, on average, managed to beat the annual CHF 30 million AuM production target. But there is substantial variation in performance at the individual CRO level. The bar chart shows that a few 'heavy hitters' have generated up to CHF 195 million in annual AuM production. Still, the classes of 2003 and 2004 have significantly exceeded the target, which is a sign perhaps that, with its growing reputation, EFG can hire more productive CROs and increase its share of wallet.

The performance on the gross margin target of 110 bps has been more mixed across the CRO classes. The class of 1999 has the highest margin on their incremental AuM production from 1999 to 2005 (132 bps).

EFG has a large degree of flexibility to improve the profitability of underperforming CROs. In particular, it can reduce the CRO's salary expense and/or bonus payout. If, for example, the CRO has not broken even for an entire year by the end of year three, the CRO's salary is adjusted to break even. That also enables the bank to avoid firing CROs, which is important given the relatively small and reputation-based nature of the private banking market.

The bank also has incentives in place for CROs to manage their retirement with minimal loss to the group. First, a retiring CRO has the opportunity to choose a successor. Second, for the three years following retirement, bonuses on the legacy stock of AuM are fully paid to the retiree, provided that their revenue contribution does not decline. During those years, the successor is paid on incremental net contribution, inheriting the full contribution after three years.

Other distinguishing features

Four other key factors differentiate EFG International from other Swiss private banks:

1. *Exclusive focus on private banking.* EFG has refrained from expanding into areas such as brokerage or corporate finance, unlike many of its Swiss competitors such as Julius Baer, Sarasin and Vontobel. Risk is kept low, with no proprietary trading.

2. *Global orientation.* Following the completion of its recently announced acquisitions, EFG will have 33 offices and 12 booking centres worldwide. It targets clients worldwide and, as at mid-2005, high-growth Asia is its second-largest market (61 CROs) after Switzerland (68 CROs).
3. *Fully integrated, global operating platform.* EFG's role is to provide common infrastructure for the CROs, using a 'hub-and-spoke' model. Processing, brand awareness, legal, accounting and compliance are all centralised. Its integrated IT platform (based in Geneva), together with strong IT project management, has contributed to EFG's very low non-compensation cost–income ratio of 16%, which will help with scaleability. Also, the IT platform's flexibility has helped EFG to integrate acquired businesses efficiently.
4. *Slick, 'industrialised' M&A execution.* Globally, EFG aims to close several small bolt-on acquisitions a year, including financial advisory firms, mid-sized private banks and product specialists. On acquisition targets, its key principles include: (a) knowledge of the target business beforehand, (b) strong development potential and (c) quality individuals that are known to EFG. In terms of financial discipline, it refuses earnings-dilutive transactions, does not attach a value to the target's brand or IT infrastructure or to revenue synergies, and emphasises earn-out schemes.[6] Integration, using a dedicated in-house team, typically takes around 3–4 months.

Impact

EFG's business model has had considerable success to date. Its AuM grew by 15.9% to CHF 25.6 billion ($19.5 billion) in the first half of 2005, and EFG is now believed to be the sixth-largest private bank in Switzerland. Over the period 2000–2004, while most Swiss banks were struggling, EFG was able to increase AuM by 45% a year on average and its pre-tax profits by 65% a year (albeit partly driven by inorganic growth). In addition, it has yet to lose a single profitable CRO from its recruits.

Looking ahead, as EFG absorbs more staff and AuM, a key issue for management will be whether to become more bureaucratic. One suggestion is to spin off successful regions in order to crystallise their value and encourage independence.

For universal banks, the bulk of the wealth management value-creation opportunity lies in their existing book of business – in particular, their retail- and business-banking franchises. As competition has increased in recent years, they have increasingly looked at ways of maximising intragroup synergies by, for example, dissolving operational silos and providing incentives for the various business units to work together (see Chapter 8).

UBS was a first-mover here and that, together with an aggressive push onshore (organically and via a series of small 'bolt-on' acquisitions – see Chapter 9), has given it critical mass and helped it accelerate away from the pack. It is now the industry's clear leader, with particularly impressive net new money growth, given its size. To put that into perspective, in 2004 it attracted CHF 89 billion, which is a full 46% more than Julius Baer's entire private banking AuM. It is easy to forget that just five years before, UBS was being viewed skeptically by the market, having suffered net outflows of AuM following a difficult merger with Swiss Banking Corporation.[7]

---

[6] Deferred consideration linked directly to future net profit.
[7] Some remember a notorious e-mail attachment that circulated around the investment community. It featured the replica of the poster of 'Saving Private Ryan' with the picture of the then CEO, Marcel Ospel, substituted for Tom Hanks, and the movie renamed 'Saving Private Banking'.

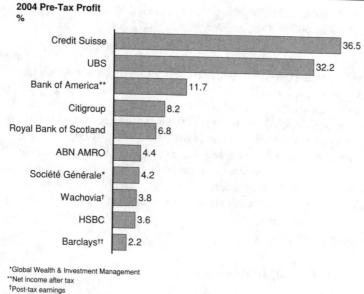

2004 Pre-Tax Profit
%

Credit Suisse	36.5
UBS	32.2
Bank of America**	11.7
Citigroup	8.2
Royal Bank of Scotland	6.8
ABN AMRO	4.4
Société Générale*	4.2
Wachovia†	3.8
HSBC	3.6
Barclays††	2.2

*Global Wealth & Investment Management
**Net income after tax
†Post-tax earnings
††Private Clients

Figure 6.2   Wealth management contribution to universal bank profits
Source: Annual reports; author's analysis.

Box 6.2   High-profile retrenchments

A number of the online-oriented wealth management ventures that were launched amid much fanfare towards the end of the dot-com boom have retrenched. Many are no longer with us. Here are three examples.

Lloyds TSB's 'Create'

In February 2001, Lloyds TSB announced Create, a new UK wealth management business targeting individuals with either GBP 100 000 in liquid assets or GBP 60 000 in annual income. It offered three main services: (a) an 'all-in-one wealth management account', offering account aggregation, loan interest offset and access to funds from 20 providers; (b) access to Goldman Sachs' PrimeAccess global equity brokerage platform, offering equities trading, settlement, custody and research access; and (c) advice on investments under four categories:

- 'Create Self', which allowed a 'do-it-yourself' approach.
- 'Create Portfolio', a fund-of-funds service for clients requiring straightforward financial management without in-depth personal advice.
- 'Create Partner', which gave the client access to a relationship manager.
- 'Create Private', offering similar services to that of a traditional private bank.

The Internet was to be the dominant channel, and it was originally planned, like so many similar ventures at the time, to expand from the UK into Continental Europe. It had set a target of 250 000 clients by the end of 2002, from a UK mass affluent population which it estimated at 4 million. The objective was to double Lloyds TSB's wealth management profitability to GBP 600 million by 2005.

It finally launched in October 2001. However, it quickly suffered senior management defections amid talk of disagreements over strategic direction. It was closed in April 2002, after reportedly gaining only a few hundred clients. Lloyds TSB reasoned that 'the strategy of Create is equity-based, but the whole equity market situation changed late last year'.

The original plan was to absorb Lloyds TSB's existing private bank into the operation. Instead, the bank said it would focus its wealth management effort on the 40 000 clients in its existing private bank, who held around GBP 11 billion in AuM.

Overall, the dominant factor here was the equity market downturn, which is arguably when clients need good investment advice the most. By relying on the Internet as the main channel, the venture was unable to meet that need adequately. Also, given the conventional skill base of a retail bank and clients' (rational or otherwise) fragmentation of assets across providers, another issue was whether affluent clients really value their high-street bank as a financial one-stop shop.

Merrill Lynch–HSBC (MLHSBC)

In the first quarter of 2000, HSBC and Merrill Lynch committed $1 billion of capital over 5 years to a new 50:50 global online wealth management joint venture. The idea was to marry Merrill Lynch's fund management and research expertise with HSBC's mass affluent client base. At one stage, some thought that the initiative could have been the prelude to a full-blown merger between the two financial services giants.

It targeted self-directed mass affluent clients, with a minimum investment of around $100 000 (though the account minimum was subsequently reduced to as low as GBP 10 000 in the UK). $100 million was earmarked to back its launch in late 2000 in Australia and Canada, and in the UK in May 2001. Germany and Japan were the next countries on the list.

The service itself offered integrated banking and investment, including multicurrency bank accounts, online equity and ETF broking, funds and investment research. In the UK, there was a quarterly GBP 18 portfolio fee, though that was later eliminated.

But first came the announcement, in November 2001, that the planned expansion to Germany and Japan was being abandoned. Then, in May 2002, Merrill Lynch pulled out of the venture altogether. MLHSBC attracted fewer than 4 000 clients in the UK and, in the end, the entity was absorbed within the HSBC group.

Again, the reasoning was the deterioration in stock market conditions that had fundamentally changed the logic of the original strategy. MLHSBC had also overemphasised the size of the self-directed investor market in the UK and elsewhere, and the willingness of clients to rely primarily on the Internet for wealth management. It had also been insufficiently tailored to local markets.

myCFO

myCFO.com launched in Silicon Valley in May 1999. Backed by Netscape founder Jim Clark, Northern Trust and venture capitalists Kleiner Perkins, it was a one-stop advisory firm, catering to the local overnight self-made UHNWIs with net worth ranging from $10 million to $2 billion. Selling no products of its own, myCFO had a pure fee-based business model.

It was essentially an updated and technologically enhanced version of the family office. myCFO was a pioneer in leveraging the Internet in wealth management, offering proprietary web-based expense management and accounting applications, together with account and asset aggregation (including wine and art investments). It did, however, subsequently open physical offices.

In terms of client segments, its minimim investment was $10 million, though its median account size was $60 million in 2001. Half to three-quarters of its clients were said to have sourced their wealth from technology or Internet firms. Its original plan was to extend the offering to HNWIs with $1 million–10 million in net worth, and then to the mass affluent.

But needless to say, the bursting of the dot-com bubble took a particularly heavy toll on myCFO. Its current Chaiman noted that 'we had clients worth $1 billion, but then they woke up and had nothing left – and they left, or we asked them to leave'. By 2003, its number of clients had fallen to 200, from a peak of around 360 in 2001.

In addition, one product that myCFO is reported to have been involved with is tax shelters – an area that grew rapidly during the 1990s in the US. One disgruntled client signed up to a scheme that is reported to have left him owing millions of dollars following a US government crackdown on tax cheats. Shortly after this shelter began to fall apart, in November 2002, most of myCFO was sold off to Bank of Montreal's Harris Bank. One piece of myCFO that the bank did not touch is the entity that handled tax shelters, which is currently being liquidated.

The name lives on (albeit now without the '.com'), as Harris myCFO. But it is a shadow of its former self. Since being acquired, it has deliberately reduced its number of clients, transferring lower-value clients to the group's private bank; at the end of 2004, it had 156 clients and $29 billion under advisement.[8] It still offers comprehensive family office services (its average account size is a whopping $186 million and minimum investment $25 million) but, as you would expect, it is now less Internet oriented – in terms of client base and channels, with many more relationship managers ('client directors') and more offices. Indeed, its current President has said that 'comprehensive family office' is what the 'CFO' in the company's name actually stands for. Management are reported to expect it to be profitable in 2006.

---

[8] *Source*: 'Multifamily Offices', Special Report, Bloomberg Wealth Manager, September 2005.

6.1.3 Financial advisers

In Europe in particular, the financial adviser network – whether independent or tied to an institution – has shown itself to be a highly effective vehicle for serving the financial planning and investment needs of the affluent client segment. Almost three-quarters of Europe's major retail banks now own or have a special distribution agreement with a financial advisor network.

A good example is Banca Fideuram. Owned by Sanpaolo IMI, it is one of Italy's largest (4 300 financial advisers and €177 million pre-tax profit in 2004), targeting affluent and HNW clients (accounting for 21% and 51% of its AuM respectively). One of its key success factors has been its ability to attract and retain strong advisers, who are among the most qualified in the Italian market. Its recruiting model consists mainly of enticing traditional banking employees to a more profitable financial advisor career.

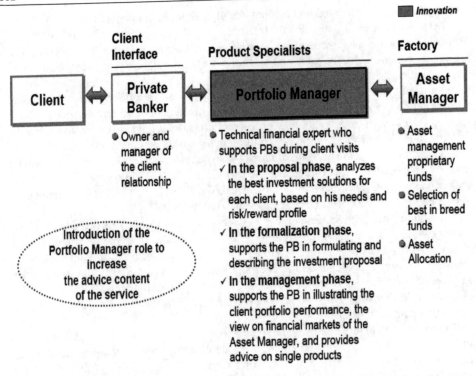

Figure 6.3 Financial adviser innovation and specialisation – Fideuram example
Source: Banca Fideuram.

Going forward, Fideuram's 2005–2007 business plan outlined a more specialist approach towards HNW clients. In particular, it plans to introduce a new product specialist role to support the private banker (Figure 6.3). It also plans to introduce a limited number of HNW offices and to recruit 1000 private bankers over the next three years, mainly from local private banks. Its aspiration is to become 'the reference private bank in Italy for HNW clients'.

6.1.4   Investment banks

Investment banks have become large wealth managers in their own right, particularly in the US. According to Barron's US wealth manager rankings 2005, Goldman Sachs is number 9 (with AuM estimated at $130 billion), JP Morgan number 14 and Lehman Brothers/Neuberger Berman number 15.

Invesment banks are increasingly recognising the benefits of (U)HNWI clients. For example, a wealth management business enables investment banks to:

1. Leverage their product manufacturing/structuring and risk management capabilities (which can also be white labelled for other wealth managers).
2. Access a pool of readily available liquidity for new issues and other deals.
3. Retain investment banking clients who are liquidating or restructuring their businesses.

4. Offer add-on services to existing clients, e.g. HNW capital introduction to hedge fund clients in the investment bank's prime brokerage and tax planning for investment banking clients.

To help develop wealth management businesses, investment banks have been using various approaches. For those players that are part of larger groups, many have been reorganising so that the wealth management business is integrated with the investment bank to a greater extent. Barclays Capital is a recent example. These types of reorganisation need to be handled sensitively to ensure they deliver the desired benefits (see Chapter 8).

Other players have been using acquisitions to add product capability, which can then be leveraged through their existing HNW distribution networks. An example of this is Goldman Sachs' 2003 acquisition of Ayco, a financial consultant that offers fee-based financial planning services to executives at US companies. Its advisers were able to access the investment bank's resources and Goldman's wealth managers were able to offer Ayco's portfolio of services to their existing clients.

Another inorganic approach is Lehman Brothers' acquisition of an HNW-oriented asset manager, Neuberger Berman, in 2003. The motivation here was to acquire a wealth management capability and an existing HNW client base into which a range of investment banking products could be sold.

Most recently, investment banks have started to take ownership stakes in hedge funds. For example, in September 2004, JP Morgan acquired a majority stake in Highbridge Capital, an $8 billion hedge fund. That will provide JP Morgan's existing HNW clients with ready access to Highbridge's range of high-performing funds. In April 2005, Lehman Brothers acquired 20% of Ospraie Management, a hedge fund focused on commodities and basic industries.

6.1.5 Family offices

Family offices are particularly well developed in the US, but much less so in Europe. Hard data are difficult to find, but one recent estimate suggested there are around 4 000 family offices in the US, and perhaps 500 in Europe. The difficulty arises because there are different family office models and no common definition within each. The models include:

- *Single-family office*, invented by John D. Rockefeller in 1882.
- *Multifamily office*. These started to emerge in the mid-1970s, driven by single-family offices seeking economies of scale, either by opening their doors to new clients (e.g. Bessemer Trust in 1974) or through mergers of single-family offices (e.g. Sentinel Trust, which was the product of a merger between the Fruehauf and Flowers single family offices). The multifamily office clearly appeals to clients who cannot justify having a single family office (estimated to require at least $100 million).
- *Multiclient family office*, or *private investment office*. These are designed to overcome some of the potential problems with multifamily offices, such as whether the original needs of the office meet those of new clients. The private investment office avoids this issue by having no attachment to a specific family. Examples include Lord North Street, Unigestion and Heritage Bank & Trust. Many of these are, in effect, small private banks.

Many of the large private banks have recently been setting up dedicated multifamily offices of their own. Indeed, all of the players ranked in the 'best provider of family office services' section of the *Euromoney* 'Private Banking Survey' were large private banks (headed by UBS,

Pictet and JP Morgan). That reflects the deliberately low profile of the independent family offices, and probably the hefty marketing effort of the large banks. Family offices can therefore be thought of as having 'product', as well as player, channel and client-segment characteristics.

Another trend is for some of the US family offices to expand into Europe. An example is Bessemer Trust's investment in Europe's Stanhope Capital in 2004. As these organisations expand, a key challenge for them (as for most wealth managers) is the need to maintain high levels of service and intimacy. It is rare for multifamily offices to serve more than around 12 families.

Family offices can represent attractive acquisition opportunities for private banks. Recent examples include UBS's acquisition of Germany's Sauerborn Trust in November 2004, Deutsche Bank's acquisition of Wilhelm von Finck in January 2005, and Standard Chartered's acquisition of a 20% stake in Fleming Family & Partners in December 2005.

The Bloomberg Wealth Manager US multifamily offices survey 2005 found that the median multigenerational family assets is $650 million. But it also noted that some of the multifamily offices have minimum assets as low as a few million dollars.

Bank consolidation, perceived conflicts of interest, the relentless product marketing push, less personalisation and more intense competition among providers have left many wealthy individuals feeling that their interests no longer always come first, particularly at the larger private banks. These factors are attracting more clients to small traditional banks and family offices.

One interesting recent development is that family office offshoots are starting to emerge. Some of the larger clients are choosing to take matters into their own hands – side-stepping wealth managers altogether – assisted, in some cases, by high-end 'investment clubs' such as UK-based Pi Capital and by new peer networks (see Box 6.3).

Box 6.3   Peer networks

Wealthy individuals and families are discovering a new source of financial advice: each other. In the US in particular, a number of private peer-to-peer network organisations are being formed to bring these individuals together and facilitate collaboration and the exchange of investment ideas and advice.

The networks are mostly drawn from UHNWIs, but membership is starting to broaden. In addition to regular ideas exchange, the networks offer members access to investment opportunities and financial products, often on favourable terms because of their collective buying power. Examples of these networks include TIGER 21, Met Circle, CCC Alliance and the Institute for Private Investors.

TIGER 21 stands for The Investment Group for Enhanced Returns in the 21st Century. It was formed in 1998 and currently has 59 members – mostly former Wall Street partners, retired CEOs and entrepreneurs – who have a collective $5 billion in assets. To join, members must have more than $10 million in assets and satisfy the partners that they have 'something to offer in terms of expertise'. They are charged an annual fee of $25 000. Members are allocated to a circle of no more than 12 individuals, which meets for a full day each month for knowledge sharing and a 'portfolio defense'. Here, a circle member confidentially subjects his or her entire portfolio to a rigorous peer review, which involves other members challenging the presenter's investment decisions and suggesting alternative strategies.

TIGER 21 is the most 'deal-oriented' network. Members often co-invest selectively and have created their own hedge fund; one circle even bought an oil well. TIGER 21 receives discounts on financial products, which it passes on to members. However, it does not receive commissions from companies that sell products to its members and does not allow corporate members or sales pitches. It is one of the fastest growing networks and hopes to increase its membership to 300 within 5 years. It is also reported to be considering renting office space to members and selling them concierge services.

Met Circle comprises around 100 families, mostly with assets of at least $100 million. Families are charged around $1 000 a year and meet twice monthly to exchange advice. It too has a no-vending policy.

CCC Alliance was built 'by families, for families'. It currently comprises around 50 families, again mostly with assets of at least $100 million, which are charged $12 000 a year. Families exchange advice over a confidential electronic system and attend meetings once a quarter. By combining the considerable buying power of its members, CCC Alliance is able to negotiate attractive rates on important services that no single family could achieve independently. It benchmarks fees, negotiates preferential rates with financial service and family office providers, and is often able to negotiate lower investment minimums. It has also recently teamed up with the Wharton School in the Wharton Global Family Alliance, which provides members with access to cutting-edge research and broadens the peer network.

The Institute for Private Investors comprises around 310 family members, with minimum wealth of $10 million which are charged $2 000–$9 000 a year. It differs from the other networks in that it is run more like a business, generating around half its revenue from 175 corporate members.

Overall, if peer networks catch on, they could represent a threat to conventional wealth managers, not least because of their collective buying power and because group members often subject wealth managers' ideas to the scrutiny of fellow members. For example, several members of TIGER 21 discovered that they were being charged different fees for similar services at the same wealth manager – and one of them subsequently negotiated a halving in his fee. Other group members simply avoid using wealth managers altogether. As TIGER 21's co-founder, Michael Sonnenfeldt, points out, 'Private bankers may be great gatekeepers, but they aren't experts. Here, we are collectively wealthy enough that we don't need a private banker to open doors to deals for us.'

6.1.6   Regional perspective[9]

6.1.6.1   North America

The US wealth market is dominated by brokerage firms, trust banks, family offices and independent financial advisors (IFAs). Most operate locally, but some are now trying to build out their networks to provide a more nationwide presence. In Canada, the large local banks dominate.

In terms of foreign players, UBS, Deutsche Bank and HSBC are the most prominent, having made significant wealth management acquisitions; Barron's 2005 survey ranked them at numbers 3, 19 and 25 respectively in terms of US HNW AuM. The private banks of BNP and ABN AMRO are also recognised, at least by peers (for example, the *Euromoney* Private Banking Survey 2006 ranked BNP at number 12, but neither of them featured in the more quantitative

---

[9] Appendix 1 provides a more detailed country-by-country analysis.

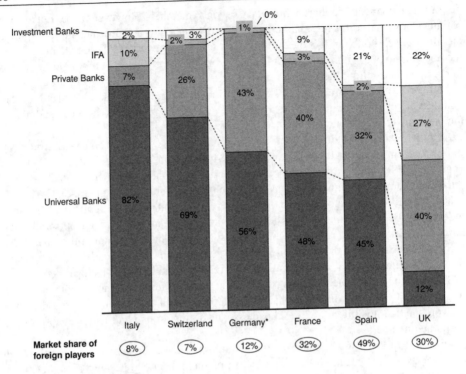

Figure 6.4 Western European competitive landscape (share of 'private banking' services market)
Source: McKinsey & Company (2002).

Barron's top 40), probably linked to some extent to their US regional-banking franchises. Beyond that, most other foreign banks that have tried to develop a US presence organically have struggled to develop sufficient scale (and, in some instances, product breadth). The many examples include Barclays,[10] which sold its New York and Miami operation in 2002; and Julius Baer, which, despite its locally well-respected brand, sold its US private banking business to UBS in December 2004.

6.1.6.2 Western Europe

There is considerable variation in the competitor landscape across countries (Figure 6.4). The wealth market remains multidomestic and, outside the UK, the universal banks dominate in most European countries. Switzerland and Germany are characterised by a high number of small, unlisted players, some of which are merging or are starting to be acquired by larger

---

[10] In 2004, Barclays integrated its wealth business with its investment banking and institutional fund management arm. Recent press statements from Barclays Wealth Management's new management suggest that a product-led re-entry to the US is under consideration, on the basis that the US is too large a market to ignore for an aspiring global bank.

players. Independent private banks have a strong position in most countries except Italy. There are very few players that operate on a pan-European basis. Traditionally, European clients have tended to use the US global players only as their second bank – so, for example, Spanish clients might mainly use Santander, relying on Merrill Lynch or Citigroup for their global needs. The US global players are under-weight in Europe and are looking to make acquisitions.

6.1.6.3   Eastern Europe

The wealth markets in most Eastern European countries are dominated by foreign players. Citigroup and some of the large German and Austrian banks are particularly strong. In Russia, some of the large local players, e.g. Sberbank and Zenit Bank, are currently developing private banking services. Among the foreign players, Citigroup is leveraging its retail network, while many of the large Swiss and global players have opened representative offices.

6.1.6.4   Asia-Pacific

The local players are finding it hard to compete as the large global, US and European players have muscled in aggressively in recent years, some of which are adopting a pan-regional strategy (Figure 6.5). UBS, for example, now claims to serve around half of Asia's billionaires. There was not a single local player in the top 10 Asian private banks in *Euromoney*'s 2006 survey. Also, the *Asiamoney* 2005 private banking poll found that 80% of HNWIs are multibanked, with 10% using five or more banks.

Local players lack appropriate product expertise, which is in particularly strong demand in Asia. Going forward, that, together with the fact that much of the wealth is still sitting in local

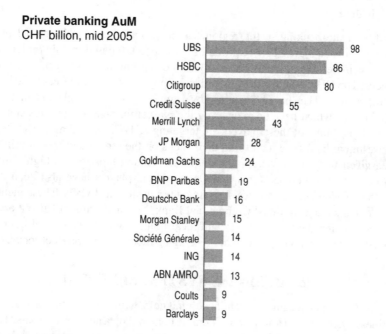

Private banking AuM
CHF billion, mid 2005

UBS	98
HSBC	86
Citigroup	80
Credit Suisse	55
Merrill Lynch	43
JP Morgan	28
Goldman Sachs	24
BNP Paribas	19
Deutsche Bank	16
Morgan Stanley	15
Société Générale	14
ING	14
ABN AMRO	13
Coults	9
Barclays	9

Figure 6.5   Largest Asia-Pacific wealth managers
Source: Morgan Stanley (2006); company data.

retail banks, ought to make this natural joint venture territory. A recent example is Merrill Lynch's tie-up with Mitsubishi Tokyo Financial Group in Japan (see Chapter 10). In some countries, such as India, regulatory restrictions have also encouraged banks to go down this route. US players are advantaged because most clients look for dollar exposure. Also, Asian clients are comfortable with foreign brands, which are typically regarded as aspirational. In some countries, a colonial legacy has advantaged some foreign players. For example, ABN AMRO, ING and Fortis Private Banking are large players in Indonesia, thanks mostly to the country's Dutch colonial heritage. Going forward, the non-specialist mid-sized foreign players are likely to lose share as the Asian wealth market develops and these players' competitive advantage starts to wane.

6.1.6.5   Latin America

In 2003, many foreign players withdrew from the region, or scaled back their operations, driven by economic recession and the accompanying wealth destruction. The market is now dominated by the global players and the large Iberian banks. Santander has been acquiring banks in the region, and is now reported to have the bulk of its private banking business there, rather than in Spain. ABN AMRO has recently been acquiring banks to strengthen its position in Brazil, where it is now the fifth-largest bank. Banco Itau is the key local player in Brazil, having grown through acquisitions; other strong foreign players include Royal Bank of Canada and BNP Paribas. Some foreign players, such as EFG International, run their Latin American operations mainly from Miami and New York (60%–70% of the region's offshore assets are estimated to reside in the United States).

6.1.6.6   Middle East

Historically, private banking in the region has been dominated by the global players and some specialist product providers (e.g. Man Investments), focused mainly on UHNWIs. But competition is increasing and new entrants have been piling in. Most of the existing players remain focused on UHNWIs, and have been developing their onshore presence and buiding new Islamic propositions. They have been joined by a number of European players, including Pictet and BNP Paribas, which have been entering the market through local representative offices and partnerships. Many of these players are targeting HNWIs as well as UHNWIs. Many of the US investment banks are increasing their focus on the region and are, in principle, well positioned given that family wealth and corporate relationships remain highly intertwined; favoured entry routes include Dubai and Quatar. Local players have also been developing their wealth management capabilities, focusing more firmly on HNWIs. These include (a) the leading local banks (e.g. National Commercial Bank, National Bank of Kuwait and Samba), which are leveraging their client bases and local brands; and (b) new local boutiques (e.g. Arcapita and SHUAA Capital), which are leveraging their regional product focus.

6.2   BUSINESS SYSTEM UPHEAVAL

Driven by technological changes, client needs and cold, hard economics, the wealth management business system is undergoing considerable upheaval on a number of fronts. This section focuses on three: value chain disaggregation, business model convergence and divestment of non-core businesses.

6.2.1 Value chain disaggregation

Technology will continue to transform the wealth management business system. That should lead to reduced client-interaction costs. But it can clearly also lead to higher IT investment requirements. Both effects, together with clients' demand for open product architecture, should accelerate further unbundling of the value chain, which can already be observed today in mature and fragmented private banking markets.

Broadly, there are two main types of unbundling, aimed at:

1. Provision of fully independent advice.
2. Outsourcing of certain elements of the value chain to benefit from economies of scale of larger providers.

A good example of the first type of unbundling is Coutts, which introduced a multimanager approach for discretionary portfolio management in 2001 (see Chapter 4). A number of smaller players have outsourced various elements of their business system; e.g. Bank Hapoalim Switzerland set up an agreement with Pictet for the management of its discretionary accounts. Outsourcing is discussed in detail in Chapter 7. Unbundling, in turn, enables a new type of private banking player to become established: the 'independent orchestrator'.

Independent orchestrator banks (IOBs) focus on client relationship management, managing a network of various providers for each type of product and service such as research, discretionary portfolio management, mutual funds, trust, tax advice, etc. The IOB aggregates these services to an overall value proposition for its clients. The idea of the network also applies to client acquisition, which could occur over multiple cannels.

Setting up an IOB could be an attractive option for smaller players with established brand names and experienced advisors that lack sufficient scale to compete in an environment that demands ever-larger IT investments and where competition moves to a regional/global level. Alternatively, one could imagine new entrants in the form of IOBs. Examples include New York Private Bank & Trust, BBR Partners and some of the other multifamily offices.

6.2.2 Business model convergence

As noted above, there is an increasing degree of business model convergence among the different types of players. Most are converging on the holistic advisory model in various forms.

In part, this reflects a need to build the strengths of their competitors into their service models. For example, on the one hand, many private banks and trust companies, driven by the sophistication of newly wealthy clients in particular, are adding capital market products by building, buying or outsourcing expertise. On the other hand, investments banks and brokerage firms, also spurred by client demand, are placing greater emphasis on advisory services, including trusts.

For the US retail brokers in particular, this is a significant shift (Figure 6.6). It has been driven, in part, by client needs and by economics. Pre-tax profit margins in US retail brokerage are 20% at best, which is less than half that achieved by UBS and Credit Suisse in their private banking businesses. The key flaw in the US model is that much of the economics are captured by the financial adviser. High payout rates to financial advisers (FAs) and high retention payments for recruiting FAs from competitors leads to long breakeven periods for FAs and destroys the operating leverage of the business.

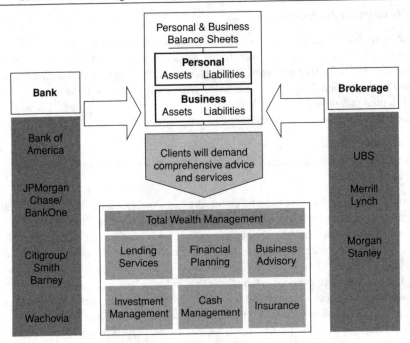

Figure 6.6 Bank/brokerage business model convergence – US example
Source: UBS.

That key flaw has combined with low organic account growth, limited consolidation opportunities and the prospect of a sustained, relentless decline in trade pricing. To help counter the impact of these factors, many brokers are shifting to team-based coverage models. Many are also seeking to broaden their asset base beyond portfolios of tradeable securities. On the product side, the main push is into banking products such as mortgages, deposits and credit cards. These products carry a lower effective payout to the FA than stocks and mutual funds. Morgan Stanley estimates the effective payout on banking-oriented products to be 15%, compared with 35%–40% for stocks and mutual funds. That is because a significant portion of the revenue from these products (mainly the ongoing spread income) does not fall on to the FAs' production 'grid', from which they receive their payouts. While the US will never move entirely towards a Swiss private banking model, the successful firms will succeed in 'institutionalising' a greater proportion of their revenue streams.

The most successful example of a bank product push is Merrill Lynch between 2001 and 2003, shortly after it introduced a deposit-sweep account and focused on mortgage origination. Morgan Stanley estimate that around half of the 8.4 percentage point increase in operating margin over that period came from the increased earnings in its Utah-based bank.

Focusing on recurring and fee-based revenue streams, which now account for as much as half of total revenue at Merrill Lynch and Citigroup/Smith Barney, is leading to higher and more stable returns. That trend is likely to continue, driven in particular by those brokerage firms that are owned by a bank, such as Citigroup/Smith Barney, UBS Wealth Management USA/Paine Webber and Wachovia/Prudential. Looking ahead, to help capture some of the assets that will be freed up through generational transfer, some of the traditional retail brokerage firms may acquire trust and estate-planning capabilities.

It is possible that the convergence of the bank and brokerage business models in the US, together with the relative success of the bank/broker mergers, could lead to more banks buying brokerage operations. In addition, the weak returns and operating metrics generated by the regional brokerage firms relative to the large, diversified brokerage firms brings the sustainability of the standalone brokerage model into question.

6.2.3   Divestment of non-core businesses

In the face of cost pressure and perceived conflicts of interest, some Swiss wealth managers in particular have been reviewing their participation in non-core businesses. The main areas that have come under the microscope are brokerage and corporate finance, each of which tend to have high fixed costs.

Brokerage margins have come under pressure in recent years, linked to market weakness and intense competition. During the period 1999–2002, the Julius Baer international brokerage business had a negative impact on the group's cost–income ratio, partly because of development costs around the turn of the millennium and also because of the subsequent downturn in the stock market. In 2001 and 2002, the business suffered losses, and Julius Baer withdrew from international brokerage in the Spring of 2003. In addition, shortly after Julius Baer announced its deal with UBS in 2005 (see Box 6.4 below), it closed its in-house sales and trading operation. It will, in future, outsource that activity from UBS and Citigroup. Pictet has also decided that brokerage is not part of its core business and plans to outsource that activity to its Helvea subsidiary. It plans to completely reduce its stake in Helvea by the end of 2008 in order to focus on its four core business lines (private banking, institutional asset management, custody and family office).

Corporate finance is a specialist game and wealth managers that are still active in this business are unlikely to generate higher than average returns, even though earnings momentum has picked up a little recently. If wealth managers continue to experience cost pressure and the stock market environment does not improve significantly, corporate finance will also face the threat of being restructured or closed down altogether by a number of wealth managers. It will, however, be difficult to find buyers for these businesses. One option would be for several wealth managers to merge their corporate finance activities.

For example, in Spring 2005, Vontobel significantly scaled back its corporate finance activities. Although Vontobel does not want to abandon this business altogether, most commentators think that the group is likely to find it difficult to reestablish a strong foothold.

6.3   CONSOLIDATION

Most players continue to focus on organic growth strategies. But recall from Chapter 1 that the wealth management industry is extremely fragmented: UBS controls around 3% of the market, whilst the number 10 competitor, HSBC Private Bank, controls only 0.6% of the market. Many players have, over recent years, recognised that they lack scale, particularly in the back-office area. That, in part, has driven increasing focus on consolidation. Indeed, the KPMG private banking acquisition survey in 2005 (KPMG, 2005) showed that it is hard to find a player that does *not* intend to pursue an acquisition over the next three years.

This section looks at recent consolidation activity, examines the key drivers and provides some best-practice implementation guidelines.

6.3.1   Recent consolidation activity

According to Berkshire Capital, there were 60 wealth management acquisitions in 2005, down marginally from 64 in 2004 (Figure 6.7). Domestic transactions continue to dominate wealth management M&A activity, with buyers mainly seeking to strengthen their presence in an existing territory or add particular expertise. Most of the transactions were small and strategic.

WEALTH MANAGEMENT TRANSACTIONS*	2000	2001	2002	2003	2004	2005
Number of Transactions	44	41	50	51	64	60
Combined Value ($b)	6.7	2.2	2.0	6.3	2.1	2.8
Total Seller AUM ($b)	186	53	63	189	94	169
Average Deal Size ($m)	153	53	39	124	33	46
Average Seller AUM ($b)	4.2	1.3	1.3	3.7	1.5	3.3

Source: Berkshire Capital Securities LLC

Domestic and cross-border deals as a proportion of private banking transactions globally (percent)

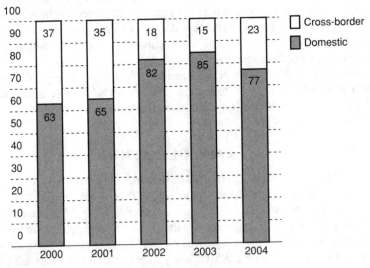

* Survey includes all deals for which seller's AuM > $100 m.

Figure 6.7   Global wealth management M&A activity
Source: Berkshire Capital Securities LLC; Thomson Financial Data SDC; KPMG (2005). Reproduced by permission.

From a legal, cultural and regulatory standpoint, domestic acquisitions are less challenging, but still require careful execution (see below). The majority of acquisitions are valued at less than $50 million.

Regionally, the KPMG private banking acquisition survey 2005 found that Asia-Pacific and North America were the most active regions accounting for 73% of deals in 2004. By contrast, the proportion of deals in Europe has fallen for the fourth consecutive year. That reflects the relative maturities of the regions and the relative scarcity of available targets at realistic prices in Europe. Most of the small Swiss players, for example, cherish their independence and are particularly averse to the idea of having a foreign shareholder, which they perceive as being a key bar for many clients.

6.3.1.1 Specific deals

Turning to specific deals (Tabel 6.2), they broadly fall into two main categories: large buys small and small buys small. The deals that have occurred have had very little impact on the market shares of the largest players. What we have not yet seen are deals among the large banks; Chapter 10 offers some suggestions for potential marriages there.

Table 6.2 Selected global wealth management deals, 1997–2004

Date	Target	Buyer	Currency	Prices (mn)	AUM (mn)	Bv (mn)
Dec-04	Sauerborn Trust	UBS	€	120–150	6,000	N/AV
Nov-04	Caixabank Banque Privée	BNP Paribas	€	N/AV	300	N/AV
Oct-04	Banco Atlantico Gibraltar	EFG Private Bank	€	18	N/AV	N/AV
Sep-04	Chiswell Associates	Sarasin	N/AV	N/AV	N/AV	N/AV
Sep-04	CenE Bankiers (ING)	Van Lanschot	€	250	N/AV	168
Sep-04	Bank von Ernst (Monaco)	BNP Paribas	€	N/AV	360	N/AV
Sep-04	Societe Monegasque de Banque Privee	BNP Paribas	€	N/AV	630	N/AV
Mar-04	Credit Agricole Indo. Private Banking Italia	Banca Intesa	€	60	1,400	N/AV
Jun-04	Vontobel (12.5%)	Raiffeisenbank	SFr	220	49,400	939
Jun-04	Bank Jenni & Cie (Bank Sarasin)	MBO team and Geneva Mirabaud & Cie	SFr	N/AV	1,140	N/AV
Mar-04	Puilaelco	Almanij (Kredietbank Luxembourg)	€	N/AV	3,400	51
Mar-04	AP Anlage und Privatbank	Parex Bank	SFr	20	N/AV	N/AV
Mar-04	Atlantic Wealth Management	Singer & Friedlander	€	29.8	1,200	N/AV
Feb-04	Schmidt Bank Acquisition	Commerzbank	€	60	N/AV	N/AV
Feb-04	Scott Goodman Harris	UBS	N/AV	N/AV	N/AV	N/AV
Feb-04	Bank of Bermuda	HSBC	US$	1,300	134,700	662
Feb-04	Laing & Cruickshank (Crédit Lyonnais)	UBS	£	160	5,100	N/AV
Feb-04	Leopold Joseph	Butterfield	£	52	N/AV	32
Feb-04	Tempus Privatbank	M.M. Warburg	N/AV	N/AV	N/AV	N/AV

Table 6.2 (*Continued*)

Date	Target	Buyer	Currency	Prices (mn)	AUM (mn)	Bv (mn)
Jan-04	Schoellerbank (BA-CA)	Kredietbank Luxembourg	€	N/AV	5,000	N/AV
Dec-03	BethmannMaffei (HVB Group)	ABN AMRO	€	110	5,400	N/AV
Dec-03	Bankhaus Lobbecke	M.M. Warburg & Co.	€	90	N/AV	N/AV
Dec-03	HSBC Private Banking Italy	Banca Profilo	€	10.8	650	N/AV
Nov-03	Worms' Nivard, Flornoy, Fauchier Magnan, Durant des Aulnois (NFMDA)	Oddo & Cie	€	N/AV	1,000	N/AV
Nov-03	Banque Notz Stucki	Ferrier Lullin & Cie	SFr	N/AV	2,000	N/AV
Oct-03	Bank von Ernst & Cie (HVB)	Coults Bank (RBS)	£	228	6,000	78
Oct-03	Merril Lynch's German Private Client Operations	UBS Wealth Management	US$	N/AV	1,400	N/AV
Oct-03	Gerrard Management Servies	Barclays Bank	£	210	12,500	N/AV
May-03	Compagnie Bancaire Geneve	Société Générale	SFr	450	11,600	219
May-03	Banque Edouard Constant	EFG	SFr	N/AV	6,000	N/AV
May-03	Lloyds TSB (France)	UBS	€	N/AV	1,000	N/AV
May-03	STG (Swiss Life)	LGT	SFr	197	7,000	N/AV
Mar-03	Rued Blass	Deutsche Bank	SFr	275est	7,100	N/AV
May-02	Henderson	Newton IM (Mellon)	£	20	836	N/AV
May-02	Cie Monégasque de Banque	Mediobanca	£	348	3,800	N/AV
Sep-02	Delbrueck	ABN Amro	€	58	N/AV	N/AV
Mar-02	Rabobank PB	Sarasin	SFr	523	17,000	272
Mar-02	Sarasin	Rabobank	SFr	3,319	38,900	N/AV
May-01	Kempen	Dexia	US$	1,053	6,700	222
Mar-01	Bank Austria Schweiz	Aargauische Kantonalbank	£	50	600	N/AV
Dec-00	Marcaud Cook	Anglo-Irish Bank	£	50	700	N/AV
Oct-00	Banque Worms	Deutsche Bank	£	N/AV	4,300	N/AV
Oct-00	WestLB	Swiss Life	£	83	1,000	N/AV
Jul-00	CIBC (Suisse)	Banque Indosuéz	£	93	1,200	N/AV
Apr-00	CPR Gestion Privee	Lloyds TSB	US$	40	1,200	N/AV
Mar-00	Labouchere	Dexia Belgium	US$	896	1,700	190
Dec-99	STG	Swiss Life	SFr	N/AV	9,000	N/AV
Sep-99	Safra/Republic	HSBC	US$	10,495	57,739	1,973
Aug-99	Banque Vemes	Artesia	US$	34	865	44
Apr-99	Robeco (Suisse)	Rabobank	£	N/AV	1,000	N/AV
Mar-99	Banca del Goltardo	Swiss Life	SFr	2,400	30,800	898
Mar-99	Merck Finck	Kreditbank	US$	282	4,076	181
Jul-98	BSI	Generali	SFr	1,920	31,000	652
Jun-98	Banque du Louvre	CCF	US$	61	N/AV	25
Jun-98	BMP	BIL SA (Dexia)	US$	109	N/AV	79
Aug-97	SMH	UBS	DM	350	15,326	238

Source: Huw van Steenis, Morgan Stanley. Reproduced by permission.

HSBC's acquisition of Republic New York and Safra Republic Holdings in 1999 doubled the size of its private banking assets and represented a key initial step in creating one of the few global private banks. In that sense, it is described by some as an industry-shaping deal. HSBC followed that up by acquiring Credit Commercial de France, the specialist private client tax business of Arthur Anderson in the US, Property Vision in the UK and, most recently, Bank of Bermuda in 2004 (making it the world's largest private client trust business).

UBS has been a particularly active onshore acquirer (see Chapter 9). Its $12.2 billion acquisition of Paine Webber in 2000 enabled it to access the US, the biggest onshore wealth market in the world and significantly shifted its geographic focus away from Switzerland. It has since followed that up with a series of small acquisitions, mainly in Europe. UBS's AuM have more than doubled over the last eight years.

Among the various Swiss transactions, three landmark deals, all announced in 2002, stand out. First, in March 2002 an announcement was made of a 'strategic alliance' between Basel-based Sarasin and Rabobank. That followed a sharp deterioration in Sarasin's financial performance: its net profit fell by 46% in 2001, driven by a 6% fall in AuM and a rise in the cost–income ratio to 77%. Rabobank, one of the largest banks in the Netherlands, with roots in the agricultural sector, was looking to enter the Swiss market and wanted a platform to expand in northern and central Europe. The transaction was structured in two parts:

1. The sale of 28% of Sarasin to Rabobank in exchange for Rabobank's international private banking franchise (Switzerland, Luxembourg, Guernsey and Asia).
2. The purchase by Rabobank of a 7-year call option on 100% of Eichbaum Holding, the entity via which Sarasin partners control the bank.

Sarasin's announcement made clear:

> There are certain key criteria that any Swiss private bank must fulfil if it wishes to secure its future – criteria that we could not realistically meet on our own, or through organic development alone. We are thinking here of a necessary critical mass of assets under management, of the resources and distribution network required to develop a substantial international onshore business, of the economies of scale required in logistics, and of the opportunity to use our expertise in related business areas and product lines to round out our core business.

The second landmark deal was the May 2002 acquisition of Discount Bank & Trust Company (DBTC) by Union Bancaire Privée (UBP). Here, the main objective was to reduce the cost base and also leverage complementarities between the banks, which were largely geographic in nature (UBP was present mainly in the north of Switzerland; DBTC more in the south) and product driven (DBTC was more conservative; UBP more dynamic).

The third landmark deal was the June 2002 'merger' of Lombard Odier and Darier Hentsch, two prestigious Geneva-based partnerships.[11] Darier Hentsch had suffered a blow in October 2001 when one of its senior partners was forced to step down because of his involvement in

---

[11] The history here is interesting. Hentsch was the oldest Geneva-based private bank, founded in 1796. For the first two years of its life, the bank was, in fact, called Lombard Hentsch. The banks separated into Lombard Odier and Hentsh in 1798. Darier, another Geneva-based bank, was founded in 1837, and merged with Hentsch in 1991.

Swissair's collapse. The two banks described the merger as fulfilling the need for 'optimum size, allowing it to stand out and compete against the ever-growing competition'.

Box 6.4   Julius Baer

By mid 2005, Julius Baer, like many other mid-sized Swiss private banks, found itself with a cost problem and non-existent AuM growth. In addition, a new share structure had cut the Baer family's voting power from 52% to 18%. The bank's imminent takeover seemed assured. But in September 2005, much to many analysts' surprise, Julius Baer announced the acquisition from UBS of GAM, the world's largest fund-of-funds provider, and three independently operated Swiss private banks, for CHF 5.6 billion.[12]

The deal's value creation will be driven by (a) cost savings; (b) cross-selling of GAM products; and (c) a higher profit margin (the acquired banks are around three times as profitable as the Julius Baer private bank). A large number of the new senior management are transferring from UBS, and many analysts have likened the deal to a reverse management takeover.

Through this acquisition, Julius Baer has become Switzerland's largest pure-play wealth manager (Figure 6.8) and its CEO has said that, going forward, the group expects to play a leading role in the market's continuing consolidation. Julius Baer's CEO also said on the announcement of the deal that 'our strategy is largely an offshore strategy and will continue to be so'. It will, however, also be important to reinvest for growth (Figure 6.9). But first comes the difficult bit: integrating the acquired banks, as smoothly and quickly as possible.

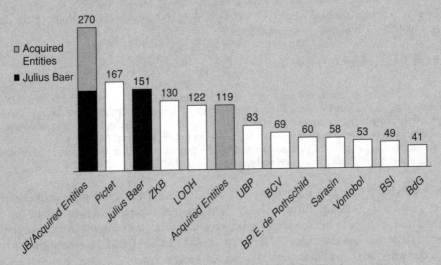

Figure 6.8   AuM of selected Swiss private banks, end-2004. (CHF billion)
Source: Julius Baer.

[12]In February 2003, UBS combined Basel-based Bank Ehinger, Bern-based Armand von Ernst, Zurich-based Cantrade Privatebank, Geneva-based Ferrier Lullin, Lugano-based Banco di Lugano and London-based GAM into a new holding company. The first three private banks were subsequently merged to form Ehinger & Armand von Ernst. These private banks were acquired by UBS and SBC mainly during the 1970s and 1980s. GAM was founded in 1983 by Gilbert de Botton, and acquired by UBS in 1999.

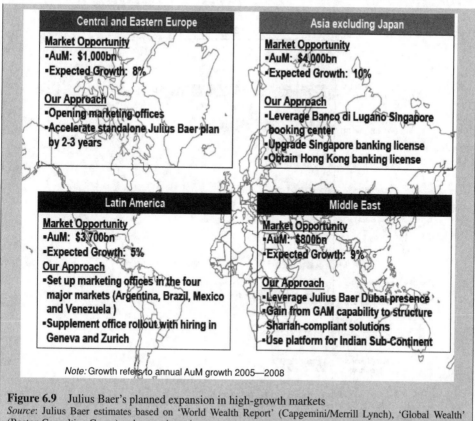

Figure 6.9   Julius Baer's planned expansion in high-growth markets
Source: Julius Baer estimates based on 'World Wealth Report' (Capgemini/Merrill Lynch), 'Global Wealth' (Boston Consulting Group) and expert interviews.

In the US, a key recent deal was Charles Schwab's acquisition of US Trust in 2000. It is an example of a mass-affluent-oriented player extending its reach into the HNW market. Through this acquisition, Schwab was able to offer its relatively young, upwardly mobile customers a full-service offering once they 'graduate' from the low-cost discount model. In addition, the acquisition gave US Trust a wider range of proprietary products for its strong distribution platform, including research (an original goal of the transaction, though it did not actually happen in the end). The benefits of the transaction are less clear for US Trust clients, although they include access to a stronger trading desk and better technology.

Most recently, Mellon Financial has been a particularly active acquirer. Between 2000 and 2004, it acquired seven wealth management firms, including three acquisitions in three separate US regions in 2004. It is seeking to deepen its national footprint and now has 60 offices operating under the Mellon brand.

The above has concentrated on outright acquisitions of entire firms. Clearly, consolidation can take a variety of other forms, including team lift-outs, acquisitions of client portfolios and joint ventures or alliances. For example, Schroder Private Bank, aware of the need for a cultural fit, has focused on team lift-outs such as a structured product team from Kleinwort

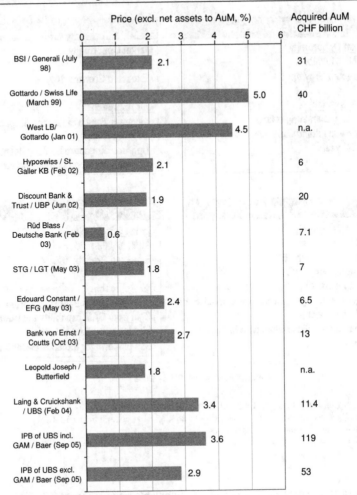

Figure 6.10   Private banking acquisition valuations – Swiss examples
Source: Sarasin; Millenium Associates.

Benson Private Bank in order to offer more sophisticated financing and investment strategies
to its HNW clients.

6.3.1.2   Deal pricing

Prices for takeover candidates fell sharply during the stock market downturn. But in the last
three years, valuations of private banking acquisitions – measured as the price paid in excess
of the AuM as a percentage of the AuM – have recovered well (Figure 6.10). In particular,
onshore distribution and specialist product providers command a premium. Looking ahead,
given the focus of most players on acquisitions, there is unlikely to be any softening of pricing
in the near term.

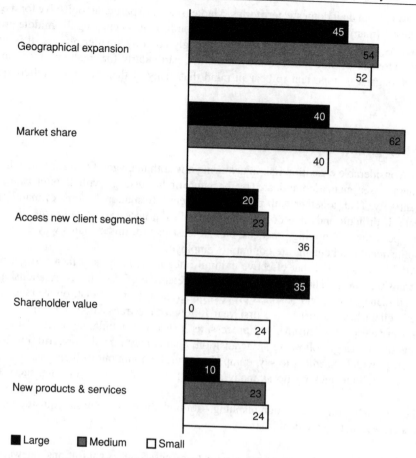

Figure 6.11 Main objectives of acquisition strategy
Source: KPMG (2004). Reproduced by permission.

6.3.2 Consolidation drivers

Clearly, scale is the primary transaction motive, particularly for smaller banks. But there are a number of other important drivers, which tend to vary by size of player and the region in which it operates. Many players are using M&A as a defensive strategy to help them cope with regulatory and other challenges (see Chapter 9). That is particularly the case in Europe and Switzerland.

Others view M&A as a means of accessing new growth opportunities (Figure 6.11). Geographic expansion is cited by players of all sizes as the number one objective of their acquisition strategy. Within that broad objective, most US players, for example, are interested in achieving a greater presence across the key wealth centres within the US. Northern Trust, for example, has been buying up boutique firms; and Bank of America's 2003 acquisition of FleetBoston was motivated in part by Fleet's 28% share of the lucrative private banking market in the wealthy Northeast. Larger players, by contrast, are more interested in accessing growth away from their domestic territories. Market share is a particular objective for medium-sized players (many of which presumably feel uncomfortable occupying the middle ground), while access to new client segments is most strongly cited by smaller players. It is surprising that shareholder value ranks so low on the list, particularly for small and medium-sized players, though it is important to bear in mind that many of them are not publicly quoted companies.

6.3.3 Best-practice implementation

There is considerable execution risk in acquiring a wealth manager. For a start, due diligence and synergy assessment is complicated by the nature of the business, with its emphasis on client confidentiality. That, together with poor management information systems of many players, can make it difficult and time consuming to obtain the necessary data on the client base, business performance, pricing practices, etc. At least in part, this explains why earn-out and price-adjustment mechanisms are commonly employed.

KPMG's survey found that effective cultural integration is the key factor to get right in post-acquisition work. That was followed by the retention of key clients, relationship managers and management, and business process integration. It found that, on average, 10% of a target's client base is lost in the first year following the transaction. For clients, switching their private bank is an involved process, as it involves liquidating assets. However, as contracts often change following an acquisition, clients may take the opportunity to reconsider their provider. Needless to say, competitors will be going out of their way to make the most of any fallout, picking up as many of the clients and relationship managers as they can.

To be successful, implementation planning – for both the pre- and post-acquisition phases – should start well before the deal is struck:

- *Pre-acquisition.* Spend the necessary time to discuss both organisations' views on risk taking, future acquisitions and the role of the combined entity within the Group. Consider drafting a combined statement of business principles. It is also important to assess the management team's ability to execute, recognising the significant management resources required. Develop a detailed execution plan (covering the first 100 days in detail, and beyond), including ownership, accountability, dependencies and key milestones.
- *Post-acquisition.* The key priority is to balance internal and client communication. Key professionals should be managed and motivated by communicating quickly, making the process inclusive, soliciting regular feedback from 'coal-face' employees and adopting a 'what's best for the client?' perspective. On the client side, expectations need to be managed carefully, and it is important to ensure a consistent message. In particular, the branding decision should be made quickly and definitively to avoid creating unnecessary confusion among clients and other stakeholders. With regard to IT integration, a dedicated integration team should be formed as soon as possible.

The KPMG private banking acquisition survey 2004 provided a set of guidelines for enhancing acquisition success (Figure 6.12).

Setting the Acquisition Strategy

- Be rigorous in setting acquisition criteria that meet your objectives.
- Set out clearly what should be achieved and why this is right for the business.
- Rigorously analyse potential acquisitions against these requirements.

Obtain Maximum Comfort During Due Diligence

- While honoring confidentiality constraints, obtain maximum comfort on client profile and client profitability. Insist on discussions with key relationship managers on client profile analyses, commission fee structures and other key areas.
- Caliber of senior management:
  - Obtain detailed job descriptions and curricula vitae.
  - If permissible, conduct interviews through a human resources consultant.
  - Objectively assess the individual's performance in his/her respective field.

Integration

- Begin the integration process early.
- Develop an integration plan as early as possible in the pre-completion phase, in particular to bridge the management vacuum which commonly arises in the initial period following completion. Devote more time and management attention in the pre-completion phase to prepare for integration.
- Integration plan should focus on value: preserving it, realizing it and creating it.
- Recognize that integration is a complex project and treat it accordingly, devoting appropriate resources and skills.
- Communication is key. Acquirers should not underestimate the human factor in all acquisitions: communication can be critical to employee retention.

Retention of Key Clients

- Prepare a formal retention plan, particularly in the major onshore markets where client loyalty tends not to be as strong.
- Ensure that earn-out structures are subject to levels of client retention.
- Understand what drives the target's customer base, addressing such questions as:
  - Which types of client does the target's brand attract?
  - Will the target's clients be attracted by our brand?
  - How does our bank compare to the target in terms of reputation and approach?
  - Will the target's client base prefer the services offered by a smaller bank or a larger bank?
  - Can we determine the target clients' appetite for new products?
- Access to, and communication with, clients at the earliest opportunity is critical. Organize meetings with clients in the immediate post-completion period.

Retention of Key Client Advisers

- Include key employee retention clauses in the sale and purchase agreement.
- Avoid surprises: check whether any special arrangements or guarantees have been awarded to a client relationship manager that he/she will expect to continue post-acquisition.
- Relationship managers are typically attracted by share option schemes and performance-related remuneration, particularly when it is tied only to the wealth management unit.

Measuring Success

- Link the measures of acquisition success with the acquisition objectives.
- Apply selected measures to track success; don't simply ask the question 'Is the business growing?'.
- Develop a performance management process that links right into the pre-acquisition valuation assumptions.

Figure 6.12   Enhancing acquisition success: agenda for action
Source: KPMG (2004), pages 18–19. Reproduced by permission.

ADDENDUM: FINANCIAL DATA OF SELECTED PRIVATE BANKS

Gross margin

in bps	2000	2001	2002	2003	2004
UBS Wealth Management	101	96	98	101	104
o/w EWMI[13]	n/a	88	85	72	68
Citigroup Private Bank	96	99	104	109	98
Credit Suisse Private Bank	130	131	118	131	137
Northern Trust – PFS	116	119	124	120	111
HSBC Private Bank	112	114	103	106	113
Julius Baer Private Bank	87	76	78	74	74
Sarasin – Entire Firm	108	101	79	83	80
Vontobel – Private Bank	n/a	n/a	88	87	93
Société Générale – Private Banking	84	75	80	84	99
Credit Agricole – Private Banking	n/a	n/a	57	58	72
CASA: Latam Business Sold in 2004	104	100	92	93	95
EFG International	110	112	104	139	114

Source: Company data.

Cost–income ratio

	2000	2001	2002	2003	2004
UBS Wealth Management	49.7%	53.0%	60.6%	61.1%	54.8%
o/w EWMI[13]	n.a	212.8%	283.3%	277.5%	188.6%
Citigroup Private Bank	62.9%	61.2%	59.1%	59.3%	63.7%
Credit Suisse Private Bank	42.5%	56.4%	71.9%	62.5%	58.3%
Northern Trust – PFS	59.0%	60.5%	62.3%	62.6%	64.5%
HSBC Private Bank	n/a	65.9%	69.9%	69.3%	67.6%
Julius Baer Private Bank	65.7%	72.5%	70.0%	76.3%	75.3%
Sarasin – Entire Firm	n/a	70.0%	84.6%	80.1%	73.4%
Vontobel – Private Bank	n/a	n/a	73.1%	74.2%	71.5%
Société Générale – Private Banking	69.1%	74.7%	65.1%	64.0%	61.3%
Credit Agricole – Private Banking	n.a	n/a	89.5%	84.1%	83.7%
EFG International	70.2%	89.7%	84.5%	81.3%	73.6%

Source: Company data.

Net new money

% of prior-year-end AuM	2000	2001	2002	2003	2004	H1 2005
EFG Bank	–	–	–	–	–	14%
Vontobel	–	–	0.0%	−4.2%	1.1%	n/a
Julius Baer	13.9%	3.1%	−3.4%	1.3%	−1.2%	−1%
Sarasin	–	–	−4.3%	6.3%	1.3%	–
Credit Suisse PB	–	7.8%	3.7%	3.9%	5.2%	7%
UBS PB	0.2%	2.9%	2.4%	5.2%	6.5%	9%
o/w Switzerland	−2.5%	0.6%	−1.1%	0.0%	0.9%	2%
o/w International	1.2%	3.3%	2.6%	4.5%	6.0%	8%
o/w EWMI[13]	100.0%	56.0%	47.5%	38.6%	29.6%	31%

Source: Company data.

---

[13] European Wealth Management Initiative.

Market valuation[14]

Local currencies		Price	Mkt Cap (mn)	2005e	2006e	P/E 2006e	P/BK 2004	AuM (bn)	Price/AuM
Swiss stocks									
Julius Baer	BAER VX	90.6	3,434	22.2x	18.2x	15.2x	2.2x	140/270	2.5%
Vontobel	VONN SW	37.8	1,695	17.5x	16.3x	14.6x	1.5x	52.9	3.2%
Sarasin	BSAN SW	2645.0	1,162	17.3x	16.2x	14.2x	1.4x	57.8	2.0%
Average				**19.0x**	**16.9x**	**14.7x**	**1.7x**		**2.6%**
European stocks									
Man Group	EMG LN	1805.0	4,228	13.1x	11.9x	10.9x	3.3x	22.1	19.1%
Fideuram	BFIIM	4.6	3,678	23.1x	209x	19.7x	5.9x	59.5	6.2%
AMVESCAP	AVZ LN	393.5	2,600	19.4x	17.6x	15.8x	1.4x	199.0	1.3%
Schroders	SDR LN	891.0	2,230	17.1x	15.4x	13.6x	2.0x	105.6	2.1%
Fineco	FCO IM	7.9	1,794	18.4x	16.6x	14.3x	2.2x	37.0	4.9%
Isis (F&C)	FCAM LN	191.0	1,186	12.2x	12.8x	14.4x	1.5x	124.8	1.0%
Azimut	AZM IM	6.2	570	28.5x	18.0x	10.9x	4.3x	8.2	6.9%
Rathbones	RAT LN	892.0	348	15.6x	14.5x	12.8x	3.2x	7.7	4.5%
Average				**18.4x**	**16.0x**	**14.0x**	**3.0x**		**5.7%**
US stocks									
Franklin Resources	BEN	95.5	13,922	20.5x	18.1x	16.6x	2.7x	361.9	3.8%
Northern Trust	NTRS	51.7	10,642	19.6x	17.7x	16.0x	3.2x		n.a.
T. Rowe Price	TROW	70.8	8,062	22.7x	20.0x	16.7x	4.7x	235.2	3.4%
Janus Capital Group	JNS	18.6	3,941	36.1x	26.6x	20.3x	1.4x	139.0	2.8%
Eaton Vance Corp	EV	26.4	2,910	23.2x	19.3x	n.a.	6.5x	98.0	3.0%
Gabelli Asset Mgmt	GBL	44.7	1,399	22.1x	22.0x	n.a.	4.2x	28.7	4.9%
Average				**24.0x**	**20.6x**	**17.4x**	**3.8x**		**3.6%**
Combined Peer Group Average				**20.5x**	**17.8x**	**15.4x**	**2.8x**		**4.0%**

Price as at close on 18 November, 2005.
Source: Fox-Pitt, Kelton (2005). Reproduced by permission.

---

[14] Includes selected asset managers.

7
Operational Excellence

This chapter takes a look underneath the wealth management bonnet. In particular, the focus is on how modern wealth management businesses should be run from an operational point of view.

It is fair to say that the wealth management industry is not known for its cost consciousness. Indeed, at a structural level, costs in wealth management tend to be relatively fixed and sticky, which has been made worse in many cases by wealth managers traditionally taking a 'revenue-at-all-costs' approach. That, in turn, has left them with high cost bases, which have, in some cases, become unsustainable. For many wealth managers, their existing operating models lack scalability, which places a real constraint on profitable growth.

Wealth management businesses are growing increasingly complex. A typical player must deal with multiple client requirements, business locations, booking centres, operating models and platforms. Business complexity, in turn, leads to higher costs. Driven in large measure by recent pressure on economics, wealth managers the world over are taking a more proactive approach to operational efficiency and effectiveness. The main aim here is to re-engineer the cost side of their businesses – to produce a lower, flexible, more variable and scaleable cost base. Another aim, just as important for some, is to improve the quality and effectiveness of client service delivery.

Many wealth managers are finding that a joined-up, well-aligned operating model provides an opportunity to:

1. Reduce business complexity and costs, and better manage capacity across the business.
2. Improve client service quality.
3. Support strategic priorities and provide a platform for profitable growth going forward.

Operational efficiency improvements, in turn, enable banks to free-up back-office resources and reallocate them to more productive front-office functions. For example, by keeping non-client-facing functions very lean, UBS has been able to invest heavily in its front line: from 2000 to 2005, its number of client advisers was up by 70%, compared with growth of just 22% in non-advisory staff.

The value chain provides a useful framework for analysing wealth management activities (see Figure 7.1). Given the labour-intensive nature of client relationship management, it is unsurprising that front-office costs represent the largest proportion of total costs.

There are very few wealth managers with what one would consider world-class operations. Figure 7.2 provides an indicative performance grid against which to assess a wealth manager's back office.

Aggressive management of technology and operational spending has traditionally taken a back seat to meeting the needs of the front line. However, this proved to be expensive, with technology and operations spending currently accounting for an average of 25 basis points of assets under management, and up to 36 basis points for some players. Leading firms are taking a hard look at all of their operations, determining which functions are strategic, and using multiple approaches to reducing costs. Ahead of any operational enhancement work, it

	Support functions	Back office	Middle office	Front office
Main activity	Business administration	Transaction processing	Product manufacturing & management	Client relationship management
Key component functions	• Executive mgmt. • Finance • Planning & strategy • HR • Marketing & branding • Legal • Compliance • Audit • Risk • IT • Change	• Operations – Processing – Payments – Custody – Settlement – Clearing – Trust admin. – Reconciliations • Client reporting	• Investment mgmt. – Research – Asset allocation – Trade execution • Product mgmt. – Proposition development – Wealth structuring – Product sourcing • Sales administration – Sales performance mgmt. – Sales compliance – Channel mgmt.	• Relationship mgmt. – Advisory – Sales • Client servicing • Sales planning & business development
Indicative % of total cost*	15	32	8	45

* Note: there is substantial variation across business models and individual players

Figure 7.1   The wealth management value chain
Source: Author's analysis.

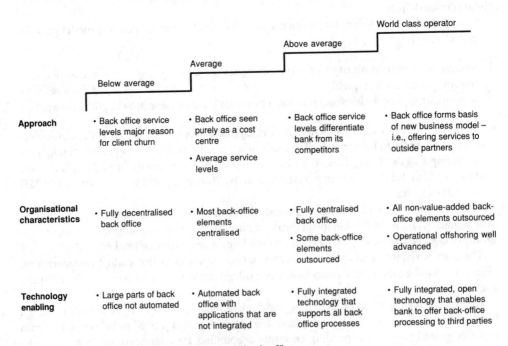

Figure 7.2   Assessment of a wealth manager's back office
Source: Author's analysis.

is useful to undertake a product simplification exercise (outlined in Box 4.6) to help ensure that the benefits are captured in full.

This chapter focuses on the four most effective disciplines that characterise wealth management operational leaders:

- Smart operational sourcing (including outsourcing and offshoring).
- Lean operations.
- Technology transformation.
- Value-added support services.

7.1 SMART OPERATIONAL SOURCING[1]

Historically, wealth managers have taken the view that the constraints of client confidentiality, risk management and control mean that most operational activities must be performed in-house. But there is growing disaggregation of the value chain and specialists have appeared that can deliver the same (or better) services at lower cost and greater scale. Wealth managers therefore need to rethink which services they genuinely need to operate in-house and which services they can source effectively from players better equipped to deliver them. Moreover, they must think about where they will source such services. Given the significant differences in cost between the Western world and lower cost locations, such as Asia, the location of a provider is becoming as critical as its service offering.

In addition to doing everything in-house with a fully integrated operating model, wealth managers have a number of sourcing options. While the boldest players are already experimenting with operational offshoring, and the number of successful outsourcing deals is growing by the month, some players have chosen a shared service centre approach. That is also known as the 'utility model' – typically a joint venture between two or more banks with the main aim of increasing economies of scale. It is possible to merge back offices and achieve substantial cost savings while preserving organisational autonomy and continuing to distribute own-branded products and services.

There are good examples of shared service centres in Switzerland. For instance, Lombard Odier has, since 2001, provided mainly back-office support for Bern-based Valiant Privatbank, covering settlement, IT, research and trading activities. The two banks also jointly develop and distribute funds and other products. In 2003, Märki Baumann set up a collaboration agreement with Zuger Kantonalbank (ZK) in which the private bank takes on the responsibility for securities administration, the execution of securities transactions and portfolio management functions on behalf on ZK.

In 2004, the Swiss-based Raiffeisen Group transferred the processing and administration of its entire securities business to Vontobel in order to gain economies of scale.[2] As part of the cooperation agreement, Vontobel became the exclusive provider of investment services to Raiffeisen's 2.5 million clients through its 1 200 Swiss branches, and Raiffeisen provides mortgages to Vontobel's clients. In the next phase, Vontobel is also due to take on transaction bank tasks such as management of client custody accounts and securities positions in the name of the Raiffeisen banks and is subject to Swiss bank client confidentiality regulations. Vontobel has subsequently invited other smaller banks to share its back office, which has arguably put it in a position to participate in sector consolidation on its own terms.

---

[1] The focus here, and throughout this chapter, is on operations. Product sourcing and open product architecture approaches are covered in Chapter 4.

[2] This extended the partnership in the investment fund business which had existed between the two banks since 1994.

That has resurrected the idea of a Swiss transaction bank, which was under discussion at the start of the millennium. A transaction bank or IT collaboration could now be easier to implement given that many reputable Swiss wealth managers – including the Raiffesen transaction bank of Vontobel, Julius Baer, Rahn & Bodmer, La Roche and Pictet – have all selected Avaloq integrated banking software. Such an organisation could be modelled after Bankers' Bank in the United States or the Sparkasse in Germany, which offer (generic, not wealth management specific) back-office and treasury services to all member institutions.

Another interesting model is that of EFG International. It operates a 'hub-and-spoke' model: relationship managers own a portion of the equity, but work semi-independently from the bank as entrepreneurs, with EFG providing the support infrastructure (back- and middle-office services) and brand. It is a unique, highly efficient, way of operating, and is achieving strong bottom-line growth. That model is discussed in more detail in Box 6.1.

7.1.1   Operational outsourcing

One specific area that has been receiving increasing attention from wealth managers is outsourcing. That is the process whereby managerial control of the provision of certain services is transferred to another legal entity – the service provider – not fully owned by the bank. The transfer is on a long-term basis and is governed by a service level agreement (SLA).

Demand for outsourcing is growing within the wealth management industry, driven by recognition of a variety of associated benefits. In principle, outsourcing:

1. *Reduces costs and creates a more flexible expense structure.* In many cases, wealth managers' primary goal in adopting outsourcing is to lower the cost of operating administrative processes and create a more flexible cost structure. Vendors typically believe they can reduce the costs of many processes by at least 10%–20%. As vendor pricing is typically variable, and as system investments become the vendor's burden, outsourcing should make the wealth manager's cost structure more variable.
2. *Enables reallocation of resources towards the core business.* Wealth managers are increasingly looking to allocate scarce resources to revenue-oriented activities. That makes non-core operations prime candidates for outsourcing.
3. *Provides access to expertise and scale.* Increasing product and business complexity requires administrative capabilities that wealth managers may not have. Also, without sufficient scale in these areas, overcoming the investment in infrastructure can substantially extend the profitability cycle times. Key product areas here include alternative investments and separate accounts. More generally, improved service quality and performance can be important drivers, e.g. in areas such as tax advice, asset management, corporate finance and the finance function.
4. *Provides flexibility to respond to external changes.* Flexibility to respond cost effectively and quickly to external changes is becoming increasingly valuable. For example, outsourcing may prove more cost effective than upgrading and expanding an existing system for those wealth managers that face capacity constraints in growing assets, volumes, accounts or products. Outsourcing may also be deployed by wealth managers facing increased systems investments driven by regulatory change (e.g. need for increased reporting disclosure) and technological changes (e.g. shift to straight through processing). Greater flexibility gained through outsourcing can be a change driver enabling accelerated transformation of legacy business and operational processes and structures.

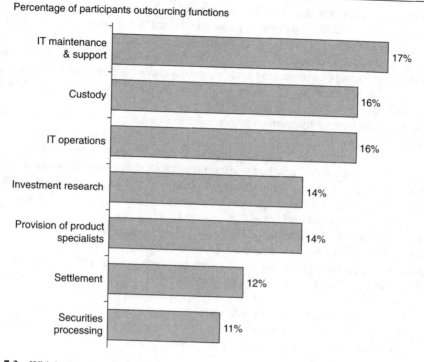

Percentage of participants outsourcing functions

IT maintenance & support — 17%
Custody — 16%
IT operations — 16%
Investment research — 14%
Provision of product specialists — 14%
Settlement — 12%
Securities processing — 11%

Figure 7.3 Which operations do you currently outsource?
Source: IBM Consulting Services, European Wealth and Private Banking Industry Survey 2005. Reproduced by permission.

Outsourcing can also play a key role in addressing the wealth management industry's ethical concerns. If in-house resources are insufficient to monitor trading practices or if there are potential conflicts of interest, outsourcing can provide an objective, third-party overseer to verify that all compliance issues are dealt with properly.

Specific outsourcing drivers vary across the value chain. For example, economies of scale are particularly relevant to back-office functions; improved service quality and access to new or better competencies may be more relevant for middle-office and support functions. As shown in Figure 7.3, the most frequently outsourced functions are currently IT maintenance and support, custody and IT operations. More than half of participants in Mercer Oliver Wyman's European Wealth Management Survey 2004 had outsourced some activities.

There can be substantial differences among the functions outsourced to third-party vendors and those shared with other parts of the parent group via a shared-service centre. When working with a shared-service centre, major outsourced components are settlement processes followed by custody and payments.

A good example of an outsourcing arrangement is a wealth manager choosing to transfer the completion of clients' standard, less-complex tax returns to a large specialist vendor. That results in (a) a lower cost per tax return, by taking advantage of the vendor's scale and by being able to reduce the number of in-house staff dedicated to basic tax returns, and (b) only the larger, more complex tax returns being handled in-house, so the remaining staff are able to focus on processing the more complex returns and expert tax resources can be deployed to offer tax advice and planning and to capitalise on cross-selling opportunities.

Similarly, an in-house trading department, while often a core activity for institutional clients, seems less important for private clients. Private clients tend to deal in much smaller trade sizes and in more liquid securities. Some banks already outsource trade execution, through a system of automatic placement of orders up to a specific size. For some wealth managers, such as Julius Baer and Vontobel, outsourcing trade execution may make less sense given the size of their client assets and their dependency on institutional business. These banks could, however, take on trade execution for private banking competitors.

Yet outsourcing is currently mostly confined to selected products, rather than entire activities. That leaves many wealth managers continuing to run areas – such as post-trade activities – that add little value and in which they have little specialist competence. Most wealth managers also intend to keep the 'core' of client portfolio management in-house, although it is already possible to outsource this function to more efficient players at lower cost. Hence, while the outsourcing drivers seem compelling, wealth managers have not, it is safe to say, traditionally been at the cutting edge of developments in this area.

For a long period historically, growth and profitability resulted in wealth managers largely ignoring rising costs in pursuit of revenue growth. The nature of private banking, with its traditional emphasis on secrecy, led to a concern that outsourcing could compromise client data confidentiality. More generally, players questioned the availability of credible outsourcing-solution vendors – and whether outsourcing would generate real cost savings, whether it would provide genuine service enhancements and whether it could lower the risk profile.

From the wealth manager's perspective, the key specific feasibility barriers hindering the value capture from outsourcing are as follows:

- *Vendors' capabilities.* There is a real or perceived lack of providers able to offer services at required service levels and at a sufficiently lower cost. Many banks remain unconvinced that providers have the capabilities to deliver services adequately. In particular, larger wealth managers that have spent a great deal of time and investment in improving the quality of various services are typically less willing to believe service quality can be enhanced by outsourcing. This real or perceived lack of capable providers, especially in operations, refers not only to the available offerings but also to whether providers can meet banks' requirements, such as the high-security levels demanded for client account data. Depending on the function, vendors are not always able to deliver enough cost reduction to justify outsourcing. That is particularly the case for more complex outsourcing arrangements that require a significant amount of customisation or in cases in which the vendor's scale is not large enough to offer sizeable efficiencies. In many cases, processes across wealth managers remain disparate enough that standardised vendor platforms cannot deliver the certain unique components regarded as important by wealth managers. When the costs of customisation are prohibitive in these cases, the value proposition of outsourcing is diluted. Going forward, this concern could dissipate as vendors' platforms include more functionality and as wealth managers become more willing to compromise certain features of their processes to save costs.
- *Wealth managers' readiness.* This may be influenced, in part, by the degree of internal transparency on internal costs and service levels. Banks may be inadequately prepared and lack specific expertise to enter into and manage an outsourcing arrangement. Many do not have a formal outsourcing policy and strategy in place, and internal service transparency is often inadequate (e.g. process documentation is lacking, cost structures and unit costs are unclear and service levels have not been formalised). Thus, it is difficult to determine the scope of an outsourcing opportunity and set cost and service-level targets. Moreover,

business cases for outsourcing opportunities are not systematically developed, and they may contain inaccuracies and gaps due to the difficulty of measuring value and feasibility. Organisationally, staff transfers can be a tough issue to manage. To avoid conflicts, staff are often not correctly redeployed or transferred to where they can add real value.

- *Sustainability.* This can be the cost and complexity of reversing or changing an outsourcing relationship. While wealth managers would prefer to hand off administrative decisions in an outsourcing arrangement, the question remains as to who is liable when something goes wrong. Mostly for this reason, wealth managers want to retain control over decisions that affect service quality. They remain concerned that they would also lose flexibility in making strategic decisions if entire operations were outsourced and the vendor was not able to make the necessary adjustments. Issues can arise concerning interface management, such as how to handle change requests or deciding which of the partners is accountable for which steps along the value chain. Part of the problem of sustainability is what to do when a partnership proves unsustainable; reversing or changing deals is often complex and costly because of contractual penalties or long changeover periods.

In addition, while most wealth managers are interested in creating a more variable cost structure, many are hoping that the current pick-up in financial markets and product demand will help leverage their current fixed operating cost structure into improved operating margins.

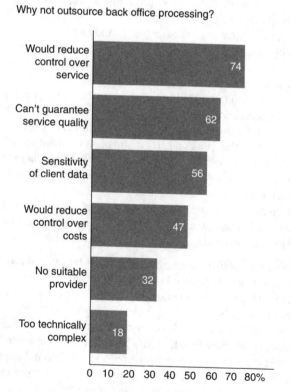

Figure 7.4   Barriers to implementing outsourcing
Source: SEI Investments (2004a); Continental Research. Reproduced by permission.

The above is supported by industry surveys. Figure 7.4 shows that the top concern of wealth managers is the risk of jeopardising client relationships from losing direct control over service levels and costs. This is particularly relevant in the current market environment, where many client relationships remain under strain. Surveys also reveal a real ongoing concern among wealth managers about the risk involved in handing over confidential data to third parties. Overall, many wealth managers are concerned about the cost–benefit tradeoff, though there are signs that this is changing.

Outsourcing patterns vary by region. North American wealth managers are the most advanced adopters of outsourcing, ahead of both Europe and Asia-Pacific. To some extent, this reflects relative market maturity, as well as cultural considerations; historical performance pressures also contributed to early acceptance of investment management subadvisory arrangements.

Outsourcing is also clearly influenced by the supply side. Many traditional and innovative new vendors have been aggressively selling their services. Many US vendors are now actively targeting the European market. Their success has so far been mixed, linked, in part, to wealth managers' concerns over whether these vendors' systems and processes are sufficiently tailored to local-market requirements. That reflects a more general problem for vendors in that different market and product structures, as well as different regulatory and compliance regimes, have made it difficult for them to generate scale economies. Wealth managers are also becoming increasingly discerning and selecting best-of-breed vendors. They are also adopting a selective approach to outsourcing, even though vendors push 'global' deals, which cover several services.

For many wealth managers, a major cultural shift is now under way, gradually helping them to overcome their resistance to outsourcing. Smaller players have been most active in outsourcing. But with cost pressure rising in recent years, there is now a clear trend among medium and larger players at least to deepen their understanding of outsourcing.

In considering whether to outsource, at the outset, banks clearly need to weigh up the case for external service provision compared with the potential value generated through internal improvements. Having selected the activities to be outsourced, the first step is to get them into a position to be outsourced; failure to do so will mean that the service provider captures the bulk of the value. It is important that banks clearly distinguish between the effects of this service 'clean-up' (a one-off project) from the effects of outsourcing (ongoing service improvement) to enable proper value attribution between the two phases. That establishes the basis for fair value sharing between the bank and the provider.

Outsourcing can create significant value. However, capturing that value requires excellent preparation, implementation and execution. There is no single path to success, but McKinsey propose a three-phase, best-practice approach to outsourcing deals:

1. *Create the conditions, establish transparency and define the opportunity.* The basic principle is for a bank to outsource only what it knows and controls. It is key to establishing internal transparency, identifying inefficiencies and benchmarking performance in order to set clear cost and service-level targets.
2. *Analyse and assess the opportunity.* It is critical for banks to build their own independent business cases based on net present value (NPV) calculations. Moreover, alternatives must be considered and the case for outsourcing compared with the internal improvement potential. In evaluating the provider landscape, banks should focus the screening and tendering process on the key criteria of service delivery, including obtaining service and industry-relevant reference cases, and the potential for creating a trust-based relationship with a particular provider.

Box 7.1   Wealth management insourcing

Specialists such as SEI, SunGard and State Street dominate the provision of wealth management outsourcing services. But large-scale wealth management players with world-class operations also have the opportunity to provide business-to-business services to other banks. In doing so, they are able to leverage their own infrastructure and systems by insourcing processes and volumes.

UBS is a good example of one of the more active insourcers. Under its 'Bank for Banks' initiative, UBS offers banks access to its products, operations and international onshore and offshore booking centres. Indeed, UBS can provide bank partners with a complete 'virtual private bank' solution. That enables bank partners to expand their geographical reach and service offering, while retaining client servicing in-house. Specific services offered by UBS include:

- Market intelligence and decision support:
  (a) Private investor research.
  (b) Trading research.
  (c) Portfolio brokerage service.
- Business execution and liquidity provision:
  (a) Portfolio management.
  (b) Private placement funds.
  (c) International private banking services.
  (d) Collateralised lending.
- Processing:
  (a) Private banking service platforms.
  (b) Client reporting and performance analytics.
- Client servicing
  (a) Non-competitive joint client servicing.

The services are modular and can be tailored precisely to the partner bank's needs, enabling it to optimise specific parts of the value chain. Many of these services are usable as part of an integrated, front-to-back solution, and provide access to UBS infrastructure through a fully automated interface. UBS has developed a range of insourcing business models, including a transparent fee-sharing concept or service-based pricing.

Under such an arrangement, the insourcer gains a new revenue stream and further economies of scale, which can lower unit costs and make its operations more efficient. The partner bank improves its operational efficiency and gains cost-effective access to new services, backed by state-of-the-art technology, and can focus on its core competencies. The partner bank's clients also gain access to a broader range of world-class products and services.

Banks intending to offer insourcing clearly need to overcome other banks' understandable reluctance to outsource parts of their business to a potential competitor. Insourcing will also mean extensive systems upgrades for banks, as well as the need to develop new organisational skills for professional service delivery (e.g. contract management, sales orientation, service level definition, client reporting, systems integration and project management).

3. *Implement the deal to capture the full value.* Banks need to actively manage the deal and implement formal, detailed interaction processes, and rigorously track performance. For the worst-case scenario, it is in a bank's own interest to improve the reversibility of the deal by building clear exit clauses into contracts and to determine the support that the provider must supply in such a situation. It should be stressed that entering into an outsourcing deal necessitates significant organisational change. In order to shift the focus successfully from execution and service delivery to managing the provider's service quality, new roles need to be established and processes adjusted, and the required mix of staff will change.

In the longer term, IBM expects leading industry players to move to more on-demand-oriented models, which they define as an enterprise in which business processes are integrated end to end across the company and with key partners, vendors and customers. That will enable wealth managers to respond with speed to any client demand, market opportunity or external threat. These future models are an evolution of previous business process improvements combined with value-added technology enablers. IBM expects incremental movement in this direction as technologies evolve.

Going forward, wealth managers expect to outsource mostly in the support arena, while selective outsourcing of middle- and front-office processes are also under more active consideration. The trend towards open product architecture (whether in the form of selective picking of products and services or the broader definition of seeking best-in-class solutions) is also likely to fuel more demand for outsourcing services in the near future.

Those wealth managers who take the lead in outsourcing and overcome apparent concerns over confidentiality and service have potential opportunities to achieve a cost advantage, at least temporarily; they may also be able to build long-term structural cost improvements that become competitive advantages. As downward pressure on margins continues, wealth managers need to assess more rigorously how these barriers – real or perceived – can be overcome.

7.1.2   Operational offshoring

For the more adventurous wealth managers, a new solution to the operational dilemma has emerged in recent years: offshoring, i.e. the internationalisation of operations to cross-border hubs in low-cost locations such as India, China, the Philippines, and select locations in Latin America, Eastern Europe and South Africa. Overall, offshoring can deliver a sustainable cost reduction of 30%–60%. The main sources of operational benefit are largely twofold:

- *Cost arbitrage.* The first and most prominent benefit is lower labour costs. In well-chosen locations, the availability of skilled labour is plentiful and increasing. The manpower is available at somewhere between 20% and 40% of the cost in advanced Western economies. Put another way, for any given level of wage cost, the skill available is much greater offshore. The fear that offshore locations would compromise service quality has been dispelled by the early experiences of global leaders (see below). Historically, the labour-cost advantage was largely offset by inadequate and more expensive telecommunications. But in recent years, locations outside the Western hemisphere have made radical improvements in that area.
- *Access to scarce skills.* For some activities, e.g. software development, the labour advantage of offshoring is not just a lower unit cost per skill level but the sheer availability of staff with the necessary skills. Offshoring to India has proved particularly successful, given that over the last five years, its number of IT professionals has more than doubled. Similarly, Ireland offers a large pool of investment professionals.

For the many wealth managers that have operations in multiple locations, offshoring creates an opportunity to concentrate activities into a single centre or into a few hubs, each supporting business activity in multiple countries.

Offshoring, particularly for the first time, poses significant logistical challenges. There is a wide gulf between formulating the business case for offshoring – which in most circumstances is robust – and the successful delivery of high-quality, low-cost operational capability in a new location. It is helpful to analyse the offshoring decision across six components: opportunity scoping, location, operating model, commercial model, partner selection/contract negotiation and setup/rollout:

1. *Opportunity scoping.* Several dimensions need to be addressed in assessing the potential scope of the opportunity: first, obtaining clarity of business logic for selecting processes to offshore; second, assessing the financial advantage from offshoring the processes selected; and third, determining the sequences and phasing, so as to reflect the bank's priorities and risk assessment.
2. *Location.* The main drivers of country selection are twofold: first, labour, including cost, quality and type of skills, and fluency in the required language; and second, economic and political geography, including infrastructure, time zone, investment incentives and political risk. Across all the locations, India, the Philippines and China are emerging as the leading low-cost countries in which to locate offshore.
3. *Operating model.* The operating model needs to address microlevel operational issues. Primary among them is the coordination of activities between the onshore and offshore locations. Setting the right SLA is important, as is deciding on risk contingency and disaster recovery plans. It is critical to ensure that quality control is applied to offshore operations as stringently as it is to onshore operations. The operating model also needs to address issues of operations structure, in particular the degree of centralisation, the appropriate number of hubs and which business locations they serve.
4. *Commercial model.* The commercial model addresses high-level organisational issues, including whether to outsource to a third-party vendor or to set up a captive operation offshore. There is no common best practice model here; instead, commercial arrangements need to be tailored to banks' individual capabilities and objectives. Early movers adopted the captive model, reflecting the absence of credible outsourcing vendors at that time. Today, a wide choice of commercial models is available, ranging from arm's-length outsourcing to a captive service company, and including several intermediate partnering options such as strategic investment, joint venture and assisted build-out.
5. *Partner selection and contract negotiation.* The issue of partner selection is necessarily intertwined with the choice of commercial model. The availability and financial terms of a potential partner will be one of the key drivers of model choice. As with any outsourcing or operational partnership arrangement, a highly disciplined and fact-based evaluation of partners is necessary, followed by due diligence and contract negotiation. The total process of evaluation and negotiation can take from three to six months.
6. *Setup and rollout.* The final step is setting up a pilot and then rolling it out to full-scale operation. That involves several disciplines: governance, microlevel process transition management, performance management, human resource management, operational risk management and communication.

The activities amenable to offshoring are already wide ranging, and their scope will increase as wealth managers gain in confidence from early experimentation. Looking further ahead, in principle nearly all wealth management processing, functional support and remote client contact activity could be performed offshore.

7.1.2.1 Offshoring examples

- *HSBC.* The HSBC Group is an offshoring pioneer, having begun in 1996. It now uses a global operating model involving more than 10 000 employees across India, China and Malaysia. Its private banking business uses six processing centres located in Hyderabad, Bangalore, Pune, Guangzhou, Malaysia and Shanghai. Many processes have been migrated from HSBC Banking Offshore Services (based in the Isle of Man and Jersey). The main private banking activities relocated include fund clearing, international payments, pre-authorised payments and closures, stops and transfers.

  HSBC has mainly adopted the captive model, driven by concern over sharing proprietary information and systems, the need for sufficient global scale and its inherent familiarity with low-cost locations such as India, China and South-East Asia.

  The global operating model has been a considerable success. At the group level, overall cost savings have been estimated to be 40%–60% relative to UK onshore operations. Other benefits include a productivity increase of around 20% and higher quality service, e.g. a 3 percentage point improvement in payment processing accuracy. HSBC has also gained from being able to realise greater synergies from cross-border mergers and acquisitions, e.g. CCF in France.

  Going forward, HSBC has plans to migrate the bulk of its private banking operations to India. More generally, it plans rapidly to scale up its offshore contact centres and to relocate more high-end activities such as research. It has no plans to outsource business processes to third-party providers, but it does see potential to serve other banks via insourcing arrangements.
- *American Express.* American Express is another offshoring pioneer. It now uses a global operating model involving more than 6 000 employees in India and the Philippines. In private banking, it has relocated some brokerage advisory capacity to serve selected mass affluent and HNW clients. Like HSBC, it has plans to relocate more high-end and knowledge-based processes such as client information management. AmEx's overall model has evolved to a mix of captive and third-party vendors. For private banking activities, it uses the captive model, driven mainly by confidentiality concerns. Overall, the global operating model's realised benefits include cost savings and productivity and service-quality uplifts.
- *Other examples.* The most common private banking activity to be relocated offshore is IT application development and maintenance, mainly to India via third-party outsourcing arrangements. Examples here include Goldman Sachs, Merrill Lynch, UBS and Credit Suisse.

7.2 LEAN OPERATIONS

Wealth management clients require flawless and prompt transaction execution. In this context, wealth managers (indeed, most financial institutions) have much to learn from industrial manufacturers. World-class manufacturers have long applied the principles of lean manufacturing to optimise their operations. These principles focus on eliminating waste, variability and inflexibility from the production process in order to minimise costs and time involved in production and to maximise process quality. There are a number of related techniques, ranging from straightforward core-process redesign to more sophisticated quality assurance concepts such as Six Sigma (see Box 7.2).[3]

Box 7.2   Six Sigma

In their strive for continuous operational efficiency improvements, some wealth managers – including Citigroup, Credit Suisse and Merrill Lynch – are employing Six Sigma techniques. Six Sigma is a long-term company-wide strategic approach to optimising processes. (A sigma is a statistical term that measures the extent to which a process deviates from perfection: three sigma equals 66 807 defects per million opportunities; Six Sigma equals 3.4 defects per million opportunities – virtual perfection.)

Example: international funds transfer

An international private bank faced increasing client dissatisfaction as a result of inefficiencies in its international funds-transfer operations. The problems included delays in transferring funds, transmission of funds to the wrong target account and transmission of the wrong amount. Clients were inconvenienced by the bank typically having to call them back to confirm orders and correct errors. They also complained about the bank's mid-afternoon cut-off time for requesting funds transfers, which was much earlier than that of competitors. These inefficiencies led to high funds-transfer processing costs.

To help solve these problems, the bank put together an internal team, with members drawn from every unit that contributed to the process. Due to their close vantage point, these employees could offer valuable insight. Management empowered the team to implement the changes that they developed.

The team's first task was to diagnose the problem. It developed a detailed process map, describing the functions involved in each step of the funds-transfer process. That uncovered inconsistent processes for initiating funds transfers, which resulted in incorrect processing instructions, incomplete information and missing signatures. The majority of transfers were subjected to re-work, including laborious retyping from faxes and verification by two separate offices. One in four transfers contained an error. Relationship managers used different methods of processing transfers. In addition, one-off errors had, over the years, led to the introduction of unnecessary checks and balances, including frequent call-backs to clients.

Overall, these inefficiencies resulted in an average processing time of 47 minutes per transaction. In addition, the early cut-off time resulted in some 20 transfer requests per day being held over until the following day.

To identify the impact of each of these individual problems, the team used simple analytical tools such as the Pareto chart. Analysing the bank's funds transfers by client, including volume and amount, the team found that the 25 most active clients initiated 15% of transfers, clients with AuM of less than $100 000 accounted for 30% of transfers and clients

---

[3] Lean operations and Six Sigma are, in principle, distinct but complementary concepts: lean was originally designed to tackle waste; Six Sigma was originally targeted at variability. In practice, lean is a participative process, whilst Six Sigma is driven by a central group of resources. Lean can, in some instances, be combined with Six Sigma. See Drew, McCallum and Roggenhofer (2004).

with AuM of more than $1million accounted for 27% of transfers. Yet error prevention and resolution procedures did not take these patterns of activity into account.

That analysis enabled the team to implement a series of quick wins, such as extending the cut-off time to the industry standard. They also developed a plan to tackle the root causes of the problems and to prevent their recurrence. The low-tech, high-impact implementation included standardised forms for clients and bank personnel to eliminate duplicated work, standardised procedures to eliminate variations among country groups and streamlined policies to greatly reduce client call-backs.

In terms of impact, the transfer cycle time fell from 47 minutes to 22 minutes. That increased efficiency, cut the cost per transaction by over 50% and enabled the bank to lower its transaction fees. The reduction in duplicated work and number of errors has also enabled the client service department to operate on the principle of single-call resolution for any problems that do arise. Equally important, the bank is well positioned for the long term to undertake further automation of the funds-transfer process.

The principles of lean manufacturing are just as applicable in a wealth management service environment. The wealth management back office is similar to manufacturing in that paper and data are moved through an end-to-end operational process, similar to the way a physical product moves in a manufacturing environment. Other similarities include:

- Error-prone processes where quality control is important.
- Repetitive tasks.
- People-intensive processes.
- Standardised (or 'standardiseable') process steps.
- Variety of subprocesses included in each process step.
- Multiple hand-offs.
- Volume of work may vary, but is relatively predictable over any given time period.

It follows that the potential for improvement through application of lean production principles is particularly high in the back office.

Examples of lean manufacturing applications are as follows:

- *Establishing service factories*. Service factories are the conceptual equivalent of call centres for distribution, i.e. a managed environment where wealth managers can centralise and industrialise their processes. It is all too common for a private bank to have a number of operation centres doing essentially the same thing, but each falling short of achieving the critical scale and quality. Hence, the challenge is to consolidate these multiple, fragmented operating centres into centralised factories in which industrial disciplines can be established (one way of doing this, regionalisation, is discussed in Chapter 8).
- *Advanced process mapping and redesign*. To ensure the cost efficiency of service factories and to identify improvement opportunities throughout the entire value chain of a private bank requires a continuous process improvement programme. That involves taking an end-to-end perspective, from the client all the way through to the operational process, with a view to re-engineering as a way to reduce cost and cycle time and increase quality. An important principle here is straight through processing (STP), which should be implemented whenever possible. STP has taken root in wholesale banking, but wealth management lags behind. There is an urgent need to redesign processes to eliminate hand-offs and reduce errors and

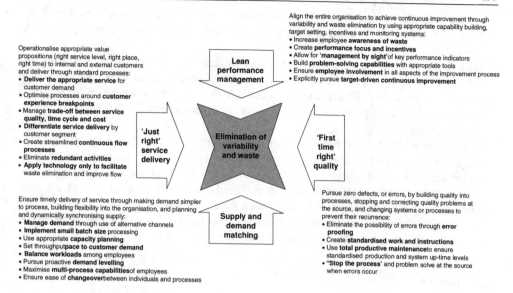

Figure 7.5   The lean operations platform for wealth managers
Source: McKinsey & Company. Reproduced by permission.

cost, not just fix up existing processes. That applies to the whole range of wealth management processes from account opening to transaction processing.

- *Introducing client- and product-specific target service levels.* It is equally important to tailor service levels according to client segment, thereby aligning cost-to-serve with client value. That can result in fundamental changes to service levels. A good example here is Merrill Lynch, which has successfully migrated its mass affluent clients to a call-centre-oriented service model (or 'financial advisory centre'), with centralised advice.

7.2.1   Four lean principles

To achieve best practice, wealth managers need to pursue simultaneous improvement against the time, cost and quality parameters by applying the four lean principles of 'just right' service delivery, supply and demand matching, 'first time right' quality and lean performance management to eliminate variability, inflexibility and waste from processes and end products (see Figure 7.5):

- *'Just right' service* refers to delivering the right end product or right service level to the right place, in the right amount, at the right time, every time. The objective is clearly and directly to link the bank's processing to customer requirements and delivering these requirements. One of the largest levers to achieve this is creating streamlined, continuous-flow processes.
- *Supply and demand matching* entails smoothing inputs where possible (e.g. channel management and processing small, frequent 'batches' rather than large batches) and matching capacity to demand.
- *'Right first time' quality* reduces variability and eliminate re-work waste. Again, this has positive cost and timeliness impact, but the potential impact on quality should not be underrated, as quality typically suffers when work must be reprocessed. The specific levers

include a number of error-proofing systems to ensure that mistakes cannot be made and that, if they are made, they are addressed as rapidly as possible by stopping processing where the mistake took place.

- *Lean performance management* ensures that improvement keeps occurring over time. That contrasts with historic performance improvement initiatives, which have very often been exercises in headcount reduction and process redesign with the objective of cutting costs today, but that lacked a perspective on the long-term impact on process flexibility and a view towards strategic change.

To a greater extent than in other parts of the value chain, back-office improvements are fundamentally driven by building employee problem-solving skills and their awareness of the impact of the back-office on customer service levels. Experience suggests that back-office staff have neither been trained nor empowered to problem solve and, as a result, their capabilities to drive improvement have not been realised. Lean operators track performance in a highly visible and transparent way ('management by sight') and teach as many people in the organisation as possible to recognise and eliminate waste.

7.2.2   Benefits

A lean back office delivers high-quality results through a consistent process and service delivery the first time, every time. That has three clear benefits: rapid and tangible cost reduction, optimisation of service delivery capabilities and the potential for new strategic options.

7.2.2.1   Rapid and tangible cost reduction

In private banks, the use of lean principles is relatively new but has already led to a very positive impact. Average cost reductions on the order of 15%–25% are the norm, not the exception. Given that the back office typically comprises 25%–35% of the total cost base, this translates into a significant bottom line impact through an improvement in the operating efficiency ratio of 2–4 percentage points.

The general approach in a lean transformation is to make near-term step-change improvements and, in the process, build the awareness, involvement and capabilities of the workforce to instill an ongoing performance improvement mindset. A lean transformation is distinctive in that improvements are systematically applied to deliver benefits across the entire process, not simply to establish local islands of excellence with little hope of sustainable impact. Typically, 70% of short-term savings are implemented in the first year and all of the short-term savings are implemented in 18 months,[4] with the expectation that continuous improvement activity will realise additional annual cost improvements of at least 5%. As an added bonus, the investments needed to capture these benefits are typically minimal.

7.2.2.2   Accurate, high-quality service delivery capabilities

Instilling the lean philosophy and principles and applying its tools and techniques can simultaneously improve cost performance, cycle time, and quality of the process and end product. That is achieved by focusing the back office on working with the rest of the organisation

---

[4] Though it is possible to capture the bulk of the initial benefit within as little as three months for a single process, achieving an *ongoing* benefit requires a change in management mindsets and behaviour which takes considerably longer.

to understand business priorities, translating them into explicit service-level agreements and adapting processes to deliver the service in the lowest cost manner. Thus, while generating huge benefits in terms of the bottom line, cycle time reductions of 50% or more are frequently achieved. Because one of the main lean principles is accurate service delivery the first time, every time, quality is also dramatically improved as process variability is eliminated and errors are captured and corrected in real time rather than through re-work processes. In this way, client service levels are also improved.

Lean back offices can also provide the flexibility in service levels required to support highly segmented client service strategies such as CRM strategies. An appropriately structured CRM programme can result in a 10%–20% increase in revenue per client, but only if the back office can deliver the operational capacity and responsiveness needed to deliver on client response to new business campaigns. Otherwise, campaign conversion will falter and any learning will not be captured because the measures of success (or failure) are not accurately recorded.

7.2.2.3   Springboard for the pursuit of long-term strategic options

Clearly, achieving low-cost operator position can act as a springboard to pursue long-term strategic options. For example, a scalable lean platform can be used to enter new product lines or new geographies without an enormous negative impact on the operating efficiency ratio. Alternatively, it can be used as a way to create new market opportunities in terms of taking over aspects of other institutions' operations through infrastructure and process management services such as those being offered by UBS (see Box 7.1 above).

Wealth managers that outsource their own back-office operations can also benefit from implementing lean principles. As noted above, successful outsourcing of back-office operations depends on seamless integration of processes between the outsourcer and the service provider. Achieving seamless integration depends on the client bank having an understanding of best practices, adequate operations and excellent handover capabilities. Lean operations can help wealth managers meet these conditions so that they maximise the value created from outsourcing their operations.

7.2.3   Implementation

Applying lean approaches to the back office is not easy. It requires a major cultural change and training effort and, on occasion, process upheaval during the change period. Therefore, it is vitally important that top management commits to and leads the change process.

The typical improvement process involves diagnosing the current situation (clarifying the high level 'current state'), developing an overall improvement programme, including a 'burning platform for change' and choosing and carrying out performance improvement on selected pilot areas. The work in the pilot areas is done by first stabilising and ensuring a consistent 'current state' and then optimising, i.e. creating a blueprint for and beginning to convert to the 'future state'.

Best-practice wealth managers recognise that there is no improvement without first achieving standardisation and stabilisation of processes. Without standard processes, it is impossible to improve on any dimension or, for that matter, to measure improvement.

Once processes are stabilised, i.e. variability is eliminated, 'waste' elimination can begin. In lean terminology, 'waste' is a non-value-added activity of which there are eight types (see Figure 7.6). Eliminating waste improves productivity and reduces costs, reduces throughput

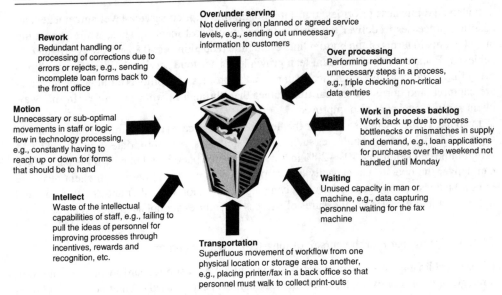

Rework
Redundant handling or processing of corrections due to errors or rejects, e.g., sending incomplete loan forms back to the front office

Over/under serving
Not delivering on planned or agreed service levels, e.g., sending out unnecessary information to customers

Over processing
Performing redundant or unnecessary steps in a process, e.g., triple checking non-critical data entries

Motion
Unnecessary or sub-optimal movements in staff or logic flow in technology processing, e.g., constantly having to reach up or down for forms that should be to hand

Work in process backlog
Work back up due to process bottlenecks or mismatches in supply and demand, e.g., loan applications for purchases over the weekend not handled until Monday

Intellect
Waste of the intellectual capabilities of staff, e.g., failing to pull the ideas of personnel for improving processes through incentives, rewards and recognition, etc.

Waiting
Unused capacity in man or machine, e.g., data capturing personnel waiting for the fax machine

Transportation
Superfluous movement of workflow from one physical location or storage area to another, e.g., placing printer/fax in a back office so that personnel must walk to collect print-outs

Figure 7.6   Types of waste in production environments
Source: McKinsey & Company. Reproduced by permission.

time (i.e. no wasted valuable processing time on non-value-added activities) and increases quality (i.e. employees have clarity abound how their responsibilities affect the end client). Thus, by focusing on waste, cost reductions are not pursued at the expense of quality and timeliness improvements, but rather simultaneously.

A significant part of the total potential impact on the performance of the back office can be achieved without significant IT investment. IT investments may, however, be necessary to reach the next level of operational performance, since modern back offices are heavily automated. Successful IT investment depends on the organisation first optimising the processes that it is automating.

Additionally, realising operational improvements from major IT investments is significantly more costly, time consuming and risky than improving operations without major IT changes. Therefore, best practice is to first optimise operations without incurring IT investments. Thereafter, IT investment should be justified on the basis of further improvement potential. For example, one best-practice player envisages achieving large improvements in the unit cost of transaction processing in the back office through first re-engineering processes, then automating these processes and finally capturing benefits of scale.

Ensuring a lean operating platform is much more than just carrying out a set of process steps to generate cost-reduction measures. Instead, it requires transfer of knowledge and tools to ensure that savings continue over the long term. For this reason, the emphasis needs to be on skill building and organisational transformation, not just cost reduction, throughout the process.

7.3   TECHNOLOGY TRANSFORMATION

Technology has increased in complexity and cost. Key IT issues and trends include: client reporting, managing high IT costs (and dealing with limited funding) and enabling straight-through processing and the ability to accommodate regulatory and business change. More generally, there is a need to deal with increasingly complex system architecture. Robust links to third-party systems are seen as increasingly important going forward.

Customised and sophisticated client reporting has become an essential building block in the branding of wealth managers in their desire to communicate their added value. A related IT issue is how to provide relationship managers with a single, integrated view of client product holdings.

As wealth managers move to share more activities and functions, the interplay among business components and IT becomes ever more important. Connectivity among partners requires more end-to-end integration among people (collaboration), processes (workflows) and information (data management) across businesses and with partners in the extended network.

Four basic IT organisational models have emerged:

- Core private banking package model, where a universal private banking package covers all major processes and functions of the private banking operations. There are only a few satellites for special purposes (e.g. regulatory reporting).
- Product split model, where different IT systems are in place for selected banking products. These support the processes horizontally from front to back, e.g. for payments, securities and credits. A common customer relationship management (CRM) application, however, integrates the front-office functions.
- Functional split model, where different vertical IT systems are in place for selected functions along the bank, e.g. one system for the front, one for trading, one platform for the whole back office and another software package for accounting.
- Mixed model, in which there are strong vertical CRM and portfolio management and trading systems, with horizontal systems for backbone processes.

The core private banking package and the mixed model are the most commonly used. Large wealth managers and private banks have a tendency to rely more on the mixed model, while smaller players are more focused around a single-core private banking package. An additional issue to consider with the mixed model is which components are actually owned specifically by the private bank and which are shared with the parent group and/or outside third parties. In this context, there is a risk in large organisations to seek to standardise too much, leading to the suboptimisation of the client experience.

Wealth managers have struggled to realise the added value generated by significant investments and most particularly in enabling the delivery of services to the front office. Senior executives have traditionally had difficulty in understanding the return on their investments in this area. IBM estimates that almost a third of all investment in IT has at best failed to deliver full value and at worst delivered no value at all. Limited funding has become an issue as players seek to maximise value from their existing investments and focus their investments in new systems on those areas where they can justify expenditure in terms of short-term, tangible, bottom-line impact. A related issue is the need for large initial investments followed by regular upgrades as technological cycles shorten.

A successful technological transformation should address infrastructure (including all production-related IT hardware, facilities and people), applications and architecture (including the separation of applications, databases and presentation). The business/technology interface must also be considered. It is notoriously difficult for the business side to specify its requirements in such a way that the IT side can deliver them accurately. A dialogue between the two is needed to ensure the right priorities and service levels. To start such a dialogue, certain basics should be in place. First, transparent pricing for the products offered by IT has to be agreed.

Second, jointly developed service level agreements have to clarify the needs of the business side. Third, continuous budget and cost control should be installed to focus IT and business efforts effectively.

7.4 VALUE-ADDED SUPPORT SERVICES

Support services are functions that do not generate revenue directly; they include finance, compliance, HR, audit and legal. Despite significant belt-tightening over the past few years, these services currently account for around 15% of a typical wealth manager's cost base. The best firms have eliminated all non-essential corporate services and consistently deliver high-quality, low-cost support to the organisation.

The right approach to use to capture cost savings in these areas varies by type of firm. For firms that have grown organically (versus by acquisition), substantial cost reduction in the overhead functions typically requires a 'clean-sheet' approach, in which the specific activities of each overhead function are assessed to determine if their value exceeds their costs and whether they should be insourced or outsourced. For firms that have been built up via merger, there are often substantial savings to be realised by combining duplicated support activities across managers and business areas.

A key step for any restructuring should be to find the right size for these services. An oversized support area sends the wrong signals to the entire organisation about what is important and where the real power lies. If too many important second- and third-level positions are located in this area and if there are more support services positions than client-facing positions, then the laws of gravity dictate that a bank will focus more on its internal affairs than on those of the client. A bloated support area tends to appropriate power from the front line, thus hindering fast, market-oriented decision making. Also, high support-area costs have to be allocated to business units – a process that ends up being a source of unproductive debate.

Though not exclusively within support services, external or purchase costs also have strong savings potential. These costs include real estate, telephony, travel and office supplies, which together can represent 10%–20% of a wealth manager's cost base. While retailers and manufacturers have been ruthless about the management of suppliers, wealth managers (indeed, most financial institutions) have been relatively lax. Starting from a thorough understanding of the existing purchase cost base, the key lies in a rigorous approach to three main sources of opportunity:

- *Vendor management.* Typically, banks have a large number of suppliers who can be squeezed by introducing new suppliers (or by consolidating existing ones) and applying open-price bidding for key contracts. By applying another tool from manufacturing – the 'total cost approach' – banks can actively identify cost-reduction potential along the entire product/service supply chain and renegotiate prices with vendors, especially vendor-related costs for ordering and delivery.
- *Demand management.* A simple, central revision of the purchase database using internal and external benchmarking usually reveals unnecessary – yet somehow institutionalised – spending, such as on support services office space. Banks need to define a purchasing behaviour code and enforce compliance with its policies (e.g. eliminate maverick buying by using a list of official suppliers and refusing to settle accounts with non-official suppliers).

- *Purchasing processes and organisation.* An appropriate segmentation of purchasing processes, according to the importance and complexity of spending, is essential for a powerful purchasing organisation. In excellent organisations, around 80% of purchasing is centralised; in the average wealth manager, centralisation varies from 20% to 50%. A major advantage of better segmentation is the separation of negotiation from administration in purchasing, with skilled central staff to manage the negotiation of all high-impact contracts and technical specialists to set the specifications. Banks should also consider investing in relevant skills by hiring core people with solid purchasing backgrounds.

7.5 INSTILLING OPERATIONAL EXCELLENCE

Operational excellence and cost management are not about one-off initiatives or ad hoc measures. The focus must be on creating and sustaining a cost management culture and demonstrating the disciplines described above. That is easier said than done. More often than not, the challenges are internal: targets are unclear, costs are opaque, responsibility is diffused across organisational silos, and top management, which is usually well versed in strategy, may not be as familiar with operations and technology. Expect to see more manufacturing-style chief operating officers (COOs) in wealth managers who are serious about operational efficiency.

Cost leaders will thrive, but cost laggards are unlikely to remain independent. Consequently, the drive to operational excellence must come from the top, with clear aspirations, accountability, transparency and relentless focus. Figure 7.7 shows three horizons of operational efficiency. While short-term cost improvements are comparatively easy to achieve, the second and third horizons require a quite fundamental operational redesign and changes in the cost culture.

7.5.1 Operational redesign

A fundamental operational redesign effort starts by considering where and how to participate across the value chain. That is the first step of a journey in which the wealth manager is focusing

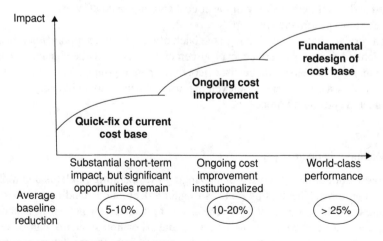

Figure 7.7 Operational efficiency horizons
Source: Leichtfuss (2003). Reproduced by permission.

on the simplification of complex business processes and aiming to change the economics of their operating model dramatically by moving to a more variable cost base.

That review should not only consider the visibility and importance of their various activities to clients, but also how the firm's ability to deliver on such activities compares to current and emerging alternatives. It should also include an assessment of future investment needs (to upgrade administrative systems, for example), which can tip the balance in favour of a more virtual model. Successful players will make sensible, economically based decisions about value-chain participation, make intelligent use of open architecture, seek active approaches to partnering and reorganise the business into 'modules' that focus individuals and teams on specific value-adding activities, paving the way for further disaggregation of the value chain.

Many players start with legacy infrastructure that is often not up-to-date, well designed and fit for its purpose. Component business units often have their own dedicated back-offices, IT and support functions, and they operate in overseas locations with their own back offices. As wealth managers continue to expand geographically, the necessity to integrate multiple back-office entities becomes an additional challenge. That has typically led to system fragmentation as IT, back-office and administration tools are not always able to cope with local requirements.

On top of that, many wealth managers have to deal with the aftermath of mergers – of the conventional M&A variety and/or internal group reorganisations – where the nuts and bolts of integrating supporting infrastructure have often been postponed for fear of losing good relationship managers and their clients. The result again can be a series of near-independent operating models being run in parallel for an extended period, with very little front-end or back-end integration. (Post-merger integration and process re-engineering – even belatedly – can have a significant impact on cost structures. Up to 70% of post-merger cost savings come from back-office integration, provided integration efforts are executed effectively.)

Increasingly, the optimal operating model must be flexible and robust enough to respond to the industry challenges, such as constant new product development, the need to address new regulatory requirements and penetration of new markets. The end point is a clearly defined operating model – built for tomorrow and sized to the market opportunities. Its key components are as follows:

- A unified and simplified model with lower cost and improved effectiveness.
- An agreed set of governance principles.
- Common service company with integrated back offices, IT and support functions.
- Clearly defined and agreed service level agreements (SLAs) between business units and the service company – whether that be elsewhere in the parent group, an outsourced third-party vendor or a separately managed joint venture arrangement with an industry partner.
- Re-engineered end-to-end processes.

7.5.1.1   Making it happen

At the outset, it should be recognised that changing the operating model is a complex, often multiyear, programme. The starting point is to gain a deep understanding of where value is created, component by component. The objective is to determine whether these activities are generating value, are core versus non-core, are standard or non-standard, can be centralised within the parent or an outside provider or need to remain local for regulatory or firm-specific reasons.

1. *Diagnosis.* The first step is to agree on a set of priorities and initial hypotheses, followed by focused, fact-based analysis. A key output of this exercise will be a cost baseline, including current costs, number of full-time equivalent employees (FTEs) and current service levels by component business, by function and by geography. In conjunction with internal and external benchmarks, this will enable identification of high-cost areas. Informed by research and interviews, the analysis should also identify other key issues to address, such as service-level weaknesses and speed-to-market (including root causes, where possible).

2. *Option generation, validation and evaluation.* The next step is to prioritise issues by strategic and financial importance. That involes defining and agreeing a set of principles to guide the future operating model, aligned to client requirement and business strategies. It is important to consider how options could work together in a joined-up approach. Implications for support functions need to be modelled, and any remaining gaps and enablers identified. Key issues to consider include:

   - How many client segments are targeted?
   - How many distinct channels?
   - How much sharing of support, product and service models?
   - What type of organisational reporting models?
   - How much sharing of platforms and infrastructure?

   One additional issue is to what extent regulatory, tax and client considerations preclude combinations of onshore and offshore operational elements.

3. *Recommendation and high-level design.* The final step is to model the lead options in detail and refine them with key stakeholders. The final recommended operating model should include: people and locations, systems and platforms, customer service operations (including call centres), processing and support functions.

Looking ahead, wealth managers are likely to continue to restructure and reposition themselves along the value chain. Most are expected to specialise increasingly on distribution, with client and fund administration contracted out to large-scale administrators. That fundamental shift towards a more virtual operating model has implications for industry consolidation. Some argue that this could, in fact, reduce the pressure on wealth managers to consolidate, enabling players to boost their cost efficiency through more structural and focused routes, rather than through blanket scale efficiencies alone.

8
Organisational Design

This chapter focuses on organisational design – an issue that is of increasing interest to many wealth management players. As noted in Chapter 6, most successful private banks are part of relatively large and internationally active universal banks and/or combine their private banking activities with other business lines such as asset management and stock broking. That raises a number of opportunities, but also brings challenges.

In principle, the selected organisational design should follow from the specific business model adopted. Yet, in practice, many players have traditionally tended to run their wealth management businesses as stand-alone, autonomous entities. For some players, this partly reflects the relatively small size and specialist nature of these businesses. But many players are reassessing the optimal location and fit of wealth management within their group structures (both functionally and geographically), and are also considering how best to structure the wealth management unit itself.

The chapter is split into three sections:

- Organisational structure.
- Business unit interfaces:
  (a) Asset management.
  (b) Retail bank.
  (c) Investment bank.
- International dimensions.

8.1 ORGANISATIONAL STRUCTURE

A key organisational trend among financial services players is the shift towards greater integration of wealth management with other areas of the group, such as retail banking, investment banking and asset management. The integrated model means that each platform of the firm can service the clients of another platform via its own products. The aim is to capture synergies. On the revenue-growth side, the synergies are largely based on client referrals (Citigroup refers to this as its 'golden Rolodex'). On the cost-saving side, the synergies include infrastructure sharing, centralisation of common activities, and leveraging economies of scale. There can also be some risk-diversification benefits.

UBS was one of the pioneers in this area, starting in 1998, and some now regard it as one of the group's most powerful advantages. Its aim was to 'deliver the firm' in order to meet or exceed client needs via a 'one-firm approach' (or 'professional firm model'). To do so, it encourages the relevant business units to work together efficiently across organisational boundaries. This is, of course, easy to say but extremely difficult to achieve in practice.

The McKinsey European Private Banking Economics Survey 2004 found that private banks currently share most back-office applications with their universal bank parent (see Figure 8.1). But there remains significant potential for private banks to share more of the asset management functions.

Percentage of private banks which are part of universal bank

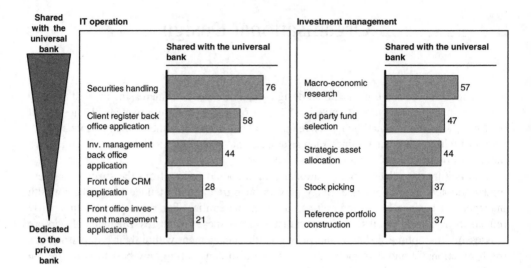

Figure 8.1   Private banking functions shared with the universal bank parent
Source: McKinsey European Private Banking Economics Survey 2004. Reproduced by permission.

A good recent example of the trend towards greater bank-wide integration, away from siloed business units, is Credit Suisse's 'One Bank' group integration initiative, originally announced in June 2004. It means that instead of operating with two banking licences – one for Credit Suisse Financial Services and one for Credit Suisse First Boston (CSFB), the group's investment bank – there will be just one. The group now operates with three core divisions: Private Banking (including the group's wealth management businesses, plus corporate and retail banking); Investment Banking (the former CSFB); and Asset Management, which will combine the various asset-management businesses of the group. The new Private Banking division is outlined in Figure 8.2.

The key aims of this initiative, which is expected to take 18 months to 2 years to complete, are to:

- Improve and broaden client relationships by delivering the group's combined skills and expertise (making use of a new 'global currency', which tracks how much revenue a given client produces acrosss the group).
- Strengthen the group's global product know-how through centres of excellence and cooperation across businesses.
- Exploit opportunities for growth in targeted markets.
- Create more opportunities for the group's employees.
- Make the group's shared services infrastructure more effective and efficient.

8.2   BUSINESS UNIT INTERFACES

The trend towards greater internal integration has increased the importance of ensuring that the interfaces between business lines are structured appropriately, including elements such as transfer pricing, incentives, procedures, and roles and responsibilities. Success here is driven

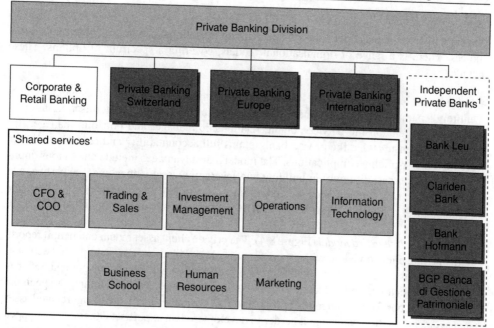

Figure 8.2 Credit Suisse Group organisational structure
Source: Credit Suisse.

more by the correct execution of a specific model than by the selection and structure of the model itself.

As many banks have found – and as with all issues that revolve around client ownership – this is a notoriously difficult thing to get right. There is no unique answer. Much depends on group strategy and objectives, as well as existing arrangements, business performance levels and internal cultural/political considerations. At the outset, it is important to create a shared vision within the group on how to serve HNW clients and to set clear objectives.

Experience suggests that for cross-divisional collaboration to have any chance of success, the private bank needs a strong, influential figurehead capable of convincing the group board that the private bank deserves attention ahead of competing proposals from other business units. Having secured buy-in from the group board, the private banking leader must be able to work constructively with other divisional directors and gain their ongoing commitment to change existing working practices.

Senior management commitment must be clear. Details of accountability, objectives, targets, action plans and resourcing need to be agreed at the outset by all relevant parties. This commitment must be effectively communicated to the relevant employees. They need to be able to see the benefits from change and the commitment of their management to implementation.

We first examine the interface with asset management in some depth, given the important functional overlap with private banking. We then turn to the interfaces with retail banking and investment banking, which are driven more by client overlaps.

---

[1] At the time of writing (April 2006), Credit Suisse announced plans to combine these banks (plus the securities dealer, Credit Suisse Fides) into a single entity – Clariden Leu – which will be Switzerland's fifth-largest bank (behind UBS, Julius Baer, HSBC and, of course, its parent).

8.2.1   Asset management

Players with asset management and private banking operations face important organisational choices. There is a range of organisational models, covering a spectrum of options. These include:

- *Independent model* (Figure 8.3). Private client and institutional asset management are kept entirely separate. This typically enables greater private client product customisation/tailoring and a closer relationship between client, relationship manager and portfolio manager. Independence ensures that the private bank retains full accountability and control, and there are no transfer-pricing complications. The model's disadvantages include an obvious duplication of resources, difficulty in building and leveraging asset management expertise, and the associated risk of inconsistent and poor long-term investment performance. Overall, this model is most applicable when the product demands of private and institutional clients are very different.
- *Private client integrated model* (Figure 8.4). The private client asset management unit reports to the private client division, with strong functional coordination between private client and institutional asset management. That increases coordination with asset management, reduces resource duplication and enhances the investment processes, whilst retaining a specialist private client portfolio management proposition. On the other hand, the disaggregated asset management function can make it harder to develop product expertise. Other disadvantages include continued duplication of asset management resources and difficulty in ensuring investment performance consistency. Overall, this model is most applicable when a high degree of customisation is required for private client products and/or the fit with the asset management business model is limited.
- *Asset management integrated model* (Figure 8.5). Asset management is centralised, with dedicated private client asset managers who liaise closely with the private bankers. This model enables a strong focus on product development and customisation, provides for more consistent investment performance and makes it easier for the private bank to implement

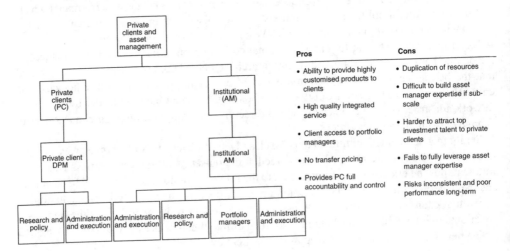

Figure 8.3   Independent model
Source: Author's analysis.

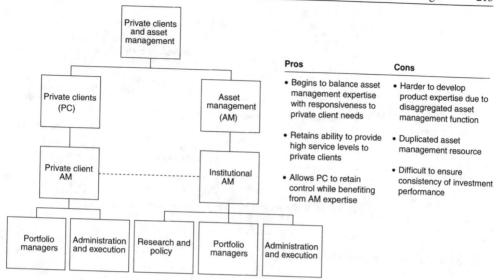

Figure 8.4 Private client integrated model
Source: Author's analysis.

open architecture. It also largely avoids any duplication of resources and lowers costs by, for example, allowing the realisation of operational synergies in the back and middle offices. But the model makes it more difficult to forge a close relationship between portfolio managers and investment managers, and the private client portfolio managers may lack clear accountability. Also, a formal transfer-pricing mechanism is required. Overall, this model is most applicable when the private bank is focused strongly on investment performance and product competitiveness.

- *Manufacturing–distribution model* (Figure 8.6). A centralised asset management unit serves institutional and private client distribution channels. This model offers the greatest degree

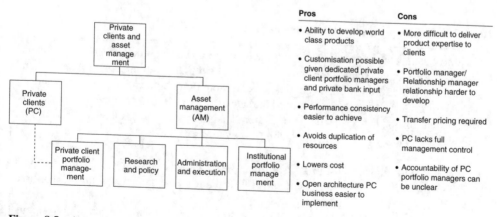

Figure 8.5 Asset management integrated model
Source: Author's analysis.

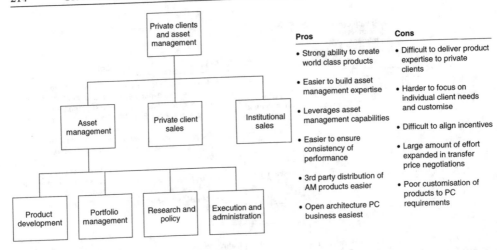

Figure 8.6   Manufacturing–distibution model
Source: Author's analysis.

of integration and hence scope to realise synergies. It enables a strong focus on product development and provides for more consistent investment performance. It also makes it easy for the private bank to implement open architecture, and for asset management products to be distributed through third-party channels. On the other hand, client relationship management can become relatively impersonal and sales oriented. It is more difficult to focus on individual client needs and to customise products. In addition, a formal transfer-pricing mechanism is required, and it can be difficult to align incentives. Overall, this model is most applicable when private client needs are similar to those of institutional clients. It is typical of brokerages and asset management groups building private client distribution channels with minimal tailoring of their existing products. Credit Suisse has recently moved to a version of this model.

Box 8.1   Citigroup's asset management exit

Should asset management manufacturing and distribution be combined under one roof in the first place? For many years, conventional wisdom held that combining asset management and distribution offered strong synergies. Clients were thought to value a 'one-stop shop'.

But in June 2005, Citigroup announced the sale of much of its asset management business in exchange for the broker-dealer private client business of Legg Mason. The $3.7 billion deal was structured as an asset swap, with the key terms as follows:

- Citigroup will transfer most of its asset management business, which had AuM of $437 billion, turning Legg Mason into the worlds fifth-largest asset manager, with $830 billion AuM.
- In exchange, Legg Mason will transfer its 1 400 brokers, which will give Citigroup an advisory team of around 14 000 (including 500 private bankers) – just behind Merrill Lynch, which has the largest advisory force in the world.

- The asset swap includes a 3-year exclusive distribution agreement under which Citigroup will become the primary domestic provider of Legg Mason's equity product family. As Legg asset management president Mark Fetting put it, the two sides want to create an asset management version of 'Intel inside', i.e. of selling Citigroup advice based on its access to Legg products.
- Citigroup will retain a 14% stake in Legg Mason. It does not, however, intend to be a long-term investor, and will sell down its stake over the next two years.

Citigroup has chosen to focus more on distribution, even though the brokerage business is inherently more volatile than asset management. In doing so, it was motivated by two key factors.

The first was to remove any perception of conflict of interest. In the current regulatory environment, with watchdogs seeing conflicts of interest everywhere, the two businesses may no longer be compatible. In recent years, companies such as Citigroup – along with Merrill Lynch, Morgan Stanley and others – have seen a sharp drop in the proportion of in-house mutual fund products sold by their brokerage arms (at Citigroup's Smith Barney, the proportion was down to around 15%). In part, this reflects the regulatory crackdown on incentives for brokers to push in-house products. Another reason is that, if in-house products perform badly, brokers often feel that clients will be more unhappy than if they had bought a third-party product with the same performance. The overall impact is that nowadays in-house products face a positive disadvantage: having manufacturing and distribution under the same roof has become something of a liability.

The second factor was the problem Citigroup had in running the asset management business itself. The division's net income fell by 34% in 2004, with AuM falling slightly over that period. Citigroup's product range was thin and underperforming, reflecting the challenge of motivating asset management staff in a large financial services group. As Chuck Prince, Citigroup's CEO noted, 'Our performance in asset management has not been what we had hoped for it to be. We are not a leader today in that business and, while we could be, the resources would be better directed elsewhere.' In addition, stand-alone asset managers tend to command higher earnings multiples.

This landmark transaction highlights the serious reflection going on within the industry as to whether it still makes sense for asset management and distribution to be combined under one roof. Above all, removing in-house asset management gives Citigroup the additional advantage of appearing more independent. Needless to say, a number of other large financial groups are considering whether they too should quit manufacturing.

Todd Thomson, Chairman and CEO of Citigroup Global Wealth Management, argues that, 'This transaction changes the game. This makes it very clear who we are working for. We are working for our clients. We're no longer in the business of selling product to clients. We're in the business of solving problems for clients, and finding the best solutions in the market place. I think others will follow. I don't think others will have a choice.'

It is, however, worth pointing out that Citigroup did *not* include its alternative investments business in the sale to Legg. Indeed, the movement here is very much in the opposite direction, with wealth managers keen to develop their in-house hedge funds and alternative investment groups. Some are even seeking to acquire successful funds. Examples include JP Morgan Chase taking a majority stake in Highbridge Capital Management in 2004 and Lehman Brothers' recent abortive discussion with GLG Partners.

8.2.1.1   Key organisational trends

A number of key organisational trends are emerging among major players. Most institutions are moving to centralise asset management, using the private bank as a separate distribution arm. Many of these institutions are, in turn, developing dedicated private client portfolio management units within asset management. A limited number of insitutions maintain independent organisational structures for asset management.

By centralising asset management, the group is able to leverage the investment process rigour of the institutional asset management unit across all client segments. For private client portfolio managers, this is typically a much greater level of investment discipline and gives HNW clients access to institutional asset management capability and performance. Centralisation enhances operational efficiency in product development and delivery. It also allows for greater consistency of investment performance across client segments and allows the private bank to focus more on relationship management and sales.

Centralisation can also help build the business in two ways. First, it enables more cost-effective penetration of new geographies and client segments, as asset management capability does not need to be duplicated. Second, given the scarcity of investment and sales talent, it allows for more focused recruiting, skills development and career paths.

Institutions that have moved private client portfolio managers from the private bank to a centralised asset management group include Merrill Lynch, Northern Trust and JP Morgan. For those institutions with centralised asset management, creating a dedicated private client portfolio management unit within asset management can have a number of benefits. Above all, it enables the private bank to maintain a strong client focus, particularly in the area of product development. It also enhances the private bank's ability to retain tight linkages between product manufacturing and distribution. More generally, it creates consistent investment performance for private client portfolios relative to the portfolios of other client segments. Institutions that have dedicated private client portfolio management groups within asset management include JP Morgan and Merrill Lynch.

A limited number of institutions maintain an independent organisational structure between asset management and private banking. That can be optimal in cases where the institution's business model focuses on providing transaction-like services (e.g. IPOs, brokerage), rather than developing the more traditional private-banking-like services such as portfolio management, trust and credit. Examples include bulge-bracket investment banks, which focus on taking HNW entrepreneurs from wealth creation to wealth management. They have created integrated structures that increase the HNW managers' ability to identify and establish a relationship with the client during the wealth-creation stage.

The independent model can also be optimal in cases where the markets in which the institution operates are less sophisticated (e.g. European HNW). That typically requires high-touch service and/or a greater focus on wealth preservation rather than on pure investment performance. For example, Deutsche Bank employs an independent, relationship-oriented model in Europe, while being centralised and product driven in the US.

But is important to note that many of these institutions are considering a move to a manufacturing–distribution model.

8.2.1.2   Interface design

The choice and key features of the interface between asset management and private banking should be driven by the strategies, business models and target client segments of the respective business units. The specific decision drivers vary across the different components of the business system:

- *Product development, marketing and business management.* It is important to ensure that the private bank's strategic demands can be accommodated within overall resource allocation. Product development interface positioning will depend on the nature, economics and delivery of the product set and the required degree of responsiveness to client needs. The degree of marketing integration will depend on the value propositions of the private client and institutional segments, product similarity and existing marketing spend. With regard to profit and loss account (P&L) arrangements, there are various models (see below) with key decision drivers including specific reporting lines, degree of unit integration, group management information system (MIS) policies and revenue/cost matching.
- *Research and investment policy.* The key tradeoff here is the requirement to balance the needs of customers against the need for excellence in research and consistent investment performance. The decision as to whether the research function is centralised or fragmented should be driven by the degree of independence required in the investment policy, as well as by cost considerations. The degree of independence in the investment policies of private and institutional clients should, in turn, be driven by commonalities in respective investment styles/processes, nature of the specific client bases and by the motivation of private client portfolio managers.
- *Portfolio management.* The role and responsibilities of portfolio managers should be driven by the demands of the relationship management model, the nature of the investment process and the need for an attractive career proposition. The location, size and structure of the private client portfolio management function should be influenced largely by the nature and degree of desired contact with clients and relationship managers, the need to exploit asset management synergies and by the relationship management model. The degree of investment policy independence given to private client portfolio managers should be driven by the demand for product customisation and by the coverage and relevance of the institutional investment policy. The career paths of the different portfolio managers serving private clients and institutions may differ depending on the nature of the different roles and the need to attract and retain private client investment talent.
- *Administration, support and execution functions.* The organisation of middle-office and support functions needs to balance cost effectiveness and the specific requirements of the two business units. In particular, the decision on whether to centralise or run customised, dedicated functions for each unit should be driven by cost efficiency as well as factors such as commonality of business requirements, service standards, number of locations and requirements for reporting independence. On the systems side, the decision on whether to integrate or run them independently should again be driven by cost efficiency, and also by commonality of specification requirements, the need for compatability and the IT strategy of the organisation.
- *Client management.* The portfolio manager and relationship manager roles are sometimes combined; in other cases, the portfolio manager has no involvement in the client relationship. That decision should be driven mainly by client demand, the relationship management model, and other specific responsibilities of the portfolio managers. The nature of the relationship between the portfolio manager and the relationship manager should be driven by the relationship management model and the relationship manager's level of investment expertise.

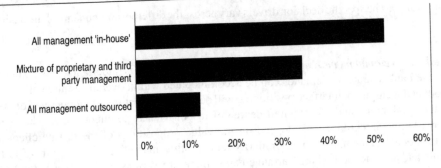

Figure 8.7   Portfolio manager roles
Source: Mercer Oliver Wyman (2005). Reproduced by permission.

Indeed, the role of the portfolio manager can differ substantially within the various organisational models. In some cases, e.g. UBS, client access to the portfolio manager is restricted
to UHNW clients only, who may be offered regular meetings. In general, most private banks
do not encourage direct contact between portfolio managers and clients (see Figure 8.7). On
the portfolio management side, portfolio managers may not exclusively manage private client
assets; e.g. only the largest segregated accounts may have specialist private client portfolio
managers. In cases where portfolio managers are dedicated to private clients, the degree of
discretion over asset allocation and model portfolio weightings is typically very limited.

8.2.1.3   Transfer pricing

On transfer pricing, a wide variety of models is available, and choice should be driven largely
by the business unit strategies. Four of the more widely used models are as follows:

- *Cost allocation.* The asset management unit allocates costs to the private bank. The basis
  of cost allocation is typically linked in some way (i.e. proportional, fixed/variable element)
  to AuM or product demands. While this has the benefit of being relatively simple and can
  be externally benchmarked, it suffers from the drawback that it can be difficult to identify
  accurately and allocate costs, and there is no direct incentive for the asset management unit
  to manage costs efficiently.
- *Double counting.* The asset management and private banking units recognise all revenues
  (though recognition may vary according to product and fee types). The advantage of this
  model is that it is easy to execute. It also aligns incentives within the organisation as a whole,
  and reduces negotiation and management involvement. A key drawback is that, by definition,
  it will not reflect the true economics and increases MIS complexity to some extent.
- *Distribution fees.* The asset management unit receives revenues and pays the private bank a
  distribution fee (with, in some cases, some sharing of the management fee). This is similar
  to some third-party distribution arrangements and has the advantage of aligning revenues
  with the relevant value added. But the negotiations involved in establishing an appropriate
  fee level can often be complex.
- *Wholesaler.* The private banking unit receives revenues and pays the asset management unit
  an institutional management fee (which typically varies across the different products). The

advantage of this model is its simplicity and the incentive it gives the manufacturer to control costs. A key drawback is that it can be difficult to benchmark fees.

8.2.2   Retail bank

A universal bank's private and retail banking businesses may be integrated to varying degrees. The McKinsey European Private Banking Economics Survey 2005 examined four organisational models employed by onshore universal banks. It found that organising the private bank as a separate business line is the most successful model, as measured by AuM growth (see Figure 8.8).

At least as important as the organisational structure is the quality of execution. Here, experience suggests that a proactive, structured approach is the best way to leverage a retail branch network as a source of client referrals (or so-called 'feeder network'). McKinsey has identified six key success factors for private banks wishing to leverage retail networks (see Figure 8.9):

1. *Distinctive value proposition.* In the first instance, it is important to secure the retail bank senior management's buy-in and raise their awareness of the private bank's value proposition. It is also important that the private bank's products, services and channels are sufficiently distinctive from those of the retail bank to help ensure that the transfer of a client from the retail network creates genuine value.
2. *Communication.* It is essential to establish a clear service level agreement (SLA), i.e. the plan, agreed by retail and private banking executives, detailing target clients by business unit, level of service provided and accounting rules governing client transfer. The SLA objectives should be discussed at the regional level and mechanisms established to track progress region by region. Retail branches should be clearly allocated to the relevant private

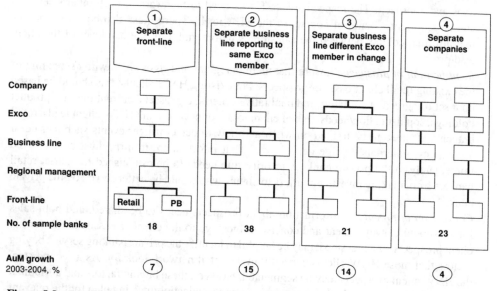

Figure 8.8   Retail banking interface models
Source: McKinsey European Private Banking Economics Survey 2005. Reproduced by permission.

1. Distinctive value proposition

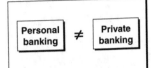

- Is value proposition of private banking division distinctive compared to personal banking?
- Does a transfer of a client create genuine value?

2. Communication

- Do the sales forces know the SLA*?
- Do the sales forces know each other s services/ target clients?
- Is there enough informal contact?

3. Identification of prospects

- Is there regular and complete screening of existing client prospects?
- Are hot leads transferred fast enough?
- Is a clear meeting plan established?

4. Conversion of prospects

Client   Retail Banker   Private Banker

- Is all information about prospects shared?
- Do both sales forces convey a clear message to the prospect/ client?

5. Compensation

Retail Banker

- Are the incentives transmitted to the right level of the organization?
- Are the objectives of subsequent years neutralized?

6. Reporting

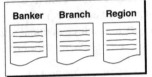

Banker   Branch   Region

- Do all levels of management receive regular and actionable reporting on the progress of the collaboration?

*Service Level Agreement (SLA): plan established by retail and private banking executives, detailing target clients per business unit, level of service provided, accounting rules for client transfer

Figure 8.9   Key success factors for leveraging a retail network
Source: McKinsey & Company. Reproduced by permission.

banking teams, with the most important branches identified and informed about the objectives and approach. The respective salesforces need to be aware of each other's services and target clients – and, of course, of the SLA itself. There must also be sufficient formal/informal contact between the salesforces before and after the handover of the client lead/prospect.

3. *Identification of prospects.* Ensure that there is regular and rigorous trawling/screening of the existing retail client base for prospects. For existing HNW clients, this should be based on a set of agreed quantitative and qualitative criteria, e.g. assets, current margin, product holdings, sophistication/needs, risk of client loss. For new-to-bank HNW client leads, retail branch staff need to be trained on when and how to detect trigger events such as sale of a company, inheritance, large deposit, etc. That information, in turn, must be conveyed immediately to the private bank. A priority rule needs to be established to restrict retail bankers from making investment offers to clients who would be better served by the private bank.

4. *Conversion of prospects.* Information about prospects needs to be shared, and both sales forces should convey a clear and consistent message to the client. To assist in converting client prospects, as a first step it may be helpful to identify the private banking service buying factors that those HNW clients currently in the retail network look for. As a second step, the HNW client prospects may be segmented, based on these buying factors and attitudinal criteria. A third step would then be to design a communication/meeting plan for the relevant clients, with tailored scripting geared to the individual client segments. The meetings are likely to be conducted by a joint branch manager and private banking team (relationship

manager and, where necessary, relevant product specialist). In preparing and scheduling the meetings, priority should be given to clients with the most important assets to transfer. A first meeting with the client would communicate the strategy of the group, present the private bank in a tailored way and, if possible, finalise the client transfer. Additional cultivation sessions and/or formal meetings may then be necessary to react to client queries and provide more information. The aim should be to complete the client transfer within around 2 months of the initial meeting.

5. *Compensation.* To ensure incentives are aligned, the retail bank needs to be compensated for the loss of the HNW client's associated economic contribution, both for the current and subsequent years. Again, there is no single solution. For example, some banks use incentive thresholds, which may vary by branch and/or by the amount of assets transferred. Another example is to leave the assets in the retail bank, but enter a service and money management agreement with fee sharing. To the extent that the client continues to use the retail bank's branches, some banks set up a shadow P&L, to ensure appropriate revenue sharing. To ensure objectives are aligned, it is important to ensure that the incentives are applied and tailored to the appropriate levels of the retail bank (such as region, area, branch, sales person). Also, the right balance needs to be struck between ensuring that the incentive is easy to communicate while ensuring it reflects, as accurately as possible, the economic value of the client. Properly designed incentives also need to focus the retail and private banks on successful client transfer and client satisfaction.

6. *Reporting.* Transparent reporting needs to be introduced across the retail and private banks, to analyse and track the progress of the collaboration. Key metrics include: number of prospects approached, conversion ratio and average assets transferred.

The rewards can be large for banks that get this right. Many top performers generate a high proportion of their inflows from their retail banking divisions.

Some of the US regional banks have been particularly successful in this area. For example, Wachovia has moved to a more systematic referral strategy to migrate wealthy individuals from the retail bank into its private bank, where their profitability improves dramatically. Transferring qualified customers from the branch to the private bank is reported to increase customer profitability by 26% on average and by 57% for the top 20% of customers. Retail bankers are compensated with a percentage of the customer's first-year profitability to help offset the lost retail earnings from that customer.

BNP Paribas encourages referrals from both its retail network and its small business (small-to-medium sized enterprise, or SME) banking unit. The key to BNP Paribas's referrals process is the way its organisation is structured. It organises its retail, SME and private banking businesses geographically, with a regional manager responsible for the associated consolidated P&L. The regional manager is assessed on this consolidated P&L, and is therefore keen to encourage client referrals that generate net revenue uplift.

Coutts maintains a small team of people dedicated to finding and realising synergies between it and its parent Royal Bank of Scotland Group.

Westpac currently maintains distinct private banking and business banking units. It has recognised, however, that such a structure can introduce conflicts of interest. It therefore seeks to service clients within one business unit, as far as possible, by adopting a hybrid approach. To do this, the business banking unit has private banking advisors that can help clients with personal financial solutions that fall outside usual business requirements. Similarly, its private bank has several financial planners who focus exclusively on the business issues of wealthy clients. This ensures that the client has, as far as possible, a single point of contact, based on the predominant financial needs of the individual. Yet the bank is flexible and remains alert to instances in which a client would be better served by a fully fledged team of specialists.

A large US commercial bank locates private bankers in or near its high-asset branches to facilitate referrals from branch managers to the private bank. This proximity increases clients' comfort with, and use of, the referral process.

Many banks have focused only on the retail interface. But some banks have gone further, by actually moving the relevant wealth management unit closer to the retail bank. A good example of such a move is Barclays Premier, the group's mass-affluent business. Formerly part of the Private Clients cluster of businesses, it was moved to the Small Business Banking part of the UK retail bank in 2003. The rationale was largely business-model related: a high proportion of Barclays Premier's existing customers were business owners, and there were obvious revenue synergies, e.g. from cross-referrals and collaborative coverage. In a similar spirit, UBS has, since 2002, organised its wealth management and business banking units under the same business group. In 2004 alone, some $5.5 billion of invested assets were funnelled into its private bank from the retail network.

Such moves need to be handled sensitively. Though not primarily cost driven, there are limits to the types of infrastructure and applications that can be shared. For example, applying a standard retail CRM system to a wealth management business can be inappropriate.

8.2.3 Investment bank

As many HNW clients increase in sophistication, synergies between the investment banking market and private banking businesses have increased significantly. These synergies have man-ufacturing and distribution elements. On the manufacturing side, private banks are increasingly keen to tap investment banks' product-structuring skills. Cross-selling of complex, high-margin structured products into private banking client bases improves private banking margins and generates additional structuring fees for the investment bank. On the distribution side, in both the primary issuing business and secondary markets, the investment bank is typically keen to leverage the private bank's client base. In addition, from the investment bank's perspective, integration enables it to amortise costs over a much broader client base than those competitors without a private banking franchise.

BCG notes that one technique used by private banks is marketing to owners of companies before their IPOs (see Figure 8.10) by, for example, joining the investment bankers in client meetings. One US investment bank employs senior staff to screen managers and owners of client companies to recruit them into its private client group. It then coordinates its sales activities with its investment bank's IPO team. The private bank is advantaged in securing these new relationships due to the institution's early knowledge of an impending transaction.

Goldman Sachs estimates that UBS's investment bank earns 15% of its security revenues from the private banking business. This 'captive revenue' allows UBS to offer a more compre-hensive service to institutional clients than those of its competitors without significant private banking units. That, in turn, has helped UBS win market share in the institutional securities businesses (e.g. cash equities).

Also, a large pool of stable private banking earnings increases the investment bank's ability to leverage risk in trading operations. Goldman Sachs have argued that a player's risk capacity is increasingly defined by reference to its earnings stream, as opposed to just its capital base.

Bankers and Brokers Share Relationships

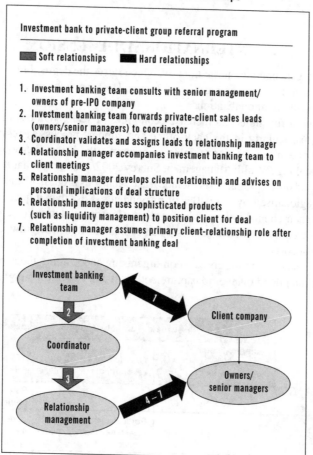

Investment bank to private-client group referral program

◼ Soft relationships   ◼ Hard relationships

1. Investment banking team consults with senior management/ owners of pre-IPO company
2. Investment banking team forwards private-client sales leads (owners/senior managers) to coordinator
3. Coordinator validates and assigns leads to relationship manager
4. Relationship manager accompanies investment banking team to client meetings
5. Relationship manager develops client relationship and advises on personal implications of deal structure
6. Relationship manager uses sophisticated products (such as liquidity management) to position client for deal
7. Relationship manager assumes primary client-relationship role after completion of investment banking deal

Figure 8.10   Investment bank to private client group referral programme
Source: BCG (2001a). Reproduced by permission.

That is clearly beneficial to integrated investment banks, given the lower volatility of earnings associated with private banking revenue streams.

A good recent example of the integrated investment banking model is Barclays. The entire Private Clients business (which includes the Private Bank, Stockbroking and Financial Planning) is being integrated into Barclays Capital and Barclays Global Investors, under a single CEO. The main aim is to increase revenue synergies among these business units.

That said, the investment banking interface is not without risks and needs to be handled with care. As one recent *Private Banker International* editorial (November 2005) noted,

'at some players, the investment banking operation could be only too eager to see the private client as 'product fodder'... at worst, the private client may prove the last link in a sausage machine, stuffed with the toxic detritus of deals dreamed up by the investment bankers and otherwise unsellable'.

The recent controversy over sales of European constant maturity swap-linked products is a case in point.

8.3   INTERNATIONAL DIMENSION

Most wealth managers operate internationally, which raises the degree of organisational complexity. A number of trends are emerging in this area. Here we touch on three: regionalisation, integration and offshore rationalisation.

Regionalisation of functions can increase economies of scale. While some regionalisation has taken place, particularly in the back-office and support processes, regionalisation rates have traditionally been low. Taking Asia as an example, the PricewaterhouseCoopers Asia-Pacific Private Banking /Wealth Management Survey 2002/2003 notes that the functions most frequently managed on a regional basis include trust, securities processing and IT management. Yet these were regionalised by only 40% of respondents. Less than a quarter of respondents had regionalised their client administration or client reporting functions (see Figure 8.11). But going forward, anecdotal evidence suggests that regionalisation will grow, driven largely by the need to control costs.

Wealth managers are increasingly keen on organising and running their international businesses in a more integrated manner to capture both cost and revenue synergies. A good recent

	Current extent of regionalisation by respondents		
	Regionalised by 41%-50% of respondents	Regionalised by 20%-40% of respondents	Regionalised by less then 20% of respondents
Front Office			Relationship management client making
Asset management & product provision	Trust	Portfolio management Investment management products	Banking and cash management Other products
Middle Office		Trading/execution Treasury Research Trust administration	Tax advice
Back Office	Securities processing	Client accounting/ reporting FX-processing Payments Credit administration Settlement Custody	Client administration
Support processes	IT management	Finance/planning/ controlling Risk management Internal audit Human resources Marketing Regulatory & compliance	

Figure 8.11   Processes and functions currently regionalised – Asia Pacific example
Source: PricewaterhouseCoopers (2002–2003). Reproduced by permission.

example of this was the July 2005 announcement by UBS that UBS Wealth Management USA (i.e. heritage Paine Webber) is to be integrated with the core private bank.

A key revenue driver is to deepen its penetration of the top 15%–20% of relationships within the US private client base, which is where much of the untapped onshore HNW wealth lies. Specifically, the aim is to train the top segment of brokers to approach their clients in a way more like a private banker. The challenge is to encourage the broker to open his most lucrative relationships up to multiple points of contact with UBS's group-wide product platform. This holistic approach, bringing in, for instance, tax specialists or investment banking capabilities, is something the firm has been working on already within the core private bank. That will now be extended to Wealth Management USA. Typically, when the wealth level reaches 'key client' status ($30 million of invested assets), the client becomes 'multidomestic' rather than merely 'international'. Therefore, much of the need to connect the client with the global wealth management platform is driven by the clients themselves. Also, the ability to service the HNW client on a multidomestic approach is something that few US competitors can replicate. That initiative has already been piloted with 200 brokers, with SFr 2 billion (c.$1.7 billion) of asset inflows so far.

The US integration should also provide UBS with cost-saving opportunities, e.g. in product design, more cost-effective purchasing and common processes. Overall, the integration should help reduce the performance gap between UBS Wealth Management USA (with a 12% operating margin) and Merrill Lynch and Citigroup (with c.19%–20% operating margins).

The third, related, trend concerns offshore businesses. Given the external pressure that many offshore financial centres are now under (see Chapter 9), many players are thinking hard about their offshore strategies. One immediate issue is how to retain assets within their organisations in the face of growing demands by offshore clients to shift assets onshore. Integrated offshore/onshore propositions can be effective for some clients. The challenge is to ensure that the organisational interface is seamless. Going forward, a related issue is whether the offshore entities should remain as stand-alone businesses in their own right or whether they should be regarded more as pure custodial businesses.

9

Regulatory and Tax Issues

The aims of this chapter are to:

- Review the reasons why wealth management is vulnerable to money laundering.
- Outline recent key international regulatory developments, which focus on money laundering and corporate governance.
- Discuss recent international tax initiatives.
- Put forward practical approaches and best-practice action that wealth managers should take in responding to these regulatory and tax developments.

The chapter does not aim to provide an exhaustive review of regulatory and taxation developments. Rather, the aim is to pick out the key initiatives and themes and then to suggest a practical action plan for wealth managers.

The widespread financial deregulation that began in the 1980s is largely over. In recent years, there has been a wave of regulatory resurgence, which has led to heightened and more globally coordinated regulatory and compliance pressure on wealth managers, particularly on the offshore side.

Overall, the main result of the international regulatory and taxation initiatives is more declared offshore money and a quickening in the march towards complete elimination of the conventional distinction between onshore and offshore wealth management. That has particularly stark implications for Switzerland, the world's largest offshore financial centre. It also has implications for the tradeoff between the optimal commercial structure and leading-edge compliance.

9.1 MONEY LAUNDERING VULNERABILITY

Much of the regulatory activity has focused on money laundering – the process in which assets obtained or generated by criminal activity are moved or concealed to obscure the link between the crime and the assets. Money laundering is a diverse and often complex process and plays a fundamental role in facilitating the ambitions of drug traffickers, terrorists, organised criminals, insider dealers and tax evaders as well as many others who need to avoid the kind of attention that 'sudden' wealth brings.

For many years now, there has been growing evidence of private banks and other wealth management players' vulnerability to money laundering. Though the history here stretches back at least as far as the 1970s, successful prosecutions were rare. The 1994 conviction of a private banker from American Express was one example of an early wake-up call. The 1998 Casablanca undercover money laundering operation resulted in the conviction of several private bankers in Mexico. The list goes on.

Arguably, certain characteristics of private banking/wealth management make the business vulnerable to money laundering and in need of greater attention and scrutiny from both regulatory and law-enforcement standpoints. There are five key contributory factors here:

1. *Private bankers as client advocates.* Private bankers/relationship managers are the linchpin of the wealth management business. They are trained to service their clients' financial needs, to set up accounts and to manage international assets using sophisticated instruments, structures and tools. Wealth managers encourage their relationship managers to develop close personal relationships of trust with their clients – visiting the clients' homes, attending family functions and arranging their financial affairs. The result is that the relationship managers may feel intense loyalty to their clients for both professional and personal reasons, leading them to miss or minimise any warning signs. In addition, private bankers may use their expertise in bank internal systems to evade what they may perceive as unnecessary bureaucracy, hampering easy access to the services their clients want and thereby evading internal controls designed to detect and prevent money laundering.

2. *Powerful clients.* Wealthy clients may also exert political and economic influence, which may make banks more anxious to satisfy their requests and reluctant to ask questions. If the client is a government official with influence over the bank's in-country operations, the bank has added reason to avoid causing offence. A good example is the private banker who, when asked why he never questioned a client about certain transactions, replied that he felt constrained by 'issues of etiquette and protocol' because the client was a head of state.

   Moreover, verifying certain information about a foreign client's assets, business dealings and community standing can be difficult, due, for example, to a lack of independent databases. A key problem is developing tools for detecting when clients may be misrepresenting their personal assets or business dealings, or supplying inaccurate documentation. While wealth managers routinely claim that their relationship managers gain intimate knowledge of their clients, the case history evidence demonstrates that all too often that is not true.

3. *Culture of discretion and secrecy.* A culture of secrecy pervades the wealth management industry. The numbered Swiss private bank account is one of the classic examples. But there are many other layers of secrecy that wealth managers and their clients use to mask accounts and transactions. For example, private banks routinely create shell companies and trusts to shield the identity of the beneficial owner of a bank account. Private banks also open accounts under code names and will, when requested, refer to clients by code names or encode account transactions. This can adversely impact those banks that aim to capture and leverage client data for CRM purposes.

   In addition to shell companies and codes, a number of private banks also conduct business in offshore jurisdictions, such as Switzerland and the Cayman Islands, which impose criminal sanctions on the disclosure of bank information related to clients and restrict regulatory oversight. The secrecy laws are often so tight that they even restrict internal bank oversight. For example, if a bank's own employee uncovers a problem in an office located in a secrecy jurisdiction, that employee is barred from conveying any client-specific information to colleagues in the United States, even though they are part of the same banking operation. The bank's auditors and compliance officers operate under the same restrictions: any audit or compliance report sent out of the country must first be shorn of any client-specific information. In a recent strategic review of the global business of a European bank, it proved impossible to get any relevant transaction data from the Luxemburg operations.

If a bank employee in the United States wants more information about a problem in a secrecy jurisdiction involving specific clients, he or she must fly to the secrecy jurisdiction to discuss the matter face to face, or review documentation. Even then, the restrictions continue. For example, before allowing an employee to travel to Switzerland, private banks such as JP Morgan and Citibank require their employees to sign a non-disclosure agreement, reminding them that Swiss law prohibits disclosure of client information acquired in Switzerland to anyone, even their fellow bankers in the United States.

Bank regulators operate under similar restrictions. Once a matter becomes the subject of a criminal investigation, many secrecy jurisdictions provide a disclosure exception for law-enforcement enquiries. But that exception may be invoked only by law-enforcement personnel, acting in an official capacity through designated channels. It cannot be used by bank regulators.

4. *Culture of lax anti-money-laundering controls.* As well as a culture of secrecy, wealth management operates in a culture that can be indifferent or resistant to anti-money-laundering controls, such as due-diligence requirements and account-transaction monitoring. The fundamental problem is that relationship managers are asked to fill contradictory roles: to develop a personal relationship with a client and increase their assets under management, while also monitoring their accounts for suspicious activity and questioning certain transactions. Human nature makes these contradictory roles difficult to perform, and anti-money-laundering duties often suffer.

Wealth management firms have dealt with this problem by setting up systems to ensure that relationship manager activities are reviewed by third parties, such as supervisors, compliance personnel or auditors. However, while strong oversight procedures exist on paper, in practice relationship manager oversight can be absent, weak or ignored. Audits, compliance reviews, repeated deadlines and bonus threats are just some of the tools wealth managers have used to coax their relationship managers to improve their client-due diligence.

5. *Strong competition and profitability.* A final factor creating money laundering concerns is, as earlier chapters have discussed, the ongoing competitive intensity of the wealth management industry, linked to its perceived high profitability. That is manifesting itself, not least, in aggressive expansion and client-acquisition plans by many incumbents and industry newcomers. The dual pressures of competition and expansion are powerful disincentives for relationship managers to impose tough anti-money-laundering controls that may discourage new business or cause existing clients to move to other institutions.

In addition to the five general factors above, the actual products and services offered by wealth managers can also create opportunities for money laundering. These include:

- *Multiple accounts.* One striking feature of wealth management accounts is their complexity. Wealth management clients often have multiple accounts at multiple banks in multiple locations. Though this is now changing, until recently, it was very rare for a wealth manager to be able to aggregate all of the information related to an individual client. That lack of comprehensive understanding of their own clients' accounts creates a vulnerability to money laundering. It also complicates regulatory oversight and law enforcement by making it nearly impossible for an outside reviewer to be sure that all wealth management accounts belonging to an individual have been identified.

- *Secrecy products*. Most wealth managers offer a range of products and services that shield a client's ownership of funds. They include offshore trusts and shell companies, special name accounts, etc. Shell corporations, often referred to as 'private investment corporations' or PICs, are usually incorporated in offshore jurisdictions that restrict disclosure of a PIC's beneficial owner. Private banks then open bank accounts in the name of the PIC, allowing the PIC's owner to avoid identification as the account holder.

  It is not unusual for private bank clients to have multiple PICs and use them to hold accounts and conduct transactions. Some private banks will open accounts only for PICs they incorporate and manage, while others will do so for PICs incorporated and managed by someone else, such as the client. These so-called 'client-managed PICs' create additional money laundering risks because the private banks do not control and may not even know the activities, assets and complete ownership of the PIC holding the account at the private bank.

- *Movement of funds*. Client account transactions at wealth management firms routinely involve large sums of money. The size of client transactions increases the bank's vulnerability to money laundering by providing an attractive venue for money launderers who want to move large sums of money without attracting notice. In addition, most wealth managers provide products and services that facilitate the quick, confidential and hard-to-trace movement of money across jurisdictional borders. For example, private banks routinely facilitate large wire transfers into, out of and among client accounts, in multiple countries. Such transfers can take place with minimal or no notice from the client and sometimes involve parties and accounts with which the relationship manager is unfamiliar. That is a situation that invites money laundering.

- *Credit*. Another common – and growing – wealth management service involves the extension of credit to clients, often using deposits as collateral (see Chapter 4). This practice also creates vulnerabilities to money laundering by allowing a client to deposit questionable funds and replace them with 'clean' money from the loan. In addition, since the client's loan is fully collateralised by assets on deposit with the bank, the bank may not scrutinise the loan purpose and repayment prospects as carefully as for a conventional loan, and may unwittingly further a money launderer's efforts to hide illicit proceeds behind seemingly legitimate transactions.

9.2 REGULATORY INITIATIVES

In the late 1990s, the international community became increasingly concerned about money laundering and tax evasion. As a consequence, there has been a large number of high-profile cases. Take just two recent examples.

In the late 1980s, Citibank in London accepted as clients two young 'commodity and oil dealers', Ibrahim and Mohamid Sani Abacha. Bank files recorded the brothers as the sons of Zachary Abacha, 'a well-connected and respected member of the northern Nigerian community', but no mention was made that Abacha senior (later head of state) was a general in the Nigerian army and chairman of the country's Joint Chiefs of Staff. By 1998, the Sani Abachas had deposited $60 million with Citibank. They and other members of the Abacha circle allegedly stole an estimated $4.3 billion over a number of years – about half of it from the Nigerian central bank. The web of banks and jurisdictions implicated in these thefts is wide and tangled. So far, more than $1.4 billion has been found and frozen in banks in Liechtenstein, Luxembourg and Switzerland. Several major Swiss banks were publicly 'named and shamed' by the Swiss Federal Banking Commission; a number of UK banks were also identified as having handled some of the funds involved.

Table 9.1   Main official international anti-money-laundering forums

Organisation	Role
OECD	The Financial Action Task Force (FATF) spearheads the global effort against money laundering
Bank for International Settlements	The Financial Stability Forum (FSF) established an ad hoc Working Group on Offshore Financial Centres in April 1999
European Commission	Various Directives have addressed the financial system and anti-money-laundering.
United Nations	UN Security Council resolutions call on member states to strengthen global efforts to control money laundering
Egmont Group	An informal organisation of Financial Intelligence Units, set up in 1995, that supports national anti-money-laundering programmes by facilitating the exchange of intelligence and communication among its members
World Bank and IMF	Multilateral donor banks have recently instituted anti-money-laundering action plans that are being shared with sovereign governments and against which the IMF will conduct assessments of capabilities

Source: Author's analysis.

The second example was, of course, 11 September 2001, which placed the spotlight on the funding arrangements of terrorist organisations.

These cases, and others, have led various international committees to take concerted action (see Table 9.1).

The Financial Action Task Force (FATF), established in 1989, is the organisation with primary responsibility for developing a global anti-money-laundering (AML) framework, in close cooperation with relevant international organisations. It is an intergovernmental body, currently consisting of 29 countries (including the major financial centre countries of Europe, North and South America, and Asia) and two international organisations. Its responsibilities include examining money laundering techniques and trends, reviewing actions already taken at national and international levels, and setting out additional measures to be taken to combat money laundering.

The 'FATF 40 Recommendations', issued in April 1990, set out the basic framework for AML efforts and were designed with universal application in mind (see Appendix 2). The basic issues addressed by the Recommendations relate to:

- The criminalisation of money laundering.
- International cooperation in investigating, prosecuting and extraditing of crime suspects.
- The existence of adequate supervisory policies, practices and procedures, including 'know your customer' rules, which shield banks from being used by criminal elements.
- The international exchange of information regarding suspicious information.

Over time, the Recommendations have been revised to reflect new developments in money laundering and experience. The most recent review is currently nearing completion.

After 11 September 2001, the FATF expanded its mission beyond money laundering and agreed to focus its expertise on the worldwide effort to combat terrorist financing. In October 2001, it issued new international standards, designed to supplement the 40 Recommendations, called the 'Eight Special Recommendations to Combat Terrorist Financing' (see Appendix 3).

Post 11 September, there was a dramatic global gear shift on money laundering and other illegal fund transfers. For example:

- G7 countries and Russia agreed to work more closely together to track the funding of terrorist groups.
- The FATF established standards for the prevention of terrorist financing, for the tracking down of terrorist assets and for the pursuit of individuals and countries suspected of participating in or supporting terrorism.
- The Basel Committee issued guidelines on monitoring money laundering.
- The European Union adopted the second AML Directive, widening the range of offences and extending the obligations of the 1991 Directive to a range of non-financial activities and professions (including lawyers and accountants).
- The Wolfsberg Group of 12 major international banks agreed to increase the resources allocated to internal AML procedures.
- Interpol and Europol agreed to exchange information on international crime, including money laundering and fraud.

Table 9.2 provides a more detailed global overview of recent initiatives in individual countries.

9.2.1 Offshore financial centres

Offshore financial centres (OFCs) may be broadly defined as jurisdictions that attract a high level of non-resident financial activity. They are popular with wealth management clients for a number of reasons:

- Protection. Clients in countries with weak economies may want to keep assets offshore to:
  (a) Protect them against the collapse of their domestic currencies and banks.
  (b) Keep assets outside the reach of existing or potential exchange controls.
- Confidentiality. If these clients also seek confidentiality then an offshore account is often the vehicle of choice.
- Tax planning.
- For some clients, geographic proximity to major financial centres.

Wealth managers also find OFCs attractive because the regulatory and tax burdens have typically been less stringent. Here, the specific attractions may include:

- More convenient fiscal regimes. For example, those with no capital gains tax, no withholding tax on dividends or interest, no tax on transfers, no corporation tax and no exchange controls, which lower explicit taxation and give much higher net profit margins.
- Convenient regulatory frameworks. These include light and flexible supervision and less stringent reporting requirements, which reduce implicit taxation and hence also increase net profit margins.
- Minimum formalities for incorporation.

But things are changing. The fact that many OFCs exist in loosely defined regulatory and supervisory environments has increased the focus of policy makers and regulators on the possible role played by OFCs in the process of tax evasion and money laundering. For example, in mid-2000, both the FSF and the FATF issued reports on the state of money laundering with a focus on various OFCs. They used various criteria to determine the degree of 'cooperation' with

Table 9.2   Anti-money-laundering initiatives, pre and post 11 September

Country/ government body	Pre 9/11	Post 9/11
AMERICAS		
Canada	The Proceeds of Crime (Money) Laundering Act was passed in June 2000. Requires financial entities to report, *inter alia*, to a new agency – Financial Transactions Reports Analysis Centre (FinTRAC)	The Anti-Terrorism Act became law in December 2001. Provides measures to identify, prosecute, convict and punish terrorists. Gives law-enforcement and national security agencies tools to gather intelligence and evidence against terrorists and terrorist groups
Cayman Islands		Enacted measures to prohibit/freeze funds that would benefit Osama bin Laden, Taliban or associated persons; prohibits financial services to terrorists
United States	The Bank Secrecy Act applied to banks; Suspicious Activity Reports (SARs) required of banks (large broker–dealers and some insurance firms voluntarily filed SARs); Office of Foreign Assets Control reports required of all; Form 8300 required trades and business cash reporting over $10 000	USA PATRIOT Act was signed into law in October 2001. Major expansion of anti-money-laundering obligations for all financial services institutions; attempts to move towards consistency across the financial services industry
Mexico	Money laundering prohibited by Penal Code and financial regulation. Specific measures published for know your customer, detection and reporting of abnormal transactions	New regulations to report transactions that could be related to Osama bin Laden, Taliban or associated persons
ASIA-PACIFIC		
Australia	Anti-money-laundering laws in place	Strengthened laws, expanded to civil forfeiture/confiscation of property intended for use in terrorism; funding of terrorism explicitly criminalised in Code
Japan	Financial institutions must notify the Financial Services Authority of suspected illegal activities	Proposals to require financial institutions to identify customers, address anti-terrorism measures
New Zealand	Financial Transactions Reporting Act of 1996.	No new legislation or regulatory action
Singapore	Prevention of Misuse of the Singapore Banking System for Drug Trafficking for Money Laundering Purposes Act 1990; Monetary Authority Guidelines on Prevention of Money Laundering Act 1999; Corruption, Drug Trafficking and Other Serious Crimes Act, Chapter 65A, revised 2000	The relevant authorities published lists of names of Al-Qaeda related persons and organisations; financial institutions are required to report on activities or suspected activities associated with these organisations

(cont.)

Table 9.2   (*Continued*)

Country/ government body	Pre 9/11	Post 9/11
Thailand	Cash transactions through financial institutions in excess of Baht 2 million ($46 000) must be reported to AMLO, the government Anti-Money Laundering Office	
EUROPE/AFRICA		
Belgium	Money laundering is prohibited by Penal Code; Law of 11 January 1993 to prevent use of the financial system for money laundering purposes	Ministerial decrees restricting transactions with Taliban; strict enforcement of reporting by FSIs to FIU; cooperating with G10 and EU initiatives
Czech Republic	Prohibition on opening anonymous accounts	No new legislation or regulatory action
France	Money laundering prohibited by Penal Code	New policies, including cap of €8000 for transactions originating/passing through nations or territories in non-compliance with international anti-money-laundering rules
Germany	Money Laundering Act and Guidelines of the Banking Supervisory Office concerning measures to be taken by credit institutions to combat and prevent money laundering, established 1998/1999	Anti-Terrorism Act became law in December 2001. The Banking Supervisory Office published lists with names of potential terrorists, asked credit institutions for research. New regulations to be issued in 2002 to improve/tighten existing anti-money-laundering rules
Italy	Money laundering prohibited by Penal Code. Other measures provided by Law N. 197 of 5 July 1991 and by Bank of Italy additional Regulation of December 2001	Plans to comply with EU Directive 2001/97
Luxembourg	Laws of 5 April and 11 August 1993 setting know-your-customer obligations and obligations to inform and cooperate with authorities for financial institutions and professionals; and several circulars issued by different supervisory authorities	Issued new directives for financial institutions in fight against money laundering. Draft law in preparation to extend anti-money-laundering provisions to financing terrorism
South Africa	Prevention of Organised Crime Act 1998 (to be repealed and replaced by Financial Intelligence Centre Act 2001)	Financial Intelligence Centre Act 2001 application, duties of various institutions and persons, secrecy and confidentiality; also establishes Financial Intelligence Centre
Switzerland	Since the 1980s, a series of laws and regulations was implemented in the form of penal and administrative provisions, specific banking regulations applicable to banks and non-bank financial institutions	Published lists with names of potential terrorists; Al-Quaeda officially declared as a prohibited organisation

Table 9.2   (*Continued*)

Country/ government body	Pre 9/11	Post 9/11
Turkey	Anti-money-laundering laws enacted 1999	No new legislation or regulatory action. Enhanced role for the financial regulator in combating money laundering
United Kingdom	Primary legislation (applicable to all) contained in six Acts. Financial services institutions also covered by Money Laundering Regulations 1993, addressing internal controls and communications, know-your-customer procedures, recognition and reporting of suspicious transactions, training and record keeping	Anti-Terrorism, Crime and Security Act 2001 allows monitoring and freezing of accounts. Also, restraint, seizure or forfeiture of terrorist assets; 'objective knowledge' test for the regulated sector. Required to conform with EU Directive 2001/97

Source: Deloitte Touche Tohmatsu (2003). Reproduced by permission.

tax authorities and/or the adequacy of legal and supervisory systems relative to international standards.

The FATF evaluated 26 non-member countries or territories using 25 criteria drawn up on the basis of the 40 Recommendations. These criteria can be grouped into four main areas:

1. Loopholes in financial regulations.
2. Obstacles raised by regulatory requirements.
3. Obstacles to international cooperation.
4. Inadequate resources for dealing with money laundering activities.

Of the 26 countries and territories initially evaluated, 15 were declared to be non-cooperative (NCCT), meriting economic sanctions if they failed to reform their money laundering laws and procedural implementation by June 2001.

In general, being declared cooperative did not exclude the need to improve on measures to address money laundering, through, for example, supervision and regulation, but rather that the country or jurisdiction had been taking measures to address any shortcomings. The report identified detrimental rules and practices that obstructed international cooperation against money laundering.

Since the issuing of the report in 2000, several countries have indicated that their financial sectors have suffered owing to the adverse publicity. The FATF recommended that financial institutions pay special attention to transactions with non-cooperative countries, essentially increasing the scrutiny paid to those transactions that are more likely to be related to money laundering.

The FATF keeps its black list of non-cooperative countries or territories (NCCTs) under regular review; an updated list is published annually. In June 2001, the FATF reviewed the progress made by the countries identified as non-cooperative. At that time, among others, the Bahamas and Cayman Islands were removed from the list.

Both the Bahamas and Cayman Islands enacted significant modifications to existing legislation as well as new laws to address their identified deficiencies. In the case of the Bahamas, a major improvement was the establishment and adequate staffing of a financial intelligence unit (FIU). The FIU was designed to request, receive, analyse and disseminate disclosures of financial information in order to counter money laundering. In addition, the existence of anonymous accounts and bearer shares was banned, and measures were implemented to improve international cooperation. In the case of the Cayman Islands, a more ambitious financial inspection programme has been initiated, identification of all pre-existing accounts is required and all banks licensed in the Caymans must maintain a physical presence. In February 2001, the Cayman authorities ordered 62 private banks to open and staff offices in the Caymans and to maintain records there if they wanted to remain licensed.

As of February 2006, the NCCT list contained two countries: Myanmar and Nigeria.

9.2.2   USA PATRIOT Act

The USA PATRIOT Act[1] was signed into US law on 26 October 2001. It strengthens the AML provisions in existing regulations and augments them to cover a range of financial services companies that were not previously affected. One of its most important effects is to encourage the US Treasury Department to exercise much more vigorously the authority it already had been granted through the Bank Secrecy Act of 1970. The Act also increases the power of the US Justice Department in enforcing the Criminal Code and somewhat broadens the role of the Internal Revenue Service.

Within the Act, the definition of money laundering is expanded to explicitly include financing terrorism. The Act requires all financial institutions to have had an AML programme by 24 April 2002. This means that all wealth managers must develop internal policies, procedures and controls, designate a compliance officer, run training programmes, and conduct independent audits of their compliance programmes. It raises the standards for 'know your customer' due diligence by requiring this suspicious activity be reported. Private banks are among the first group of financial institutions to have to comply. This requires the involvement of virtually every business unit and support area. The Act also permits greater sharing of information between the authorities and financial institutions and among financial institutions about suspected money laundering.

Box 9.1   Basle II

Another key regulatory development, which will have potentially far-reaching consequences for the wealth management industry, is the new version of the 1988 Basle Capital Accord – so-called Basle II. That sets the minimum regulatory capital requirements for banks around the world.

The objective of Basle II is to foster a strong emphasis on risk management and to encourage ongoing improvements in banks' risk-assessment capabilities. The Basle Committee believes this can be accomplished by closely aligning banks' capital requirements with modern risk management practices and by ensuring that this emphasis on risk makes its way into supervisory practices and into market discipline through enhanced risk- and capital-related disclosures.

---

[1] The Uniting and Strengthening America by Providing Appropriate Tools Required to Intercept and Obstruct Terrorism Act.

Basle II may have a disproportionately large effect in Europe. The European Union's third Capital Adequacy Directive (CAD 3) will stretch the provisions of Basle II to cover the asset management industry explicitly. The Basle II draft agreement is due to take effect at the end of 2006, and the CAD based upon it, though currently very much under discussion, should become law around the same time.

Overall, the impact of Basle II is expected to be broadly neutral on the level of most wealth managers' regulatory capital: the credit risk benefit will most likely be offset by the new operational risk-related capital requirement. The key elements are as follows:

- Changes to the treatment of *credit risk*, including a wider definition of credit instruments and changes to the calculation of the associated capital requirement. (Recall from Chapter 4 that wealth managers are increasingly offering lending products in response to strong client demand.) Given that private banking clients are, by definition, highly solvent, private banks should benefit from a lower capital requirement. In practice, however, it can be difficult for private banks to build statistical models to support the more sophisticated ratings-based approach because historically they are unlikely to have had many defaults. Large exposures to a small number of individual clients can also complicate the calculations.
- Introduction of a new explicit capital requirement to cover *operational risk* – exposure to losses from inadequate internal processes and systems (e.g. technology failure and trade-settlement errors) and from external threats (e.g. fraud). That, at the very least, is forcing a re-evaluation of the view that wealth management is effectively a 'risk-free' business. For Swiss private banks using the standardised approach, operational risk will incur a level of capital adequacy of 10%–15% of gross income.
- For European wealth managers, recognition of *goodwill*. The UK Financial Services Authority's consultation paper CP173 confirms that goodwill will be excluded in the calculation of regulatory capital. Hence, for those private banks that have been highly acquisitive in the past, CAD 3 could significantly reduce their measured capital.

Basle II has therefore caused concern among asset managers, particularly in Europe. Some argue that Basle II has the potential to reshape the industry's profile altogether. Asset managers falling under the Directive who do not form part of a larger banking group may choose to relocate outside the EU or be forced to rebuild their balance sheets. For example, Amvescap, the UK's largest quoted fund management group, said in April 2003 that it might move its headquarters and delist from the London stock exchange because of the Directive. Banks that own asset managers may even decide that the costs involved in meeting the new regulations are simply too high and exit the wealth management business altogether (see Box 8.1, 'Citigroup's asset management exit' in Chapter 8).

Another issue is the uneven geographical application of Basle II, at least initially. In Europe it will be applied to the entire financial services sector. In the US, however, regulators require only the largest banks and those with significant assets abroad to comply. Meanwhile, banks in some emerging markets, including China and India, have opted out entirely, claiming that Basle II is too complex.

But Basle II mostly prescribes good banking and business practice. Looking further ahead, for those banks that do comply, the prescribed improvements in risk management practices should yield long-term benefits of many times the initial compliance costs.

9.2.3 Wolfsberg anti-money-laundering principles

One of the aims of AML measures is to encourage bankers to know their clients sufficiently well to be able both to identify and report suspicious transactions. The Wolfsberg Group is a private-sector forum comprised of 12 major international private banks.[2] The banks came together essentially to fine-tune the 'know your customer' rules. In October 2000, it issued a set of global AML guidelines (see Appendix 4). The guidelines state at the outset: 'Bank policy will be to prevent the use of its worldwide operations for criminal purposes. The bank will endeavour to accept only those clients whose source of wealth and funds can be reasonably established to be legitimate.'

The principles deal with diverse aspects of 'know your customer' policies that pertain to relationships with wealthy clients and the private banking departments of financial institutions. They also deal with the identification and follow-up of unusual or suspicious activities.

Provisions in the new guidelines, for example, relate to the efforts of bankers to secure the accurate identity of individuals opening private banking accounts. From time to time, individuals may seek to secure anonymity for themselves and use third parties to represent them on opening accounts. The guidelines state clearly: 'Beneficial ownership must be established for all accounts.'

The Group expect that the principles will be seen by regulators as representing a standard that all banks engaged in international private banking should be encouraged to adopt. The principles act as a powerful reputational incentive for compliance. The fact that other banks now wish to sign up to them underlines the extent to which reputational issues have become central to international wealth management.

9.2.4 Implications of regulatory initiatives for wealth managers

What does all this mean for wealth managers? To begin with, wealth managers clearly need to have a deep understanding of the new regulatory environment and how it affects them. As one panellist at a recent roundtable put it, 'This is a period where you have to take a more conservative tack. There's not a lot of tolerance in the system right now.' The recent forced closure of Citigroup Private Bank Japan is a good example (see Box 9.3).

The commercial impact of money laundering – real or just suspected – on wealth management businesses can be significant. Involvement in money laundering, however inadvertent, means large fines, as well as other sanctions from the authorities. Even more seriously, wealth managers could also face:

- Sharp decline in profit.
- Adverse publicity and weakened client and market confidence.
- Untold and lasting damage to corporate and professional reputations, goodwill and careers.
- Costly civil or criminal litigation.
- Long prison sentences.

In short, for the wealth management institution itself, the issues at stake here can be nothing short of life threatening. The recent saga at Riggs Bank provides a telling example (see Box 9.4).

---

[2] ABN AMRO Bank NV, Bank of Tokyo-Mitsubishi Ltd, Barclays, Citigroup, Credit Suisse Group, Deutsche Bank AG, Goldman Sachs, HSBC, JP Morgan Private Bank, Santander Central Hispano, Société Générale and UBS AG.

Box 9.2   International accounting standards

From 1 January 2005, all quoted companies in the EU will either be permitted or required to present their accounts according to international financial reporting standards (IFRS). The move to IFRS actually goes beyond the EU since several other countries are also mandating an equivalent move, and outside Europe there is increasing adoption of IFRS. For example, Australia will also adopt IFRS in 2005. In all, post-2005 there will be over 90 countries that either mandate IFRS, permit domestic companies to use IFRS or base local accounting standards on the IFRS rules. The US is an important exception. The aim is to raise accounting transparency and make it easier to compare financial performance across companies.

The adoption of IFRS in Europe is perhaps the most significant and dramatic change in accounting ever seen. Switching to the new standards will alter not just what companies and their auditors do with financial information but how firms run and report on their businesses. IFRS shifts the focus of accounts from historic costs to fair-value accounting: the fluctuations of everything from pension promises to property portfolios will be reflected in profit statements. The ongoing impact will therefore be to make reported profits much more volatile than in the past.

The standards likely to be of most relevance to wealth managers are IAS 39 'Financial Instruments: Recognition and Measurement' and its companion standard IAS 32 'Financial Instruments: Disclosure and Presentation'.

Some of the biggest changes will occur when firms merge. Wealth managers will be impacted disproportionately, given the ongoing consolidation within the industry. So-called merger accounting – favoured by acquisitive companies because it flatters the enlarged group's profits – will no longer be permitted. Nor will firms be able to write off goodwill (the value of a business to an acquirer over and above that of its physical assets) over a period of, say, 20 years. Instead, they will have to carry the full amount of goodwill on their books and test its value each year to establish the extent to which it may be 'impaired'. Under IFRS, there are also stricter rules on how to measure the value of businesses that are sold or discontinued.

The impact of the IFRS changes on performance metrics will vary by company and in many cases is unpredictable. For example, expensing of stock options will be a general negative, but the elimination of goodwill amortisation, in aggregate, should more than offset this at the net income level (although most investors currently exclude goodwill amortisation from adjusted earnings).

To comply with the new rules, as a starting point, wealth managers have had to identify the data they need for IFRS, which has meant substantial upgrading of systems and data-collection processes. That has put IT departments under considerable resource strain, not least because wealth managers typically operate multiple systems across multiple geographies.

Despite these initial implementation issues, going forward IFRS can be turned into a benefit if approached properly. The data consolidation required to produce IFRS reports can also be used to improve performance and reduce costs.

Box 9.3   Citigroup Private Bank Japan

On 17 September 2004, Citigroup was ordered by the Japanese regulator, the Financial Services Agency (FSA), to cease all private banking client transactions and close the private banking unit's operations by October 2005. That judgement was the result of what the FSA described as 'fundamental problems' with compliance and governance systems. The action followed a less severe August 2001 order by regulators that cited – and warned the company about – similar problems.

The key compliance shortcomings identified by regulators included the following:

- 'Acts injurious to public interests'. Primarily a failure to adhere to know-your-customer and suitability standards.
- 'Violations of laws and regulations'. Insufficient record-keeping (incomplete or infrequent suspicious-transaction reporting), sales practices (risk disclosure), and unlawful non-banking transactions with other Citi entities in Japan.
- 'Unfair transactions'. Improper markups and ill-advised customer transactions to drive increased profits for the private bank.
- 'Improper transactions'. Transactions structured to shield illegal activity by customers.

Governance issues highlighted in the FSA's report focused on the lack of management supervision from 'bank headquarters', in addition to inadequate internal controls to monitor and review operations. The FSA also cited violation of securities law with respect to the sale of private placements, including linking the provision of credit to the purchase of securities.

It was not long before conspiracy theories began to spring up. Did jealous domestic players connive with the FSA to drive their powerful foreign rival out of the market? Were the authorities planning a wealth tax, and hence concerned about private banks creating clever tax avoidance schemes? Some even wondered if it may have been linked to the prospective privatisation of Japan Post, which could cause a destabilising deposit flight to private banks.

Conspiracy or no conspiracy, the resulting business and career damage was real and swiftly felt. Chuck Prince, Citigroup's chief executive, admitted that senior staff in the private bank had put 'short-term profits ahead of the bank's long-term reputation' and broken the law. Three senior executives were asked to leave the firm, including a Citigroup vice chairman, the chairman and chief executive of the global investment management division, and the head of the private bank.

Citigroup had claimed to be the market leader in Japan – the largest single private banking market outside the United States for Citigroup. Thus, operations in the country were a significant contributor to overall private bank financial results. Around 17% (i.e. c.4 000) of the firm's private bank clients were located in Japan, including some of Japan's wealthiest investors. Guy Moszkowski, analyst at Merrill Lynch, estimated that a similar percentage (i.e. 15%–20%) of the unit's net income was sourced from the region (Citigroup Private Bank accounted for c.3% of the group's total earnings). Thus, the potential direct annual earnings impact could conceivably be of the order of $100 million. In addition, many wealthy clients served by the private bank have corporate interests that are an important source of business for other parts of Citigroup, including the investment bank.

Of much greater potential significance is any associated reputational fallout. In prestige-conscious Japan, it seems likely that a meaningful number of local clients will take their business elsewhere. The reputational impact could also harm efforts to enter and penetrate emerging Asian markets in China and India. South Korean regulators immediately examined Citigroup's private banking operations in Korea to look for the kind of problems discovered in Japan.

The news clearly takes some of the shine off the private bank's image and operations – a business that has generated top-of-class returns and solid organic growth for the firm. Going forward, the pullback from Japan removes a significant avenue of growth for the firm's private bank.

Needless to say, competitors did not waste any time in taking full advantage. For example, UBS and Société Générale stepped up their aggressive push into the Japanese private banking market, hiring about 35 former Citigroup relationship managers in the immediate aftermath.

Mr Prince has been vocal about steps he is taking to try to prevent another such disaster. Compliance officers, for example, no longer answer to business heads, but report up an independent chain of command directly to the head risk officer in New York. Mr Prince says he plans to revamp employee training to focus on ethics, and is considering changing the compensation system to tie individual pay more to the health of the entire Citigroup franchise. He is reported to have begun lecturing employees about a new way to think about the franchise, in which its DNA no longer means 'deliver numbers always'.

On a more positive note, wealth managers can, in principle, gain solid business benefits from improving their ability to know their customers. Not least among them is the improved capacity to cross-sell products and services. In addition, clients may become more reluctant to switch institutions, due, in part, to the more thorough screening process and the associated 'hassle factor'. More generally, many clients may take comfort from a more thorough approach to regulatory compliance.

Fundamentally, a number of core principles are widely recognised as being critical to any AML programme:

- Compliance with the relevant AML laws of the appropriate jurisdiction.
- Knowing your customer, including the source of wealth.
- Cooperating with various law enforcement and supervisory agencies.
- Communicating the firm's AML programme through policies, procedures and staff training.
- Continuous and sustainable risk assessment across the enterprise.

Yet, as Figure 9.1 indicates, wealth managers need to do a lot more in this regard.

At the practical level, suspicious money needs to be identified at the outset of the business relationship, before it actually gets into the financial system. Wealth managers need to ask themselves whether they are satisfied that their relationship managers know their clients. In terms of account opening procedures, for instance, wealth managers need to ensure that there are effective know-your-customer checks in place. Typical questions to be asked include: 'Can the individual's identity and address be verified'; 'Why does the individual want to open the account'; and 'Where has the customer's wealth come from and what will the likely pattern of transactions be?'.

Box 9.4   Riggs Bank

For almost 170 years, Riggs National was the bank of choice for the great and good of Washington DC and the world. The 'bank of presidents' managed the accounts of 21 first families, including those of Abraham Lincoln and Dwight Eisenhower, financed the Mexican War and the purchase of Alaska, and handled most of the accounts of the diplomats and embassies in the US capital.

But along with the great and the good, it transpired that Riggs also banked for the shady and sordid. That started to come to light following the terrorist attacks of 11 September 2001. Key elements of the scandal are as follows:

- *Saudi money transfers*. The FBI, and later the 9/11 Commission, ultimately stated that transfers from Riggs' customers' accounts were not intentionally being routed to fund terrorists. But investigators were surprised to see how lax the safeguards at Riggs Bank were. Several Saudi accounts were discovered to have financial improprieties, including a lack of required background checks and a consistent failure to alert regulators to large transactions, in violation of the law. Many of these transactions involved transfers of over $1 million at a time.
- *Pinochet's frozen funds*. Augusto Pinochet, the former dictator of Chile, has been widely accused since 1973 of corruption, illegal arms sales and torture. In 1994, Riggs officials invited Pinochet to open an account at Riggs Bank. A recent US Senate report revealed that Riggs' executives helped Pinochet disguise millions of dollars that had been stolen from the Chilean people, although some of Pinochet's supporters have claimed that the money came from supporters outside Chile. By using shell companies and hiding accounts from federal regulators, Riggs illegally allowed Pinochet to retain access to much of his fortune. The Senate report also indicated that regulators were negligent in holding the bank accountable.
- *Equatorial Guinean funds*. In July 2004, the US Senate published an investigation into Riggs Bank, into which most of Equatorial Guinea's oil revenues were paid until recently. The report showed that accounts based at the embassy to the United States of Equatorial Guinea were allowed to make large withdrawals without properly notifying federal authorities. At least $35 million were siphoned off by the long-time dictator of Equatorial Guinea, Teodoro Obiang Nguema Mbasogo, his family and senior officials of his regime.

In May 2004, Riggs was fined $25 million by the US Treasury Department for violating money laundering laws. Subsequently, in January 2005, Riggs pleaded guilty and paid a further $16 million fine for violations of the US Bank Secrecy Act. In February 2005, the bank agreed to pay $9 million to Pinochet victims for concealing and illegally facilitating movement of Pinochet money out of Britain. Members of the Albritton family, long-standing controllers of the bank, were forced to stand down from the bank's board.

February 2005 marked the final chapter of this saga. PNC Bank acquired Riggs Bank and closed its embassy business in order to refocus on retail banking. All Riggs Bank branches now bear the logo of PNC – quite a come-down for the former bank of presidents.

% of respondents

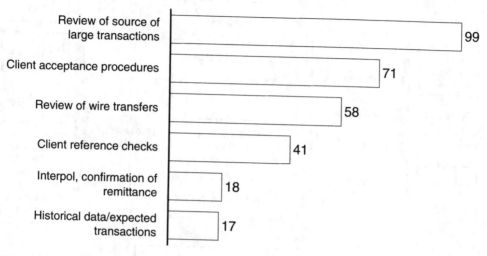

Figure 9.1 Activities in place to detect money laundering
Source: Ernst & Young Private Banking in Australia Survey, November 2002. Reproduced by permission.

Once the business relationship is up and running, wealth managers need to understand whether the actual transactions are in line with initial expectations. They also need to be prepared to investigate changes in account activity.

Many wealth managers start by making sure they understand not just the rules and regulations, but also the 'expectations' of each jurisdiction in which they operate. The next step is to compare them with the existing group-wide policy. That helps in identifying any gaps in local systems and controls, policies and procedures to meet local requirements and expectations. They then fill the gaps through specific initiatives, such as staff training backed up by the necessary manuals and compliance arrangements. The latter might involve monitoring, either by internal audit or by a dedicated resource, to oversee key activities such as procedures for account opening and for monitoring transactions.

But there is growing recognition that wealth managers need to develop a more comprehensive strategic response to the threat of money laundering. That is a proactive, enterprise-wide solution to managing the risk across business lines and in multiple jurisdictions, which is fully integrated into their business system. As a result, wealth managers may have greater assurance that their AML programmes are sufficiently robust to face the continuously evolving regulatory environment. This reflects the view that implementing AML controls is more than just a compliance issue. It cannot be addressed in isolation from the business itself.

That framework, illustrated in Figure 9.2, allows for enhanced all-purpose use of client data in a cost-efficient manner, while seeking to achieving enterprise-wide compliance with regulatory and legal requirements. Wealth managers can even achieve some cost savings by adopting this type of approach. Data collection and aggregation costs can be substantially reduced if a common data model is used for all purposes. Similarly, the know-your-customer data required for AML efforts originates at the account opening point.

The most obvious link here is to CRM. Embedding know-your-customer procedures into the sales and marketing process enables the front office to obtain more comprehensive information

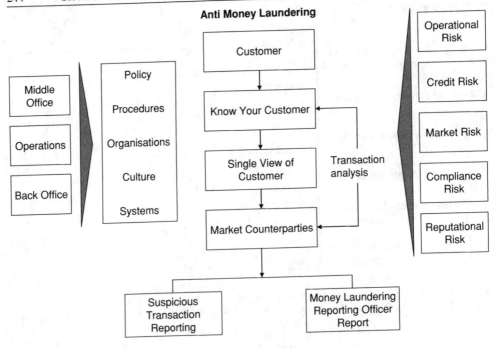

Figure 9.2 Defining the anti-money-laundering vision
Source: PricewaterhouseCoopers. Reproduced by permission.

about their clients' financial circumstances and thus sharpens the marketing focus. It also increases the incentive to update and validate information regularly.

Although clearly important, costs are not the only factor to consider. Data quality for all applications is improved if it originates from a single source, maintaining integration between source systems. Analytical solutions can also be substantially streamlined where there are fewer interfaces. In addition, if CRM data are considered when designing the common data layer, CRM solutions that provide effective cross-selling across channels and products become more economic.

The key components of a modern AML programme include:

1. *Strong corporate governance.* Wealth managers must demonstrate that senior executives and the board are properly overseeing the institution's AML programme and that it is integrated into effective risk management.
2. *Enterprise-wide policies and procedures.* An AML programme must be universal and consistent and span business lines, products and services, jurisdictions and technologies. Written policies must state the organisation's commitment and goals.
3. *Designated AML officer.* A global designated AML officer should be appointed, supported where necessary by local AML officers for each jurisdiction. The global AML officer should have access to top management and should report periodically to the board on the status of AML rules, regulations and trends, and on the organisation's initiatives to address any new developments.
4. *Good intelligence and communication.* Good-quality information and effective, enterprise-wide communication are essential to create and maintain strong internal controls. Larger

organisations should consider establishing FIUs to gather and analyse information and inform senior management and the board of potential problems.

5. *Effective employee training.* Continuous AML training of employees at all levels is essential. Training is not a one-size-fits-all undertaking; it should be:
   - Organisation-wide and tailored to fit resource functions.
   - Ongoing and require employee certification.
   - Offered through a range of delivery channels, including the Web.

6. *Technological solutions.* Technology should be leveraged to support all the elements of a wealth manager's AML programme. Such technology includes transaction monitoring software, and data-capture and reporting systems. But it is important to bear in mind that technology should act as a complement, never a substitute, for good judgement.

7. *Continuous maintenance and refinement.* The authorities increasingly look for wealth managers to have robust action plans for ongoing maintenance and improvement of their AML programmes.

9.2.4.1   Regulatory costs

Over the last three years, compliance costs have risen by more than 60%, driven by the following factors:

- New regulations force banks to overhaul their IT platforms and/or to buy new software in order to facilitate compliance work.
- Products often have to be adapted to comply with the new regulations.
- Work processes often have to be changed.
- In some cases, business strategy may have to be adapted to the modified conditions. These tasks tie up management resources.

Recent work by the Swiss Banking Institute at the University of Zurich has examined wealth managers' regulatory burden in detail. Compliance costs account for c.80% of the regulatory burden, with the remainder made up of incremental auditing and direct costs (see Table 9.3).

Table 9.3   Costs of regulation in wealth management (CHF thousands, per employee, 2002)

	Large banks	Securities dealer – securities trading	Securities dealer – wealth management	Small banks
Compliance costs	**10.9**	**11.6**	**15.3**	**24.3**
Prevention of money laundering	5.1	0.1	4.9	8.4
Risk management	2.5	4.8	2.4	3.5
Equity/ liquidity/ accounting	1.6	4.5	2.1	5.4
Other	1.8	2.1	5.8	7.0
Incremental auditing costs	**1.2**	**2.0**	**3.0**	**4.3**
External audit	0.4	1.1	2.2	1.6
Internal audit	0.8	0.9	0.9	2.7
Direct costs	**0.1**	**0.6**	**0.3**	**0.1**
Total regulatory burden	**12.2**	**14.2**	**18.6**	**28.7**
Number of employees	>100	<100	<100	<100

Source: Swiss Banking Institute, University of Zurich.

Given the largely fixed nature of compliance costs, it is not altogether surprising that small banks bear a disproportionately large share of the regulatory burden. Small banks' average compliance costs per employee amount to some CHF 24 000, or 9.8% of operating expenses. That compares with CHF 11 000 per employee, or 4.1% of operating expenses, for the larger banks. In addition, relationship managers are reported to be spending an average of 1.5 hours per day dealing with regulatory issues.

Compliance departments' resource requirements have therefore increased in recent years. Compliance is an area in which banks could potentially collaborate to spread fixed costs and share expertise. In Switzerland, for example, one solution might be an umbrella organisation, similar in character to the Swiss Bankers Association, which undertakes the compliance tasks of wealth managers that participate in the scheme. Potential obstacles include the different IT systems and resistance to disclose client information. Hence, this may only become an option if the regulatory cost pressure on wealth managers continues.

9.3   TAX INITIATIVES

This section outlines four recent tax-related initiatives, which are having a profound impact, particularly on offshore wealth management: the OECD's project on harmful tax practices, the US qualified intermediary regime, the EU Savings Directive and international tax amnesties.

9.3.1   OECD project on harmful tax practices

As part of its work to promote good governance in a globalised economy, the OECD has, for several years now, been engaged in a project on harmful tax practices. These it defines as practices designed to encourage people to evade the tax laws of other countries.

The project's first report was published in 1998. That report developed criteria to identify harmful aspects of a particular regime or jurisdiction. In particular, it focused on factors that could cause harm by undermining the integrity and fairness of tax systems. These factors included:

- No or nominal taxes in the case of tax havens and no or low effective tax rates on the relevant income in the case of preferential regimes.
- Lack of effective exchange of information.
- Lack of transparency.
- No substantial activities, in the case of tax havens, and ring fencing, in the case of preferential regimes.

The OECD's 1998 report was followed by a progress report in 2000. That report:

- Identified 47 potentially harmful preferential tax regimes in OECD countries.
- Listed 35 jurisdictions found to meet tax haven criteria.
- Proposed a process whereby tax havens could commit to eliminate harmful tax practices.
- Made proposals for associating non-member economies with the harmful tax practices project.
- Proposed elements of a possible framework of co-coordinated defensive measures designed to counteract the erosive effects of harmful tax practices.

The OECD has had considerable success since then. Eleven jurisdictions – Aruba, Bahrain, Cayman, Cyprus, Isle of Man, Malta, Mauritius, Netherlands Antilles, San Marino, and Seychelles – have committed to eliminate their harmful tax practices. In 2002, the OECD published a list of uncooperative tax havens, describing them as 'a threat not only to the tax systems of developed and developing countries but also to the integrity of the international financial system'. The list includes Andorra, Liechtenstein and Monaco. More than 30 other OFCs have pledged to work with OECD countries to counter harmful tax practices.

The finance ministers of the G7 countries at their summit in Halifax, Canada, in June 2002 called on 'all countries to permit access to, and exchange, bank and other information for all tax purposes'. It said that progress in this area is a priority and urged the OECD countries to lead by example.

9.3.2 US qualified intermediary regime

On 1 January 2001, new tax rules were introduced in the United States, which changed the withholding tax and reporting procedures that apply to income from US sources and certain other payments. The changes were intended to ensure that US citizens and residents properly report and pay tax on their income and that all non-US recipients of US source income pay the appropriate rate of withholding tax.

The new regulations contain more stringent documentation requirements to determine the status of investors (US or non-US). To streamline the processing of these complex documentation requirements, the US government allows non-US financial institutions to enter into an agreement directly with the Internal Revenue Service (IRS) to become a Qualified Intermediary (QI) – a conduit between the client and the IRS.

The QI's responsibilities include:

- Obtaining documentation to establish the identity and tax status of the beneficial owner of US source income.
- Reporting of US source income.
- Withholding and remitting of US non-resident alien and backup withholding taxes.

Those foreign institutions that become QIs essentially make it impossible for US taxpayers to hold US securities and instruments anonymously offshore.

A key advantage of becoming a QI is the ability to pass on an applicable lower rate of withholding tax to foreign beneficiaries (assuming the IRS is provided with sufficient information and/or representations concerning the ultimate beneficiaries of the US source payments). It also enables a more streamlined administration of withholding tax and information reporting. In addition, the QI's clients are likely to receive a somewhat more efficient service, such as speedier income reporting.

By contrast, institutions that choose not to become QIs are required to charge the highest withholding tax rate provided by the IRC (31%). They have also been warned that they might have their access to US markets and exchanges denied on the grounds that their refusal to enter the QI regime might be evidence of complicity with US tax evaders.

But QI status is a complex undertaking. In order to attain – and, more importantly, maintain – QI status, there are considerable compliance policies and procedures. IRS regulations also require that continuing compliance with the withholding and reporting obligations of the QI agreement be tested in the second and fifth year of the agreement by an independent external auditor. Failure to pass these independent audits could lead to the surrender of QI status, causing damage to the institution's reputation.

Many of the QIs are now reported to be concerned that the audit requirements will result in considerable additional costs. Additionally, their initial concerns about the effects on banking secrecy requirements have not abated, and may well become more of a worry should their external audits reveal problems with their QI compliance, ultimately resulting in direct IRS contact. More time will be needed to determine if the QI regime has achieved its initial goals of reducing US tax evasion and proper withholding tax rate allocation.

9.3.3 European Union Savings Directive

The EU is pursuing a slightly different approach in this regard. It has, for many years now, been trying to encourage cooperation among fiscal authorities and create a more level tax playing field. In 1997, the European Union (EU) introduced 'a package to tackle harmful tax competition in Europe'. That package consists of the code of conduct, the directive on cross-border interest and royalties, and the savings directive (the Directive).

The Directive focuses on effective taxation of interest income paid to individuals within the EU on their cross-border savings. The Directive aims to stamp out bank secrecy, fraud and evasion of tax on savings income by individuals who have savings in other countries and simply do not declare it.

The Directive came into force for existing EU countries on 1 July 2005 (EU accession countries are likely to have to apply the Directive from 2007). After this time, EU countries will either exchange information on non-residents' savings or operate a withholding tax regime, for a period not exceeding 7 years after the Directive is adopted. Luxembourg, Belgium and Austria have already announced that they will operate a withholding tax regime, starting at 15% from 1 July 2005 and rising to 20% from 1 July 2008 and 35% from 1 July 2011. They will share the revenue with the country of residence (handing over 75% and keeping 25%).

The EU is aware of the risk that if the EU countries adopt the Directive, the savings in question may easily flow out of their current EU locations to more tax-efficient jurisdictions. Therefore, the European Commission entered into discussions with the US, Switzerland, Liechtenstein, Monaco, Andorra and San Marino to promote the adoption of similar measures, including the exchange of information. EU countries will also promote the adoption of the same measures in all relevant dependent or associated territories including the Channel Islands, Isle of Man and those in the Caribbean.

After very lengthy negotiations, Switzerland and the other offshore territories have agreed in principle to the terms of the Directive. Switzerland will operate a withholding tax at the same rates as those that will be applied in Luxembourg, Belgium and Austria, sharing revenue in the same way. These three countries, in turn, have agreed to begin automatic exchange of information on non-residents' savings:

- If and when the European Commission enters into an agreement with Switzerland, Liechtenstein, San Marino, Monaco and Andorra to exchange of information upon request as defined in the OECD Agreement on Exchange of Information on Tax Matters (developed by the OECD Global Forum Working Group), applying simultaneously the withholding tax rate.
- If and when the European Commission agrees that the US is committed to exchange of information upon request.

By the end of the first full fiscal year following the entry into force of that agreement, Austria, Belgium and Luxembourg will cease to apply a withholding tax with revenue sharing.

The EU Commission has stated that it has reached a satisfactory agreement on equivalent measures with the US authorities. The US will provide information on request, but it will not be automatically exchanged on a year-on-year basis.

The current debate is focusing on potential practical issues in implementing the Directive. These include:

1. *Loopholes.* The relatively narrow scope of the Directive's definition means that private banks can mitigate its effects (at least partially) in three main ways:
   - Product innovation. Many banks are developing specialised products to mitigate the effects of the Directive. These include:
     (a) Funds or direct holdings of 'grandfathered' bonds. Under the terms of the Directive, income arising from certain bonds is not liable to tax until the end of 2010. Qualifying bonds must have been issued prior to March 2001 and must not have been reopened since March 2002. Clearly, over time, the price of such bonds should adjust to reflect their tax-advantaged status. One example is Bank Leu's Euro Bond fund.
     (b) Deferred interest accounts. Interest accrued on such accounts is not credited until the account is closed. In this way, the tax liability is deferred until the account is closed. For individuals anticipating a reduction in tax band or change in tax residency, such accounts can be attractive. That type of product has been particularly popular in the British Isles; early pioneers include Britannia International and Alliance & Leicester International.
     (c) Life assurance products. Unit-linked bond products, for example, enable clients to hold investments in cash, corporate and government bonds within an investment bond wrapper. In principle, it is possible to move money from a deposit account into an investment bond wholly invested in a cash fund, thereby avoiding a tax liability under the Directive, while retaining the risk profile of the investment.
   - Developing trust and company structures. Given that the Directive is not generally applicable to discretionary trusts or companies, an individual who receives interest through such structures may not be exposed to information exchange or withholding tax. These structures are likely to be more relevant to genuine HNW clients, so it is the affluent clients that are likely to be most affected by the Directive.
   - Managing assets from other jurisdictions. The ability of the largest players to manage client portfolios from non-EU jurisdictions provides another way to mitigate the impact of the Directive. Private banks with offices in Asia are particularly advantaged in this regard.
2. *Non-participating OFCs.* The Directive may have the effect of driving capital to non-participating OFCs such as Panama, Hong Kong and Singapore. For example, Germany's decision to introduce a withholding tax in 1987 led to immediate capital flight to Luxembourg and was very quickly revoked.
3. *Enforcement.* The Directive contains no specific reference to audit requirements or enforcement procedures. Though the Directive includes minimum policy standards, there are concerns among financial institutions that there will be differences in the way it is implemented in different countries.
4. *Administrative burden.* Financial institutions will need to adapt their IT systems and back offices, communicate to clients the impact of the new rules and invest in staff training. BCG

Table 9.4   Recent tax amnesties

Country	Timing	Tax rate applied (%)	Repatriated assets (€ billion)
Italy	Aug 01–Jun 02	2.5	60
	Jan 03–Jun 03	4.0	20
Israel	Jan 03–Apr 04	15	n/a
Portugal	Dec 02	n/a	1
South Africa	Jun 03–Feb 04	5–10	5
Germany	Jan 04–Dec 04	25	} c.4
	Jan 05–Mar 05	35	
Belgium	Jan 04–Dec 04	6–9	6
Cyprus	Sep 04–Feb 05	5	4
Greece	Feb 05–Aug 05	3	n/a

Source: Press cuttings.

estimates that the Directive has created an average cost burden of 2–3 basis points for each institution.

5. *Other issues.* At the time of writing, there are a number of other issues outstanding, such as: the extent of evidence needed about the recipient, the definition of interest, which appears impracticably wide, transitional arrangements, and the effect of double tax treaties.

The EU Commission is expected to enter talks over the next 7 years with other important financial centres to discuss the adoption of equivalent measures. The major target of those discussions is likely to be the Asia-Pacific region, especially the OFCs of Singapore and Hong Kong. In the meantime, as noted above, Asia will be a major beneficiary of funds from EU individuals who wish to avoid having their income disclosed to the tax authorities or having withholding tax applied on their savings. Whether the Asia-Pacific countries will be willing to forgo this influx of funds in return for greater cooperation with the EU remains to be seen.

Going forward, in principle, the case could be made for the Directive to be extended to cover dividend and other types of taxable income. Indeed, the EU has already publicly admitted that the Directive is likely to be reinforced over time.

9.3.4   International tax amnesties

Driven by rising budget deficits in recent years and the consequent need to boost tax revenue, some governments are employing tax amnesties to encourage people to repatriate offshore assets (see Table 9.4). The first to do this was Italy in 2001. Under the terms of the amnesty – also known as the Tremonti law, or the *scudo fiscale* – individuals were able to 'come clean' by making a tax payment without fear of additional tax and criminal penalties. The rate of tax was set at 2.5% of the assets held offshore on 1 August 2001. (Alternatively, the individual could opt to subscribe to special state bonds for an amount equal to 12% of the value of the relevant assets.) The amnesty's original deadline of February 2002 was later extended to June 2002.

Individuals could opt to return assets in two ways:

• 'Repatriation' of financial offshore investments. Under this scheme, the offshore assets must be deposited in Italy in a special account with a qualifying financial intermediary. Relevant investments included cash, shares, bonds, mutual funds and insurance policies.

- 'Regularisation' of financial and non-financial offshore investments (including real estate, works of art and precious items). Under this scheme, the offshore assets continue to be held outside Italy and are simply declared to a qualifying financial intermediary.

Overall, the amnesty captured some € 60 billion of assets, around 10% of the target. Of these assets, around 20% were regularised, 50% repatriated to Italian banks (reflecting, in part, the decision by some onshore banks to reimburse clients' amnesty tax payments) and 30% repatriated to Swiss banks in Italy – in particular, Credit Suisse and UBS. Indeed, the scheme was so successful that the Italian government launched a second tax amnesty in 2003, this time with a higher tax rate of 4%. That captured a further € 20 billion of assets.

In the light of Italy's success, various other countries have followed suit, including Portugal, Germany, Belgium, South Africa, Israel and Cyprus. In most cases, the associated tax rates are relatively high, particularly in Germany (25%–35%), where the amnesty has been widely viewed as a failure. Russia has tentative plans for a six-month tax amnesty in January 2006, and is expecting to repatriate assets of around $15 billion. A number of other countries, including France, Switzerland, Portugal and India are reported to be considering tax amnesties of their own.

9.3.5   Implications of tax initiatives for wealth managers

The regulatory and tax developments outlined above clearly represent an escalation in the multifronted assault against offshore wealth management. These factors reinforce the other key drivers of global onshore asset growth, which include:

- More stable macroeconomies (price and currency stability).
- Greater confidence in domestic banking systems.
- Profitable onshore investment opportunities.
- Possible waning appeal of offshore/Swiss banking brands, particularly among the younger generation of clients who place greater emphasis on performance, cost and transparency.

This has led many to believe that, going forward, managing wealth offshore will be considerably less attractive to clients. The outcome could be a dramatic falloff in growth – if not, outright absolute shrinkage – in global offshore assets. As an indication of the magnitude of change, McKinsey estimates that European HNW clients' offshore assets as a proportion of their total assets could fall to around 24% in 2008 from 29% in 2003. Merrill Lynch analysts expect annual growth in offshore assets to average 4.1% over the next 5 years, compared to growth of 7% for onshore assets.

Once Switzerland and other offshore centres adopt full information exchange for EU citizens, banking secrecy is effectively eliminated. In that case, clients are likely to move their assets out of the European offshore centres – either onshore, particularly if there is a favourable tax amnesty, or, if still possible, to another offshore centre outside Europe. That is likely to be an option for only the wealthiest individuals. Analysts at Dresdner Kleinwort Wasserstein calculate that for client portfolios less than € 2 million, it will be cheaper to pay the withholding tax than to make one annual trip to monitor an offshore account in Singapore for example.

That, at least, is the current orthodox view. Yet, can we really be certain that offshore wealth management is dead? Though directionally correct, the goodbye may turn out to be more protracted than some currently envisage and the impact is likely to be far from even across the various OFCs. For example, most of the negative impact is likely to be felt by some of the smaller European OFCs, which are less able to compete on the basis of other, non-fiscal advantages.

Much depends on the reasons why specific clients use OFCs. Offshore banks can do other things besides providing a tax haven. For example, a lot of Taiwanese money is managed out of Singapore because Taiwanese cannot invest in China directly. For some clients, particularly those based in countries with unstable political regimes, offshore assets will remain a key part of their portfolios. Many clients have, in any case, become more willing to bundle their wealth in onshore locations and use offshore selectively for tax efficiency, while declaring their holdings for domestic tax purposes. The desire to move to an offshore location purely for tax reasons has, in some cases, waned as governments have brought down their tax rates to increase the tax take.

Some OFCs view the greater global scrutiny as an opportunity as well as a threat. OFCs now have some of the most advanced and robust regulatory frameworks in the world. While some argue it will drive away account holders seeking privacy, others claim higher standards will make legitimate investors feel more comfortable.

In any event, competition among OFCs will undoubtedly grow. Hence, to compete effectively, they will need to reinvent themselves, rather than simply rely on their traditional tax, secrecy and safety advantages. There is no single business model for today's OFCs. Long-term success now depends on having much more clearly defined business lines and the infrastructure to support them. Potential approaches they could adopt here include:

- Leveraging/developing specific expertise (e.g. in trust and estate planning, and in fixed-income fund management).
- Providing higher service levels.
- Delivering superior investment performance.
- Targeting themselves at specific client segments/geographies.

The withholding tax will mean that European clients face a reduction in cash and bond returns (equities, recall, are not covered). But banking confidentiality is maintained for now. During the transition period, in the absence of a tax amnesty, clients are likely to keep their assets offshore and shift the allocation to assets that are not subject to the withholding tax. Over this period, for the largest players with strong brands, the key Asian OFCs of Hong Kong and Singapore represent the greatest opportunity to reorientate their offshore businesses.

9.3.5.1   Offshore-oriented wealth managers

In this tough emerging scenario, offshore-oriented wealth managers, such as the traditional Swiss players, need to take a highly proactive strategic stance. They need to pursue one or more of the following strategies:

1. *Defend*: Stay within existing OFCs and retain and deepen relationships with existing clients
   - Bolster offshore wealth management propositions by:
     (a) Leveraging specialist expertise.
     (b) Focusing on selected product/client segment niches (e.g. expatriates) and providing exclusivity.
     (c) Differentiation through superior client service.
   - Increase economies of scale through:

(a) Relationship manager team lift-outs.

(b) Acquisition of asset portfolios.

(c) Outright M&A activity.

2. *Attack*: Grow beyond existing OFCs

- Offshore:

(a) Increase their presence in one or more of the Asian OFCs.

- Onshore:

(a) Develop selective complementary onshore presence or distribution capability.

(b) Offer an integrated onshore/offshore proposition.

(c) Tailor propositions to the needs of local markets.

For the attacking option, a number of offshore-oriented wealth managers have decided to go onshore in Europe. Here, they have essentially three options: (a) build it from scratch by recruiting and training relationship managers; (b) buy it through outright acquisitions of individuals, teams or entire firms; and (c) 'rent' it by entering joint ventures and by developing feeder networks. None of these options is easy. For example, the build option is both costly and difficult to execute; for the buy option, even now there are relatively few quality acquisition candidates available at non-dilutive prices.

Onshore expansion needs to be guided by an assessment of the size of the target market, the breakeven market share and the availability of high-quality staff. Though a new service centre can be set up relatively cheaply, a strong presence in the major cities and an appropriately tailored offer is a far more considerable undertaking, typically requiring new dedicated infrastructure, including a booking centre and back office. The execution risk is considerable.

With that in mind, it typically takes 5–10 years for a new geographic location to break even. That is mainly due to ongoing and substantial investments in the franchise (including processing platforms, physical sites, advertising and IT) and new hirings. It also reflects the fact that gross margins tend to be rather low at the start as, initially, clients typically only bring part of their wealth and request low-margin products; UBS management think it takes clients up to five years to mature to a broad relationship. An analysis of Credit Suisse's expansion into the Italian private wealth management market suggests that even with an acquisition to accelerate entry, breakeven is around the four-year mark, and requires at least around €10 billion in assets. There is a classic 'hockey-stick' path to profitability with significant cumulative losses in the early years of such a project. The relatively long timescales present a major problem for publicly listed wealth managers, because of the relentless pressure to deliver short-term earnings growth for their shareholders.

These large initial losses probably explain why few of the mid-sized players have fully committed to such an aggressive business plan. Pictet took 27 years to be successful in Japan, but now claims to be one of the leading foreign wealth managers in the Japanese market. In 2002, Vontobel entered the German onshore private banking market. Julius Baer started doing business in the newly established Dubai International Financial Centre (DIFC) in September 2004; it also plans to break into Germany's onshore private banking market.

For the small and medium-sized offshore players, with lower resources, the response has been limited largely to joint ventures, partnerships and distribution agreements. Such onshore alliances allow these offshore players to avoid building a physical onshore presence that in all likelihood would be subscale. Depending on the country, other possible JV targets include networks of independent financial advisors. One example was Julius Baer's 2003 link-up with

Table 9.5 Recent wealth management acquisitions by UBS

Date	Target	Country	AuM (US$ billion)
Jan 2005	Etra SIM	Italy	0.5
Dec 2004	Dresdner Bank Lateinamerika	Latin America	7.1
Dec 2004	Julius Baer North America	US	3.4
Nov 2004	Sauerborn Trust	Germany	8.0
Nov 2004	Amex Luxembourg	Luxembourg	0.4
Jan 2004	Scott Goodman Harris (IFA)	UK	9.5
Jan 2004	Laing & Cruikshank (Credit Lyonnais)	UK	9.2
Oct 2003	Merrill Lynch's German private client activities	Germany	1.4
May 2003	Lloyds TSB's French wealth management business	France	1.0
Jul 2000	PaineWebber	US	533

Source: Merrill Lynch; UBS.

Credito Valtellinese in Italy. Based in Milan, the new venture was called Julius Baer Creval Private Banking. But such cross-border JVs need to be managed carefully: in August 2005, Julius Baer abandoned the JV, reasoning that its expectations regarding local business had not been fulfilled.

For the buy strategy, acquisitions would need to focus on HNW clients without bringing unwanted baggage in the form of an inefficient branch network, for example. The UBS acquisition of the US-based Paine Webber in 2000 represents one of the few relative success stories. It has since followed this up with a series of other acquisitions (see Table 9.5), increasing its AuM by around $40 billion.

On the whole, quality acquisitions are very difficult to find at reasonable valuations. Though valuations have fallen from their late 1990s highs, earnings dilution is still a real concern. In addition, top-class integration skills are essential. The management time and resources needed to rationalise and integrate cross-border banking operations, in particular, will prove at best a challenge and at worst a serious drain on resources.

Targeting the right client segments will be a crucial factor in determining the success or failure of offshore banks' onshore asset-gathering strategies. For example, UBS has stated that its target clients are individuals with more than $500 000 in investable assets. Such clients have acquisition costs that are higher on a per-client basis, but lower on a per-asset basis, than those of mass affluent clients. By contrast, Credit Suisse had said it was willing to consider clients with assets as low as just €50 000. But that changed in 2002 as it reviewed its Pan-European onshore expansion strategy. It now focuses on high-end clients and has cut back on the scale of its planned onshore expansion.

In terms of propositions, the offshore model cannot easily be exported to onshore markets. Notwithstanding the ability to leverage offshore investment expertise and specialised services, a high degree of local tailoring is essential.

Overall, the effect will be to sharpen the divide between the largest, globally active offshore-oriented players and the rest. Some of the smaller offshore-oriented wealth managers may, in the end, be forced to exit the market altogether.

9.3.5.2   Onshore-oriented wealth managers

Conversely, the regulatory and tax developments, in principle, represent a huge opportunity for onshore-oriented wealth managers. The key challenge here is for players to upgrade their propositions and investment performance to ensure that they capture a high share of the repatriating assets. That will require them to upgrade their quality of advice and improve their relationship management skills. They will also need to consider selling any non-core offshore businesses. As noted above, they represent attractive partners for offshore wealth managers to share in the repatriation of assets.

10

The Future

With Philip Molyneux

The global wealth management industry has experienced marked changes over the last few years and is faced with a variety of future challenges. Private banking firms need to develop their businesses models and change (or enhance) their strategic focus in order to take advantage of the opportunities afforded by higher growth markets and product segments. A key source of profit growth is expected to be mid-market HNWIs in the developed wealth management markets of North America and Europe, with a stronger growth potential in the newer emerging markets of Asia, the Middle East, Latin America and Eastern Europe. Various global private banks are actively developing activities in the three key markets of China, India and Russia. Growth in the offshore wealth management area is expected to lag that of onshore business; Singapore and Hong Kong are perceived as markets that offer the greatest potential here, given their advantages in attracting Asian wealth. (Some rather ambitious forecasts even suggest that Singapore could replace Switzerland as the major private banking offshore centre by 2010.)

The industry is also gradually restructuring – similar to the consolidation process that occurred in the global investment banking industry during the 1990s. A three-tier system is emerging headed by large global private banks that offer a full range of onshore and offshore services, followed by medium-to-large operators that typically have a regional focus and then specialist (or boutique) operators. Consolidation is an ongoing theme in the industry, although the majority of deals to date have been relatively small, with many of the global players buying up some of the smaller players. If the consolidation trend follows that in investment banking it is almost inevitable that larger deals will take place between global and mid-market operators – especially as the latter are, to some extent, being squeezed by the global operators on the one hand and by small specialist, high-touch operators on the other.

In order to generate greater returns from existing clients, and to attract new business, private banks need to focus aggressively on enhancing client relationships, generating greater value-added from these relationships while boosting client loyalty. They need to place more emphasis on monitoring and managing client satisfaction, enhancing the functions and effectiveness of client relationship managers, providing better tailored products and services and developing more cost-effective production and distribution channels. They also need to improve their pricing structures and internal performance measurement in order to evaluate the value-adding capacity of relationship managers and product lines.

Overall, that adds up to a more demanding operating environment for the private banking industry in the years to come. This chapter examines these main issues and concludes that the firms most likely to succeed will be those that most effectively understand and meet increasingly exacting client needs while optimising (from both the bank and client perspectives) the long-term wealth management relationship.

The chapter is split into the following sections:

- Introduction: recap of key trends.
- Sources of new profitable growth:
  (a) Geographic participation.
  (b) Client relationship deepening.
  (c) New propositions.
- Future industry structure.
- Critical success factors.

10.1 INTRODUCTION

The strategic focus of the global wealth management industry in recent years has shifted from an industry characterised by sales-led solutions of (usually limited) proprietary products and services to one that emphasises the trusted-advisor role, offering a much broader spectrum of value-added solutions. Standard products and services are likely to be produced in-house, although specialist services (such as alternative investments, structured products, various advisory services) are just as likely to be obtained from third-party providers. The trend towards the greater use of open architecture structures to both produce and distribute wealth management services seems inevitable as clients become increasingly discerning in their demands for best-value solutions. The effective delivery of such solutions should also ultimately feed through to enhanced client relationships.

Figure 10.1 highlights some of these trends. Other features of the changing environment relate to increasing consolidation in the industry and the growing relative importance of onshore wealth management. Note also the emphasis on the 'full client balance sheet', wealth managers providing 'holistic' investment and other advisory services in order to capture a greater share

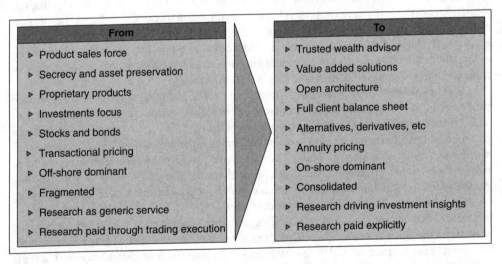

Figure 10.1 Transformation of wealth management
Source: Presentation by Todd S. Thomson, Chairman and Chief Executive Officer, Citigroup Global Wealth Management, UBS Asset Gathering Conference, 31 March 2005.

of the client's wallet. The focus on managing a client's total wallet enables private banks to generate greater returns from existing relationships as well as helping them to prospect for new business (by, for example, identifying links between client and extended family wealth). In short, it is inevitable that industry participants will focus much more on building brands around the 'trusted wealth advisor' concept (very much emulating the family office service) in order to generate greater value from existing clients and at the same time prospect for new business in high growth markets.

10.2   SOURCES OF NEW PROFITABLE GROWTH

The rapidly changing wealth management environment is increasingly forcing market participants to take a hard look at their own operations and consider new ways of boosting growth. Key sources of new profitable growth include:

- *Geographic participation.* Potential growth opportunities in established and new markets.
- *Client relationship deepening.* Increasing the penetration and loyalty of existing clients, and targeting new client segments.
- *New propositions.* Developing product and service innovations and personalising the wealth management advisory role.

10.2.1   New geographies[1]

There has been a number of forecasts published that aim to identify the markets that are perceived to offer the best growth potential for wealth management firms. While forecasts of the growth of HNW assets under management (AuM) in different markets vary, a generally accepted view appears to be that new emerging markets offer the most attractive opportunities. Particular attention has focused on the 'BRIC' economies – Brazil, Russia, India and China – in particular the latter three economies, given the projected economic growth over the coming decades. Figure 10.2 shows that these economies could become an important source of new global spending in the not-too-distant future. For example, India's economy could be larger than Japan's by 2032 and China's larger than the US by 2041 (and the second biggest economy in the world by 2016). The Goldman Sachs forecasts show that the combined BRIC economies will be larger than the current G6 (US, Japan, UK, Germany, France and Italy) by 2039. Figure 10.3 shows the ten largest economies in 2050, ranked by GDP.

The substantial expected growth in the aforementioned and other emerging economies is reflected in the changing pattern of global HNW wealth. Figure 10.4 shows the figures from the Capgemini/Merrill Lynch (2005) 'World Wealth Report.' Global HNW wealth is expected to grow at an average annual rate of 6.5% between 2004 and 2009. Emerging markets are generally expected to experience the fastest growth: Middle East 9.1%, Asia Pacific 6.9% and Latin America 6.4%.

The one area where forecasts of HNW wealth appear to vary is for the US and Europe. Figure 10.4 shows that North American HNW wealth will grow on average by 8.4% a year between 2004 and 2009. But other forecasts suggest that such growth will be much more

---

[1] More detail on specific countries mentioned in this section can be found in Appendix 1.

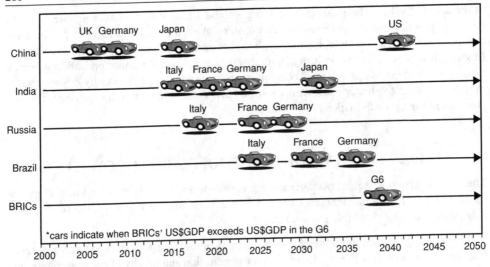

Figure 10.2   Overtaking the G6: when BRICs' US$GDP would exceed G6
Source: Goldman Sachs (2003). Reproduced by permission.

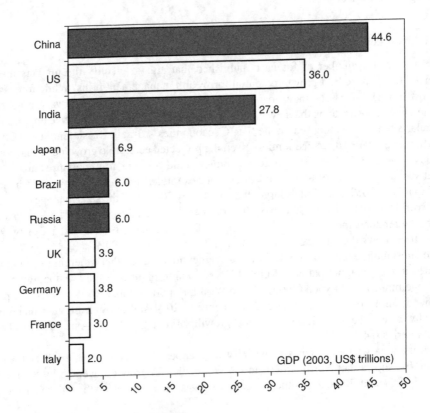

Figure 10.3   The largest economies in 2050
Source: Goldman Sachs (2003). Reproduced by permission.

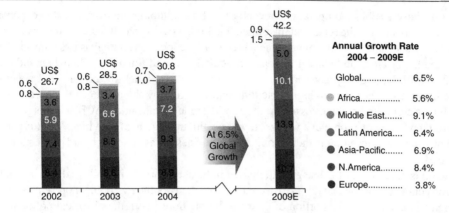

Figure 10.4 HNWI financial wealth forecast by region, 2004–2009E (US$ trillions)
Source: Capgemini/Merrill Lynch World Wealth Report 2005. Reproduced by permission.

modest; Boston Consulting Group (2005b), for example, projected an average annual growth of 4.1% over the same period. Similar differences also occur in the forecasts of European wealth. Capgemini and Merrill Lynch expect relatively low growth of 3.8%, whereas BCG forecast 6% annual growth in HNW wealth. Taking a crude average of these projections of HNWI wealth gives average annual growth in North American wealth of around 6% and European wealth of around 5% over the next five years.

Despite differences in the forecast growth of HNWI wealth, there is a strong consensus that:

- Growth of private banking business in North America and Europe will predominantly come from established clients. The North American wealth market will grow faster than that of Europe and, because of its sheer size, will still remain a key market.
- In emerging markets (Asia, Eastern Europe and Latin America), growth will come from emerging (generally entrepreneurial) clients. In the Middle East, growth is mainly expected to come from inherited wealth as well as from clients that have businesses linked mainly to the energy sectors.
- China, India and Russia, plus possibly Brazil, are the most attractive growth markets.
- Offshore wealth will grow slower than onshore wealth, particularly in Europe, driven mainly by regulatory pressures relating to transparency and disclosure of activities, and by initiatives relating to the cross-border taxation of investment income.

The geographical markets that are expected to yield the greatest growth potential are those of China, India and Russia. While all these markets remain relatively small, the prospects for growth in their economies and the subsequent increase in wealth of mainly entrepreneurial clients is expected to be substantial:[2]

- *China* HNW wealth is believed to have been around $530 billion in 2004 and this is expected to grow to just over $1 trillion by 2009 – an annual growth rate of 14%. Many large foreign

---

[2] Forecasts for China, Russia and India are from The Boston Consulting Group (2005b).

banks have established operations recently in China, although the focus of this expansion has mainly been in the retail and investment banking areas. Typically, this is the precursor to offering specialised wealth management services. The location strategy is to set up activities in the major cities and coastal regions, particularly around Shanghai, Shenzhen and other cities with large entrepreneurial activity, as this is where much of the personal wealth is concentrated. Various banking restrictions will be lifted by the end of 2006, according to China's commitment on accession to the World Trade Organisation (WTO). Foreign banks will then be freer to conduct a wider array of wealth management activities. Various private banks are also developing their Hong Kong businesses as a springboard into mainland China.

- *Russia* is perceived as the key growth market in Eastern Europe. HNWI wealth is estimated at around $300 billion and this is expected to more than double by 2009. At present, Russian clients hold a substantial portion of their wealth offshore, given the historical political and other uncertainties associated with the domestic investment climate. However, there are signs that economic and political stability is returning to the country, the banking system is being overhauled and the general investment climate is improving. Risk-adjusted returns from the Russian market have been relatively high over recent years, providing good investment opportunities. This is one of the major factors that are expected to drive development of the wealth management business.

- *India* is also widely touted as a market with substantial growth potential. HNW wealth is estimated at around $150 billion and the market is expected to grow by 11% annually to $253 billion by 2009. (Other forecasts[3] suggest that growth in UHNW clients could be even higher, suggesting a doubling of wealth over the next four years.) Given the strong economic growth prospects, demographic changes and the increasing number of entrepreneurial HNWIs, the demand for more sophisticated wealth management solutions is seen as inevitable, especially given the perceived limitations of the domestic banking system. As in the aforementioned markets, foreign banks have been rushing to establish operations in the Indian market, where banks such as Citigroup, BNP Paribas, SG Private Banking and HSBC all now offer some form of wealth management service.

While these emerging markets are viewed as having particularly strong potential, other regions such as the Middle East and Latin America (particularly Brazil) are also often cited as geographical areas that have stronger growth opportunities than the European and North American markets. That raises various issues for wealth management firms, not least the different distribution and asset allocation approaches that need to be employed. Investors in emerging markets typically take a less balanced approach to asset allocation than their Western counterparts, focusing more on property investments, for example. In addition, as the bulk of HNWIs have accumulated their wealth through entrepreneurial activity they are often more familiar with complex financial products. They are therefore often more prepared to employ alternative investments as part of their overall portfolios. Quite often they require wealth management solutions that combine low- and high-risk assets as opposed to more traditional balanced investments.

---

[3] KPMG (2005), pages 19–22.

Box 10.1   Japan

Japan has the second-largest pool of HNW wealth in the world, with around 1.3 million US dollar millionaires[4] and c.$5 trillion AuM (around 16% of the global totals), and is home to some of the world's wealthiest families. Japanese wealthy households controlled around $11 trillion in 2003, or 20% of the global total.[5] UBS expects the market to grow by 4.5% a year on average from 2004 to 2008. Whatever the merits of Asia's other economies, Japan demands attention, if only for its scale and breadth. Yet Japan does not have a private banking market, at least not in the conventional sense.

Drivers of underdevelopment

Restrictive regulations, limited product offerings and conservative investment attitudes have stifled this potentially attractive private banking market. In addition, Japanese investors have been averse to concentrating their assets in a single financial institution because of trust and privacy concerns. The incentive to fragment financial relationships increased recently by the capping of deposit insurance at ¥10 million ($90 000). Unusually for an advanced economy, around 63% of household assets are invested in postal and bank deposits, and only around 15% in securities and mutual funds.

Above all, the Japanese remain understandably cynical about financial institutions. During the late 1980s, securities firms had manipulated the stock market to favour institutional clients at retail customers' expense. In the early 1990s, insurance companies guaranteed returns on client investments, only later to cut promised returns to help counter their own mounting losses. During this period, banks provided low rates to depositors to generate cheap corporate funding; retail banking became a sideshow. That fuelled excessive speculation, a bubble and a recession, the effects of which are still being felt today. For example, a middle-aged woman who inherited lucrative properties that had been in her family for generations, received a flurry of investment proposals from private bankers at domestic and foreign institutions. But she steadfastly refused all of them saying 'I never give any of them even a quick look at my asset portfolio.'

While HNW Japanese have been keen to protect their savings, they have demonstrated little interest in diversifying their investments internationally or in less traditional investment products, where their understanding is limited. For example, potential clients who have been targeted by private bankers for single stock hedges have often declined on the basis that such solutions may fall into a 'legally grey' area. The limited offshore investment that did take place was typically conducted through organised 'private banking tours', which enabled Japanese HNWIs to meet directly with banks in Geneva, Zurich, Luxembourg and other offshore centres.

A strong preference for secrecy surrounding personal finances had made educating potential clients on the benefits of new products difficult. That secrecy, combined with the fallout from Japan's scandals, has frustrated attempts for much of the 1990s to serve clients with a single relationship manager. Instead, clients have preferred to hedge themselves by spreading their investments across institutions on a product-by-product basis.

[4] Source: Capgemini/Merrill Lynch.
[5] Source: Boston Consulting Group (2004b); refers to household wealth >$100,000.

By 1998, the leading foreign players in Japan had less than $5 billion in private banking assets. All were starting from a small base, but several were gearing up to take a real crack at the Japanese market. The efforts of the most aggressive were perhaps best exemplified by Merrill Lynch and the SBC side of the newly merged UBS. After exiting Japan in the early 1990s, Merrill Lynch Private Clients re-entered in 1997 with its purchase of Yamaichi's retail brokerage arm. Merrill pulled out of this brokerage business in 2001, amid heavy losses, as clients had proved unwilling to move their savings into mutual funds and securities. Merrill Lynch subsequently retained only the wealthier clients. UBS/SBC, in 1997, entered into a partnership with the Long Term Credit Bank of Japan (LTCB) in the expectation of bringing its expertise to its partner's network of personal relationships. LTCB's financial problems, which became apparent in 1998, resulted in UBS/SBC acquiring the private banking business of the partnership. However, it too shut the business down in 2002 because, according to the bank, 'the market was not quite ready to appreciate the kind of services it was trying to offer'.

Potential market catalysts

Looking ahead, more liberal foreign investment and financial services distribution regulations should help. Japanese regulations traditionally meant that private banks needed licences for each service they offer, from securities broking, to tax and inheritance advisory, discretionary asset management and deposit-taking services. With the recent revision of securities law, banks can now act as agents for securities firms and sell their products to clients. As a result, for institutions that operate a separate bank and securities firm, it is much easier to offer securities products to their clients. But under the current regulations, there is no way of creating a full one-stop-shop private bank in Japan. In particular, the regulations that surround the giving of advice are complex for institutions that are not asset managers or securities companies. In addition, banks in Japan cannot make money on brokerage fees through the sale of securities products, which is a problem because these revenues typically represent 20%–30% of a typical private bank's revenue in most other countries. Overall, regulatory wise, there have been improvements, but private banking remains somewhat in a grey area.

Local banks are under government pressure to boost their profitability and fee income, and are increasingly focusing on strengthening their businesses with retail customers, particularly with wealthy clients. It is conceivable that the privatisation of Japan Post, scheduled to start in 2007, will lead to some deposit flight to private banks, as postal savings currently represent around 23% of total deposits.

Clients are becoming increasingly frustrated with the consistently poor returns offered by real estate and traditional bank deposits. Yen devaluation remains a concern among some HNW investors, but could help bring Japan's long battle with deflation to an end. Going forward, Japan's rapidly ageing population will require higher returns to retire comfortably.[6] There are signs that wealthy clients are reconsidering how to manage their money, with many becoming more comfortable investing in riskier assets such as equities, fixed-income mutual funds (known locally as investment trusts) and non-yen instruments.

---

[6] Japan's dependency ratio, at c. 30%, is already one of the highest in the world. By 2050, it is expected to have reached c. 70%.

Taking all these factors together, this is likely to help spur onshore private banking development – but only gradually.

Recent activity

Citigroup Private Bank's forced exit from the Japanese private banking market in September 2004 (see Box 9.3 in Chapter 9) undoubtedly shook local clients' already fragile confidence in wealth management and foreign providers. Citigroup was the market leader, though its market share was thought to be less than 1%. There is, however, no shortage of domestic and foreign firms looking to fill this gap and develop the private banking market. Merrill Lynch and UBS, both of which are on their second or third attempts at cracking this market, are, together with Société Générale (SocGen), among the more high-profile foreign players.

SocGen acquired an operating platform (Chase Trust Bank) in 2002, which enabled it to operate under a relatively wide-scope trust licence. It currently has some 700 HNW clients and aims to have $5 billion in AuM by the end of 2007. UBS re-entered the market in late 2004, and has so far taken an organic approach to business building.

Some foreign banks are collaborating with local players. For example, Merrill Lynch and Mitsubishi Tokyo Financial Group (MTFG), Japan's second-largest bank, are establishing a 50:50 private banking joint venture. It will operate as a secutities company and is expected to start operations in 2006. Merrill Lynch Japan Securities will contribute its existing private clients business, including 8 000 client accounts, and private banking expertise. MTFG will provide access to its HNW client base. Nikko Cordial, Japan's third-largest brokerage house, has tied up with Banque Privée Edmond de Rothschild to offer trust, asset management and custody services. JP Morgan is reported to be planning private banking expansion in Japan in 2006.

Some local players are choosing to 'go it alone'. Mizuho, Japan's largest bank, had joint venture proposals from various foreign players, but recently launched a wholly owned private banking subsidiary, Mizuho Private Wealth Management. Targeting clients with assets of more than $4.6 million, its product offer will include mutual funds from Wells Fargo, Wachovia and Bank of New York. It also has partnerships with art galleries and importers of luxury cars. The unit will be headquartered at Mizuho's main branch in central Tokyo, where clients will have a dedicated reception room. Shinsei Bank is offering high-end retail banking (leveraging its business banking unit for client referrals), by opening lounge-style offices in Tokyo's Ginza district and Osaka's Umeda district exclusively for 'platinum members', or those who have deposits of $90 000 or more, aiming to cultivate wealthy customers. The offices are modelled after airport executive lounges and are located on quiet upper floors with views; they feature electronic bulletin boards and clients can consult in private rooms, relax after shopping and take wine classes. (Shinsei has also spun off a separate HNW business, which has product tie-ups with US Investor Select Advisors and CDC of France.) Sumitomo Trust & Banking has set up a new unit, STB Wealth Partners, which will offer fee-based consulting services to HNW clients in such areas as asset management and inheritance planning. Its referral partners include accountants, lawyers and the fine-art firm M&I Art System. At the UHNW end, Diamond Private Office, another division of the Mitsubishi group, was established in 2002, and now has 550 clients each with assets averaging $20 million.

Other foreign players are also establishing or expanding their wealth management activities. Standard Chartered, which is active in Japanese wholesale banking, is launching a retail banking venture. That will target affluent individuals with more than $180 000 to invest, through an up-market retail branch in the Marunouchi district of Tokyo. The service will focus on banking activities such as no-commission foreign currency deposits and relatively high-return structured deposits. HSBC Private Bank is reported to be seeing improved business activity in Japan.

Winning in Japan

The battle for assets will be between (a) the leading foreign players, which have the private banking expertise and relatively high credit ratings, but limited access to clients; and (b) the large local banks, which have deep client relationships from years of business lending but high organisational inertia when its comes to implementing new ideas.

In addition to the four key generic success factors (client segmentation, product innovation, cost management and organisational critical mass), competitors in Japan need to undertake aggressive staff training, build client confidence and implement a broad programme of client education. Competitors in Japan must have a clear vision of which client segments they want to penetrate. That clarity will provide a focus for the massive programme of banker and client training that must occur in Japan. The biggest challenge in developing this latent private banking market is client trust. All private banks in Japan must demonstrate to potential clients that they offer something different that clients need. Private banking is still not well understood by most wealthy individuals. Internal training must give relationship managers the skills to educate potential clients on the strengths of their institution and products.

Institutions wishing to excel in Japan must evaluate their ability to carry out wide-scale internal staff education, client confidence building and client education. The large local Japanese banks house much of the personal wealth and have the personal relationships, but are still only just beginning to grapple with the organisational and skill-building challenges of setting up new private banking operations. Many will try, but only a few are likely to emerge as true leaders in Japan's future private banking landscape. The magnitude of the challenges and the complementary capabilities of foreign and local players argue strongly, we feel, for collaboration. Needless to say, victory in Japan will come to those who demonstrate staying power in the battle to win client trust. In the coming years, private banking in Japan should finally begin to mirror other parts of Asia. Given the potential impact of only relatively small shifts in HNWIs' investment behaviour, Japan should, in time, be an arena for significant business growth.

So far we have focused largely on prospects for the onshore wealth management industry. There are also major changes expected to take place in the offshore market, with the perceived attractions of Switzerland forecast to lose out to Singapore, as shown in Table 10.1.

Singapore is already an important private banking centre, with around $150 billion in assets booked by many private banks with operations in the city. Its chief competitor in Asia is Hong Kong, with around $300 billion in booked assets. Hong Kong used to be the offshore centre of choice for money from China, Taiwan and the Philippines. However, its attractiveness as a neutral and confidential haven, particularly for overseas Chinese and Taiwanese demanding discretion, has eroded since the 1997 handover by Britain to China of sovereignty over the territory. As a consequence, money is increasingly flowing to Singapore, which has long been the preferred parking space for wealth from Indonesia, Malaysia and Thailand.

Table 10.1 Growth in offshore private banking assets – Singapore's ascendancy

What do you believe will be the most important offshore centers in terms of growth of private banking assets in two years' time?

Offshore centers in 2005	Rank	Offshore centers in 2007
Switzerland	1	Singapore
Singapore	2	Switzerland
Hong Kong	3	Hong Kong
UK	4	UK
Luxembourg	5	Luxembourg
Cayman Islands	6	Cayman Islands
Bahamas	7	Bahamas

Source: IBM Consulting Services (2005). Reproduced by permission.

Singapore has further strengthened its position over Hong Kong by luring money from Europeans looking for an alternative to Switzerland, the traditional premier offshore private banking centre that has come under pressure from EU countries to reduce secrecy and provide greater assistance in tracking down tax evaders (see Chapter 9). In the future, Hong Kong and Singapore are likely to vie for money flowing out of Japan in search of higher returns.

10.2.2 Client relationship deepening

Given the demographics and growth prospects of the traditional wealth management markets of North America and Europe, most commentators believe that opportunities to boost performance by attracting new clients will be severely limited. As few are predicting another imminent wealth-creating IT boom or similar event, the name-of-the-game here is cultivating new business mainly through existing client relationships and focusing aggressively on intergenerational wealth transfers, especially for mid-range HNWIs (ranging from $1 million to $30 million of AuM). That is because the wealth of mid-market clients is expected to grow by more than that of less wealthy clients. In addition, attempts to access the mass affluent market by wealth management firms has not been a success and this segment is now perceived increasingly as more of a financial-advisor/retail-banking-oriented activity.

In the North American and European markets the focus is to extend the range of services on offer to mid-level HNWIs, expand the advisory role to encompass intergenerational wealth transfer (product life-cycle) products and services and develop broader family wealth relationships with established clients. The ultimate aim is to offer a wider range of tailored services that not only meet an individual client's investment needs but span the entire spectrum of family business relationships as well as inheritance and estate planning. Therefore younger family members of established clients represents a key 'new' client segment.

We noted in Chapter 4 the trend towards private banks promoting intergenerational wealth transfer issues by hosting various educational programmes to illustrate to family business members and potential inheritors various wealth management issues and opportunities. That is all part of the ongoing strategy to nurture the next generation of clients and to squeeze more value (a bigger share of wallet) out of existing clients. The increased focus on developing such

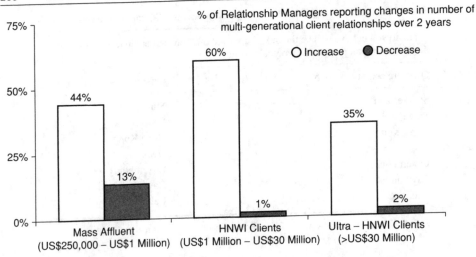

Figure 10.5 Growth of multigenerational client relationships, by client type, 2002–2004
Source: Capgemini/Merrill Lynch World Wealth Report 2005. Reproduced by permission.

relationships is illustrated in Figure 10.5, which shows that client relationship managers of the mid-market HNWI segment are dealing more with intergenerational wealth transfer issues than their poorer (or richer) counterparts.

As already noted, the genuine new clients will emanate primarily from those economies expected to have the greatest economic growth potential, namely Russia, India and China. It is expected that the bulk of these will have created their wealth through entrepreneurial activity and will seek services that reflect their greater familiarity with more complex financing options coupled with relatively strong protection elements.

10.2.2.1 Increasing client penetration and loyalty

A key driver of profit growth is boosting revenue from established clients, and especially the wealthier segment that is perceived to have a greater need for such value-added services. The difficulty for wealth managers is that clients are becoming increasingly sophisticated and demand greater performance and security from their assets. That requires searching across a wider range of investment opportunities, both traditional and relatively new (e.g. hedge funds, private equity, property and commodity products, structured investments and so on). Growing regulatory oversight and compliance issues also pose challenges to firms promoting some of the newer investment alternatives as well as for pensions and other intergenerational products and services. Clients are becoming more performance and price sensitive, are more likely to switch provider if not satisfied and demand bespoke tailored best-practice wealth management solutions across an increasingly broad spectrum of areas.

To promote client penetration and greater loyalty wealth managers will have to focus more on:

- *Understanding the needs and aspirations of clients.* This seems an obvious point, although there is only limited evidence that wealth mangers undertake systematic surveys of clients (or client groups) to assess levels of satisfaction associated with their service delivery, product offering, pricing and other aspects of their business. Similarly, we are not aware of any cases where wealth managers seek to optimise product and service offerings based on such survey evidence.

- *Focusing on higher-value clients.* While client segmentation is an overriding theme in private banking, there is strong evidence that many wealth managers have a significant proportion of unprofitable clients, particularly those with low balances. The increase in competition has encouraged many firms to take on uneconomic clients with the hope of these generating future returns. But most of the time the anticipated higher returns fail to materialise, at least not without concerted effort. As noted in Chapter 3, clients are segmented in many different ways: mainly by AuM, risk preferences and geography, but also through their source of wealth, etc. Segmentation on the basis of value-creation criteria, however, has rarely been used. In order to boost performance, wealth mangers are likely to focus much more on the value-generating attributes of various HNWI clients. Loss-making (or low-return) clients – typically those that have been accepted with low assets – are likely to be charged cost-plus fees, or the services on offer need to be reduced/standardised to enable these clients to be served more efficiently on an economic basis. That was the approach recently taken by ING in Belgium, which transferred its low-value clients to its retail division.
- *Creating value-added services for clients.* Focus on delivering relevant value to targeted clients. That, of course, requires wealth managers to understand the needs and expectations of clients and also really demands that the relationship manager understands more precisely what clients value. Confidentiality, security and performance are important value-enhancing propositions. Linked to this is the need to be able to offer a broad array of traditional and innovative products and services. Being able to provide genuine 'independent' advisory services is also seen as key to enhancing value to clients.

While it is reasonably easy to identify the broad approaches that wealth managers can take to strengthen client relationships and promote loyalty, such a process is difficult to manage. It requires placing much greater strategic emphasis on systematically analysing client needs, the client–relationship manager relationship, and identifying the performance of the whole spectrum of product and service propositions. Most wealth managers do, however, have only relatively small numbers of clients (compared to retail banks, at least), have closer connections and rapport with clients, and have a variety of customer relationship, product and financial planning tools (such as RiskMetrics WealthBench), which can be used to help analyse the performance and other attributes of the service being offered.

10.2.3 New propositions

Product innovation is an important aspect of the wealth management offer. However, as in other areas of the financial services industry, private banks appear dependent on other parties to create such innovations – typically investment banks or/and other specialist firms. The relatively recent embrace of hedge funds and private equity investment vehicles as part of the product armoury of private banks is a good example. Product innovation rests mainly outside private banks so they need to leverage other providers or other parts of their organisations. In fact, it is difficult to identify any high-value new product innovations that have come from within the sector. Wealth managers primarily offer a range of services that have commercial banking, investment banking, brokerage and various other professional advisory characteristics in a manner that is attractive to certain client groups. That is complemented with up-market service delivery elements and 'dusted' with an exclusive brand image.

Box 10.2   Emerging client segments

As well as deepening relationships with existing clients, there are opportunities to target various emerging client segments. This box focuses on two: affluent women and ethnic groups. Some of these types of clients have a greater resonance with advisers from their own segments. Hence, to target these segments successfully, wealth managers will need to recruit more relationship managers from these segments in order to reflect the changing balance of their client base.

Affluent women

The financial services world, and wealth management in particular, has traditionally been very much a male domain. But that is changing. There is little in the way of global data, but some regional and country-specific stylised facts provide evidence that affluent women represent a key emerging wealthy client segment.

In North America, Merrill Lynch estimate that women make up 43% of the affluent segment, with that percentage set to rise. The Spectrem Group estmate that the number of wealthy women has been growing by 68%, while the number of wealthy men grew by only 36%. Women now own and run 26% of America's companies, with the number of women-owned businesses growing at twice the rate of the total number of US firms. In the UK, the story is similar. One-quarter of HNWIs are women, with Brewin Dolphin estimating that there are around 360 000 women in the UK worth more than $900 000. Research by the Centre of Economics and Business Research shows there are more women millionaires aged between 18 and 44 than men. By 2025, women are expected to own more than 60% of the UK's personal wealth. In Australia, National Australia Bank has reported a 5% increase in the number of new female clients over the last year, which exceeds the growth of male clients. In the Middle East, as noted in Chapter 1, there are growing levels of wealth in the hands of women. In Saudi Arabia, the region's largest wealth market, women are reported to own 40% of private wealth and account for more than half of all university graduates.

Overall, wealthy women are growing in number as they delay marriage to pursue professional and personal goals. Most wealthy women are likely to be enterpreneurs and professionals; some may be seeking to take control of their finances following bereavement or divorce. A growing number of wealthy women are filling senior executive posts.

Relative to men, women tend to:

- Generally live longer, frequently earn less pay and often receive less in the way of pension (on average, a woman takes about 12 years 'off' to care for children or elderly parents compared with less than 2 years for a man).
- Have a different attitude towards money (financially more conservative, rational and more risk-averse investors; trade less often; more inclined to follow a consistent, long-term approach to investing).
- Be traditionally less sophisticated financially; they want financial advice and education given within a more supportive environment; they also value superior listening skills as much as technical expertise.
- Show greater loyalty to their financial services provider.

Some wealth managers are now starting to recognise this opportunity. Examples include:

- *Citigroup*. Women & Co. is a division of Citigroup, launched in February 2001. It offers bundled product and services designed specifically for upper-income professional women. Product features include: personal financial consultation and access to a team of financial advisors; access to a toll-free number for financial and tax-related questions; a comprehensive financial education programme, including seminars, newsletters and a members-only knowledge library; discounted mortgages, childcare and other products; online nanny referral service; and household help in tax planning.
- *Bramdiva*. This is a new women-focused wealth management service launched in the UK by Bramdean Asset Management and UBS. Its full asset management service will be available to HNW clients, and the minimum investment for the company's multimanager fund is $170 000. It will also offer its clients a series of social and networking events around the UK.
- *Wachovia*. In 1997, Wachovia created a director of women's financial advisory services within its capital management group. The idea was to understand women's financial needs. Its has run targeted direct-mailing campaigns and, following a two-year pilot, made a number of modifications to its marketing to make it more women friendly. For example, it has produced a very well received series of money management guides aimed at women clients, is active in supporting various womens events and holds a number of financial education seminars of its own.

Ethnic groups

As globalisation takes hold and mobility rises, particularly among the affluent, ethnic groups represent a growing opportunity for wealth managers. Ethnic groups include people sharing common and distinctive racial, national, religious, linguistic or cultural heritage. By their very nature, many ethnic groups have specific needs, which are very different to those of the rest of the population.

For example, Asian-Americans and Hispanic-Americans are the two fastest-growing populations in the US, but have divergent investment approaches. Generally, Asian-American HNWIs embrace a more 'do-it-myself' attitude to investment. Conversely, Hispanic-Americans are more inclined to solicit advice from financial advisors. Merrill Lynch[7] found that only 52% of Asian-American HNWIs used a primary advisor compared with 67% of Hispanic-Americans. That attitude is also reflected in Hispanic-American HNWIs' greater use of financial plans: 33% compared with 24% of Asian-Americans. These behavioural differences are not based on different levels of investment knowledge, as both groups view themselves as fairly educated in financial matters concerning traditional products, such as stocks and bonds. It is more likely that differences may be attributed to varying cultural backgrounds. Also, when choosing an advisor, Asian-American HNWIs put a much greater emphasis on advisor personality compared with Hispanics.

For Asian-American and Hispanic-American HNWIs, wealth growth and preservation are both key financial goals. The difference is in the motivations behind these two goals. When asked about the primary goal of estate planning, supporting family and spouse were two of the top goals for Hispanic-Americans. Conversely, a majority of both Asian-American

[7] 'Hispanic/Asian Affluent Study', April/May 2003.

and general US HNWIs saw tax planning as their primary estate planning goal. It should be noted that almost half of affluent Asian-Americans and more than 40% of affluent Hispanic-Americans did not have an estate plan.

In the US and elsewhere, certain ethnic groups share key characteristics and have similar financial needs. For example, many Muslims require Islamic private banking (see Box 4.1 in Chapter 4). Many ethnic groups are entrepreneurs or self-employed, and can therefore require close working relationships between their wealth management and business banking providers.

A good example of a wealth manager targeting ethnic groups is Merrill Lynch's Multicultural and Diversified Business Development Group, which is focused on specific segments of the US population. The aim is to establish the firm as the preeminent wealth management provider among diverse and multicultural markets. It currently focuses on the South-Asian-American and African-American segments. For example, it offers non-resident Indians (one of the fastest-growing segments in the US) networking events and access to the Indian financial markets via its Indian subsidiary.

One major challenge relates to managing the product life-cycle. As in the investment banking area, products that were once considered exotic and of high value soon become commoditised, thus encouraging a new wave of product and service innovation. That is also the case in private banking where structured products have become the norm, with an ever-increasing number of variants vying for clients. Product life-cycles are shortening and the associated regulatory/compliance and tax issues are becoming more onerous. Increasingly, wealth mangers will have to manage these product life cycles more effectively to meet client needs. In addition, they will have to become more aggressive in removing under-used, low-value commoditised products from their 'shelves'. Traditionally, banks proliferate products but are loathe to get rid of them. The same can be said about wealth management firms – much greater focus needs to be paid to stripping out low-value products and services and focusing more on value-creating business. That, of course, will involve the adoption of different production and distribution channels and a fuller embrace of open architecture.

10.2.3.1 Non-financial 'lifestyle' services[8]

Lifestyle services are an umbrella term referring to a wide range of services designed to support, facilitate and improve the lifestyles of wealthy clients. Lifestyle services can be classified into four major categories, as follows (see Figure 10.6):

1. Lifestyle organization services aimed at assisting in organizing and facilitating aspects of individuals' lives such as leisure, entertainment, shopping and event planning.
2. Travel services aimed at supporting and arranging individuals' travel requirements.
3. Property and home services aimed at assisting with individuals' household and property requirements including finding, purchasing, moving and maintaining the home.
4. Luxury asset acquisition services aimed at helping wealthy individuals in the purchase and management of large-scale luxury items.

---

[8] This section draws heavily from Datamonitor's work in this area – in particular, from its report, 'Incorporating Lifestyle Services into the Wealth Management Proposition Survey', May 2003.

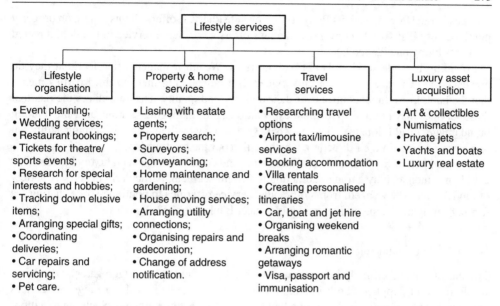

Figure 10.6 Lifestyle services
Source: Datamonitor, 'Incorporating Lifestyle Services into the Wealth Management Proposition Survey', May 2003, Reproduced by permission.

In their efforts to provide superior levels of service, some private banks and wealth managers and more particularly family offices at the ultra-high net worth level have long provided specific non-financial services to their clients, mainly as a component of their client service proposition. However, these have generally been offered as perks and rarely considered as an additional or integrated component of the wealth management proposition. In this respect the trend towards offering lifestyle services is still very much at an embryonic stage in both the US and, more particularly, Europe.

The relative novelty of these types of services means that in the client's mind there is, as yet, no single established best source for lifestyle services. Wealth managers are in a relatively strong position to supply such services as they (a) have access to the client segment that is more likely to require lifestyle services; and (b) can often have strong and trusted relationships with their clients, which makes them credible 'referees' for these types of services. From the wealth manager's point of view, the main reasons for developing such services relate to:

1. *Revenue diversification*. In the current choppy financial market conditions, wealth managers need to develop new sources of revenue.
2. *Incremental revenue opportunities*. For example, by offering to help wealthy clients buy luxury items, wealth managers can maintain a post-acquisition role in the management of the acquired item.
3. *Increase client loyalty*. Lifestyle services can increase client loyalty and deepen client knowledge. That, in turn, enables wealth managers to respond more effectively to client needs and spot new opportunities for relationship expansion.

Examples of wealth managers providing such services include Northern Trust, which is reported to be dabbling in high-end travel. HSBC Private Bank offers a range of property services in the UK thorough its Property Vision subsidiary. It offers clients advice on property purchases of GBP 400 000 upwards. Barclays offers a concierge service in London, directed at clients living outside the UK.

Providing lifestyle services is not without risks. Wealth managers often feel that they do not have the expertise to offer such services. But outsourcing them to third parties means that the bank loses direct control over their delivery and quality. This introduces the risk that these services may not live up to client expectations, thus damaging relationships and diluting brand image. In addition, the client may believe that the wealth manager is pushing additional unwanted services in their direction, which could sour the relationship.

A related possibility is that of more interesting and creative tie-ups with luxury brands. That could, in principle, play a role in attracting the youth segment, particularly in Asia. A variety of models can be envisaged, from co-branded service offerings to boutique-space sharing – a form of 'up-market supermarket banking'. Gucci Bank, anyone?

10.2.3.2   Aggregator role

The industry is increasingly being viewed (and talked about) as an 'aggregator', whereby a whole range of suppliers, both internal and external to the bank, offer a range of services that can be offered individually or bundled together to meet client needs. Such 'aggregation' activity means that wealth managers have to be much more nimble and efficient in sourcing, distributing and identifying value-enhancing services (for both the client and the bank).

The 'aggregator' function of wealth managers, and the growing focus on value-added advice-led sales, has encouraged (or forced) the industry to consider developing their business along similar lines to the family office, with the aim of offering holistic and independent advice. Providing advisory services across the full range of wealth management areas is viewed by many as a key profit driver going forward. The stronger and more proactive the advisory function, the greater information the wealth manager can glean about the needs and future demands of clients and their families, businesses and so on. The provision of such advice, however, is a major challenge as such services can often come from specialists outside the private bank. However, the potential benefits can be substantial: advisory services typically cannot be commoditised and are more likely to result in higher-value specialist solutions and improve client loyalty. Figure 10.7 illustrates the main differences between the traditional private bank approach and the family office style of operation.

In order to boost performance, it is widely accepted that the wealth management industry will have to embrace the main aspects of the family office model, given its growing 'aggregator' and advisory service function. Figure 10.8 illustrates how the industry is expected to evolve using many elements of the family office model to develop the trusted advisor role. While the US is expected to remain the largest family office market, we think Europe will see major growth as it is still underdeveloped (for Asia, it is probably a little too soon to be going down the family office route).

10.3   FUTURE INDUSTRY STRUCTURE

The global wealth management industry has experienced a wave of M&A activity in recent years as many banks have sought to acquire new clients in both established and new markets. In general, however, the consolidation trend has not had a marked impact on the industry as most of this activity has focused on large firms acquiring relatively small operators. So far, most of

Characteristics	Traditional FSI* Approach	Family Office Model
Wealth Management Methodology	• Product-oriented • Investment-management focused • Advice centered on "in-house" portfolio only • Little or no coordination/collaboration with third-party providers • Service oriented toward individual mid-tier millionaires	• Product neutral • Investments are managed in the context of the family "balance sheet" • Advice reflects a full view of client's assets • Coordinates/collaborates with all providers to develop an integrated wealth strategy • Service focuses on the mid-tier millionaire family "entity"
Process & Pricing	• Transaction-based pricing now moving towards AUM or "by service" fee-based model • Ad-hoc investment process; reacts to market conditions • Portfolio reviews based on standard templates	• Historically AUM-based pricing • Investment process is often documented and standardized, according to agreed-upon investment policy • Portfolio reviews are regularly scheduled and customized, according to client's needs and preferences
Products & Services	• **Advice & Planning to develop personalized wealth management plan:** - Set objectives - Develop strategy - Implement solutions - Review progress • **Banking Services:** - Direct deposit, check writing, funds transfer, etc. • **Business Financial Services:** - Integrated cash management, business banking, etc. • **Credit & Lending** - Home, personal, investment and business financing • **Estate Planning:** - Trust services, tax assessments, etc. • **Investment Management** • **Retirement planning**	• **Chief Advisor:** Oversees relationships with all product and service providers, external counselors/advisors; provides personalized service, technical expertise and creative business leadership • **Investment Manager:** Manages, analyzes and reviews family's financial capital, including: investment policy, manager selection/review, asset monitoring/review and due diligence • **Financial Administrator:** Ensures asset allocation mirrors client's investment philosophy; tax compliance; financial control; project management and financial reporting • **Trustee:** Educates and mentors; administers family trusts, ensures timely communications; and oversees philanthropic management • **Back Office Manager:** Provides investment and partnership accounting, client reporting, internal controls and technology support

*Financial Services Institution

Figure 10.7 Private banking and the family office model
Source: Capgemini/Merrill Lynch World Wealth Report 2005. Reproduced by permission.

the consolidation activity has been among domestic firms, followed by within-region deals. Figure 10.9 illustrates that there have been few cross-region acquisitions. This pattern emulates the same trends that occurred in European commercial banking in the second half of the 1990s. The reason for this is that banks, on the whole, were prioritising consolidation in their domestic markets followed by overseas expansion. Few intercontinental deals have occurred and those that have mostly relate to US and European firms making acquisitions in Asia.

While the consolidation trend does not appear to have had a major impact on the industry so far (mainly because of the lack of mega mergers), what has emerged is an industry characterised by a handful of global players, a range of medium-to-large mainly regional operators and various specialists/boutiques. In fact, the structure of the wealth management industry is, in many ways, now similar to that of the investment banking industry.

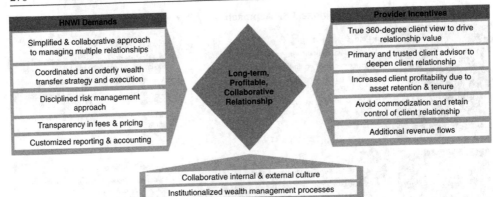

Figure 10.8   Evolving to the next level of a global trusted advisor
Source: Capgemini/Merrill Lynch World Wealth Report 2005. Reproduced by permission.

Proportion of private banking transactions per region by volume (2002–2004)

● Inter-regional acquisitions (acquirer and target in different regions*)
☐ Acquisitions where acquirer and target are in the same region*
▨ Domestic acquisition

* Regions are defined as North America, South America, Europe, Africa and Asia Pacific

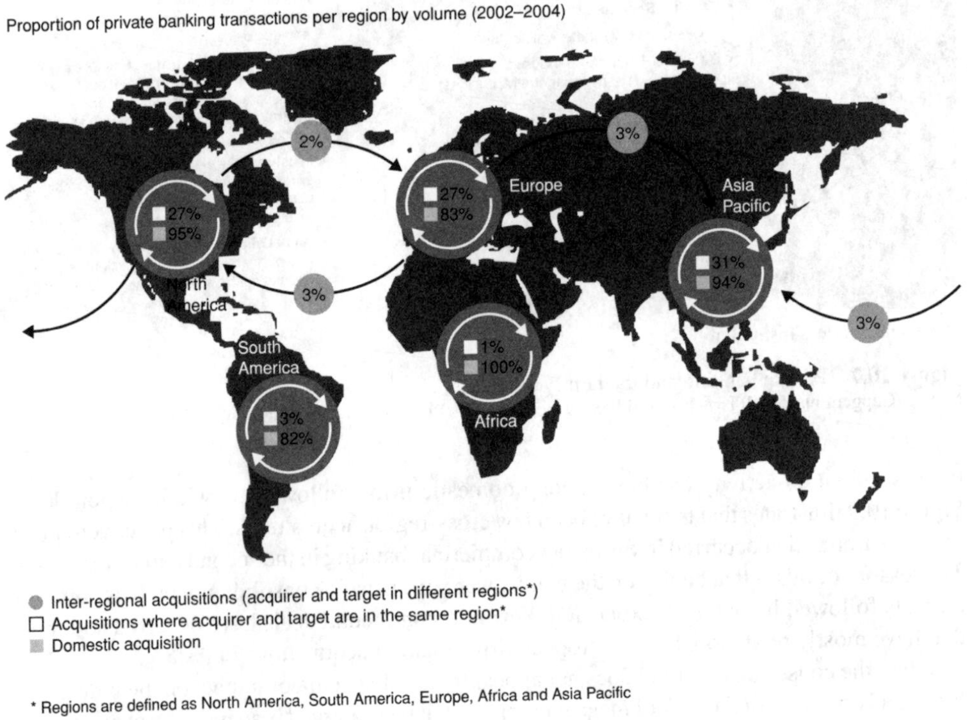

Figure 10.9   Private banking M&A
Source: KPMG (2005). Reproduced by permission.

One widely suggested potential candidate for an industry-changing, intercontinental merger is UBS. It has been linked with Northern Trust and Charles Schwab amongst others, which fit with the group's strategic willingness to improve its UHNW platform in the US. Merrill Lynch equity analysts[9] have argued that Northern Trust is 'the obvious number one choice'. Its wealth management franchise is, after all, very strong at the top end of the HNW band (versus the more mass-affluent franchise of legacy Paine Webber) and its presence in asset management has strong synergy potential. The concerns would be Northern Trust's relatively high price and its size, which would not quite get UBS to a 51% revenue base in the US. As for Schwab, the Merrill Lynch analysts view the company as 'way too expensive . . . and could risk bringing the UBS brand somewhat downmarket'. Moreover, there are fewer obvious synergies than with Northern Trust. In the US, a roll up of smaller players, by contrast, should also not be discounted.[10] UBS has also been linked with Standard Chartered, which would enable UBS to (a) join the ranks of global banks such as Citigroup and HSBC, (b) claim a higher multiple, based on a higher growth profile, and (c) rebalance its business mix towards Asia, securing growth for the decade to come.

The industry structure is set to become more polarised over time and could eventually come to resemble the industry structure of other professional markets such as law and accountancy. Various commentators suggest a number of different possible future structures, but in our view the industry is likely to resemble the following:

- *Global 'champions league'*. Strong global wealth management giants such as UBS, Credit Suisse, Citigroup, Merrill Lynch and HSBC. These target multiple onshore and offshore locations and are developing their businesses in both mature markets and emerging high-growth regions.
- *Regional 'premier league'*. Medium-to-large players with strong domestic and regional brands such as BNP Paribas, Deutsche Bank, Santander, Bank of America, etc. They offer a wide range of products and services, but lack a genuine global presence.
- *Small specialised players*. These operate mainly locally or focus on niche product or client segments. They include EFG International, Wegelin & Company, Sal Oppenheim, Hoare & Co, family offices, etc. They are mainly distributors and rely entirely on client relationships as their main asset, with heavily outsourced production, operations and technology.

Figure 10.10 highlights the view of industry participants. Private banks that are part of large banking groups are likely to be the most successful over the next three to five years, followed by independent financial advisors and stand-alone private banks. Other future structures of the industry have been suggested, as illustrated in Figure 10.11, but the main point to note is that a more polarised industry structure is likely to emerge.

Some have argued that for the largest players, such as Citigroup, it may actually make financial sense to break them up.[11] The argument is that scale is overrated in financial services and that smaller, focused players tend to outcompete large, diversified ones. Extracting the global wealth management business would, the argument goes, be much more credibly conflict free and be a way of releasing meaningful value.

---

[9] See, for example, Merrill Lynch Global Equity Research (2005a).

[10] Its April 2006 acquisition of the private client branch network of Piper Jaffray (90 branches, 842 advisors, $52 billion invested assets) may represent an important first step in that direction.

[11] See, for example, Tom Brown (2005).

Biggest winners and losers
Who will be the biggest winners and losers in European Wealth Management over the next 3-5 years?

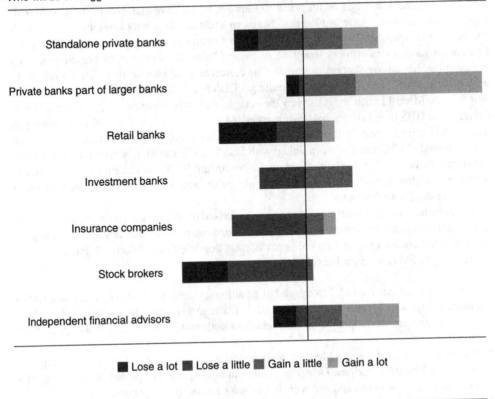

■ Lose a lot ■ Lose a little ■ Gain a little ■ Gain a lot

Figure 10.10 Winners and losers in European wealth management over the next 3 to 5 years
Source: Mercer Oliver Wyman (2005). Reproduced by permission.

10.4 CRITICAL SUCCESS FACTORS

Whether the wealth management firm is a global or a niche player, all operators need to develop a common skill set to meet client demand, drive profit growth and to secure a sustainable competitive edge. These skills relate to:

- Building client relationships and developing a proactive and flexible response to increasingly complex needs.
- Networking, for both production and distribution purposes.
- Marketing, co-branding and enhanced target client focus.
- Improving operational efficiency.
- Implementing value-based pricing and client management.

The common skill set for identifying and meeting client needs is shown in Figure 10.12.

In order to deliver value-adding propositions, wealth managers also need to develop their network or 'aggregator' skills in the most effective manner. The industry will increasingly have to embrace the open architecture structure even if various commentators are currently rather

Global/European scale dominators - The future looks bright for those few firms that have achieved critical mass along the entire value chain, boast strong brands, can build and buy high-quality products and are investing in advanced marketing and customer management. But very few such behemoths exist, and this would be an unrealistic strategic choice for any firm that is not already very nearly there.

Relationship-focused pure-play assemblers - This is the virtual business model writ large, the next logical step for firms that have already built a strong 'front end' and embraced open architecture, but are subscale in other areas. Most wealth managers will find this model as much of a conceptual challenge as a practical one.

Standardized low-cost wealth managers - Much of the cost in wealth management comes from the production of complex products. Adopting a simpler approach based on standardised products and advice will inevitably offer cost savings that can be reinvested for growth.

Advice-focused assembler boutiques - If there is one client proposition that today stands above all others, it is advice. That creates scope for firms who excel in this area: they will resemble today's IFAs, but concentrate most of their resources in the provision of high-quality advice rather than brand or distribution. The nature of the offering means that this group is likely to remain fragmented.

Pure product producers - We expect to see scale product producers emerge to complement the activities of distribution and advice specialists, such as the advice focused boutiques mentioned above. It is likely that much of this activity will be white-labelled to limit perceived problems.

Niche production specialists - In this business, scale is more effective at the product/fund level than in the aggregate. Every niche will attract competitors capable of serving the needs of many distributors: in this way open architecture will promote the survival of a fragmented investment management industry focused on delivering product to individuals.

Scale administration specialists - We will also see the continued development of scale players in administration. Some US players are already moving into the European market. We should also see deals involving the consolidation of existing back-office activities.

We are confident that these are the basic forms that successful future businesses will take. What is also clear is that the traditional integrated private bank operating at small scale will not be a winning model going forward. Such firms will be faced with both intensifying competition from new structured products that offer fit more closely with private clients' needs (and which will be hard to replicate) and with subscale operating economics.

Private-banking 'winners' will increasingly focus on the front end, typically by strengthening their brands and customer relationships, looking to others to create innovative products and offer efficient administration. Today's private banks can survive and prosper, but will need to radically overhaul their participation in the value chain to do so.

Figure 10.11   Future structure of the wealth management industry
Source: Mercer Oliver Wyman (2005), Reproduced by permission.

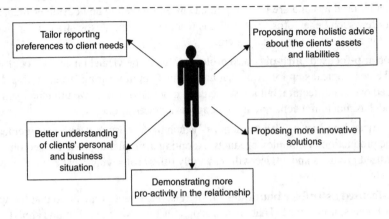

Figure 10.12 Common skills – building relationships
Source: IBM Consulting Services (2005). Reproduced by permission.

sanguine about the prospects of this approach.[12] The evolution of this approach is highlighted
in Figure 10.13, suggesting a move to higher value-added services if the open architecture
approach is fully developed.

As competition increases, and new clients become increasingly scarce in North American
and European markets, increasingly the industry will have to engage in targeted marketing
and other promotional events. Building brand image will be a key theme developed through
high-profile generic marketing campaigns plus greater sponsorship of up-market sporting and
cultural events as well as growing links to high profile 'ambassadors', especially those who can
promote the attractions of independent advisory-led services that focus on high-value clients
and solutions. Greater promotional effort is also likely to put into educational and advisory
'road-shows' for HNWIs and their offspring.

In addition to enhancing client relationships, marketing and building network capacity,
wealth managers need to focus much more on improving their overall efficiency in terms of
cost, revenue and capital deployment:

- Cost efficiency can be improved by initiatives such as centralising and outsouring operations, shedding low-value clients, more aggressive product management and more rigorous
  management of human resources (e.g. remunerating managers more on the basis of value
  created).
- Revenue efficiency can be boosted by initiatives such as applying more systematic value-
  added pricing models tailored to specific client segments, increasing investment thresholds for unprofitable clients, identifying areas for effective cost-plus pricing and promoting
  higher-margin specialised advisory services.
- Capital efficiency directs capital resources to the highest value-adding areas of the business,
  with a relentless focus on value creation across all product and business areas. The focus

---

[12] PricewaterhouseCoopers (2005) note that, 'Open architecture is still a masquerade for many wealth managers and in reality only
exists at the margin. Most wealth managers still manufacture products either themselves or via their parent'.

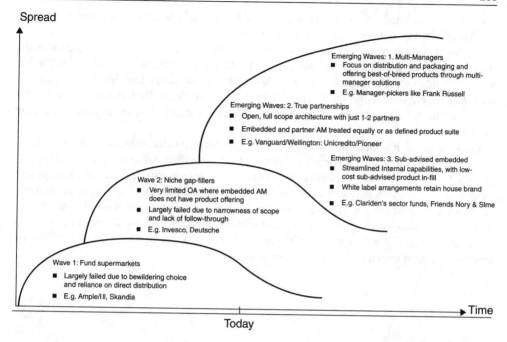

Figure 10.13   Open architecture waves – where we're at and where we're going
Source: Mercer Oliver Wyman (2005). Reproduced by permission.

was on areas that generate returns in excess of some margin above the cost-of-capital and ditch or restructure those areas that fail to hit benchmark returns.

All in all, the private banking industry has been relatively slow to develop such aggressive strategies, as there has been the view that if such an approach is adopted it could worsen client relationships and destroy brand value and image. In our view this is a misguided perception, especially as investment banks and many other financial firms have pursued such strategies with success over the last decade or so. Wealth managers, whether they like it or not, will certainly have to embrace these changes if they are to be successful in the future.

10.5   CONCLUSIONS

In conclusion, the key for the private banking industry is to take a holistic approach and to deliver wealth management solutions in an efficient and appealing manner. Most wealth managers are currently trying to meet this need by offering a broad range of products that are mainly manufactured in-house.

But most clients are unhappy with this approach. Clients want the personal touch and to know and trust their relationship manager. In some ways, we seem to be reverting to the old-school private banking model – but an updated, transparent version with a broader proposition and much higher and more consistent service standards. Clients clearly need their wealth manager to guide them through the bewildering range of products and market uncertainties and the constant financial scandals we see these days, as well as to take care of more traditional concerns around things like inflation and taxes. Can this really be done by institutions the size of UBS, Citigroup and Merrill Lynch, for example?

Further increases in account minimums are likely to be necessary for many players to make the economics of genuine private banking work. We think family offices and strains thereof will really take off, and the mass affluent who cannot afford such a high level of service will stick with the big wealth managers in particular. A key issue then will be whether family offices can grow and still maintain the personal touch, and have enough clout to get access to the top product providers.

Looking ahead, it is clear that substantial profit potential remains: there is more wealth to be made in wealth management. For most players, emerging markets are critical to unlocking that potential – and are no longer simply a 'nice to have'. A range of different wealth management models can thrive, with the most successful ones likely to be built to a large extent around one or more client segments. Many clients are underserved and, in the end, it will be the players that can meet those needs efficiently and cost effectively, whilst making the right organic and inorganic moves, that will capture the 'pot of gold'. The best wealth managers will then enjoy prosperity, perhaps even to the same extent as their clients.

Appendices

APPENDIX 1: COUNTRY WEALTH MARKET ANALYSES

North America

- United States
- Canada

Western Europe

- Germany
- UK
- Italy
- France
- Spain
- Netherlands
- Switzerland
- Belgium

Eastern Europe

- Russia
- Czech Republic

Asia-Pacific

- Japan
- China
- Taiwan
- Hong Kong
- Australia
- South Korea
- India
- Singapore

Latin America

- Brazil

Middle East

- Saudi Arabia
- United Arab Emirates
- Israel

Africa

- South Africa

Key Data Sources

The Boston Consulting Group; McKinsey & Company; Datamonitor; Capgemini/Merrill Lynch; IMF; World Bank; United Nations; central banks; official statistics; UBS; Economist Intelligence Unit; *Euromoney*; national and international press cuttings; interviews with local experts. All data are for 2004 unless otherwise indicated. US dollars.

USA

Social and economic indicators

GDP	$11 734 billion
Population	298.2 million
GDP per capita	$39 935
Growth in GDP per capita (2000–2006)	3.9% CAGR

Wealth market size

HNW wealth	$8 600 billion
Number of HNWIs	2 498 000
HNW wealth growth projection	10% p.a.
Gini coefficient (2000)	0.408

Wealth market characteristics

- The world's largest, most mature and competitive wealth market.
- Onshore oriented; wealth concentrated in regional pockets: e.g., California (technology, entertainment), New York (finance, industry), Florida (retirees), Texas (oil) and Illinois (agriculture).
- Higher degree of wealth concentration than in most other mature markets.
- 'The Forbes 400' wealthiest Americans, 2005: collective net worth $1.13 trillion (9.6% of GDP); all but 26 are billionaires; lowest had net worth of $900 million.
- Offshore wealth management negatively impacted by the USA PATRIOT Act and other regulations, key traditional destinations: Luxembourg, Cayman Islands, Switzerland, Bahamas, Bermuda.
- Clients seeking high-quality, objective advice.
- Equities (mainly managed funds) form a relatively high proportion of clients' portfolios.
- Market for structured products less well developed than in Europe and Asia.
- Large generational transfer of wealth to baby boomers under way.

Wealth management players

- Traditionally, brokerages and family offices dominate; trust banks are strong regionally; many local registered investment adviser boutiques.
- Shift by brokerages in recent years towards full-service model (emphasis on advice, broader product range, fee-based pricing), driven by weaker financial markets and more complex client needs.
- Key players:
  - (a) Local: Merrill Lynch, Citigroup, Wachovia, Charles Schwab, Private Bank at Bank of America, Fidelity, JP Morgan Private Bank, Goldman Sachs, Northern Trust, Wells Fargo Private Client Services, Morgan Stanley, Mellon Financial, Lehman Brothers/Neuberger Berman, SunTrust Banks, First Republic Bank.
  - (b) Foreign: UBS, Credit Suisse (mainly via former CSFB), Deutsche Bank, HSBC Private Bank.

CANADA

Social and economic indicators

GDP	$993.4 billion
Population	32.3 million
GDP per capita	$31 134
Growth in GDP per capita (2000–2006)	7.4% CAGR

Wealth market size

HNW wealth	$700 billion
Number of HNWIs	217 000
HNW wealth growth projection	8% p.a.
Gini coefficient (1998)	0.331

Wealth market characteristics

- Onshore-oriented wealth market.
- *The Canadian Business* magazine 'Rich 100', 2005: collective net worth $123.2 billion (12.4% of GDP)
- Oil is a key driver of the wealth market.
- Strong regional concentration of HNWIs, particularly in regions such as Ontario.
- Relatively unsophisticated client needs.
- Many investors have a preference for property investments.
- Similar regulatory framework to that of the US.

Wealth management players

- Local universal banks dominate.
- Full-service brokerage firms account for around 25% of the market.
- Key players:
  (a) Local: BMO Harris Private Banking, Royal Bank of Canada, Scotia PCG, CIBC Private Banking, TD Waterhouse Private Banking.
  (b) Foreign: Citigroup Private Bank, UBS, HSBC Private Bank, Goldman Sachs, Merrill Lynch, Pictet.

GERMANY

Social and economic indicators

GDP	$2 754 billion
Population	82.7 million
GDP per capita	$33 390
Growth in GDP per capita (2000–2006)	6.3% CAGR

Wealth market size

HNW wealth	$2 356 billion
Number of HNWIs	760 000
HNW wealth growth projection	7% p.a.
Gini coefficient (2000)	0.283

Wealth market characteristics

- Europe's largest onshore wealth market.
- German HNWIs hold an estimated $500 billion offshore, mainly in Luxembourg and Switzerland.
- Four key urban markets: Hamburg, Cologne/Dusseldorf, Frankfurt and Munich.
- Recent tax amnesty unsuccessful.
- Key client segments include inheritors, retirees, business owners ('Mittelstand') and professionals.
- Most clients require wealth preservation, above all.
- Going forward, key products include inheritance and tax planning, and alternative investments; many players are actively reworking their asset allocation models.

Wealth management players

- Universal banks and large number of small independent banks dominate the market, but have relatively unsophisticated private banking offers.
- Various Landesbanks reported to be interested in entering the private banking market.
- Financial adviser networks such as MLP and AWD target mainly the mass affluent client segment.
- Foreign players have struggled to have much impact onshore, linked to inconsistent strategies.
- Key players:
  (a) Local: Deutsche Bank, Dresdner Bank, Commerzbank, Sal. Oppenheim, B. Metzler, Feri Wealth Management, Berenberg Bank, HSBC Trinkaus & Burkhardt, Delbrück Bethmann Maffei (owned by ABN AMRO), Bremer Landesbank, B. Lampe, BHF Bank, Dr. Jens Ehrhardt, Hamburger Sparkasse, Weberbank, Fürst Fugger Privatbank.
  (b) Foreign: UBS, Credit Suisse, ABN AMRO Private Banking, Merrill Lynch, Citigroup, JP Morgan Private Bank, Goldman Sachs, Bank Sarasin, Pictet.

UK

Social and economic indicators

GDP	$2 133 billion
Population	59.7 million
GDP per capita	$35 548
Growth in GDP per capita (2000–2006)	6.8% CAGR

Wealth market size

HNW wealth	$1 588 billion
Number of HNWIs	418 000
HNW wealth growth projection	9% p.a.
Gini coefficient (1999)	0.36

Wealth market characteristics

- Largest European (offshore and onshore) wealth market; London and Channel Islands traditionally strong offshore centres.
- UK HNWIs hold an estimated $600 billion offshore, mainly in Jersey, Switzerland and Luxembourg.
- 'Sunday Times Rich List,' 2006: wealthiest 1,000 individuals' combined wealth $536 billion (24.3% of GDP); 1997–2006 CAGR 13.2%; includes 54 sterling billionaires.
- Key client segments include inheritors, retirees, business owners, executives and professionals.
- HNWIs are relatively sophisticated, with a stronger equity culture than other European countries.
- Strong demand for structured products and alternative investments.
- Some local players, e.g. Coutts, expanding out of London to other areas of the UK.

Wealth management players

- No dominant player – market highly fragmented among universal banks, investment banks, IFAs, stockbrokers.
- Key players: UBS, Coutts,[1] HSBC Private Bank, Credit Suisse, Goldman Sachs, C. Hoare & Co, Barclays, JP Morgan Private Bank, Citigroup Private Bank, Schroders Private Bank, SG Hambros, Merrill Lynch, Kleinwort Benson Private Bank, Royal Bank of Canada, BNP Private Bank, Rathbones, Rothschild, Adam & Co.[1]

[1] Owned by Royal Bank of Scotland.

ITALY

Social and economic indicators

GDP	$1 680 billion
Population	58.1 million
GDP per capita	$29 014
Growth in GDP per capita (2000–2006)	8.0% CAGR

Wealth market size

HNW wealth	$1 517 billion
Number of HNWIs (households)	523 000
HNW wealth growth projection	7% p.a.
Gini coefficient (2000)	0.36

Wealth market characteristics

- Large onshore market, but private banking is relatively undeveloped.
- Wealth generation largely driven by ownership of small and medium-sized businesses, concentrated in a small number of regions in northern/central Italy; key regions: Lombardia (c.26% of HNW assets), Veneto, Piemonte, Emilia Romagna, Lazio and Toscana.
- Other key client segments include professionals, sports/media personalities, landowners and corporate executives.
- Clear preference for low-risk, fixed-income products; pick up in growth of alternative investments expected following recent rule changes.
- Tax amnesties of 2001–2003 attracted c.$100 billion in repatriated assets.
- Italian HNWIs continue to hold an estimated $225 billion offshore (mainly in Luxembourg and in Ticino, Switzerland), driven by relatively high taxation and by political and economic uncertainties.

Wealth management players

- Local universal banks and some of the (northern/central) Popolari banks have a large share of the private banking market, but most still lack distinctive private banking offers, resulting in low AuM per client at most banks.
- Other types of local players targeting higher-end clients include:
  (a) Some of the Promotori (financial adviser) networks, such as Banca Fideuram, Banca Euromobiliare and Azimut.
  (b) Local private banks, such as Banca Profilo, Meliorbanca and Banca Intermobiliare.
- Major foreign players entered the market in the late 1990s, mainly through organic growth.
- Italian private banking asociation (Associazione Italiana Private Banking, AIPB) formed in 2004.
- Key players:
  (a) Local: UniCredit, Banca Esperia (JV between Banca Mediolanum and Mediobanca), Sanpaolo IMI, Ersel, Intesa, Monte dei Paschi di Siena.
  (b) Foreign: UBS, JP Morgan Private Bank, BNP Paribas (which recently acquired Banca Nazionale del Lavovo), Citigroup Private Bank, Credit Suisse, Pictet, Deutsche Bank, Schroders Private Bank, Morgan Stanley, Merrill Lynch, Goldman Sachs.

FRANCE

Social and economic indicators

GDP	$2 046 billion
Population	60.5 million
GDP per capita	$32 911
Growth in GDP per capita (2000–2006)	7.5% CAGR

Wealth market size

HNW wealth	$1 234 billion
Number of HNWIs	363 000
HNW wealth growth projection	7% p.a.
Gini coefficient (1995)	0.327

Wealth market characteristics

- Large onshore market; c.50% of HNWIs based in Paris and Île-de-France; remainder broadly distributed across other regions and large cities.
- Key client segments include owners/managers of businesses, professionals and corporate executives.
- Taxation relatively high, and includes an explicit wealth tax, paid by individuals with total assets (including housing) of more than €732 000; threshold uplift currently under discussion.
- Life-insurance-related products account for more than half of HNW assets – driven by tax efficiency.
- French HNWIs hold an estimated $240 billion offshore, mainly in Luxembourg and Switzerland.
- Client preference for fixed-income products; alternative investments and foreign exchange products are developing rapidly, linked to recent rule changes.
- HNWIs strongly value a local presence and brand, and are generally not very receptive to foreign players.

Wealth management players

- Local universal and retail banks dominate (c.50% of HNW assets); life insurance companies, asset managers and stockbrokers c.30%); private and investment banks c.20%.
- Some foreign players have entered the market through acquisitions (e.g. HSBC/CCF, ABN AMRO/Banque NSMD and Barclays/ING Ferri).
- Key players: BNP Paribas Private Bank, Rothschild, UBS, Société Générale Private Banking, Crédit Lyonnais, Credit Agricole, Credit Suisse, Banque de Neuflize OBC (majority owned by ABN AMRO), LCF Edmond de Rothschild, HSBC Private Bank, Lazard, Merrill Lynch, Lombard Odier Darier Hentsch, JP Morgan, Banque Delubac.

SPAIN

Social and economic indicators

GDP	$1 041 billion
Population	43.1 million
GDP per capita	$25 320
Growth in GDP per capita (2000–2006)	11.6% CAGR

Wealth market size

HNW wealth	$479 billion
Number of HNWIs	141 000
HNW wealth growth projection	9% p.a.
Gini coefficient (1990)	0.325

Wealth market characteristics

- Relatively small onshore-oriented market, but private banking likely to grow robustly, driven by relatively low market penetration.
- Strong economic growth continues to be a key wealth-market driver.
- Key client segments include business owners, landowners, professionals and Spanish expatriates living abroad.
- Spanish HNWIs hold an estimated $50 billion offshore, mainly in Cayman, Switzerland and Jersey.
- Going forward, clients' key requirements are higher returns (including access to alternative investments and opportunities in emerging markets) and tax optimisation; domestic sale of hedge funds expected to be authorised soon.
- Clients tend to be relatively loyal and prefer well-known brands of local players and global private banks.

Wealth management players

- Local retail and commercial banks continue to account for a high proportion of HNW assets, but have only recently started to develop dedicated private banking offers.
- Foreign players have a relatively strong presence.
- Key players:
  - (a) Local: Santander (through both its Banco Banif and Banca Privada subsidiaries), BBVA Patrimonios, Banco Urquijo, Bankinter, Sabadell Banca Privada, Banca March, ALTAE Banco Privado (owned by Caja Madrid), Atlas Capital (part owned by Julius Baer).
  - (b) Foreign: UBS, Credit Suisse, JP Morgan, BNP Paribas Private Bank, Citigroup Private Bank, Merrill Lynch, Morgan Stanley.

NETHERLANDS

Social and economic indicators

GDP	$608 billion
Population	16.3 million
GDP per capita	$37 326
Growth in GDP per capita (2000–2006)	8.6% CAGR

Wealth market size

HNW wealth	$333 billion
Number of HNWIs	98 000
HNW wealth growth projection	7% p.a.
Gini coefficient (1999)	0.309

Wealth market characteristics

- Key client segments include business owners, corporate executives and professionals.
- Relatively large mass affluent market.
- Wealth market competitors include the large insurance companies.
- Many players are developing their onshore presence and making small acquisitions (e.g. BNP Paribas/Nachenius, Tjeenk & Company).

Wealth management players

- Relatively few foreign players.
- Key players: ABN AMRO Private Banking, Fortis Private Banking, F. van Lanschot Bankiers, CenE Bankiers, Effectenbank Stroeve, ING Private Banking, Rabobank Private Banking, Theodoor Gilissen, UBS, Merrill Lynch, Lombard Odier Darier Hentsch.

SWITZERLAND

Social and economic indicators

GDP	$358 billion
Population	7.3 million
GDP per capita	$49 300
Growth in GDP per capita (2000–2006)	6.3% CAGR

Wealth market size

HNW wealth	$256 billion
Number of HNWIs	73 000
HNW wealth growth projection	6% p.a.
Gini coefficient (1992)	0.331

Wealth market characteristics

- Remains, at least for the moment, the world's largest offshore wealth market and is, for many, the home of private banking.
- Also has a significant onshore wealth market.
- Swiss HNWIs place great emphasis on security and capital preservation.
- Limited net new money inflows in recent years, with several players experiencing net out-flows, driven by impact of tax amnesties, EU Savings Directive and pressure on Swiss bank client confidentiality.
- Going forward, inheritance, tax and pension planning are becoming increasingly important.
- Increasing regulation is wealth managers' key concern.
- The consolidation process continues; key recent deal: Julius Baer's acquisition of UBS independent private banks in September 2005.
- Medium-sized, non-specialist players are under particular pressure.
- Competition rising.
- Swiss private banking brands continue to have international resonance.

Wealth management players

- Relatively fragmented market: more than 300 banks.
- Dominated by the two Swiss-based global universal banks: UBS and Credit Suisse.
- Foreign global banks, including: ABN AMRO, BNP Paribas, Citigroup, Deutsche Bank, HSBC, JP Morgan Chase, and Royal Bank of Scotland.
- Swiss-based private banking specialists, including: Julius Baer, Banca del Gottardo, Clariden Leu,[1] Banque Privée Edmond de Rothschild, Banca della Svizzera Italiana, Bordier,[2] EFG International, Lombard Odier Darier Hentsch,[2] Pictet,[2] Sarasin, Union Bancaire Privée, Vontobel, Maerki Baumann, Bank Jungholz, LGT Bank in Liechtenstein, and Atlantic Vermögensverwaltung.
- Private banking divisions of Swiss-based retail banks, including: Banque Cantonale Vaudoise, St. Galler Kantonalbank and Zürcher Kantonalbank.
- A large number of niche wealth managers and independent advisers, which compete with traditional private banks and provide them with business in the form of client introductions.

[1] Owned by Credit Suisse.
[2] Denotes private bank structured as partnership.

BELGIUM

Social and economic indicators

GDP	$352 billion
Population	10.4 million
GDP per capita	$33 866
Growth in GDP per capita (2000–2006)	8.0% CAGR

Wealth market size

HNW wealth	$186 billion
Number of HNWIs	62 000
HNW wealth growth projection	7% p.a.
Gini coefficient (1996)	0.25

Wealth market characteristics

- Traditionally, a significant proportion of wealth is managed offshore (mainly in Luxembourg and Switzerland), driven by Belgium's relatively high income tax rates.
- 2004 tax amnesty was not as successful as expected.
- Belgian market attracts French expatriate HNWIs seeking refuge from the wealth tax (Belgium does not tax capital gains).
- Other key client segments include business owners, corporate executives and professionals.
- Relatively large mass affluent market.

Wealth management players

- Relatively few foreign players.
- Most of the independent private banks have been acquired.
- Key players:
  (a) Local: Petercam, Banque Degroof, Bank Delen, Fortis Private Banking, KBC, Puilaetco (owned by KBL European Private Bankers, which is part of the KBC Group), Dexia Private Banking.
  (b) Foreign: UBS, ABN AMRO Private Banking, ING Private Banking, BNP Private Bank, Credit Lyonnais Private Banking, Commerzbank.

RUSSIA

Social and economic indicators

GDP	$582 billion
Population	143.2 million
GDP per capita	$4 086
Growth in GDP per capita (2000–2006)	24.3% CAGR

Wealth market size

HNW wealth	$300 billion
Number of HNWIs	88 000
HNW wealth growth projection	16% p.a.
Gini coefficient (1998)	0.487

Wealth market characteristics

- Vast majority of the wealth management market is offshore.
- HNW market is double that of Poland, the Czech Republic and Hungary combined.
- Wealth generation heavily dependent on oil, natural gas, metals and timber resources.
- Wealth primarily in the hands of young entrepreneurial and professional HNWIs, based mainly in Moscow; growing middle class.
- 'Forbes 100 Richest Russians', 2004: collective net worth $137 billion (23.5% of GDP); includes 36 US-dollar billionaires (third-highest number in the world, behind the United States and Germany). *Finans* magazine's 2006 list of richest Russians includes 50 US-dollar billionaires.
- Most clients have a deep mistrust of banks, linked to memories of the 1998 banking crisis.
- Widespread corruption and money laundering risks; tight KYC controls are essential.
- Clients favour asset diversification (by asset class and geography); preference for low-risk, international fixed-income and real-estate assets; education trusts becoming more popular.
- Many foreign banks are entering the market, mainly by establishing representative offices in the first instance.
- Onshore market is expected to grow gradually, driven by higher risk-adjusted returns and improving client trust in local institutions.

Wealth management players

- Local universal banks are starting to develop affluent propositions (known locally as 'VIP banking'), leveraging their large customer bases and distribution networks; these players include: URALSIB, Rosbank, Zenit Bank, Sberbank, IMPEXBANK, Gazprombank, Alfa-Bank, Bank of Moscow.
- Some foreign players are leveraging their investment banking franchises to access the private banking market, e.g. Credit Suisse, which now has offices in Moscow and St Petersberg.
- Other foreign players include: ZAO Raiffeisenbank Austria, UBS, Citigroup (including onshore retail), HSBC Private Bank, Merrill Lynch, Deutsche Bank, Morgan Stanley, Pictet, Société Générale Private Banking.

CZECH REPUBLIC

Social and economic indicators

GDP	$107 billion
Population	10.2 million
GDP per capita	$10 485
Growth in GDP per capita (2000–2006)	14.8% CAGR

Wealth market size

HNW wealth	$38 billion
Number of HNWIs	11 000
HNW wealth growth projection	9% p.a.
Gini coefficient (1996)	0.254

Wealth market characteristics

- Czech market is probably the most competitive in Eastern Europe.
- In mid-1990s, clients were almost exclusively recipients of restitution property wishing to liquidate it.
- Towards the end of the 1990s, sources of wealth began to broaden, and now include: entrepreneurs, senior executives, foreign expatriates and elite athletes.
- Relatively large mass affluent market (c.100 000 individuals, c.$11 billion, projected growth c.8% p.a.).
- Changing client mix driving slightly less conservative investment preferences.
- Events-based client acquisition particularly important.
- Dedicated expatriate centres and foreign desks expanding, driven by strong client demand.
- Strong demand for additional services such as insurance, travel, legal and professional networking; some banks are considering adding real estate consulting.
- Going forward, entrepreneurial wealth expected to be key driver.

Wealth management players

- Heavily dominated by foreign banks, but some local retail banks and other specialists are emerging.
- Local key players: ČSOB (owned by Belgium's KBC), Živnobanka (owned by Italy's UniCredit), Česká spořitelna (owned by Austria's Erste Bank), Komerční banka, J&T Bank, Slavia Capital, Glisco.
- Foreign key players:
  (a) Onshore: RZB, HVB (a first mover, which has recently merged with UniCredit), Commerzbank, Citigroup.
  (b) Offshore: UBS[1], Credit Suisse, Deutsche Bank[1], Banque Privée Edmond de Rothschild (Luxembourg), Dexia Banque Internationale à Luxembourg, Bank Austria.

---

[1] Via its Austria office.

JAPAN

Social and economic indicators

GDP	$4 671 billion
Population	128.1 million
GDP per capita	$36 596
Growth in GDP per capita (2000–2006)	−0.5% CAGR

Wealth market size

HNW wealth (2003)	$4 537 billion
Number of HNWIs (households, 2003)	1 413 000
HNW wealth growth projection	6% p.a.
Gini coefficient (1993)	0.249

Wealth market characteristics

- Second-largest wealth market in the world.
- Private banking sector undeveloped and not well understood by most wealthy individuals.
- Onshore-oriented wealth market; limited offshore activity focused on Hong Kong and Singapore.
- Preference for simple, low-risk products such as bank deposits and fixed-income mutual funds (known as investment trusts in Japan).
- Emerging deregulation supporting universal banking.

Wealth management players

- Global players trying again to kick-start the private banking market; some large local retail banks are also targeting the wealth market.
- Key players:
  (a) Local: Nomura, MTFG, Sumitomo Mitsui Financial Group, Daiwa, Shinsei Bank, Nikko Cordial, Mizuho.
  (b) Foreign: Merrill Lynch (recently announced JV with MTFG), UBS, Société Générale Private Banking, Standard Chartered, HSBC Private Bank, Deutsche Bank, Credit Suisse.

CHINA

Social and economic indicators

GDP	$1 654 billion
Population	1 315.8 million
GDP per capita	$1 272
Growth in GDP per capita (2000–2006)	11.7% CAGR

Wealth market size

HNW wealth	$530 billion
Number of HNWIs	300 000
HNW wealth growth projection	14% p.a.
Gini coefficient (2001)	0.447

Wealth market characteristics

- Key wealth market drivers include high economic growth and strong potential for IPOs; key sectors: property, manufacturing, IT, finance.
- 'Hurun Report 400' list of wealthiest Chinese, 2005: total wealth $75 billion (4.5% of GDP); includes 7 US-dollar billionaires; lowest had net worth of $60 million.
- Private banking market currently at very early stage of development.
- Currently, primarily an offshore-oriented wealth market, driven by lack of easily accessible onshore investment alternatives (bank deposits 80% of retail liquid assets; mutual funds just 0.5%); key destinations: Hong Kong, Singapore, Bahamas (one incentive for Chinese individuals to take money to offshore centres is that they are then able to invest in domestic companies as a foreign investor, which has tax advantages).
- Bulk of HNWIs are concentrated in key urban centres in the eastern swath of the country.[2]
- Wealth held by 55 million Chinese diaspora is significant: they contribute c.60% of China's inward foreign direct investment.
- Banking industry expected to be opened fully to foreign competition by end-2006, in line with WTO commitments.
- In terms of foreign players, banks are likely to enjoy a head start on brokerage firms and investment banks, as regulators are hesitant of placing additional strain on deposit bases of local banks.

Wealth management players

- Many Chinese banks serve the market from Hong Kong; similarly, many foreign private banks serve the Chinese market from other parts of Asia, notably Hong Kong and Singapore.
- Many foreign players are currently seeking local partners (currently, the maximum stake a single foreign bank can hold in a Chinese bank is 20%).
- Key players: HSBC Private Bank, Citigroup, UBS, BMO Harris Private Banking, Goldman Sachs, BNP Paribas Private Bank, Société Générale Private Banking, JP Morgan Private Bank, ABN AMRO Private Banking, Merrill Lynch, Deutsche Bank.

---

[2] Including Shanghai, Beijing, Guangzhou, Shenzhen, Tianjin, Hangzhou, Suzhou, Nanjing, Ningbo, Xiemen and Fuzhou.

TAIWAN

Social and economic indicators

GDP	$305 billion
Population (2002)	22.5 million
GDP per capita	$13 451
Growth in GDP per capita (2000–2006)	1.7% CAGR

Wealth market size

HNW wealth (2003)	$369 billion
Number of HNWIs (households, 2003)	58 000
HNW wealth growth projection	13% p.a.
Gini coefficient (2000)	0.325

Wealth market characteristics

- Much of the wealth derives from ownership of small and medium-sized businesses.
- Offshore-oriented wealth market, driven by political uncertainty and tax issues.
- Onshore wealth market development impacted by restrictive regulatory regime; e.g. strong onshore demand for structured products, but the government is currently trying to impose restrictions on product design.
- Private banking businesses in Taiwan are not legally allowed to offer advice or offshore products.

Wealth management players

- Local banks are beginning to establish dedicated private banking divisions; local securities houses and asset management companies are also competing.
- Some foreign banks now moving onshore, e.g. UBS, ABN AMRO Private Banking.
- Key players:
  - (a) Local: Chinatrust Commercial Bank, Taishin International Bank, Taipei Fubon Bank, Hua Nan Bank.
  - (b) Foreign: UBS, Credit Suisse, Citigroup, Merrill Lynch, Goldman Sachs, HSBC Private Bank, Morgan Stanley, ABN AMRO Private Banking, EFG International, Deutsche Bank, Société Générale Private Banking, JP Morgan Private Bank.

HONG KONG

Social and economic indicators

GDP	$164 billion
Population	7.0 million
GDP per capita	$23 608
Growth in GDP per capita (2000–2006)	0.8% CAGR

Wealth market size

HNW wealth (2003)	$282 billion
Number of HNWIs	67 000
HNW wealth growth projection	5% p.a.
Gini coefficient (1996)	0.522

Wealth market characteristics

- Along with Singapore, Hong Kong is one of the key Asian offshore financial centres, catering traditionally to clients in China, Japan, South Korea and Taiwan; increasingly attracting funds from Europe, driven by the European Savings Directive.
- Key onshore client segments include expatriates (in particular, Japanese, British and American), entrepreneurs and executives.
- Highest number of USD billionaires per capita in the world.
- 'Gateway to China'.
- Some offshore clients concerned over Hong Kong's political risk.
- Relatively advanced hedge fund market.
- Highly competitive market.

Wealth management players

- Chinese banks advantaged in capturing offshore flows from mainland China.
- Key players: HSBC Private Bank, UBS, Citigroup Private Bank, Credit Suisse, BNP Paribas Private Banking, DBS Bank, CIBC Private Banking, ABN AMRO Private Banking, Merrill Lynch, Royal Bank of Canada, Standard Chartered, EFG International, ING Private Banking, Deutsche Bank, Goldman Sachs, Bank Sarasin.

AUSTRALIA

Social and economic indicators

GDP	$618 billion
Population	20.2 million
GDP per capita	$30 682
Growth in GDP per capita (2000–2006)	9.7% CAGR

Wealth market size

HNW wealth (2003)	$237 billion
Number of HNWIs	134 000
HNW wealth growth projection	10% p.a.
Gini coefficient (1994)	0.352

Wealth market characteristics

- Private banking market still relatively undeveloped
- Relatively low number of HNWIs
- Onshore-oriented wealth management market; despite relatively high income tax rates, Australian tax authorities are reported to be successful at minimising the flow of funds offshore.
- Wealth market concentrated in Sydney, linked to wealthy Asian immigrant population and concentration of professionals.
- Wrap accounts particularly popular, driven, in part, by compulsory superannuation regime (9% of base salary).
- Large generational transfer of wealth to baby boomers under way.

Wealth management players

- Traditionally, brokerage-oriented model.
- Preference for investments such as property has enabled the large local retail banks to become major players in the private banking market.
- Many of the foreign players run their Australian private banking operations from Hong Kong and/or Singapore.
- Key players:
  - (a) Local: ANZ Private Bank, Macquarie Private Bank, National Australia Bank, St George Private Bank, Westpac Banking Group.
  - (b) Foreign: UBS, Merrill Lynch, Goldman Sachs JBWere, ING Private Banking, Citigroup Private Bank, Deutsche Bank.

SOUTH KOREA

Social and economic indicators

GDP	$680 billion
Population	22.5 million
GDP per capita	$14 151
Growth in GDP per capita (2000–2006)	8.2% CAGR

Wealth market size

HNW wealth (2003)	$215 billion
Number of HNWIs	71 000
HNW wealth growth projection	13% p.a.
Gini coefficient (1998)	0.316

Wealth market characteristics

- Much of the wealth derives from ownership of small and medium-sized businesses.
- Historically, offshore-oriented market, driven by political and financial instability and relatively high taxation; key destinations: Singapore and Hong Kong.
- Clients tend to have very short investment horizons (a one-year maturity is considered long term); strong preference for domestic assets (traditionally, bank deposits and property).
- Clients are starting to become more comfortable with paying fees for advice.
- Number of wealthy foreign (mainly US, Chinese and Japanese) expatriates is low, but growing rapidly.
- Fairly well developed capital markets.
- Recent relaxation of product restrictions is expected to stimulate demand for structured products and alternative investments.
- Beneficiary certificates (which can include money market, fixed income and equities) are particularly popular products.

Wealth management players

- Most local banks target the mass affluent; little in the way of genuine private banking.
- Key players:
    - (a) Local: Hana Bank, Shinhan Bank, Choheung Bank, Kookmin Bank, Korea Exchange Bank, Woori Bank (product tie-ups with UBS and ABN AMRO).
    - (b) Foreign: Merrill Lynch, Citigroup Private Bank, JP Morgan Private Bank, UBS, Standard Chartered, ING Private Banking, HSBC Private Bank.

INDIA

Social and economic indicators

GDP	$665 billion
Population	1103.4 million
GDP per capita	$622
Growth in GDP per capita (2000–2006)	8.1% CAGR

Wealth market size

HNW wealth	$150 billion
Number of HNWIs	70 000
HNW wealth growth projection	11% p.a.
Gini coefficient (1999)	0.325

Wealth market characteristics

- Geographically, 70%–90% of the wealth is concentrated in the largest eight cities.[3]
- Key wealth driver is high rate of economic growth, linked to particularly strong growth in the services sector (now 56% of GDP).
- 'Forbes India's 40 Richest', 2005: collective net worth $106 billion (15.9% of GDP); includes 26 US-dollar billionaires; lowest had net worth of $590 m.
- Private banking market at very early stage of development.
- Key client segments include professionals, senior executives, entrepreneurs and retired executives.
- Increasingly onshore-oriented wealth market.
- Domestic clients are restricted from investing offshore (maximum $25 000 per person per year); Singapore is a favoured destination.
- Wealth held by c.20 million non-resident Indians (NRIs) is significant; c.150 000 are millionaires; they maintain a strong bond with India, remitting money and seeking investment opportunities; Dubai is a particularly popular location from which many banks serve NRIs.
- Traditionally, strong demand for physical assets (supported, in part, by social-caste system): real estate, gold, precious stones, high-end jewellery.
- Financial products currently largely simple and passive, but growing demand for advice; one challenge is the need to educate clients in benefits of longer-term investing and in equity-based products.
- Regulations currently prohibit banks from offering discretionary asset management – may be offered only through asset management or brokerage companies; restrictions on hedge funds and structured products.
- Indian banking market expected to be fully liberalised to foreign banks by 2009.

Wealth management players

- Local players currently lack product skills; some have JVs with international investment banks.

---

[3] Mumbai, Delhi, Bangalore, Kolkata, Chennai, Hyderabad, Ahmedabad and Pune.

- Key players:
  - (a) Local: ICICI Bank, HDFC Bank, Kotak Mahindra Bank, ING Vysya Private Bank.
  - (b) Foreign: DSP Merrill Lynch, BNP Paribas Private Bank, ABN AMRO Private Banking, Deutsche Bank, Citigroup Private Bank, HSBC Private Bank, JP Morgan Private Bank, UBS, Standard Chartered, JM Morgan Stanley.

SINGAPORE

Social and economic indicators

GDP	$107 billion
Population	4.3 million
GDP per capita	$24 740
Growth in GDP per capita (2000–2006)	3.2% CAGR

Wealth market size

HNW wealth (2003)	$144 billion
Number of HNWIs	49 000
HNW wealth growth projection	6% p.a.
Gini coefficient (1998)	0.425

Wealth market characteristics

- Along with Hong Kong, Singapore is one of the key Asian offshore financial centres, catering traditionally to clients in Southeast Asia (mainly Indonesia, Malaysia and Thailand, which are all now developing onshore markets); increasingly attracting funds from Europe, driven by the European Savings Directive.
- Key onshore client segments include non-resident Indians, Muslims (strong competition from Malaysia for Islamic private banking), expatriates, entrepreneurs (particularly Chinese) and executives.
- Onshore clients have been offered tax incentives to repatriate assets.
- Reputation for being exceptionally well regulated; trust laws comparable to international best practice (e.g. UK Channel Islands).
- Hedge funds and other alternative investment products are developing particularly strongly.
- Big shortage of relationship managers, currently.
- Singapore government offers financial incentives for banks that establish a significant presence there.
- Highly competitive market.

Wealth management players

- Local players (including the Qualified Full Banks[4]) largely dominate the onshore wealth market.
- Key players:
  - (a) Local: Development Bank of Singapore, Overseas Chinese Banking Corporation, United Overseas Bank.
  - (b) Foreign: UBS, Citigroup Private Bank, HSBC Private Bank, Credit Suisse, BNP Paribas Private Bank, ABN AMRO Private Banking, CIBC Private Banking, Fortis Private Banking, Royal Bank of Canada, Goldman Sachs, EFG International, Deutsche Bank, JP Morgan Private Bank, Coutts.

---

[4] Foreign banks that are allowed to operate largely as local banks, with limited branch networks.

BRAZIL

Social and economic indicators

GDP	$604 billion
Population	186.4 million
GDP per capita	$3 325
Growth in GDP per capita (2000–2006)	5.1% CAGR

Wealth market size

HNW wealth	$1 400 billion
Number of HNWIs	98 000
HNW wealth growth projection	7% p.a.
Gini coefficient (2001)	0.593

Wealth market characteristics

- Predominantly an offshore market; key destination: US (Miami and New York are key centres for Brazilian clients).
- Following a few tough years, the wealth market is now growing, linked, in part, to recent IPOs, M&A activity, foreign direct investment and elevated commodity prices.
- Some asset repatriation in recent years, driven by greater economic stability.
- High proportion of UHNWIs, who rely on family offices for advice.
- Most clients unwilling to give private bankers a full view of their entire portfolio.
- Clients have relatively simple investment needs, but require high-touch service.
- Continued emphasis on confidentiality and capital protection, but asset allocation is becoming more sophisticated and diversified.
- Onshore hedge funds emerging.
- Legally, banks in Brazil are not allowed to advise clients to buy foreign assets.

Wealth management players

- Market share is split broadly equally among US investment banks, international universal banks, Swiss banks and local players.
- Key players:
  (a) Local: Itaú Private Bank, Banco Pátria, Banco Pactual (recently acquired by UBS).
  (b) Foreign: UBS, Citigroup Private Bank, Royal Bank of Canada, Credit Suisse, HSBC Private Bank, JP Morgan Private Bank, ABN AMRO Private Banking, Société Générale Private Banking, BankBoston International (owned by Bank of America), BNP Paribas Private Bank, Goldman Sachs.

SAUDI ARABIA

Social and economic indicators

GDP	$251 billion
Population	24.6 million
GDP per capita	$11 065
Growth in GDP per capita (2000–2006)	8.1% CAGR

Wealth market size

HNW wealth	$280 billion
Number of HNWIs	50 000
HNW wealth growth projection	11% p.a.
Gini coefficient	n/a

Wealth market characteristics

- Saudi Arabia dominates the wealth market of the GCC region.
- Wealth market strongly driven by oil, which directly accounts for around 40% of GDP.
- Wealth largely controlled by ruling Royal family and social stratum immediately below it, typically diplomats and the families that own the top 1000 Saudi companies.
- Traditionally, the wealth market is extremely offshore oriented (US and Europe) but, post 9/11, significant wealth repatriation with growth of onshore market and investment elsewhere, particularly Bahrain and Asia.
- No personal income tax.
- High proportion of expatriates (c.50% of workforce).
- Saudi HNWIs hold around 85% of their wealth offshore; key destinations include other GCC states, US and Europe.
- High share of Islamic assets (c.21% in 2003).

Wealth management players

- Recent accession to WTO and local financial-market deregulation is attracting foreign players.
- Local players very strong; some are partnering with foreign/players, e.g. Credit Suisse/Saudi Swiss Securities,[5] National Commercial Bank/Deutsche Bank, and Arab National Bank/AXA.
- Key players:
  - (a) Local: Samba, National Commercial Bank, Saudi British Bank (part owned by HSBC), Riyad Bank, Al Rajhi, Banque Saudi Fransi (part owned by Credit Agricole), Arab National Bank.
  - (b) Foreign: UBS, Credit Suisse, Citigroup Private Bank, Merrill Lynch, HSBC Private Bank, Deutsche Bank, Pictet.

---

[5] Includes local partners: Olayan Financing Company, Ali Zaid Al-Quraishi & Brothers Company, Sheik Mohammed Aba Al Khail, Omran Bin Mohammed Al Omran & Partners Company, Dr Saleh Al Omair, and ABQ Investments Ltd.

UNITED ARAB EMIRATES

Social and economic indicators

GDP	$104 billion
Population	4.5 million
GDP per capita	$23 968
Growth in GDP per capita (2000–2006)	5.5% CAGR

Wealth market size

HNW wealth	$120 billion
Number of HNWIs	53 000
HNW wealth growth projection	14% p.a.
Gini coefficient	n/a

Wealth market characteristics

- Wealth managament focused on new Dubai International Financial Centre (DIFC); it was given 'free-zone' status in 2004, exempting it from Islamic law; currently positioning itself as the main Middle Eastern financial hub and as a bridge between Western and Far Eastern financial centres.
- Wealth market strong driven by oil, though economy has become more diversified and less directly reliant on oil (now c.30% of GDP).
- Many of the wealthy are business owners, interested in reinvesting in their businesses.
- High proportion of expatriates.
- High share of Islamic assets (c.29% in 2003).
- Most local and foreign banks offer integrated onshore/offshore propositions; Jersey, Hong Kong and Singapore are particularly popular offshore destinations.
- No personal income or capital gains tax makes the UAE an attractive offshore destination in its own right.
- Very competitive market.
- Expected to see highest growth of HNWIs in the GCC.

Wealth management players

- Local players partnering with foreign banks, e.g. National Bank of Dubai/Pictet offshore cooperation.
- Key players:
  (a) Local: National Bank of Abu Dhabi (market leader), National Bank of Dubai, Emirates Bank, Abu Dhabi Commercial Bank, Mashreqbank.
  (b) Foreign: Société Générale Private Banking, HSBC Private Bank, UBS, Citigroup Private Bank, ABN AMRO Private Banking, Standard Chartered, Credit Suisse, Royal Bank of Canada, Goldman Sachs, Coutts, Julius Baer, JP Morgan Private Bank, Merrill Lynch.

ISRAEL

Social and economic indicators

GDP	$117 billion
Population	6.7 million
GDP per capita (2000–2006)	$17 781
Growth in GDP per capita	−0.8% CAGR

Wealth market size

HNW wealth (2003)	$15 billion
Number of HNWIs (2003)	10 000
HNW wealth growth projection	Low
Gini coefficient (1997)	0.381

Wealth market characteristics

- Strong offshore orientation.
- Preference for liquidity.
- Relatively large and growing affluent population (c.$130 billion).

Wealth management players

- Many banks have integrated onshore/offshore propositions.
- Key players:
  - (a) Local: Bank Hipoalim, Bank Leumi, First International Bank, Israel Discount Bank.
  - (b) Foreign: Investec.

SOUTH AFRICA

Social and economic indicators

GDP	$213 billion
Population	47.3 million
GDP per capita	$4 587
Growth in GDP per capita (2000–2006)	9.9% CAGR

Wealth market size

HNW wealth	$259 billion
Number of HNWIs	37 000
HNW wealth growth projection	15% p.a.
Gini coefficient (2000)	0.578

Wealth market characteristics

- HNW market is primarily offshore.
- Onshore market in early stages of development, serving mainly mass affluent clients including those from emerging black middle class, linked to empowerment legislation.
- Many clients have a preference for US dollar-linked assets, property and precious metals.
- Substantial variation among banks in terms of client entry criteria.
- Many banks have relatively low minimum asset criteria; Investec, for example, targets high-potential clients with current incomes as low as $100 000.

Wealth management players

- Local universal banks dominate, with some foreign player involvement, particularly at the higher end.
- Key players:
  - (a) Local: Investec Private Bank, Absa Private Bank (owned by Barclays), Standard Private Bank, RMB Private Bank, Nedbank Private Banking, BoE Private Clients (Old Mutual/Nedcor HNW JV).
  - (b) Foreign: UBS, HSBC Private Bank, Citigroup Private Bank, Credit Suisse, BNP Paribas Private Bank, Merrill Lynch.

APPENDIX 2: FATF 40 RECOMMENDATIONS
GENERAL FRAMEWORK OF THE RECOMMENDATIONS

Recommendation 1

Each country should take immediate steps to ratify and to implement fully the 1988 United Nations Convention against Illicit Traffic in Narcotic Drugs and Psychotropic Substances (the Vienna Convention).

Recommendation 2

Financial institution secrecy laws should be conceived so as not to inhibit implementation of these recommendations.

Recommendation 3

An effective money laundering enforcement programme should include increased multilateral cooperation and mutual legal assistance in money laundering investigations and prosecutions and extradition in money laundering cases, where possible.

ROLE OF NATIONAL LEGAL SYSTEMS IN COMBATING MONEY LAUNDERING

Scope of the criminal offence of money laundering

Recommendation 4

Each country should take such measures as may be necessary, including legislative ones, to enable it to criminalise money laundering as set forth in the Vienna Convention. Each country should extend the offence of drug money laundering to one based on serious offences. Each country would determine which serious crimes would be designated as money laundering predicate offences (see Interpretative Note).

Recommendation 5

As provided in the Vienna Convention, the offence of money laundering should apply at least to knowing money laundering activity, including the concept that knowledge may be inferred from objective factual circumstances.

Recommendation 6

Where possible, corporations themselves – not only their employees – should be subject to criminal liability.

Provisional measures and confiscation

Recommendation 7

Countries should adopt measures similar to those set forth in the Vienna Convention, as may be necessary, including legislative ones, to enable their competent authorities to con-fiscate property laundered, proceeds from, instrumentalities used in or intended for use in the commission of any money laundering offence, or property of corresponding value, without prejudicing the rights of bona fide third parties.

Such measures should include the authority to: (a) identify, trace and evaluate property which is subject to confiscation; (b) carry out provisional measures, such as freezing and seizing, to prevent any dealing, transfer or disposal of such property; and (c) take any appropriate investigative measures.

In addition to confiscation and criminal sanctions, countries also should consider monetary and civil penalties, and/or proceedings including civil proceedings, to void contracts entered into by parties, where parties knew or should have known that as a result of the contract, the State would be prejudiced in its ability to recover financial claims, e.g. through confiscation or collection of fines and penalties.

ROLE OF THE FINANCIAL SYSTEM IN COMBATING MONEY LAUNDERING

Recommendation 8

Recommendations 10 to 29 should apply not only to banks, but also to non-bank financial institutions. Even for those non-bank financial institutions which are not subject to a formal prudential supervisory regime in all countries, e.g. bureaux de change, governments should ensure that these institutions are subject to the same anti-money-laundering laws or regulations as all other financial institutions and that these laws or regulations are implemented effectively (see Interpretative Notes: Recommendation 8 and Recommendations 8 and 9).

Recommendation 9

The appropriate national authorities should consider applying Recommendations 10 to 21 and 23 to the conduct of financial activities as a commercial undertaking by businesses or professions which are not financial institutions, where such conduct is allowed or not prohibited. Financial activities include, but are not limited to, those listed in the attached annex. It is left to each country to decide whether special situations should be defined where the application of anti-money-laundering measures is not necessary, e.g. when a financial activity is carried out on an occasional or limited basis (see Interpretative Note).

Customer identification and record-keeping rules

Recommendation 10

Financial institutions should not keep anonymous accounts or accounts in obviously fictitious names: they should be required (by law, by regulations, by agreements between supervisory authorities and financial institutions or by self-regulatory agreements among financial institutions) to identify, on the basis of an official or other reliable identifying document, and record the identity of their clients, either occasional or usual, when establishing business relations or conducting transactions (in particular opening of accounts or passbooks, entering into fiduciary transactions, renting of safe deposit boxes, performing large cash transactions).

In order to fulfil identification requirements concerning legal entities, financial institutions should, when necessary, take measures:

- To verify the legal existence and structure of the customer by obtaining either from a public register or from the customer or both, proof of incorporation, including information concerning the customer's name, legal form, address, directors and provisions regulating the power to bind the entity.
- To verify that any person purporting to act on behalf of the customer is so authorised and identify that person.

Recommendation 11

Financial institutions should take reasonable measures to obtain information about the true identity of the persons on whose behalf an account is opened or a transaction conducted if there are any doubts as to whether these clients or customers are acting on their own behalf, e.g. in the case of domiciliary companies (i.e. institutions, corporations, foundations, trusts, etc., that do not conduct any commercial or manufacturing business or any other form of commercial operation in the country where their registered office is located) (see Interpretative Notes: Recommendation 11 & Recommendations 11 and 15 to 18).

Recommendation 12

Financial institutions should maintain, for at least five years, all necessary records on transactions, both domestic or international, to enable them to comply swiftly with information requests from the competent authorities. Such records must be sufficient to permit reconstruction of individual transactions (including the amounts and types of currency involved if any) so as to provide, if necessary, evidence for prosecution of criminal behaviour.

Financial institutions should keep records on customer identification (e.g. copies or records of official identification documents like passports, identity cards, driving licenses or similar documents), account files and business correspondence for at least five years after the account is closed. These documents should be available to domestic competent authorities in the context of relevant criminal prosecutions and investigations.

Recommendation 13

Countries should pay special attention to money laundering threats inherent in new or developing technologies that might favour anonymity, and take measures, if needed, to prevent their use in money laundering schemes.

Increased diligence of financial institutions

Recommendation 14

Financial institutions should pay special attention to all complex, unusual large transactions, and all unusual patterns of transactions, which have no apparent economic or visible lawful purpose. The background and purpose of such transactions should, as far as possible, be examined, the findings established in writing, and be available to help supervisors, auditors and law enforcement agencies (see Interpretative Note).

Recommendation 15

If financial institutions suspect that funds stem from a criminal activity, they should be required to report promptly their suspicions to the competent authorities (see Interpretative Notes: Recommendation 15 and Recommendations 11 and 15 to 18).

Recommendation 16

Financial institutions, their directors, officers and employees should be protected by legal provisions from criminal or civil liability for breach of any restriction on disclosure of information imposed by contract or by any legislative, regulatory or administrative provision, if they report their suspicions in good faith to the competent authorities, even if they did not know precisely what the underlying criminal activity was, and regardless of whether illegal activity actually occurred (see Interpretative Note).

Recommendation 17

Financial institutions, their directors, officers and employees, should not, or, where appropriate, should not be allowed to, warn their customers when information relating to them is being reported to the competent authorities (see Interpretative Note).

Recommendation 18

Financial institutions reporting their suspicions should comply with instructions from the competent authorities (see Interpretative Note).

Recommendation 19

Financial institutions should develop programmes against money laundering. These programmes should include, as a minimum:

- The development of internal policies, procedures and controls, including the designation of compliance officers at management level, and adequate screening procedures to ensure high standards when hiring employees.
- An ongoing employee training programme.
- An audit function to test the system.

Measures to cope with the problem of countries with no or insufficient anti-money-laundering measures

Recommendation 20

Financial institutions should ensure that the principles mentioned above are also applied to branches and majority owned subsidiaries located abroad, especially in countries which do not or insufficiently apply these Recommendations, to the extent that local applicable laws and regulations permit. When local applicable laws and regulations prohibit this implementation, competent authorities in the country of the mother institution should be informed by the financial institutions that they cannot apply these Recommendations.

Recommendation 21

Financial institutions should give special attention to business relations and transactions with persons, including companies and financial institutions, from countries which do not or insufficiently apply these Recommendations. Whenever these transactions have no apparent economic or visible lawful purpose, their background and purpose should, as far as possible, be examined, the findings established in writing, and be available to help supervisors, auditors and law enforcement agencies.

Other measures to avoid money laundering

Recommendation 22

Countries should consider implementing feasible measures to detect or monitor the physical cross-border transportation of cash and bearer negotiable instruments, subject to strict safeguards to ensure proper use of information and without impeding in any way the freedom of capital movements (see Interpretative Note).

Recommendation 23

Countries should consider the feasibility and utility of a system where banks and other financial institutions and intermediaries would report all domestic and international currency transactions above a fixed amount, to a national central agency with a computerised database, available to competent authorities for use in money laundering cases, subject to strict safeguards to ensure proper use of the information.

Recommendation 24

Countries should further encourage in general the development of modern and secure techniques of money management, including increased use of checks, payment cards, direct deposit of salary checks and book entry recording of securities, as a means to encourage the replacement of cash transfers.

Recommendation 25

Countries should take notice of the potential for abuse of shell corporations by money launderers and should consider whether additional measures are required to prevent unlawful use of such entities.

Implementation and role of regulatory and other administrative authorities

Recommendation 26

The competent authorities supervising banks or other financial institutions or intermediaries, or other competent authorities, should ensure that the supervised institutions have adequate programmes to guard against money laundering. These authorities should cooperate and lend expertise spontaneously or on request with other domestic judicial or law enforcement authorities in money laundering investigations and prosecutions (see Interpretative Note).

Recommendation 27

Competent authorities should be designated to ensure an effective implementation of all these Recommendations, through administrative supervision and regulation, in other professions dealing with cash as defined by each country.

Recommendation 28

The competent authorities should establish guidelines which will assist financial institutions in detecting suspicious patterns of behaviour by their customers. It is understood that such guidelines must develop over time, and will never be exhaustive. It is further understood that such guidelines will primarily serve as an educational tool for financial institutions' personnel.

Recommendation 29

The competent authorities regulating or supervising financial institutions should take the necessary legal or regulatory measures to guard against control or acquisition of a significant participation in financial institutions by criminals or their confederates (see Interpretative Note).

STRENGTHENING OF INTERNATIONAL COOPERATION

Administrative cooperation

Exchange of general information

Recommendation 30

National administrations should consider recording, at least in the aggregate, international flows of cash in whatever currency, so that estimates can be made of cash flows and reflows from various sources abroad, when this is combined with central bank information. Such information should be made available to the International Monetary Fund and the Bank for International Settlements to facilitate international studies.

Recommendation 31

International competent authorities, perhaps Interpol and the World Customs Organisation, should be given responsibility for gathering and disseminating information to competent authorities about the latest developments in money laundering and money laundering techniques. Central banks and bank regulators could do the same on their network. National authorities in various spheres, in consultation with trade associations, could then disseminate this to financial institutions in individual countries.

Exchange of information relating to suspicious transactions

Recommendation 32

Each country should make efforts to improve a spontaneous or 'upon request' international information exchange relating to suspicious transactions, persons and corporations involved in those transactions between competent authorities. Strict safeguards should be established to ensure that this exchange of information is consistent with national and international provisions on privacy and data protection.

Other forms of cooperation

Basis and means for cooperation in confiscation, mutual assistance and extradition

Recommendation 33

Countries should try to ensure, on a bilateral or multilateral basis, that different knowledge standards in national definitions, i.e. different standards concerning the intentional element of the infraction, do not affect the ability or willingness of countries to provide each other with mutual legal assistance (see Interpretative Note).

Recommendation 34

International cooperation should be supported by a network of bilateral and multilateral agreements and arrangements based on generally shared legal concepts, with the aim of providing practical measures to affect the widest possible range of mutual assistance.

Recommendation 35

Countries should be encouraged to ratify and implement relevant international conventions on money laundering such as the 1990 Council of Europe Convention on Laundering, Search, Seizure and Confiscation of the Proceeds from Crime.

Focus of improved mutual assistance on money laundering issues

Recommendation 36

Cooperative investigations among countries' appropriate competent authorities should be encouraged. One valid and effective investigative technique in this respect is controlled delivery related to assets known or suspected to be the proceeds of crime. Countries are encouraged to support this technique, where possible (see Interpretative Note).

Recommendation 37

There should be procedures for mutual assistance in criminal matters regarding the use of compulsory measures, including the production of records by financial institutions and other persons, the search of persons and premises, seizure and obtaining evidence for use in money laundering investigations and prosecutions and in related actions in foreign jurisdictions.

Recommendation 38

There should be authority to take expeditious action in response to requests by foreign countries to identify, freeze, seize and confiscate proceeds or other property of corresponding value to such proceeds, based on money laundering or the crimes underlying the laundering activity.

There should also be arrangements for coordinating seizure and confiscation proceedings which may include the sharing of confiscated assets (see Interpretative Note).

Recommendation 39

To avoid conflicts of jurisdiction, consideration should be given to devising and applying mechanisms for determining the best venue for prosecution of defendants in the interests of justice in cases that are subject to prosecution in more than one country. Similarly, there should be arrangements for coordinating seizure and confiscation proceedings which may include the sharing of confiscated assets.

Recommendation 40

Countries should have procedures in place to extradite, where possible, individuals charged with a money laundering offence or related offences. With respect to its national legal system, each country should recognise money laundering as an extraditable offence. Subject to their legal frameworks, countries may consider simplifying extradition by allowing direct transmission of extradition requests between appropriate ministries, extraditing persons based only on warrants of arrests or judgements, extraditing their nationals, and/or introducing a simplified extradition of consenting persons who waive formal extradition proceedings.

Annex to Recommendation 9: list of financial activities undertaken by business or professions that are not financial institutions

- Acceptance of deposits and other repayable funds from the public.
- Lending.[1]
- Financial leasing.
- Money transmission services.
- Issuing and managing means of payment (e.g. credit and debit cards, cheques, traveller's cheques and bankers' drafts).
- Financial guarantees and commitments.
- Trading for account of customers (spot, forward, swaps, futures, options, etc.) in:
  (a) Money market instruments (cheques, bills, CDs, etc.).
  (b) Foreign exchange.
  (c) Exchange, interest rate and index instruments.
  (d) Transferable securities.
  (e) Commodity futures.
- Participation in securities issues and the provision of financial services related to such issues.
- Individual and collective portfolio management.
- Safekeeping and administration of cash or liquid securities on behalf of clients.
- Life insurance and other investment related insurance.
- Money changing.

---

[1] Including, *inter alia*:
o Consumer credit.
o Mortgage credit.
o Factoring, with or without recourse.
o Finance of commercial transactions (including forfeiting).

APPENDIX 3: FATF SPECIAL RECOMMENDATIONS ON TERRORIST FINANCING

I.   Ratification and implementation of UN instruments

Each country should take immediate steps to ratify and to implement fully the 1999 United Nations International Convention for the Suppression of the Financing of Terrorism. Countries should also immediately implement the United Nations resolutions relating to the prevention and suppression of the financing of terrorist acts, particularly United Nations Security Council Resolution 1373.

II.   Criminalising the financing of terrorism and associated money laundering

Each country should criminalise the financing of terrorism, terrorist acts and terrorist organisations. Countries should ensure that such offences are designated as money laundering predicate offences.

III.   Freezing and confiscating terrorist assets

Each country should implement measures to freeze without delay funds or other assets of terrorists, those who finance terrorism and terrorist organisations in accordance with the United Nations resolutions relating to the prevention and suppression of the financing of terrorist acts. Each country should also adopt and implement measures, including legislative ones, which would enable the competent authorities to seize and confiscate property that is the proceeds of, or used in, or intended or allocated for use in, the financing of terrorism, terrorist acts or terrorist organisations.

IV.   Reporting suspicious transactions related to terrorism

If financial institutions, or other businesses or entities subject to anti-money-laundering obligations, suspect or have reasonable grounds to suspect that funds are linked or related to, or are to be used for terrorism, terrorist acts or by terrorist organisations, they should be required to report promptly their suspicions to the competent authorities.

V.   International cooperation

Each country should afford another country, on the basis of a treaty, arrangement or other mechanism for mutual legal assistance or information exchange, the greatest possible measure of assistance in connection with criminal, civil enforcement and administrative investigations, inquiries and proceedings relating to the financing of terrorism, terrorist acts and terrorist organisations. Countries should also take all possible measures to ensure that they do not provide safe havens for individuals charged with the financing of terrorism, terrorist acts or terrorist organisations, and should have procedures in place to extradite, where possible, such individuals.

VI. Alternative remittance

Each country should take measures to ensure that persons or legal entities, including agents, that provide a service for the transmission of money or value, including transmission through an informal money or value transfer system or network, should be licensed or registered and subject to all the FATF Recommendations that apply to banks and non-bank financial institutions. Each country should ensure that persons or legal entities that carry out this service illegally are subject to administrative, civil or criminal sanctions.

VII. Wire transfers

Countries should take measures to require financial institutions, including money remitters, to include accurate and meaningful originator information (name, address and account number) on funds transfers and related messages that are sent, and the information should remain with the transfer or related message through the payment chain. Countries should take measures to ensure that financial institutions, including money remitters, conduct enhanced scrutiny of and monitor for suspicious activity fund transfers that do not contain complete originator information (name, address and account number).

VIII. Non-profit organisations

Countries should review the adequacy of laws and regulations that relate to entities that can be abused for the financing of terrorism. Non-profit organisations are particularly vulnerable, and countries should ensure that they cannot be misused:

(a) by terrorist organisations posing as legitimate entities;
(b) to exploit legitimate entities as conduits for terrorist financing, including for the purpose of escaping asset freezing measures; and
(c) to conceal or obscure the clandestine diversion of funds intended for legitimate purposes to terrorist organisations.

APPENDIX 4: THE WOLFSBERG ANTI-MONEY-LAUNDERING PRINCIPLES

(First revision, May 2002)

Preamble

The following guidelines are understood to be appropriate for private banking relationships. Guidelines for other market segments may differ. It is recognized that the establishment of policies and procedures to adhere to these guidelines is the responsibility of management.

1   Client acceptance: general guidelines

1.1   General

Bank policy will be to prevent the use of its worldwide operations for criminal purposes. The bank will endeavour to accept only those clients whose source of wealth and funds can be reasonably established to be legitimate. The primary responsibility for this lies with the private banker who sponsors the client for acceptance. Mere fulfilment of internal review procedures does not relieve the private banker of this basic responsibility.

1.2   Identification

The bank will take reasonable measures to establish the identity of its clients and beneficial owners and will only accept clients when this process has been completed.

1.2.1   Client

- Natural persons: identity will be established to the bank's satisfaction by reference to official identity papers or such other evidence as may be appropriate under the circumstances.
- Corporations, partnerships, foundations: the bank will receive documentary evidence of the due organisation and existence.
- Trusts: the bank will receive appropriate evidence of formation and existence along with identity of the trustees.
- Identification documents must be current at the time of opening.

1.2.2   Beneficial owner

Beneficial ownership must be established for all accounts. Due diligence must be done on all principal beneficial owners identified in accordance with the following principles:

- Natural persons: when the account is in the name of an individual, the private banker must establish whether the client is acting on his or her own behalf. If doubt exists, the bank will establish the capacity in which and on whose behalf the account holder is acting.
- Legal entities: where the client is a company, such as a private investment company, the private banker will understand the structure of the company sufficiently to determine the provider of funds, principal owner(s) of the shares and those who have control over the funds, e.g. the directors and those with the power to give direction to the directors of the company. With regard to other shareholders the private banker will make a reasonable judgement as

to the need for further due diligence. This principle applies regardless of whether the share capital is in registered or bearer form.

- Trusts: where the client is a trustee, the private banker will understand the structure of the trust sufficiently to determine the provider of funds (e.g. settlor), those who have control over the funds (e.g. trustees) and any persons or entities who have the power to remove the trustees. The private banker will make a reasonable judgement as to the need for further due diligence.
- Unincorporated associations: the above principles apply to unincorporated associations.
- The bank will not permit the use of its internal non-client accounts (sometimes referred to as 'concentration' accounts) to prevent association of the identity of a client with the movement of funds on the client's behalf; i.e. the bank will not permit the use of such internal accounts in a manner that would prevent the bank from appropriately monitoring the client's account activity.

1.2.3   Accounts held in the name of money managers and similar intermediaries

The private banker will perform due diligence on the intermediary and establish that the intermediary has a due diligence process for its clients, or a regulatory obligation to conduct such due diligence, that is satisfactory to the bank.

1.2.4   Powers of attorney/authorised signers

Where the holder of a power of attorney or another authorised signer is appointed by a client, it is generally sufficient to do due diligence on the client.

1.2.5   Practices for walk-in clients and electronic banking relationships

A bank will determine whether walk-in clients or relationships initiated through electronic channels require a higher degree of due diligence prior to account opening. The bank will specifically address measures to satisfactorily establish the identity of non-face-to-face customers.

1.3   Due diligence

It is essential to collect and record information covering the following categories:

- Purpose and reasons for opening the account.
- Anticipated account activity.
- Source of wealth (description of the economic activity that has generated the net worth).
- Estimated net worth.
- Source of funds (description of the origin and the means of transfer for monies that are accepted for the account opening).
- References or other sources to corroborate reputation information where available.

Unless other measures reasonably suffice to do the due diligence on a client (e.g. favourable and reliable references), a client will be met prior to account opening.

1.4 Numbered or alternate name accounts

Numbered or alternate name accounts will only be accepted if the bank has established the identity of the client and the beneficial owner. These accounts must be open to a level of scrutiny by the bank's appropriate control layers equal to the level of scrutiny applicable to other client accounts.

1.5 Offshore jurisdictions

Risks associated with entities organised in offshore jurisdictions are covered by due diligence procedures laid out in these guidelines.

1.6 Oversight responsibility

There will be a requirement that all new clients and new accounts be approved by at least one person other than the private banker.

2   Client acceptance: situations requiring additional diligence/attention

2.1   General

In its internal policies, the bank must define categories of persons whose circumstances warrant additional diligence. This will typically be the case where the circumstances are likely to pose a higher than average risk to a bank.

2.2   Indicators

The circumstances of the following categories of persons are indicators for defining them as requiring additional diligence:

- Persons residing in and/or having funds sourced from countries identified by credible sources as having inadequate anti-money-laundering standards or representing a high risk for crime and corruption.
- Persons engaged in types of business activities or sectors known to be susceptible to money laundering.
- 'Politically exposed persons' (frequently abbreviated as 'PEPs'), referring to individuals holding or having held positions of public trust, such as government officials, senior executives of government corporations, politicians, important political party officials, etc., as well as their families and close associates.

2.3   Senior management approval

The banks' internal policies should indicate whether, for any one or more among these categories, senior management must approve entering into new relationships. Relationships with politically exposed persons may only be entered into with approval from senior management.

3   Updating client files

3.1

The private banker is responsible for updating the client file on a defined basis and/or when there are major changes. The private banker's supervisor or an independent control person will review relevant portions of client files on a regular basis to ensure consistency and completeness. The frequency of the reviews depends on the size, complexity and risk posed by the relationship.

3.2

With respect to clients classified under any category of persons mentioned in Section 2, the bank's internal policies will indicate whether senior management must be involved in these reviews.

3.3

Similarly, with respect to clients classified as set forth in Section 3.2, the bank's internal policies will indicate what management information must be provided to management and/or other control layers. The policies should also address the frequency of these information flows.

3.4

The reviews of PEPs must require senior management's involvement.

4   Practices when identifying unusual or suspicious activities

4.1   Definition of unusual or suspicious activities

The bank will have a written policy on the identification of and follow-up on unusual or suspicious activities. This policy will include a definition of what is considered to be suspicious or unusual and give examples thereof. Unusual or suspicious activities may include:

- Account transactions or other activities that are not consistent with the due diligence file.
- Cash transactions over a certain amount.
- Pass-through/in-and-out transactions.

4.2   Identification of unusual or suspicious activities

Unusual or suspicious activities can be identified through:

- Monitoring of transactions.
- Client contacts (meetings, discussions, in-country visits, etc.).
- Third-party information (e.g. newspapers, Reuters, Internet).
- Private banker's/internal knowledge of the client's environment (e.g. political situation in his or her country).

4.3 Follow-up on unusual or suspicious activities

The private banker, management and/or the control function will carry out an analysis of the background of any unusual or suspicious activity. If there is no plausible explanation a decision will be made involving the control function:

- To continue the business relationship with increased monitoring.
- To cancel the business relationship.
- To report the business relationship to the authorities.

The report to the authorities is made by the control function and senior management may need to be notified (e.g. Senior Compliance Officer, CEO, Chief Auditor, General Counsel). As required by local laws and regulations, the assets may be blocked and transactions may be subject to approval by the control function.

5 Monitoring

5.1 Monitoring programme

A sufficient monitoring programme must be in place. The primary responsibility for monitoring account activities lies with the private banker. The private banker will be familiar with significant transactions and increased activity in the account and will be especially aware of unusual or suspicious activities (see Section 4.1). The bank will decide to what extent fulfilment of these responsibilities will need to be supported through the use of automated systems or other means.

5.2 Ongoing monitoring

With respect to clients classified under any category of persons mentioned in Section 2, the bank's internal policies will indicate how the account activities will be subject to monitoring.

6 Control responsibilities

A written control policy will be in place establishing standard control procedures to be undertaken by the various 'control layers' (private banker, independent operations unit, compliance, internal audit). The control policy will cover issues of timing, degree of control, areas to be controlled, responsibilities and follow-up, etc. An independent audit function (which may be internal to the bank) will test the programmes contemplated by the control policy.

7 Reporting

There will be regular management reporting established on money laundering issues (e.g. number of reports to authorities, monitoring tools, changes in applicable laws and regulations, the number and scope of training sessions provided to employees).

8 Education, training and information

The bank will establish a training programme on the identification and prevention of money laundering for employees who have client contact and for compliance personnel. Regular training (e.g. annually) will also include how to identify and follow-up on unusual or suspicious activities. In addition, employees will be informed about any major changes in anti-money-laundering laws and regulations. All new employees will be provided with guidelines on the anti-money-laundering procedures.

9   Record retention requirements

The bank will establish record retention requirements for all anti-money-laundering-related documents. The documents must be kept for a minimum of five years.

10   Exceptions and deviations

The bank will establish an exception and deviation procedure that requires risk assessment and approval by an independent unit.

11   Anti-money-laundering organisation

The bank will establish an adequately staffed and independent department responsible for the prevention of money laundering (e.g. compliance, independent control unit, legal).

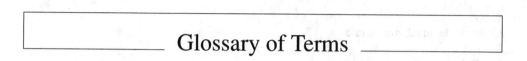

Glossary of Terms

Account minimum
Published or stated minimum balance of assets under management allowed within an individual private client account.

Administration and asset fee revenues
Revenues from annual fees and service fees related to private client wealth management; include fund management fees, mutual fund management fees, estate and trust management fees, custody fees, account management fees, and other recurring planning and advice charges.

Advisory mandate
Mandate under which the wealth manager provides advice but the client makes the investment decisions.

Alternative investments
Investments in non-traditional asset classes such as hedge funds, private equity, real estate and managed futures. Can also describe investment in physical assets such as antiques, jewellery, wine and works of art.

Asset allocation
The strategic allocation of the available capital to different asset classes, sectors, categories, countries and currencies.

Assets under custody (AuC)
All assets for which an institution acts as custodian or fulfills a securities-servicing role, such as the processing of securities trades and the safeguarding of assets; includes assets under management as well as other third-party assets held solely under a custody arrangement.

Assets under management (AuM)
All assets managed by an institution on behalf of private clients; includes directly held equities, managed funds, hedge funds, fixed income, and cash or cash equivalents.

Basis point (BP)
A measure used mainly in the statement or calculation of investment yields. One basis point is one hundredth of 1%.

Best advice
Duty on financial advisers to recommend products that can reasonably be described as the most suitable for the client.

CAGR
Compound annual growth rate.

Capital-guaranteed investments
A structured investment in the form of a fund, security or deposit that guarantees the repayment of a given percentage of the capital originally invested.

Churning
Excessive trading generated by a broker to accumulate profit from commissions; not in the best interests of the client.

Client assets and liabilities (CAL)
Sum of a client's assets under management, assets under custody and outstanding loans.

Closed-end fund
An investment company that offers a fixed number of shares traded on an exchange.

Commission revenues
Transaction-based revenues from private clients' trading (usually charged on a per trade basis); include volume-based trading charges (bond and equity markets), foreign-exchange transaction charges, fiduciary deposit charges and commission income from sales of insurance.

Discretionary mandate
Mandate under which the wealth manager usually has sole authority to buy and sell assets, and to execute transactions on behalf of the client.

Distribution
The various front-office activities required to gather and retain private client assets.

Exchange traded fund (ETF)
Open-ended index funds that trade continuously, like stocks, on major stock exchanges.

Execution-only mandate
Mandate under which the wealth manager executes, or selects brokers to execute, securities transactions on behalf of the client.

Fiduciary
An individual, corporation or association holding assets for another party, often with the legal authority and duty to make decisions regarding financial matters on behalf of the other party. These types of services typically encompass planning and structuring of trusts and estates.

Forfeiture
A loss of money, property or privileges due to a breach of legal obligation, which serves as compensation for resulting losses.

Front running
An illegal activity in which a trader takes a position in a security in advance of an action which he or she knows his or her brokerage will take that will move the security price in a predictable fashion.

Fund-of-funds
An investment fund that invests solely in other funds.

Gini coefficient
Measures the extent to which the distribution of income across individuals deviates from a perfectly equal distribution. Falls between zero, for perfect equality, and one, for extreme inequality.

Hedge fund
Actively managed fund that targets absolute returns using a wide range of investment strategies, with the ability to use asset classes and strategies not usually available to mutual funds; may include derivatives (e.g. options, futures), leverage and short positions.

Jumbo mortgage (US)
Conventional residential mortgage loan that exceeds the limit set by the US agencies. The current limit is $300 700. This type of mortgage is not eligible for sale and delivery to either Fannie Mae (Federal National Mortgage Association) or Freddie Mac (Federal Home Loan Mortgage Corporation). Also known as a 'non-conforming' mortgage.

Know your customer (KYC)
The duty to ascertain sufficient information about a customer to enable suitable advice to be given.

Lombard loan
A loan collateralised by securities, bank deposits or other realisable assets. It can be used to purchase securities, invest in life insurance and cover liquidity needs.

Managed fund/product
A pooled investment fund that is actively managed.

Multimanager
An investment structure that involves an institution investing in securities via appointed investment managers. Includes manager-of-manager and fund-of-fund structures.

Net interest income
The interest earned on assets (for instance, margin loans and private banking loans) net of the interest paid on liabilities (e.g. brokerage cash balances and banking deposits).

Net investment assets (NIA)
A broad measure of the wealth of a household: the value of the sum of listed securities held directly or indirectly through managed funds, administrative platforms, cash deposits and non-listed investments (such as equity in family businesses), less all personally held debt (such as mortgages and personal loans); excludes the value of a household's primary residence but includes other real estate investments.

Offshore
Used to designate any location foreign to an investor's country of residence and/or nationality. In respect of taxation, any location where levels of taxation or regulations governing operations are sufficiently favourable to attract funds from other financial centres.

Onshore
Used to designate the location of an investor's country of residence and/or nationality.

Open-ended fund
A regulated investment company that offers an unlimited number of shares and stands ready to buy back shares at any time. Another term for a mutual fund.

Open product architecture
Describes the system under which the wealth manager offers clients access to selected products from third parties.

PIC (private investment corporations)
Shell corporations, often referred to as 'private investment corporations' or PICs, are usually incorporated in offshore jurisdictions that restrict disclosure of a PIC's beneficial owner. Private banks then open bank accounts in the name of the PIC, allowing the PIC's owner to avoid identification as the account holder.

Portfolio manager
The person or team responsible for investing the pool of clients' assets within a fund. The portfolio manager decides which securities to hold, when to buy and when to sell.

Portfolio turnover
A measure of the trading activity in the fund's portfolio of investments; measures how often securities are bought and sold by the fund.

Private equity fund
A fund invested in the private equity or quasi-equity of companies in various stages of growth. The main types of private equity investments are venture capital (young companies), leveraged buyouts, mezzanine finance and distressed debt. See also 'venture capital fund'.

Production/manufacturing
The middle- and back-office activities required to appropriately manage the gathered assets, including transactional and administrative tasks.

Qualified intermediary (QI)
Agreement between a financial institution and the US Internal Revenue Service (IRS) to ensure that US citizens and residents properly report and pay tax on their income, and that all non-US recipients of US source income pay the appropriate rate of withholding tax.

Regulation T (Reg T)
Federal Reserve Board regulation that governs the extension of credit to clients of broker-dealers. The rules specify the amount and type of credit that may be extended or must be maintained when clients purchase, carry or trade eligible securities. It defines eligible securities and establishes initial margin requirements. Reg T does not cover the extension or maintenance of credit by a broker-dealer for clients who purchase or trade in exempt securities.

Relationship managers
Senior client-facing team members; include team members whose responsibility is to contact clients on a relatively frequent basis; excludes junior team members who have little client contact. Also known as private bankers, client relationship officers (CROs), financial advisors, etc.

Retrocession
Fee paid by the product provider to the sales agent as a sales commission and for brokering its products.

Scalping
To trade for small gains. Scalping normally involves establishing and liquidating a position quickly, usually within the same day.

Separately managed account
An individually managed portfolio that is entirely owned by the individual investor; i.e. assets are not co-mingled with those of other investors as they are in mutual funds.

SICAV
Société d'Investissement à Capital Variable. French term to describe a mutual fund.

Structured (investment) products
Standardised or bespoke investment products that combine assets, derivatives and covenants to create a specific and sometimes complex risk-return profile. Most usual are capital-guaranteed and tax-optimised products.

Tax amnesty
Government initiative to encourage individuals to repatriate assets from abroad without fear of criminal penalties.

Trust
A (tax-efficient) arrangement whereby the so-called trustees hold property for the benefit of other people called the beneficiaries.

Venture capital fund
A fund invested in the private equity of start-up or young growth companies.

Withholding tax
A tax on income deducted at source that a paying agent is legally obliged to deduct from its payments of interest on securities.

Wirehouse (US)
National or international brokerage firms whose branch offices are linked by communication networks. The term dates back to when only the largest firms had high-speed communications. The networks rapidly disperse information and research about securities and markets. Through increased technology, regional brokers and small retail firms now have the same ability. However, the designation as a wirehouse is used only to refer to the largest brokerage firms.

Wrap account
Accounts that allow the clients to make their own decisions regarding transactions. For an annual fee and relatively low transaction charges, clients enjoy unlimited trading of stocks, bonds and funds, and receive regular performance reports.

Bibliography

Accenture (2001), 'Reaching Your Goals: Navigating the Future of Wealth Management', *The Point*, 1(2).

Accenture (2002), 'Taking Off: Why Separate Accounts Are the Hottest Thing in Wealth Management', *The Point*, 2(4).

Arthur Andersen (2000/2001), 'High Net Worth Asset Management: Delivering Value in Dynamic Markets', Winter.

Banks, James, Richard Blundell and James P. Smith (2000), 'Wealth Inequality in the United States and Great Britain', Working Paper WP 00/20, The Institute for Fiscal Studies, November.

Barclays Capital (2006), 'Annual Asia Wealth Management Survey', March.

Barron's, 'Annual Survey of Top Wealth Managers in the United States', various years.

Bear, Stearns International, European Equity Research (2006), 'The Wealth Management Industry: Show Me the Money', 11 April.

Benaissa, Nasr-Eddine, Michael Wiegand and Mayank Parekh (2005), 'A Growth Model For Islamic Banking', *McKinsey on Banking*, October.

Berkshire Capital Securities LLC, *Investment Management Industry Review*, various years.

Bernstein Research (2000), 'The Future of Money Management in America', March.

Bernstein Research (2003), 'The Hedge Fund Industry: Products, Services or Capabilities?', June.

Bicker, Lyn (1996), *Private Banking in Europe*, Routledge.

Bishop, Matthew (2001), 'Survey: The New Rich: The New Wealth of Nations', *The Economist*, 14 June.

Bishop, Matthew (2006), 'Survey: Wealth and Philanthropy: The Business of Giving', *The Economist*, 25 February.

BNP Paribas (2004), 'Structured Retail Products: Global Overview, 2002–2004 and Beyond'.

Booth, Tamzin (2003), 'Survey: Asset Management: Other People's Money', *The Economist*, 3 July.

Booz Allen Hamilton (2001), 'Wealth Management: The Challenge'.

Booz Allen Hamilton and Reuters (2003), 'Defining Excellence in Private Client Servicing'.

Boston Consulting Group (2001a), 'Global Wealth 2001: Richer Prospects in Wealth Management', July.

Boston Consulting Group (2001b), 'Untapped Riches: The Myths and Realities of Wealth Management', September.

Boston Consulting Group (2002a), 'Hidden Treasure: Finding the Keys to Profitability in Wealth Management', April.

Boston Consulting Group (2002b), 'Global Wealth 2002: Prospering in Uncertain Times', July.

Boston Consulting Group (2003a), 'Global Asset Management 2003: Navigating the Maze', June.

Boston Consulting Group (2003b), 'Global Wealth 2003: Winning in a Challenging Market', July.

Boston Consulting Group (2003c), 'Crafting New Approaches to Offshore Markets', December.

Boston Consulting Group (2004a), 'The Asset Management Battle: Using Tools of Other Trades to Win', January.

Boston Consulting Group (2004b), 'Global Wealth 2004: The Rich Return to Richer Returns', November.

Boston Consulting Group (2004c), 'Global Asset Management 2004: A Restless Recovery', December.

Boston Consulting Group (2005a), 'Breaking Compromises in the Mass Affluent Market', June.

Boston Consulting Group (2005b), 'Global Wealth 2005: Searching for Profitable Growth', September.

Boston Consulting Group (2005c), 'Striving for Organic Growth in Retail Banking', December.

Boston Consulting Group (2005d), 'Wealth Markets in China: Exciting Times Ahead', December.

Bowers, Tab, Gregg Gibb and Jeffrey Wong (2003), *Banking in Asia: Acquiring a Profit Mindset*, 2nd edn, John Wiley & Sons, Ltd, Chichester.

Broby, Louise (2001), *The Wealth Management Outlook*, Reuters, London.

Brooks, David (2000), *Bobos (Bourgeois Bohemians) in Paradise*, Simon & Schuster, New York.

Brown, Tom (2005), 'The Citi is Sleeping: Break it Up!', Bankstocks.com, 21 September.

Buehrer, Christian, Ivo Hubli and Eliane Marti (2005), 'The Regulatory Burden in the Swiss Wealth Management Industry', Working Paper 39, Swiss Banking Institute, University of Zurich, February.

Capgemini (2006), 'Private Banking Systems Survey 2005', March.

Capgemini Ernst & Young (2002), 'Private Banking Systems Survey'.

Capgemini/Merrill Lynch, 'Relationship Manager Surveys', various years.

Capgemini/Merrill Lynch 'World Wealth Report', various years.

Capital Research Associates (1999), 'American Family Wealth: Analysis of Recent Census Data', 25 October.

Casserley, Dominic and Greg Gibb (1999), *Banking in Asia: The End of Entitlement*, John Wiley & Sons, Ltd, Chichester.

Citigroup (2004), 'Private Bank: Analyst/Investor Day', Peter K. Scatturro, Private Bank CEO, 10 February.

Citigroup (2005a), 'Wealth Management', Presentation by Todd S. Thomson, Chairman and CEO Citigroup Wealth Management, at UBS Asset Gathering Conference, 31 March.

Citigroup (2005b), 'Asia Wealth Management', Presentation by Deepak Sharma, CEO Global Wealth Management, Asia Pacific and Middle East, 22 September.

Citigroup Alternative Investments (2003), 'Alternative Thinking from Citigroup'.

Citigroup Global Markets (2005), 'Equity Strategy: Plutonomy: Buying Luxury, Explaining Global Imbalances', 16 October.

Citigroup Global Markets (2006), 'Equity Strategy: Revisiting Plutonomy: The Rich Getting Richer', 5 March.

Citigroup Private Bank and McKinsey & Company (2005), 'New Perspectives on Wealth Management: A Survey of the World's Wealthiest Families', January.

Citigroup Private Bank and The Wharton School (2006), 'Special Report: Protecting the Value of Real Estate-Rich Portfolios', March.

Citigroup Smith Barney (2003a), 'US Affluent Investor Survey', 3 September.

Citigroup Smith Barney (2003b), 'Swiss Private Banking: Roundtable Notes', 3 July.

Citigroup Smith Barney (2003c), 'Swiss Private Banking: Credit Suisse Private Banking to Close Gap with UBS?', 4 July.

Citigroup Smith Barney (2003d), 'US Affluent Investor Survey', 3 September.

Citigroup Smith Barney (2003e), 'UBS: From Bahnhofstrasse to Main Street USA', 9 October.

Citigroup Smith Barney (2003f), 'Why Rich Clients Matter: Private Banking Momentum at UBS, Credit Suisse and Julius Baer', 14 November.

Citigroup Smith Barney (2004), 'Affluent Investor Survey', 2 June.

Citigroup Smith Barney (2005), 'Swiss Private Banking Roundtable 2005', 12 July.

Citigroup Smith Barney/CNBC, 'Affluent Investor Poll', various issues.

Clement, Douglas (2003), 'Accounting for the Rich', *The Region*, Federal Reserve Bank of Minneapolis, June.

Cocca, Teodoro D. (2005), 'The International Private Banking Study 2005', Swiss Banking Institute, University of Zurich.

Commerzbank (2001), 'Converging on the Mass Affluent: European Financials Race for Market Share', February.

Credit Suisse, various investor presentations.

Credit Suisse First Boston Equity Research (2004), 'Swiss Asset Managers: The Art of Banking', 17 August.

Credit Suisse First Boston Equity Research (2005), 'EFG International: The Invisible Hand', 18 November.

Cruciano, Therese (1996), 'High Income Tax Returns for 1996', Federal Reserve Board of Governors.

Datamonitor, various reports.

Deloitte Touche Tohmatsu (2003), 'Financial Services and the Fight Against Money Laundering'.

Deutsche Bank (2004), 'The Morphology of Debt', Speech by Anshu Jain, Head of Global Markets, at JP Morgan Investment Banking Conference, 11 March.

Deutsche Bank Global Equity Research (2004), 'Private Banking: Quantifying the Asian Opportunity', 17 March.

Deutsche Bank Research (2003), 'EU: Taxation of Savings Income Coming Down Home Straight', *EU Monitor*, 5, 8 October.

Dew-Becker, Ian and Robert J. Gordon (2005), 'Where Did the Productivity Growth Go? Inflation Dynamics and the Distribution of Income', *Brookings Papers on Economic Activity*, 2005(2).

Díaz-Giménez, Javier, Vincenzo Quadrini, José-Victor Ríos-Rull and Santiago Budría Rodríguez (2002), 'Updated Facts on the US Distribution of Earnings, Income and Wealth', *Federal Reserve Bank of Minneapolis Quarterly Review*, summer.

Dresdner Kleinwort Wasserstein (2004), 'Wealth Management', 20 January.

Drew, John, Blair McCallum and Stefan Roggenhofer (2004), *Journey to Lean: Making Operational Change Stick*, Palgrave Macmillan: London.

EFG International (2005), *Initial Public Offering Memorandum*, 6 October.

Ernst & Young (2002), 'Private Banking in Australia Survey', November.

Errico, Luca and Alberto Musalem (1999), 'Offshore Banking: An Analysis of Micro- and Macro-Prudential Issues', International Monetary Fund, Working Paper WP/99/5, January.

Euromoney, 'Private Banking Survey', various years.

Euromoney, various issues.

Federal Reserve Board, Division of Research and Statistics (2000), 'Recent Changes in US Family Finances: Results from the 1998 Survey of Consumer Finances', January.

Financial Times, 'Survey: Private Banking', various years.

Financial Times, 'Survey: Wealth Management', various years.

Financial Times (2005), 'Survey: Wealth Management Asia 2005', 5 December.

Flemings Research (2000a), 'Beds and Bollinger: The Economics of Airline Products', 12 April.

Flemings Research (2000b), 'It's a Rich Man's World: Wealth Management in Europe', October.

Forrester Research (2001), 'Virtual Family Offices Blossom', February.

Fox-Pitt, Kelton (2005), 'EFG International: Global Pure Play Private Bank', 21 November.

Frank, Robert H. and Philip J. Cook (1996), *The Winner-Take-All Society: Why the Few at the Top Get So Much More Than the Rest of Us*, Penguin, Harmonsworth.

Goldman Sachs (2000), 'Driving the Green: Serving the High-Net-Worth Individual', 16 October.

Goldman Sachs (2003), 'Dreaming with BRICs: The Path to 2050', Global Economics Paper 99, 1 October.

Goldman Sachs (2004), 'Europe: Brokers and Asset Managers – Investment Banking Update: Private Banking: An Exciting Growth Opportunity', 1 September.

Goldman Sachs (2006), 'Switzerland: Brokers & Asset Managers – Julius Baer and EFG International: Bear with it', 19 January.

Goldman Sachs and Frank Russell Company, 'Survey: Alternative Investing by Tax-Exempt Organisations', various years.

Goldman Sachs Global Economics Group (2006), *The World and the BRICs Dream*, February.

Goldman Sachs Prime Brokerage, 'Annual Global Hedge Fund Investor Survey', various years.

Grove, Hannah Shaw and Russ Alan Prince (2003), 'The Lives and Advisors of New Millionaires', *Trusts & Estates*, 2(8), August.

Hamnett, Chris (2003), *Unequal City: London in the Global Arena*, Routledge.

Havens, John J. and Paul G. Schervish (1999), 'Millionaires and the Millenium: New Estimates of the Forthcoming Wealth Transfer and the Prospects for a Golden Age of Philanthropy', Boston College Social Welfare Research Institute, 19 October.

Havens, John J. and Paul G. Schervish (2003), 'Why the $41 Trillion Wealth Transfer Estimate is Still Valid: A Review of Challenges and Questions', *Journal of Gift Planning*, January.

Hoffman, David (2004), *The Oligarchs: Wealth and Power in the New Russia*, PublicAffairs.

IBM Consulting Services (2003), 'European Wealth Management and Private Banking Industry Survey 2003'.

IBM Consulting Services (2003), 'Indian Wealth Management and Private Banking Industry Survey 2003–04'.

IBM Consulting Services (2005), 'European Wealth Management and Private Banking Industry Survey 2005'.

Institutional Investor (2005a), 'The Hedge Fund 100', June.

Institutional Investor (2005b), 'The Fund of Hedge Funds 50', December.

International Monetary Fund (2006a), *World Economic Outlook*, April.

International Monetary Fund (2006b), *Regional Economic Outlook: Middle East and Central Asia*, 3 May.

Irvine, Steven (2005), 'View from the Top', *Asian Private Capital*, Summer.

Julius Baer (2005), 'Creating Switzerland's Largest Pure-Play Wealth Manager', analyst presentation, 5 September.

Julius Baer (2005), *Rights Offering Prospectus*, 11 November.

Kennickell, Arthur B. (1999), 'Using Income Data to Predict Wealth', Federal Reserve Board of Governors, 19 January.

Kennickell, Arthur B. (2003), 'A Rolling Tide: Changes in the Distribution of Wealth in the U.S., 1989–2001', Federal Reserve Board of Governors, 3 March.

Kennickell, Arthur B. (2006), 'Currents and Undercurrents: Changes in the Distribution of Wealth 1989–2004', Federal Reserve Board of Governors, 30 January.

Kopczuk, Wojciech and Emmanuel Saez (2004), 'Top Wealth Shares in the United States, 1916–2000', NBER Working Paper 10399, March.

Koye, Bernhard (2005), *Private Banking im Informationszeitalter: Eine Analyse der Strategischen Geschaftsmodelle*, Haupt Verlag, Bern.

KPMG (2002), 'Getting Wealth Management Right', *Frontiers in Finance*, January.

KPMG (2004), 'Hungry for more? Acquisition Appetite and Strategy in the Global Private Banking and Wealth Management Industry', May.

KPMG (2005), 'Hungry for more? Acquisition Appetite and Strategy in the Global Private Banking and Wealth Management Industry – Global Update 2005', July.

KPMG and CREATE (2003), 'Revolutionary Shifts, Evolutionary Responses: Global Investment Management in the 2000s', July.

KPMG and CREATE (2005), 'Hedge Funds: A Catalyst Reshaping Global Investment', July.

Kshirsagar, Alok E., Paul G. McNamara and Janette Weir (2001), 'A Broadband Future for Financial Advice', *The McKinsey Quarterly*, 2001 Special Edition: On-line Tactics.

Lansley, Stewart (2006). *Rich Britain*, Politico's Publishing, London.

Lazard and Mercer Oliver Wyman (2004a), 'Global Asset Management: Who Wants Performance?', 18 March.

Lazard and Mercer Oliver Wyman (2004b), 'Securities Servicing: Profiting from Outsourcing and Operational Risk', 14 October.

Lehman Brothers Global Equity Research (2005), 'EFG International: Banking on Entrepreneurs', 23 November.

Leichtfuss, Reinhold (ed.) (2003), *Achieving Excellence in Retail Banking*, John Wiley & Sons, Ltd, Chichester.

Lombard Odier Darier Hentsch Brokerage Research (2006), 'Private Wealth Management Switzerland', January.

Lucas, Stuart (2006), *Wealth: Grow It, Protect It, and Share It*, Wharton School Publishing.

Lusardi, Annamaria (2000), 'Precautionary Saving and the Accumulation of Wealth', Dartmouth College and University of Chicago, June.

Magrini, Gian Marco and Jean-Marie Thomas (2001) *e-Private Banking in Europe – Myth, Reality, and Promise, e-Business Perspectives*, PricewaterhouseCoopers, London.

Maude, David J. and Philip Molyneux (1996), *Private Banking*, Euromoney Books.

Maude, David, R. Raghunath, Anupam Sahay and Peter Sands (2000), 'Banking on the Device', *The McKinsey Quarterly*, 3.

McKinsey & Company, 'US Asset Management Benchmarking Survey', various years.

McKinsey & Company, 'European Asset Management Survey', various years.

McKinsey & Company, 'European Private Banking Economics Survey', various years.

McKinsey & Company (2005), 'India Banking 2010: Towards a High-Performing Sector', October.

McKinsey & Company (2006), 'The Asset Management Industry in 2010', March.

McKinsey Global Institute (2005), '$118 Trillion and Counting: Taking Stock of the World's Capital Markets', February.

McKinsey Global Institute (2006), 'Mapping the Global Capital Market 2006: Second Annual Report', January.

Mendelsohn Media Research (2000), 'The Mendelsohn Affluent Survey', November.

Mercer Oliver Wyman (2003), 'The New Rules of the Game: Implications of the New Basel Capital Accord for the European Banking Industries', June.

Mercer Oliver Wyman (2005), 'European Wealth Management Survey 2004: Wealth Management Strategies for Success', February.

Merrill Lynch (2001), 'Wealth Management: A Platform for Growth', Speech by James Gorman, President, US Private Client, October.

Merrill Lynch (2002), 'U.S. Private Client: Delivering Growth for the Future', Speech by James Gorman, President, US Private Client, 22 April.

Merrill Lynch (2005), 'Creating Differential Value in a Commoditized World: The Evolving Role of the Wealth Manager', Speech by Robert J. McCann, Vice Chairman and President, Global Private Client Group, 10 April.

Merrill Lynch Global Equity Research (2003), 'Private Banking Report: How Much is a Private Bank Worth?', 1 May.

Merrill Lynch Global Equity Research (2004a), 'Citigroup: Private Bank: Delivering the Firm – Poster Child for Global Platform', 11 February.

Merrill Lynch Global Equity Research (2004b), 'Swiss Banks: In Search of Broken Business Models – Private Banking', 7 September.

Merrill Lynch Global Equity Research (2004c), 'Citigroup: Downgrading to Neutral: Change is Hard and Slow', 20 September.

Merrill Lynch Global Equity Research (2004d), 'Securities Processors: Investment Manager Outsourcing: Revolution or Evolution?', 21 December.

Merrill Lynch Global Equity Research (2005a), 'Pan-European Banks: Strategy 2010 – Setting the Agenda', 6 September.

Merrill Lynch Global Equity Research (2005b), 'Securities Broker/Dealer: Searching for Sustainable Growth as Tailwinds Abate', 1 November.

Merrill Lynch Global Equity Research (2005c), 'EFG International: Stand and Deliver!', 21 November.

Merrill Lynch Global Equity Research (2005d), 'Lap of Luxury: Enter the Dragon', 2 September.

Moody's Investors Service (2001), 'Rapidly Evolving Dynamics of Today's Private Banking Industry', Special Comment, March.

Morgan Stanley Dean Witter (2000), 'Private Banking in the 21st Century: From Discretion to Performance', 8 February.

Morgan Stanley, 'European Asset Management Industry Update', various issues.

Morgan Stanley (2005a), 'Julius Baer: Restructuring Potential – Much Already Priced In', 21 February.

Morgan Stanley (2005b), 'UBS: Two Useful Signals about Shifting Business Focus', 1 July.

Morgan Stanley (2005c), 'Société Générale: Lyxor – Feeding the Equity Derivatives Machine', 19 July.

Morgan Stanley (2005d), 'Rerating Wealth Management at UBS and Credit Suisse', 7 September.

Morgan Stanley (2005e), 'Hedge Funds: Notes from the Investment Frontier', 27 September.

Morgan Stanley (2006), 'UBS: Wealth Management Roadmap – Destination North of SFr 150', 13 January.

Multinational Monitor (2003), 'The Wealth Divide: The Growing Gap in the United States Between the Rich and the Rest', May.

Neville, Laurence (2005), 'The Private Banking Edge to Basel II', Risk, 18(3), March.

Northern Trust (2005), 'Wealth in America 2006', December.

Paine Webber (2000), 'UBS Strategy Seminar', Q2 2000.

Phillips, Kevin (2002), Wealth and Democracy: A Political History of the American Rich, Broadway Books.

Pictet (2001a), 'Swiss Asset Managers: Braving a More Difficult Environment', June.

Pictet (2001b), 'Swiss Banks: In Perspective...', July.

Piketty, Thomas and Emmanuel Saez (2004), 'Income Inequality in the United States, 1913–2002', Mimeo, University of California, Berkeley, November.

Piketty, Thomas and Emmanuel Saez (2006), 'The Evolution of Top Incomes: A Historical and International Perspective', American Economic Review, Papers and Proceedings, 96(2).

Population Division of the Department of Economic and Social Affairs of the United Nations Secretariat (2004), 'World Population Prospects: The 2004 Revision', medium variant.

PricewaterhouseCoopers (1998), 'Pursuing Profitability (UK)'.

PricewaterhouseCoopers (2006), 'Corporate Finance Insights: Wealth Management: February.

PricewaterhouseCoopers (2002), 'Asia-Pacific Private Banking/Wealth Management Survey 2002/2003'.

PricewaterhouseCoopers (2004a), 'Competing for Clients', Spring.

PricewaterhouseCoopers (2004b), 'Product Provision: A Missed Opportunity', Summer.

PricewaterhouseCoopers (2004c), 'Leveraging Compliance and Risk Management for Strategic Advantage', Winter.

PricewaterhouseCoopers, 'European Private Banking/Wealth Management Survey', various years.

PricewaterhouseCoopers, 'Global Wealth Management Survey', various years.

PricewaterhouseCoopers, 'North American Private Banking/Wealth Management Survey', various years.

PricewaterhouseCoopers and the Economist Intelligence Unit (2002), 'Wealth Management at a Crossroads: Serving Today's Consumer'.

Private Banker International, various issues.

PSI Global, Consumer Information Services (2000), 'The Role of Advice and Information Among Affluent and Wealthy Investors'.

Rayport, Jeffrey F. and Bernard J. Jaworski (2005), *Best Face Forward: Why Companies Must Improve Their Service Interfaces with Customers*, Harvard Business School Press, Boston.

Roberts, Tim H.R., Oscar Rodriguez and Miguel Angel Rodriguez Sola (2002), 'Serving Europe's Affluent Investors', *The McKinsey Quarterly*, 4.

RSM Robson Rhodes (2004), 'Private Banking and Wealth Management Survey 2004'.

Sarasin Brokerage Research (2005), 'Compliance, Economies of Scale and M&A Transactions: Outlook for Swiss Private Banking', October.

Sawyer, Nick (2005), 'Satisfying Demand', *Risk Islamic Finance*, 1(1), Autumn.

Schapper, Gerhard R. (1997), *Timeless Banking: The Swiss Private Bankers and Their Challenges*, Swiss Private Bankers Association, July.

Schroder Salomon Smith Barney (2000), 'The Road Ahead: Boomers Invest, Europe Booms', October.

Schroder Salomon Smith Barney (2001a), 'Swiss Private Banking: Where Are the Bankers' Yachts?', 8 August.

Schroder Salomon Smith Barney (2001b), 'The Baur au Lac Experience: Swiss Private Banking Round Table', 17 October.

Schroder Salomon Smith Barney (2001c), 'The Future of Private Banking: Highlights on Industry Conference', 29 November.

Schroder Salomon Smith Barney (2002a), 'Swiss Private Banking: Sarasin, Rabobank and Why Scale Matters in Private Banking', 5 March.

Schroder Salomon Smith Barney (2002b), 'Money Machines: Investment Banking and Asset Accumulation – The Advantages of Global Firms', 10 May.

Schroder Salomon Smith Barney (2002c), 'An Expensive Business: Swiss Private Banking', September.

Schroder Salomon Smith Barney (2002d), 'Private Banking Roundtable – 2002', 3 September.

Schroder Salomon Smith Barney, 'Asset Manager Quarterly', various issues.

Scorpio Partnership, 'Private Banking Benchmark', various issues.

SEI Investments (2004a), 'Outsourcing and the Wealth Management Market: An Investigation into Current Practice Amongst European Private Banking Institutions', January.

SEI Investments (2004b), 'Are Private Banks Ready for Today's Wealthy Individual?', October.

SEI Investments (2004c), 'Do Banks Have to Reinvent Wealth Management to Win?', Fall.

Société Générale Private Banking Asia Pacific (2005), 'From Green Fields to Rising Harvests', presentation by Daniel Truchi, CEO of SG Private Banking (Asia Pacific), Group Investor Day, 20 September.

Sonnenfeldt, Michael W. and Richard L. Lavin (2002), 'Peer-to-Peer Groups: A New Model For the High Net Worth Investor', *The Journal of Wealth Management*, Summer.

Stanley, Thomas J. (2004), *Millionaire Women Next Door*, Andrews McMeel Publishing.

Stanley, Thomas J. and William D. Danko (1998), *The Millionaire Next Door*, Pocket Books.

Stapfer, Peter (2005), *Anreizsyteme in der Private Banking-Kundenbeziehung*, Haupt Verlag, Berlin.

Stenner Group, 'Millionaires Survey', various years.

Stenner, Thane and James Dolan (2002), *True Wealth, An Expert Guide for High-Net-Worth Individuals (and their advisors)*, True Wealth Publishing Inc.

Suss, Esther C., Oral H. Williams and Chandima Mendis (2002), 'Caribbean Offshore Financial Centers: Past, Present and Possibilities for the Future', International Monetary Fund, Working Paper WP/02/88, May.

Tax Justice Network (2005), 'The Price of Offshore', Spring.

Thebault, Ludovic, David Maude and Philip Molyneux, *Offshore Banking*, Palgrave Macmillan: London (forthcoming).

Thomson Venture Economics (2004), 'State of the Market: Venture Capital/Private Equity', Presentation by Jesse Reves.

UBS, various investor presentations.

UBS Global Equity Research (2004), 'Swiss Private Banking Review', 17 June.

UBS Global Equity Research (2005), 'UBS Asset Gathering Conference: Day 2 Highlights', 1 April.

UBS Global Equity Research (2005), 'Northern Trust: Steady Eddy', 23 May.

UBS Global Equity Research (2005), 'EFG International: High Growth – Priced In', 2 December.

UBS Global Equity Research (2006), '2006 Asset Gathering Conference Highlights', 31 March.

UBS Investment Research (2005), 'How to Think About China', six-part series.

UBS Investment Research (2006), 'How are Demographics Changing the Global Economy? – Equity Market Implications', 6 April.

UBS Warburg (2001a), 'Making Money Grow: Wealth Management in the Internet Age', 12 March.

UBS Warburg (2001b), 'Private Banking – Full Steam Ahead?', October.

UBS Warburg and Oliver Wyman & Company (2002), 'The Future of Asset Management in Europe', September.

United Nations (2005), *Human Development Report 2005*.

US Census Bureau (2000), 'Money Income in the United States', September.

US General Accounting Office (1997), 'Private Banking: Information on Private Banking and Its Vulnerability to Money Laundering', October.

US Trust, 'Survey of Affluent Americans', various years.

Van, George P. (2005), 'Hedge Fund Demand and Capacity 2005–2015', Van Hedge Fund Advisors International, Nashville, Tennessel.

Weldon, Lucy (1998), *Private Banking: A Global Perspective*, Gresham Books.

Wolff, Edward N. (2000), 'Recent Trends in Wealth Ownership, 1983–1998', Jerome Levy Economics Institute, April.

World Bank (2005), *World Development Indicators 2005*, World Bank, Washington DC.

Index